More Praise for

GLORY DENIED

"A sad, moving book about the havoc the Vietnam War wrought with one American soldier and his family." —Anthony Day, *Los Angeles Times*

"A remarkable story of survival that will take its place among the testimonies of other POWs." —*Library Journal*

"In this poignant account, Philpott has opted for the oral-history method. . . . The choice was fortuitous." —*Washington Post*

"Riveting. . . . Philpott arranges the entire story deftly." —*Publishers Weekly*

"[It] will stand forever as one of the most truthful and important documents to emerge from the Vietnam era." —*Senior News*

GLORY
DENIED

GLORY
DENIED

The Vietnam Saga of Jim Thompson,

   America's Longest-Held Prisoner of War

TOM PHILPOTT

 W. W. Norton New York | London

For information about permission to reproduce selections from this book, write to
Permissions, W. W. Norton & Company, Inc., 500 Fifth Avenue, New York, NY 10110

The text of this book is composed in Janson with the display set in Fairfield Light
Composition by Sue Carlson
Manufacturing by Maple-Vail Book Manufacturing Group
Book design by Chris Welch
Production manager: Leelo Märjamaa-Reintal
Manuscript editor: Ted Johnson

Library of Congress has cataloged the hardcover edition as follows:

Philpott, Tom
Glory denied : the saga of Jim Thompson, America's longest-held prisoner of war / by Tom Philpott.
p. cm.
Includes index.
ISBN 0-393-02012-6
1. Thompson, Floyd Jim. 2. Vietnamese Conflict, 1961–1975—Prisoners and prisons, North Vietnamese.
3. Prisoners of war—United States—Biography. 4. Prisoners of war—Vietnam—Biography. I. Title.

DS559.4T47 P47 2001
959.704'37-dc21   00-066993

ISBN 978-0-393-34281-9 pbk.

W. W. Norton & Company, Inc., 500 Fifth Avenue, New York, N.Y. 10110
www.wwnorton.com

W. W. Norton & Company Ltd., Castle House, 75/76 Wells Street, London W1T 3QT

1 2 3 4 5 6 7 8 9 0

To my mother, Mary Barbara,
who nurtured my curiosity;
my sons, Paul and Brad,
who inspire the truth;
my wife, Barbara,
who nurtures all
that I love
in life

CONTENTS

Photographs appear between pages 332 and 333

FOREWORD

by Senator John McCain

"Dying is easy. Living is the difficult thing," said a Viet Cong camp commander to one American prisoner of war after his capture. For American service personnel held captive during the Vietnam War, faith in country, God, and fellow prisoners kept our dream of freedom alive, making life worth living despite freedom's absence. For Jim Thompson, the lantern of faith would illuminate the way home from his ordeal as the longest-held prisoner of war in American history, his honor intact and his patriotism fortified. But the difficulty of living, after so courageously defying death's call in the bamboo cages of South Vietnam, haunt him in the land of the free.

Jim Thompson's story, as movingly portrayed in Tom Philpott's oral history, is in many ways America's story during a conflicted period in our proud history. Like many Americans, Jim left for Vietnam, had the most searing experience of his life there, and returned to a nation forever changed by the war in which he had been called to serve. Once home, he lamented what he perceived to be a diminished patriotism, a dampened national pride, and a popular culture that scorned his sacrifice. Like our nation, Jim suffered from the malaise that accompanies a lost cause once called glorious. In that sense, Jim's story is our own, viewed through the eyes of a man who sacrificed far more for it than most Americans would dare to imagine.

The experience of American prisoners held by the Viet Cong in South

Vietnam was very different from what those of us shot down in the North went through. The support of our peers, and the standards to which we held one another, were central to our ability to withstand our captivity. I could not have done so without it; Jim did for five years, in which he never saw another American. That he survived at all—this ghost of a man, a "skeleton with hair"—was attributed by the Americans later imprisoned with him as nothing less than a miracle.

I did not know Jim during the period when we were both in prison in Vietnam. In 1974, the year after our homecoming, Jim and I traveled to South Vietnam as guests of its government to be honored for our military service. I had heard legendary stories of Jim's fierce resistance to his captors, and of his heroic endurance under conditions that would have killed many men. Our trip together afforded me a welcome opportunity to get to know him. Never will I forget the love of country that accompanied his surviving the prison camps, his extraordinary test of patriotism, or the evident damage that years of concerted cruelty had done to this good and decent man.

Jim and other American prisoners suffered grievous harm to mind and body at the hands of their captors. But the indignity of their incarceration and the personal tragedies that would befall some as they struggled in vain to rebuild the lives they had lost at home, could not dim the glory of their wartime cause.

Before Vietnam, the truth of war, of honor and courage, was obscure to many of us, hidden in the peculiar language of men who had gone to war and been changed forever by the experience. I had thought glory was the object of war, and all glory was self-glory. Like Jim Thompson, I learned the truth in war: there are greater pursuits than self-seeking. Glory is not a conceit or a decoration for valor. It is not a prize for being the most clever, the strongest, or the boldest. Glory belongs to the act of being constant to something greater than yourself, to a cause, to your principles, to the people on whom you rely, and who rely on you in return. No misfortune, no injury, no humiliation can destroy it.

Faith sees the prisoner through. As Jim said, "Faith in God is one thing no man can take away from you. On the contrary, the more they try to destroy it, the tougher the test, the stronger becomes a man's faith." Country and family, said Jim, were other pillars of faith in that temple of horrors. So speak the quiet heroes of the camps—men whose faith would not succumb to any human power, no matter how strong and malevolent.

Like Jim, I discovered in Vietnam that faith in myself proved to be the least formidable strength I possessed when confronting organized inhumanity on a greater scale than I had conceived possible. In prison, I learned that faith in myself alone, separate from other, more important allegiances, was ultimately no match for the cruelty that human beings could devise when they were entirely unencumbered by respect for the God-given dignity of man. This is the lesson many Americans, including Jim, learned in prison. It is, perhaps, the most important lesson we have ever learned.

Jim Thompson kept the faith. This is his story.

AUTHOR'S NOTE

The interviews and perspectives that form the basis of this book were gathered over more than fifteen years. There is little question that a biography of such sensitive nature becomes a delicate balancing act. My goal was to give the most accurate account possible of the Thompson family saga without either exaggerating or trivializing the drama, sacrifice, heroism, guilt, or suffering. I chose oral history because I prized the freshness and spontaneity of remarks made by family members, friends, colleagues, and others. Their verbatim statements often seemed more honest, poignant, or jarring than any third-person narrative. I couldn't let these voices go. At some points in the story, I do use narration to set a scene, provide context, or quicken the pace. But wherever possible I rely on original statements and documents.

Several points about this form of oral history are worth noting. On rare occasions, I reorganized comments for clarity and continuity, as well as to avoid redundancy. In all such instances I took great care not to distort the meaning or violate the context of original remarks.

At various points in Part II, starting with Chapter 11, retired Special Forces colonel George Maloney provides valuable insight into the politics and culture of South Vietnam's frontiers in the early 1960s. His edited comments are unique to the book in that they came both from interviews with Maloney and from briefing materials he had prepared for Special Forces teams being assigned to isolated areas of South Vietnam in the war's early years.

The Thompsons' story is presented not only through edited interviews with Jim, his then wife Alyce, and their children—Pam, Laura, Ruth, and Jimmy—but also from the recollections of scores of acquaintances, including former POWs, neighbors, military escorts, psychiatrists, childhood play-mates, teachers, ministers, confidants, military superiors and subordinates, physicians, counselors, and friends. Every one of more than 160 persons interviewed was told beforehand that I was writing a book about the Thomp-sons. More than eighty of those "voices" have been selected to tell the story. Biographical sketches of those interviewed, and of several other personalities with prominent roles in the Thompson saga, are presented at the end of the book should the reader need to review a person's background.

I used pseudonyms for several individuals—Harold, Lois, and Justine—to protect their privacy. I also withheld current last names of Alyce, her daugh-ters, and their husbands.

Portions of the story also are told through documents provided by the Thompsons and the Army, including personal letters, official correspon-dence, service records, medicals files, and intelligence reports.

Jim Thompson's own insightful descriptions of his years in captivity were edited from lengthy interviews he gave soon after his repatriation. The inter-views originally were conducted for the 1976 book *P.O.W. A Definitive His-tory of the American Prisoner-of-War Experience in Vietnam, 1964–1973*, by John G. Hubbell in association with Andrew Jones and Kenneth Y. Tomlin-son. Thompson had sat down with Tomlinson in the summer of 1973, eight years before a stroke left Jim unable to communicate with clarity. I am indebted to Ken Tomlinson and to Reader's Digest Press, publisher of *P.O.W.*, for granting me permission to use Thompson's transcripts here to describe his captivity. They were invaluable.

Most of all, I'm deeply indebted to Jim Thompson, an American hero, and to Alyce and the Thompson children. They each showed remarkable courage in allowing their painful story to be told.

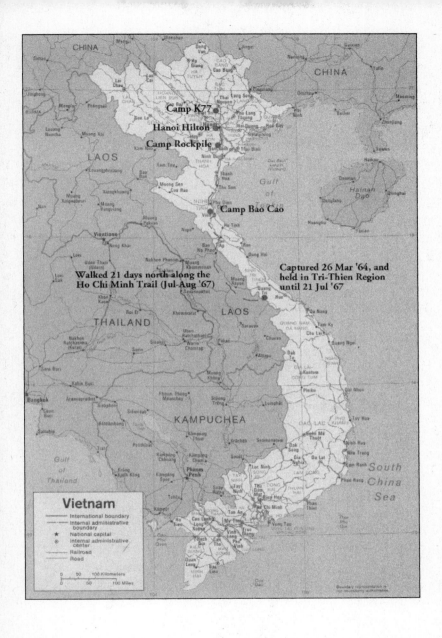

Vietnam

CHINA

CHINA

Camp K77

Hanoi Hilton

Camp Rockpile

LAOS

Gulf
of
Tonkin

Hainan
Dao

Camp Bao Cao

Walked 21 days north along the
Ho Chi Minh Trail (Jul-Aug '67)

Captured 26 Mar '64, and
held in Tri-Thien Region
until 21 Jul '67

LAOS

THAILAND

KAMPUCHEA

Gulf
of
Thailand

South
China
Sea

Vietnam
— International boundary
--- Internal administrative
     boundary
★ National capital
⊕ Internal administrative
     center
— Railroad
— Road

0   50   100 Kilometers
0   50   100 Miles

INTRODUCTION

I n the late 1960s, as public interest in the plight of American prisoners of war in Vietnam grew, journalists who asked the Pentagon to identify the longest-held American were given the name of Lieutenant (Junior Grade) Everett Alvarez, Jr., a Navy pilot shot down over North Vietnam in August 1964 during a retaliation raid following the Gulf of Tonkin incident. Army officials knew that a soldier, captured four months before Alvarez, was presumed to be still alive. They refused, however, to release his name. Floyd "Jim" Thompson was that man.

Thompson, a Green Beret officer captured in March of 1964, had spent his first five years as a prisoner in solitary confinement, mostly in rugged jungle camps in the mountains of South Vietnam and Laos. He received brutal beatings and suffered from disease, starvation, and also agonizing loneliness; it was not until 1969 that, near death, he was allowed to join other American POWs. Two years later, in 1971, he escaped and eluded capture for almost two days, a heroic act for which he was later awarded the Silver Star.

On March 16, 1973, two weeks short of nine years as a prisoner of war, Thompson's historic ordeal ended. He returned home, however, not to the fanfare of trumpets, but to a country that in many ways had turned its back on him.

Glory Denied explains why the Army kept quiet about Thompson. It tells why a POW-MIA organization was denied permission to put Thompson's name on bracelets that five million Americans wore to remember the lives of captured Americans in Vietnam. It reveals the longest-held prisoner of war in

U.S. history as an atypical hero whose tortuous journey continued long after his repatriation and the American withdrawal from Vietnam.

Thompson's story is one of sacrifice and extraordinary survival. It is a story that reflects not only the cost of war and separation, but how such trauma can bring out the best and the worst in us, and can leave the most innocent members of a family changed forever. It is the story of a family's disintegration and, in the era of this war and its aftermath, a uniquely American tragedy.

Part One

PRISONER

1 ▪ DYING

JIM THOMPSON   I don't really know how far they would have gone, whether they would have killed me or not. I don't really know. But from the 21st of July 1964, my most recent escape attempt, until the 18th of August that year, I knew one of two things was going to happen. I would either go insane or I would die. Either my mind or my body was going to crack.

One thing they harped on was "This isn't worth dying for." That more than anything preyed on my mind. I had some intelligence training, so I understood what they were doing. But even knowing, I couldn't change it. That was the hell of it. I couldn't change it. When they control your environment so completely, your morale can be manipulated at will. You can fight it to a certain point; you can minimize the effects of it. You can't completely get away from it.

Longer interrogation sessions, less and less sleep. The simple task of cutting wood became almost insurmountable. To pick up an ax, to bend down and blow on a fire, was enough to make me pass out. Just from weakness. They placed all manner of frustrating situations in front of me. Interrogation would last until well after dark. Then I had to scrounge around for wood. Or they waited to end a session until it was raining and the wood was too wet to build a fire. They took my boots and made me go barefoot in the jungle. They woke me up in the middle of the night and early in the morning and forced me to cut brush around the hut. Anything to cause me physical pain, to lose rest. It was a series of little things that together made daily life miserable.

Longer and longer interrogation sessions, more and more pressure, and finally the physical torture. Beatings, mostly, with bamboo across my back, legs, arms. An interrogator would stand in front of me and a guard behind. He would nod, signaling the guard to punctuate his remarks. Not an outright beating. Just punctuation. "You must answer!" Snap!

One day he said, "You must abide by regulations of the camp." I said I understood. He said, "The regulations are that you must not leave your hut without permission. You must obey the guards. Do you agree?"

"Yeah," I said, "I understand."

The next day he called me out and blandly said, "All right. Now we're ready to take your statement."

"What statement?"

"You agreed yesterday to answer all our questions."

"I never agreed to that!"

"You agreed to obey camp regulations! One regulation is you must do everything you're told! Now write a statement!"

"I refuse" Snap!

Far more severe than the physical abuse was the constant mental pressure. It's hard to describe in a meaningful way. I've racked my brain to figure how to portray this. But without the threat of death, you can't recreate it. I sincerely felt the end was within sight. I didn't think these people were going to stop and I didn't think I would crack. I was absolutely determined not to crack. And I believed they would continue until . . . until I died.

2 ▪ THE PIT

PASCAL BATSON   I was a young resident in psychiatry at Walter Reed Army Hospital in the fall of '77 when chosen to take on a high-profile patient. Within the Army at least, Jim Thompson was identified not only as the longest-held prisoner of war in American history but as a very charismatic and effective speaker since his return. He had found in that identity of POW a real chance to shine. So he came to us as somebody who had been a star but then had a rapid and catastrophic descent. It was because of his unique circumstances and record that Thompson was sent here at all. Walter Reed offered the best chance for a definitive evaluation of his condition. The Army already had decided his career as an infantry officer was over. Thompson was to be moved into a secondary skill, personnel management. My job was to get him well enough to fill such a position here in Washington. If I couldn't, he would be medically retired.

So Jim was a medical evacuee to Andrews Air Force Base outside Washington in late November. A medical attendant met him at the airport and accompanied him to Forest Glen, an unusual facility the Army used then for inpatient psychiatry. It was a few miles north, into Montgomery County, Maryland, from the main hospital.

RONALD ERSAY   I was a psychiatric consultant for patients with alcohol or other drug problems. Forest Glen was a fascinating place. We called it "The Army Surgeon General's Best Joke." The grounds themselves of this former women's college were crazy, adorned by odd statuary, a variety of old architecture, and a beautiful wooded landscape.

PASCAL BATSON   They tried to keep our building clean, and walls got painted regularly. But it was old. Arriving patients were led down a poorly lit stairway to a metal door with a small mesh-screen window. It felt like a cellar. This was Ward 106, also known as "The Pit."

RONALD ERSAY   Those darkened stairs were like a scene from a horror story. Visitors could get lost just trying to find the ward. Once there, they must have wondered if they could ever find their way out again. Most new patients were either so out of touch anyway or so plagued with problems they couldn't get more scared.

PASCAL BATSON   Once inside the ward, patients saw that they actually were at ground level with the rear of the building. So it wasn't really a basement. Still, the accommodations weren't deluxe. Doors and windows were locked down tight. We practiced group therapy in those days, so patients lived in open bays. The idea was that "community" is therapeutic and patients were encouraged to get involved.

FRANKLIN JONES   Forest Glen, while I was Walter Reed's director of psychiatry, had four wards altogether, up to one hundred thirty patients per ward. The average age was twenty-two. Average rank, private first class. Soldiers who had attempted suicide, like Lieutenant Colonel Thompson, were kept in the closed ward, under close supervision, until the staff knew they could be trusted. During the Vietnam War we had a ward solely for officers, but by 1977 it was no longer worth making the rank distinction.

PASCAL BATSON   Clearly the locked doors and windows, the communal living, were a replay for Jim of his prisoner status. But it was very different treatment and accommodations from what he received only four years earlier when he returned from Vietnam. No bunting decorated the walls. Patients were not greeted warmly. Though a lieutenant colonel, Jim was thrown in with a lot of young enlistees who had been in the Army a very short time, some less than a week. Most were unable to tolerate the military. As there was no discrimination between officer and enlisted, neither was there discrimination between those with a psychotic illness and those who had a major affective illness such as depression. Jim, like the other patients, wore hospital pajamas—blue blouse and pants and cloth belt. He had to keep his bunk made. Patients ate together, slept together, went to activities and therapy together. It was standard procedure that new patients be confined to the ward. So basically, Jim was stripped of rank and much of his freedom and individuality. It had a tremendous impact and brought home to him how far he had fallen.

At our first meeting, Jim didn't deny his suicide attempt. He explained he was just tired of everything going against him. He said he wanted some rest. He also made it very clear he didn't belong at Forest Glen. He was only there because he was ordered to be there, he said. He regarded it as confinement but we were not to assume we held him securely. He had escaped from prison before, he said, and this one would be very easy. "You know," he told me when we met, "I can break out of here in three minutes."

3 ■ KEY WEST

The sky stayed a brilliant blue that March morning in 1984 as I walked the seaside mile from my motel to Thompson's condominium. I should have studied the map on my place mat at breakfast, I thought, because I wasn't sure now if that was the Caribbean or the Gulf of Mexico on my left. I felt good. I carried with me not only a notepad and tape recorder but also the enthusiasm of a young journalist, hoping to shine a spotlight on a little-known but genuine American hero. I had been told that a heart attack and stroke three years earlier had almost killed Colonel Floyd James Thompson. In January 1982 the Army had retired him on full disability. He had chosen to spend his final years here in Key West.

I had first learned of Thompson four months earlier when an Army officer suggested I look into a claims case that had been quietly settled in 1983 by the Army Board for Correction of Military Records. The board routinely made its decisions available for the asking, but names were removed to protect a service member's privacy. The circumstances in this case, the officer said, were "more tragic" than *Cherry*, a court case I had covered for my newspaper, the *Army Times*. Fred V. Cherry, an Air Force pilot, had been shot down over North Vietnam in 1965. During Cherry's seven-year confinement, the Air Force had given most of his pay to his wife despite evidence it had that she was unfaithful and, indeed, had had a child by another man. In a much-publicized ruling in 1979, the U.S. Court of Claims reprimanded the Air Force and awarded Cherry $38,000 in back pay.

That painful lesson had not been lost on the Army. When a POW soldier who had been treated similarly came forward, the Army's board promptly awarded back pay to avoid its own public relations mess. But this particular soldier, I was told, was unique. He had been held captive nine years, longer than any other United States serviceman in history, yet few Americans knew his name. Even close followers of POW matters generally believed Everett Alvarez, a Navy pilot shot down and captured in August 1964, had been the longest-held.

After some digging, I learned the soldier's name: Colonel Floyd James Thompson. I contacted his friend and lawyer Michael Chamowitz, who warned me that talking with Jim would be difficult. A stroke had left him with expressive aphasia, a severe communication disability. Questions had to be asked slowly. Answers came in fractured, sometimes puzzling phrases. Thompson suffered occasional seizures too, Chamowitz said. A narrowed artery at the base of his brain had been ruled inoperable and life-threatening. No one believed he would survive too much longer, Chamowitz said, but Thompson clearly was an extraordinary survivor. Besides his medical condition, however, Thompson's personal life was in upheaval, Chamowitz said. He had had no contact with any of his four grown children for many years.

Carefully trimmed and mulched shrubs glistened from a morning shower when I arrived at the high-rise condominium complex. At the gatehouse, a guard directed me past a wrought-iron fence to a one-story office where an attractive gray-haired woman sat.

"Is Jimmy expecting you?" she said frowning.

She dialed a number, spoke softly, and listened. "Okay," she said. She directed me through a shaded courtyard, around one swimming pool, left past another, and into an elevator which still seemed to hold all of yesterday's heat. On the breezy fourth-floor terrace, I found the appropriate screen door and knocked. A gray-haired man of slender build appeared, in white polo shirt and shorts. He had a broad, tanned forehead, piercing blue eyes, and surprisingly slender shoulders.

"Come in."

I followed him down a short hall, past an immaculate kitchen on the left and bedroom on the right. As Thompson walked, his right shoulder sagged, and he limped on the same side. We settled in an elegant, formal living room, decorated in blues and whites. One wall was covered with mirrors, the others wallpapered in a tropical design. Thompson slid into a white leather easy chair. With his right arm limp at his side, Thompson used his left hand to draw a cigarette pack and lighter from his breast pocket. He jerked out a cigarette, returned the pack, and lit the cigarette with the same hand. Exhaling his first long pull, Thompson finally focused his deep-set eyes on me and waited for a fuller explanation of my visit. He seemed neither pleased nor displeased by it. Just curious. I explained how I had stumbled onto his story. Thompson strained to catch the meaning of my words. I said I wanted to learn about his experiences, to talk with family and associates. I wanted access to his service and medical records. And, I said, I wanted to interview him, often and starting immediately.

"Go ahead."

First, the captivity. What had that been like? He understood this and other questions. But in trying to respond, Thompson began to seethe with anger and frustration. It was as though the right words bounced around aimlessly in his mind, yet found no means of escape. Responses trickled out, clipped or mangled. After some effort he often would settle for "yeah" or "no." In our first hour together, the tension rose. Thompson would blurt out "Goddamn!" and clench his teeth at his inability to say what he meant, at my failure to understand. Thompson knew difficulty with speech is characteristic of many stroke victims, but it provided no consolation. Tears of helplessness finally welled in his eyes. He rose, walked across the room, and turned on an old reel-to-reel tape deck. Loud music blared through the apartment. Without adjusting the volume, Thompson returned to his seat. I was being dismissed, I thought. Suddenly, the music faded and a voice reminded listeners, "Our guest today is Colonel Floyd James Thompson, the longest-held POW in American history."

It was a radio talk show from station WCKS in Cocoa Beach, Florida, recorded a decade earlier, more than a year after Thompson's return from Vietnam but long before his stroke. As the show's hosts, a man and woman, introduced their "special guest," the disabled veteran beside me lit another cigarette and stretched back to hear the strong, confident voice that once was his.

"Listen," he told me.

MALE HOST: Colonel, your hometown?

THOMPSON: Bergenfield, New Jersey, but I've been gone for nearly twenty years. So like any Army brat, home is where I happen to hang my hat. Right now if I hung it in the Colony Inn down the block there, that would be home. I told them I would put in a plug. They're real nice folks. [*Laughing*]

MALE HOST: Are you going for thirty?

THOMPSON: Definitely

MALE HOST: How long in?

THOMPSON: Eighteen.

MALE HOST: Got it made.

FEMALE HOST: Now just go ahead. Start from the beginning so everyone will know exactly what it was like.

THOMPSON: Okay. [*Hesitating*] Well, I was drafted. A very bitter and reluctant draftee at that. I did enough in the first month to be court-martialed and thrown out with an undesirable discharge. [*Laughs*] But one very fine old master sergeant who liked me decided instead to make me a trainee platoon sergeant. At first I refused. "I'm not going to do your job, sarge," and in rather nasty language to boot. He just walked away and I wound up doing it anyway. He started ordering me, "Tell this squad to shine shoes," and "Tell this squad to clean the latrine." Finally I said to myself, "Get smart, son. He's not telling you to clean the latrine or to sweep the floor. He's telling you to tell someone else to do it." Supervise. So I sold my soul. Shortly after that I fell in love with the Army. It's my heart and soul.

After OCS, Ranger school, and airborne training, I put in a hitch in Korea. When I came back I went into Special Forces. That was my status when I went to Vietnam in 1963.

FEMALE HOST: Why solitary confinement for five years, Jim?

THOMPSON: It's part of their brainwashing technique. By separating you from contemporaries you lack the moral support of friends, someone to discuss things with, to keep things straight in your mind. You have nobody to listen to but the interrogator. You have no reinforcement from peers. This is standard brainwashing. They use it in all communist countries.

MALE HOST: Colonel, you say we should be alert. We're being saturated with propaganda.

THOMPSON: That's the main message. Since I've been back, I've been asked two or three times a week to speak to various groups around the country, to try to get people to understand. It would be absolutely ridiculous to assume a country of sixteen million people—North Vietnam—could defeat the United States on the battlefield. The only way they can defeat us is from within. There is no doubt in my mind that the entire antiwar effort worldwide, and in particular here in the United States, was communist-inspired, communist-dominated, and communist-led. Now, that doesn't mean everybody who raised his voice against the war is communist. A lot of these people are well-intentioned, well-educated. But for some reason they don't understand what's going on, don't understand how the communists fight a war today. It's a whole new ball game, not like World War II. It's not two armies slugging it out. It's a war fought on the ideological plane. It's a war of propaganda. And if we look back over the period of the sixties, it's shocking to me—it is truly shocking—to see how close they came to defeating us from within.

Our captors told us of racial unrest, unemployment, inflation, riots, demonstrations, antiwar activists. They knew all about that. They could quote speeches by Senator Morris, Senator Mansfield, Bella Abzug, and Ted Kennedy. But they knew nothing else about America.

MALE HOST: In case you're just joining us, our guest is former prisoner of war Colonel Floyd Thompson, held captive for nine years in Vietnam. Jim, there is still fighting in Vietnam. Will it go on forever?

THOMPSON: Just last March I had the privilege of meeting with the Vietnamese ambassador to the United States and the former U.S. ambassador to Vietnam at a party in Washington. They had nothing but glowing reports of South Vietnam. The country is stabilizing; the economy is stabilizing; the people are supporting their government. President Thieu ran for reelection and did rather well. The army is doing better than holding its own and I am totally convinced it is going to continue to do so.

A lot of people say we lost the war. That isn't true. We went there with a specific goal, to assist a free country remain free, to bring South Vietnamese up to a position where they could handle the job themselves. We accomplished that mission, honorably and well, and didn't come back until we had done our job.

MALE HOST: Well said.

Part II

AMERICA'S SON

1933–1963

4 ■ BERGENFIELD

That first day in Key West, Jim Thompson opened his life to me as best he could: military records, letters, uniforms, medals and awards, old photographs. On an end table in his living room was a history of prisoners of war in Vietnam, a book entitled *P.O.W.* by John G. Hubbell. To be part of that compilation of prisoner experiences, Thompson had been interviewed over several days the summer following his repatriation. Kenneth Tomlinson, an editor at Readers' Digest Press, publisher of Hubbell's book, conducted the interviews. Those transcripts, I thought, might still be available and could be valuable for telling Thompson's story. Indeed they were. Thompson, in effect, would speak to me in two voices, one of them historical and strong, the other current but disabled.

Poolside the second day of my visit, Jim and I were more relaxed in each other's company. As we warmed ourselves in the sunshine, I asked about his life.

How was your childhood?
Bus driver, you know.

Your father?
Yeah. No money at all. Bus driver first, then accident. Skull fracture. Then it's wash buses. But my father, three meals a day. Breakfast every day. Lunch every day. Supper every day.

He ate a lot?
My God, yes! Never go out. Never. And eat promptly!

A disciplinarian?
Oh my God. Awful.

Would he smack you?
Smack me, yes. But my father, only finished kindergarten, I guess. Or first grade. Barely read. If too involved, no dice. Simple words, that's it.

You two didn't get along?
Never.

What did he think of your military career?
Brand-new second lieutenant. My mother, father come down. My father new suit. Only suit. Ceremony.

They were proud.
Proud but . . . my father "No alcohol! No Coca Cola!" There at Benning, my father still must eat, "Three times a day." Dinner five o'clock! New lieutenant now. I'm at club. Eight o'clock. Awful! Terrible! Horrible! "I'm hungry." My father. "I'm hungry!"

You had just earned your commission and all he worried about was missing his evening meal?
Yeah.

———

Twins Robert and Roy Sironen were Thompson's best friends growing up in Bergenfield, New Jersey. Bernie Weisse, another classmate, was also a neighbor. Dr. Pascal Batson gained his insight into Jim's childhood while treating him as a psychiatric patient many years later.

ROY SIRONEN   Bergenfield today is a good-size town, but when we were growing up it was eight thousand people, max. A bedroom community for New York City, twelve miles from the George Washington Bridge.

BERNIE WEISSE   It was known then as "the Friendly Town." Rural with lots of wooded areas and unpaved streets.

ROY SIRONEN   My twin, Robert, and I were both close to Jim. One minute we would all be together. The next it would be one of us with Jim. Another time, Jim would be with the other. The three of us stuck together.

ROBERT SIRONEN   We met as four-year-olds picking blackberries in nearby fields. His mom made a pie from what we gathered that day. After that we ran around together for years. Of thirty kids who went to kindergarten, nineteen graduated high school together. As youngsters we'd meet to get a soda pop. As teenagers we went to football games and got drunk together.

BERNIE WEISSE   I lived on East Johnson Ave., right off Hickory. Jim was a house away from a candy store we frequented. A good guy. Never gave anybody trouble.

ROY SIRONEN   Jim's parents were elderly, maybe ten years older than ours.

ROBERT SIRONEN   His mother might have been thirty when we were in grammar school but she looked fifty. Never wore makeup.

ROY SIRONEN   She dressed plainer than other mothers, like a German schoolteacher. Wore her hair plain too and the same dresses all the time. She didn't have many.

ROBERT SIRONEN   Jim's parents didn't socialize. I suppose they talked to neighbors, but Ben Thompson didn't say a whole lot to anybody. He was a great big old Texan, husky, six foot two or three, with a tattoo on his arm that said "Miss Texas 1917." When he flexed his muscle she did a shimmy. Ben said he was related to some famous Texas outlaw who'd been around about the time the Texas Rangers became a force. Jim and his mother, by contrast, were very religious, solid members of the Old North Reformed Church in Dumont. Jim had sixteen years' perfect attendance at Sunday school.

BERNIE WEISSE   Every Sunday he'd pass our house going up to Dumont. I'd say something smart like "There he goes. Look at those medals!"—referring sarcastically to those attendance medals on his jacket. I say it now with admiration.

ROY SIRONEN   The Thompson house was small, but with three lots out back where his father had a big garden and raised rabbits for meat.

ROBERT SIRONEN   Ben had been driving for the Public Service Bus Company, a commuter line into New York. Getting out of the bus one day he slipped and landed on his head. He was unconscious a couple of days. After that he couldn't drive anymore.

ROY SIRONEN   He got downgraded and took a position as bus starter. They stand on the corner, check on the route, see how full the buses are, whether they're on time. It didn't pay much. Nobody had much money then, of course. If Jim had any he spent it. He wasn't frugal.

BERNIE WEISSE   Hickory Avenue was full of young people then. When the Second World War started we all showed our patriotism. If we saw a fellow in uniform, we talked to him.

ROY SIRONEN   Meat was rationed, and butter. Certain things we couldn't get. Everybody had a victory garden and, if they had room, raised rabbits or chickens. Our fourth-grade class knitted six-inch squares from old wool to make blankets for Army hospitals. We saved fat and tin cans and got coupons for the effort.

BERNIE WEISSE   It was such a popular war. We'd been attacked, so everybody was united and on the defensive. We couldn't wait to see the next John Wayne movie.

ROY SIRONEN   We were swept up in it, not like in Vietnam. I was saying the other day, watching a Mitsubishi move up the street, "We used to shoot at them!"

BERNIE WEISSE   When the war finally ended we got on our bicycles and raced through town, screaming and yelling to high heaven. It was a great time. I try to tell my children how it was. They can't imagine anybody would want a war.

ROBERT SIRONEN   Jim's brother, Danny, was his father's favorite. Two years older, he bullied Jim constantly.

ROY SIRONEN   Danny was like a farmer. Always outside. Always working with horses. Much tougher than Jimmy. He called Jim a mama's boy.

BERNIE WEISSE   He dressed like a cowboy, in jeans and high black boots. I guess he *was* a cowboy. Rode horses. Always seemed like he had a lot on his mind. I can't think of a single friend he had. He never mistreated me but I never knew where he was coming from. By the time we were teenagers Danny stood six feet and weighed one-eighty, one-ninety. He had a tough-guy reputation. Nobody wanted to fight him.

ROY SIRONEN   The two of them had such different personalities. Danny was rough. Physically, vocally, the whole bit. All muscle, big mouth and carrying on. Jimmy was softer. Jimmy, well, he cared about people.

PASCAL BATSON   Jim would later describe his brother's behavior toward him, referred to being tormented. I don't think Jim was beaten much physically. He may have been knocked around by Danny, maybe by his father. But it was more the psychological beatings he remembered. A very sterile existence at home. Little softness there. Sort of a minimum existence to a child with an imagination. Jim never understood why his father and brother picked on him so. It seemed they both felt any attempt at bettering one's station in life was putting on airs, being more than anyone should be.

ROBERT SIRONEN   A problem for Jimmy all through school were his ears. Everyone got on him about them. Called him Dumbo. His brother. Even his dad. Unmercifully.

ROY SIRONEN   Even we called him Dumbo. It wasn't vicious. We didn't say it that much as Jim got older. Of course, Jim never liked the teasing. He was always to be called Jim.

ROBERT SIRONEN   By late high school Jim didn't really pal around with anybody.

ROY SIRONEN   It's hard now to recall his interests and hobbies.

BERNIE WEISSE   He wasn't into sports, but he'd be the first to cheer at football games. Audiovisual aids, the yearbook staff. Sang in the choir. Things like that.

PASCAL BATSON   There was a teacher who let Jim see a better way to live. This woman broadened his horizons. She was an advocate, someone who took pleasure in his accomplishments, whereas at home his father belittled them and his mother wouldn't intervene. Only when Jim and his mother were alone did she give encouragement. His aspirations never received much nurturing at home.

————

Did your parents love each other, Jim?
I don't think so.

Why did they stay together?
My mother definitely afraid. Used to hit her. A lot.

————

ROY SIRONEN   By eleventh grade, Jim worked for A&P. He was such an organized guy. Everything methodical. He kept all the boxes in the supermarket's cellar in these long rows.

ROBERT SIRONEN   When they brought in a load, Jim priced and marked groceries. He liked it. He worked hard. He moved up from box boy to retail clerk. After high school he worked all week and then went out to party. We went to New York 'cause you only had to be eighteen to drink. Used to go to a bar called the Green Lantern and sit alongside the drunks. The bartender was a drunk himself so after ten or eleven he forgot to take our money.

BOB KEYES   Jim and I tried to drink all the breweries dry. Never did.

ROBERT SIRONEN   Jim's parents didn't drink. One New Year's Eve party we wouldn't let Jim drive home himself so we did. His mother got upset that night, saying every time we went out with Jimmy we got him drunk. Actually, it was the other way around. And Mrs. Thompson belonged to the Women's Christian Temperance Union. Jim would have a couple of drinks and go pick her up from a meeting, just to get her upset.

ROY SIRONEN   We got interested in girls our last year in high school and a lot of us were into keeping nice cars. With Jim, it was an obsession. He was always into perfection anyway.

ROBERT SIRONEN   Around 1950 Jim traded in his old car for a 1947 woody Town and Country convertible. God, that was beautiful!

ROY SIRONEN   Jim was driving that Chrysler the evening he met Alyce.

5 ■ ALYCE

In December 1984 I visited Laura, Jim Thompson's second-oldest daughter, at an apartment she shared with a rock musician in Wappingers Falls, New York. Laura, a pretty, soft-spoken woman with curly blond hair, described herself as the black sheep of the family. Years had passed since she had seen either parent. When I explained I needed to interview her mother, Laura said it wouldn't happen. Her mother never discussed her experiences as a POW's wife. The only chance I had was through Ruthie, Laura's younger sister, who lived near her mother. The two of them were close.

On the telephone, Ruth was open and friendly and spoke with a pleasing southern drawl. She too doubted that her mother would speak with me, though my odds might improve, Ruth suggested, if she broached the topic with her mother. I urged her to do so. The opportunity came three weeks later when Ruth, husband Kenny, and their two children visited Alyce and her second husband, John, on their farm in the Tennessee highlands. Ruth waited until late afternoon, when the meal was done and the rest of the family had moved outside to relax. She and Alyce were alone in the kitchen.

RUTH "Mama," I said, "this guy Tom called the other night. He wants to write a book on Dad. He talked to me quite a while and he's plannin' on comin' down here and interviewin' me. He's already talked to Laura and to Dad and he wants to talk to you too. And Jimmy. He thinks the story would be a lot better if he had everybody's side. He's interested in what you went through too."

She didn't give me a chance to say another thing. She started screamin' and cussin' and carryin' on. John come in. He looked at me and he looked at Mama and he said, "All right, what's goin' on?" Mama started cryin'.

"There's somebody tryin' to make me out to be a whore again," she said. "They're tryin' to ruin my life. That bastard in Florida. I wished he'd died when he had that stroke. He don't want to do nothin' but cause me trouble." I said, "Now Mama, stop. You're gettin' carried away."

"I don't mean that," she said. "But I do think this man is gonna be like the rest, wanting to put him up on a pedestal and make me look like trash. I ain't havin' it!"

"Now Mama," I said, "the only way he's gonna know what you were thinkin', what you were feelin', what was goin' on, is for you to tell him. The rest of us were too little."

John was on my side. "Now Ruth is right," he said. "The only way for him to know what you was thinkin' and feelin' is for you to tell him."

I told Mama, "This man sounded genuine when he said he only wants everyone's side of the story. It won't kill you to talk to him. He's gonna call next week. Give you a few days to think about it. If you want to hang up on him, okay. Nobody's threatening you."

"Go ahead and tell your story," John said. "Otherwise there's gonna be speculation on what went on instead of what really happened."

————

When Alyce answered the phone I quickly introduced myself and said I was writing about her husband. "My former husband," she corrected me. I told her I wanted to know how Jim's captivity had affected the whole family and—

"All right, Mr. Philpott," she interrupted. "I'll talk—on one condition. You let me see what he said about me."

What Jim had said, given his difficulty speaking at all, was that he had had an ideal marriage before Vietnam and came back to something else, I said.

"Prison affected Jim's mind," she said. "The marriage wasn't ideal. And when he got back he claimed I'd stolen one hundred thousand dollars. How in the name of God did he expect me to raise four children over nine years without that money? He went through hell but I went through hell too. There are certain things I did I'm not proud of. But I had to do them, for my children, for my own sanity."

One month later, in January of 1985, a blizzard struck Nashville on Super Bowl Sunday. By Monday morning, even in the brilliant sunshine, thermometers were frozen at ten degrees below zero. Businesses were closed. Highways were littered with abandoned cars. Even children rewarded with a rare snow holiday found it too cold to romp outdoors. An hour's ride beyond the city, six-foot snowdrifts narrowed the highway to single lanes. Finally I found the exit I needed, south toward the family farm.

It was a roller-coaster churn through the hilly countryside, past farms and bare orchards covered by a blinding sheet of white. At the crest of each hill, the road cut through icy limestone. Small herds of cattle dotted buried pastures. Atop every other hill, it seemed, stood a red barn and white farmhouse. I pumped my brakes furiously when I saw the turnoff to the left. I passed a clump of clapboard houses and drove up another ridge with even deeper drifts. A mile farther on I saw the small farmhouse Alyce had described. Parked beside it was a red Ford Mustang with a bumper sticker: I LOVE MY COUNTRY. A few hearty chickens pranced in the snow.

Alyce, a short woman with eyeglasses and tousled brown hair, which she brushed back from her forehead, held open the side door. I squeezed past a washing machine to enter the kitchen. John had worked all night, Alyce said, trying to unfreeze the pipes. Hand tools, gloves blackened by coal dust, and an assortment of knickknacks covered her countertop. Alyce wore slippers, dark slacks, and an olive-green sweater. She introduced me to her husband, a short, barrel-chested man with round cheeks and red beard. John had on work clothes, a ball cap, and a vest liner. At the kitchen table sat Catie, their blond, six-year-old grandchild, whom Alyce and John had adopted soon after her birth.

Alyce invited me to sit beside their woodstove. John was home because the mines were closed. He returned to the living room to watch television as Alyce fixed tea. That's all they drank anymore, she said. So, Alyce asked, what did I want to know? We began at the beginning. She was born in March 1935 to Harold and Ruth DeVries.

ALYCE   Mother and Dad lived with his parents for a time. Mother was not liked. I wasn't either because I was her child. So we soon moved to Cresskill, New Jersey, a little bungalow with a front porch, living room, two bedrooms, and a kitchen. When I was four, we moved five miles away, to Dumont, and a bigger home with a closed-in porch and a basement, which I was scared to death to go down into. Three bedrooms upstairs and a bath. Even had a piano in a little room off the dining room. Dad's brother, Uncle Lester, got it for me. He had a deal with a realtor to clean houses when people moved out. Someone left an old upright in one of 'em. I could sit down and play songs just from my ear.

BRENDA HUNTER   Alyce and I are cousins. Neither my father nor hers, Uncle Harold, got by the eighth grade. But they had the two best personalities of any men I've ever known. Harold, nicknamed Pud, was jovial and bright. He worked as a steamfitter with a salary twice what my father made as a mechanic. Aunt Ruth and Uncle Harold were my godparents. I loved her dearly. The two of them had personalities just made you feel good.

ALYCE   Dad worked for himself for a while, then he was hired at some defense plant. He'd go on the toots all the time. A heavy drinker. In the early times he just slept it off. Later it got nasty. When I was six I wanted a two-wheel red bicycle. He bought a used blue one and said he would paint it red. Well, he come home one night drunk with bright orange paint and decorated that bike. Even added black stripes. Imagine what those looked like. I was ashamed to ride it.

Still, I was close to my dad. After the Japs bombed Hawaii, Dad learned they weren't going to draft him so he joined the Seabees to help rebuild Pearl Harbor. Mother hit the ceiling. He didn't have to go, and this forced her to find a job. I missed him. He wrote from Hawaii. Even sent me a grass skirt. My mother took in a boarder to help with expenses, a young girl named Bernice. She also took in an older lady, Mrs. Stidler, to look after me while she worked in a wallet factory.

Those were pretty good years while Dad was away. I loved Stidy. She took me to the movies, bought me popcorn. She acted like my grandmother. Bernice and me dug a victory garden. Everything was rationed— tires, sugar, meat. The country was poor but we learned to do with what we had.

BRENDA HUNTER   My brother, who was serving in Hawaii with Uncle Pud, got a letter from my mother saying, Tell Pud to get home because Ruth was having a rip-roaring old time. The separation, on top of this letter, built suspicions.

ALYCE   Mom went out Friday and Saturday nights to a local bar. Played shuffleboard, had a hamburger and a couple of beers. She danced with other men. I guess, looking back, it was more than dancing.

After the war ended, we knew within a few days when Dad would be home. I was outside playing one day when I looked down the street and saw him walking toward me. Someone had dropped him off at the corner. He looked good. Handsome, about six foot tall. He'd gotten thin too. I started runnin' to him the moment I saw him. My dad loved me.

The good times didn't last, though. One night, not long after that, I was in bed when Mother came running up the stairs. She put the dresser and my bed against my door. I helped. Dad was bangin' on the door, screaming, calling her names. Said he was going to kill her. I was scared to death. I guess he found out she'd been fooling around. Mom slept with me that night, and every night after that while in that house. A few weeks later, I came home from school and Mother had our suitcase packed. I was ten years old when Dad kicked us out.

We moved into a boardinghouse and Mother began to date other men. Every weekend I had to visit my father, and he did nothing but quiz me about what Mother did all week. I grew to hate him for it. Saturday night he went out and got drunk with this lady, Louise. Sunday mornings he picked me up and took me to her house. There he sat at the table drinking beer. Louise would make dinner and he would go to sleep. Then she crabbed at me because she was stuck watching me, "the little bastard." I told Mother I would run away if she made me go anymore.

When I turned twelve, Mom met Lester Michaels, a widower with four children. Les was a carpenter, a year older than Mom, and he worshiped her. They couldn't get married until the divorce was final, but soon after they met we moved in as one family. Les's older boy, Red, was in the Army. Peggy was about to get married. Gwen was a year older than me and Jimmy, the younger son, was just two and, when we moved in, full of impetigo. I was tickled to death being there. Finally I had brothers and sisters. But we were cramped. Mother and I shared a room. Jimmy had the other with his sisters. Les slept downstairs in the living room. Les became more of a father than my own had been. When I was in my junior year of high school, he sat me down and asked what plans I had. I guess to be a secretary, I said. Les said, "What do you *want* to be?" I said a teacher. Too bad, he said. Had he known he would gladly have put me through college but by then I didn't have the necessary courses.

Mother and Les never pretended to be married. Yeah, it might have been a scandal, but people got used to it. My mother was a hell-raiser. Her philosophy was to live life and that's what she did.

6 ■ MARRIAGE

A t our first meeting in Key West, even through the verbal thicket of Jim's disability, he was able to communicate a deep affection for what he and Alyce once had, what they once were.

So, Jim, where did you meet Alyce?
New Milford. Out of high school. Working for A&P. Blind date. Robert and Roy, twins. One twin and me go out. And we swap.

You switched dates. How long after that did you marry?
One year.

In love?
Madly in love.

Happy marriage?
Happy marriage. In the Army, too, happy marriage. Life was wonderful, I guess.

ALYCE   In the beginning the marriage was good. I was eighteen, he was twenty. Young kids who had the world by the tail. We got engaged while I was still in high school. I had to be eighteen to marry, so Jim gave me the ring on my birthday. I ran upstairs to wake Mother and show her my ring. "I've already seen it," she said. That was a letdown.

But, yeah, we were in love, as much as any eighteen-year-old can be. Young, living at home, going to school, then all of a sudden I meet a guy who's got money. He has graduated. He has a woody convertible. I mean, Jim was a big deal! I graduated in June 1953, and we got married that July. It was a hot day. Oh, God, it was hot. Mother had to powder me to get me into my wedding dress. A size five which we had cut down to a four. I was tiny.

About two hundred people came to the Old North Church. Only fifty were invited to the reception. Mom and Dad did the best they could. We got a small room and a wedding cake.

At first we lived in a fairly new apartment in New Milford. Jim continued to work at the A&P. I worked payroll at *Parents Magazine*. When I couldn't make more money there I went to Remington Rand. I did statistical work and was excellent on the adding machine. My boss used to come out of his office just to watch my fingers fly.

Jim and I went dancing for entertainment. I dreaded it. Jim believed he was God's best dancer. He might have been the worst. People would stare. He'd think they were lookin' at him 'cause he was so good. But the rhythm wasn't there. You have to have some rhythm to dance. After a while I'd tell Jim I didn't feel like dancing and we'd argue about it.

Shortly after we got married, Jim still had some sort of relationship going with a teacher from his high school. He wanted to go see her Friday nights. I hated it. We'd get over there and the two of them would talk in words this long [*spreading her hands wide*]. Jim put on airs. Always had to be better than everybody else. He was always after the best. If I needed a coat he had to buy me a fur. Make a big show. Jim would drink all night sometimes and not get home till late. In a way I think he was trying to get back at his parents, who didn't drink or smoke.

His father could be so mean-spirited. I remember his dog used to chase my car. One day I hit it. I felt terrible. I brought it into the house, still alive, and said, "Come on. We can take it to the vet."

"No we won't," Ben said. He didn't want to spend the money.

"I'll pay for it."

Nope. He took the dog in the other room and let it suffer for six hours before it died.

There was no sign of love between Jim and his father. None. But Elizabeth, his mother, was very sweet, very loving. She was an old-fashioned lady. Had long gray hair that she brushed and braided every night before bed. In the morning she'd take the braid out, brush and wear her hair in a severe bun in the back of her head. Never changed in all the years I knew her. She went through hell living with that man. Once in a while we talked about it, but she had no place to go. "Ben got hurt" she'd say, "and he hasn't been the same since."

Not long after we married, Ben and Elizabeth moved up to a Lutheran camp to be caretakers. The place was gorgeous but the two of them still lived in poverty 'cause that's the way he wanted it. He collected Social Security and had some money stashed away. He picked up odd jobs. They didn't need to live like they did.

Still, the first years of marriage were happy ones. Jim talked about moving up in the A&P, becoming store manager. Eventually we wanted our own house and children. I didn't want to work all my life. But three years into our marriage, Jim got drafted. We had just signed another three-year lease on the apartment. Jim got so drunk.

Selective Service System
ORDER TO REPORT FOR INDUCTION

June 14, 1956

The President of the United States,
To Floyd James Thompson
907-A River Rd
New Milford, N.J.

Greetings: Having submitted yourself to a Local Board composed of your neighbors for the purpose of determining availability for service in the Armed Services of the United States, you are hereby ordered to report to the Local Board at 20 Banta Place, Hackensack, N. J. at 7 a.m. on the 27th of June 1956, for fowarding to an induction station.

G. M. Gillette

Remember getting drunk after receiving your draft notice?
Definitely. Horrible. [*Laughs*] Oh God. Drunk on my ass. Newark first. Screened [into the Army] and long bus trip to Dix. Commercial bus. Got off midway. Liquor store. Pooled money. Beer and hard liquor too. Drank on the bus. Drunk on my ass.

How'd the Army greet that?
Arrive at night. Lay on the ground, puking up. Find a bunk.

6 August 1956

Dear Mom and Pop,

Gee, I was really glad to hear from you. Mail Call is the brightest hour of the day. I am so happy to hear from anyone at home. I know it is hard to find time to write. Sometimes I just about get through my chores and end up writing Alyce in the crapper after 10. Although they don't bother us for this, we really need the sleep. We have a pretty rough schedule. Often our day lasts from 3 a.m. until 8 at night. I seem to be thriving on it though. Although I haven't lost any weight, my pants are getting loose and my shirts are getting tighter. I'm losing my beer belly. By the way, I did buy stamps with the dollar. A book of 24 costs 72 cents so I bought a quart of beer with the change. OK? It really tasted good.

I see Pop still likes his own cup of coffee. "Intermission. Time out for a coffee break." That's my Pop. I only wish I was there to join you. I haven't had a decent cup since I've been here. Yesterday we went to Columbus and I had some good Scotch and soda and a great big steak. I never appreciated a meal so much in my life.

As for keeping ahead, I made the highest score in the company on the transition range. The targets are in shapes of men and they pop up all over the damn place. I made 295 out of a possible 320. I still hate KP. As for sitting down, I only pulled it once, but I worked from 1 a.m. until 10:30 that night and didn't stop or sit down once.

I will be home on the first of September. We are getting a two-week leave after eight weeks basic. I can hardly wait. Right now we are only half way through because they don't count the time at Dix as basic training. At first, I was going to wait till Christmas to come home but the C.O. advised us to take the leave while the taking is good because although we expect to be here for the whole two years this army changes every 2 minutes. With the world situation in the condition it is, I might be in Burma or the Suez Canal for all I know. I'm going to take every minute I can get to be home with my family.

We had a good laugh tonight. Our C.O. berated us for not having much pride in the outfit. Our platoon is almost all married men about my age and everyone wants to get the hell out of here & get home. We'll leave this business of being a professional soldier to the other jerks who can't make a living doing honest work. I have high respect for the career Army man but the worst of the others are drunks or lazy bums who couldn't hold a job on the outside. And we are supposed to respect them or take pride in working with them? It's a laugh.

Don't misunderstand me. I am not going sour but I couldn't go around waving a flag either. I am happy here considering being separated from all

I hold dear, but I'll never be a real Army man. Part of my personality drives me to strive for the top, but that is the only reason I ever try. The reward is hardly worth the effort otherwise.

Believe me, Mom, if I couldn't talk with God at night and if I didn't have a good wife or family to come home to, I don't know what would sustain me. It took something like this to make me appreciate my background and know what a good Christian life means to a man.

I am sorry I have burdened you with some of my troubles. Please pay no attention to it. I am really doing pretty good for myself but Army life is just not for me.

Love,
Jim

7 ∎ THE ARMY

ALYCE   I moved back home when Jim went to basic. Things were bad there though. Les had drunken rages. We'd be sitting there having a nice conversation and he would change like that [*snapping her fingers*] and get a butcher knife after my mother. Weekdays I worked in New York. Weekends I'd drive up to spend time with friends, Bob and Pat Keyes, or I'd go to the country to see Jim's parents. Les thought I was whoring around. At one point he followed me, said he was taking the car keys. We had a real whoop-de-do over that. By then my real father had died from alcohol. He was dead three months before I found out. Some damn family, I'll tell you.

I'd been commuting to New York every day with a friend whose husband also got drafted. When Jim got out of basic, she and I decided we had had enough of living with our parents. We packed up and moved down to Fort Benning. Jim didn't appreciate that because money was tight.

FROM ARMY ENLISTED SERVICE RECORD

15 March 1957

I have known Private Floyd J. Thompson for one month as a member of my G3 section of the 3rd Infantry Division. In this period the section has been functioning at peak workload, particularly in several map and tactical exercises. Private Thompson has been a most valuable member of the section. He is always alert, courteous, willing and able to work long hours as an operations clerk.

I have checked his record of accomplishments and reputation in his basic training platoon and later in AG clerical school. He was considered to have outstanding potential. He has fine military bearing and appearance, initiative and ambition and leadership potential. I recommend he be enrolled in the Officer Candidate Course.

Robert J. Bigart, Lt.Col.

ALYCE   Those early military years were fun. Jim came home every night. He applied to OCS and we were waiting to hear. Finally we learned he was selected. And I got pregnant. We had talked about it. "I guess if we're going to do it," Jim said, "we might as well do it now."

29 September 1957

Dear Mom & Pop,

Forgive me for not writing sooner. We don't have enough time to think. This week I got enough demerits to make a week's restriction so I managed to get caught up with all I had to do. The pace they set here is terrific. We get up at five and lights out at eleven. Between these hours I don't think we stop once. This place is all I was told to expect and then some.

The tactical officers are hell on wheels. I've lost count of the times we've returned from training to find our room a mess. The worst was last Sunday. They came in and found the place a mess, according to their standards. They promptly inverted everything in sight and some things that were out of sight.

Accommodations here are plush for the Army. We have new three-story brick buildings with rooms for two, instead of the usual barracks. Each candidate is provided a bed, desk, chair, dresser, footlocker and wall locker and a detail SOP as to how each will be arranged.

The last time my room was inspected all the drawers in my desk, dresser and wall locker were on the floor and my bed on top. And for the coup de grace they dumped the wastebasket then gigged us for a dirty room. A good sense of humor is necessary to maintain sanity in this school.

I consider this a million-dollar experience. I wouldn't sell it for a million but you couldn't give me a million to do it again. The course of instruction is the best. The training is rugged but very necessary and very thorough. How else can we be taught responsibility? It is sometimes difficult to realize that after graduation we will be in absolute command of a minimum of forty-five men and solely responsible for their lives in time of war.

It's a heavy responsibility you carry in the service to make one think more levelly and directly on a down-to-earth basis. Incidentally, Pop, I am in a platoon with a bunch of Rebels who were bragging about their Confederate ancestors. I know you were in the Army but that is about all I do remember. How about filling me in with some retaliatory information. When were you in and what rank did you hold? We must have had someone in the War Between the States. Do you know of any? I sure would appreciate information so I can keep up with the local braggarts.

Last week Alyce and I managed to make a movie on post. Next week, if all goes well, we will be permitted to live off post, providing I don't get too many demerits. I already have six on the scoreboard from Saturday's inspection. The damn Tac Officer pulled out my toothbrush and said, "Candidate, you actually put this thing in your mouth." The case had some streaks of the toothpaste on it and you know what that looks like.

Enough about my trials and tribulations, how are things on the homefront? I hope this delinquent letter reaches you all in good health. Alyce and I get to see each other several times a week and go to church every Sunday together. Alyce's pregnancy is progressing nicely and the doctor is well pleased and predicts a normal, easy delivery. He has promised she can travel around Christmas. The school closes for the holidays and we are going to try to make it home. We both look forward to seeing the family again.

We certainly appreciate the clothes you made for Alyce. They sure save us a lot of money which incidentally is a very scare commodity. It costs me a lot to be in this school. My laundry bill alone runs $30 per month. We are expected to have a clean uniform on at all times. This means at least twice per day, the work uniform and the suntans in the evening. You never put on a uniform the second time. And the shoes must be like mirrors. The week before I entered school I spent about $100 on summer uniforms and getting my others ready for school. Since I have been here I spent money like a drunken sailor.

By the way, graduation is March 4th. It will be a happy moment in my life to have my folks pin on the first set of gold bars. And I am sure you will want to see the first son born to carry the family name. Quite a pitch isn't it? Answer by letter if you can and we can discuss it at Christmas.

For the first time in my life I feel I have a direction, a goal and something worth working for. I can't say what I will be doing 20 years from now. But if all goes well, I think I am going to make the Army my career. I feel it is an honorable and dignified profession and there is an abundance of personal satisfaction to be gained by the individual. In short, I am sold on the Army way of life and so is Alyce. I've always liked to travel and as an officer you always go first class.

I will have to close for now. I promise to write again when I have time. I would like to hear from you. Alyce reads me all your letters but once in a while it is nice to get a letter from your own folks. I'm sure you understand what I mean, sort of man to man, or parent to son or something like that. The bugler just sounded chow call. I really must go. Bye now.

All my love,
Jim

ROBERT SIRONEN   I've never seen anybody do such a turnaround. Suddenly Jim was one hundred percent Army.

BRENDA HUNTER   He was in his glory. He wanted to make something of himself. Some people can't stand to go into the office every day, see the same place, same people. That was Jim. He didn't like to be tied and he had the gift of gab. In the military he found his niche.

FRANCIS TOOMEY   As OCS roommates, Jim and I discovered we both had joined reluctantly. But things happen to people during training. Your family grows. Patriotism comes to the fore. We had a lazy crew of instructors. They harassed us but always at their convenience. During long road marches one would get in a car while the other one ran. Jim was serious and dedicated. The Army was his chance to fulfill whatever aspirations he had for his life.

JOSEPH WEAVER   Like a lot of us, Jim was neither a standout nor did he squeak by. He took OCS in stride. Alyce was one of those wives who, at a moment's call, picked laundry up for anybody. Us bachelors really appreciated that.

FRANCIS TOOMEY   Weekdays Jim couldn't wait to see his wife. He spoke of her so lovingly. Single guys like me were starry-eyed when we saw what the married guys got when wives came to visit. And there was a certain chemistry there when Alyce and Jim were together.

26 January 1958

Dear Mom and Dad,
I was very pleased to hear you're feeling better. You had me worried. This is the only bad feature with being so far from the family. Notice I said from the family and not from home. It's a funny thing but wherever Alyce and I happen to be is our home. It is better this way. I see young couples all the time pining for their home instead of making a home for them-

selves wherever they are. It certainly gives me a feeling of independence to know I am standing on my feet.

And you wouldn't believe the difference in Alyce when she is away from her people. She has never been happier or more pleasant. Pregnancy really brought out the true beauty of her. She seems to have a glow radiating from her very soul, stemming from an inner contentment she had never known before. Gone is the suspicion and the foul language and the nasty temper bred in the miserable atmosphere she has known all her life. In its place is a truly wonderful girl with the sweetest disposition and the kindest nature possible. I sincerely believe there isn't another couple as happily married as Alyce and I.

The time is fast approaching for her to enter the valley of shadows. I pray each night that, God willing, they will both emerge out of the other end. I don't know what I would do without them. You have often heard of people turning to God in times of stress. I must admit I always thought it was just a grandstand play. But I realize now that it is like a lost soul reaching out for something firm. Believe me Mom I would never be able to stand it if I couldn't share my thoughts with someone. You will be glad to hear we are still attending church as regularly as possible and are thinking of joining the choir. I don't know if this will be possible as time is very precious right now.

Did Alyce tell you she is going to be Vice President of her wives club? The last vote was a tie but it has definitely broken in Alyce's favor and will be confirmed at their meeting Wednesday. Your idea for a parcel post baby shower is excellent. Alyce was saying the other day how she missed having her friends around at this time. I am sure she would be overjoyed to hear from them

Really, you should see her. She is as big as a house. I am sure the baby will be at least eight pounds. I promise I will take some pictures this weekend and send them to you. Believe it or not she is even straining the seams of her maternity dresses.

I'm in the mood to write but I really must close as it is after midnight and 5:00 a.m. comes awfully early. Goodnight folks and God bless you both. I realize this will get there too late for your birthday, Mom, but just the same, many happy returns and my best wishes for a prosperous year.

Love,
Jim

ALYCE   It about killed Jim that he didn't graduate with that first OCS class. I was never told what happened.

FRANCIS TOOMEY   Jim got recycled about the twentieth week of twenty-two. The tac officer called us in individually and said, "We think you're a good guy but we want you to stay back. Do you accept, yes or no?" Jim and I both did well but could not compete with some guys who had more leadership experience, more maturity. OCS was a hell of a lot more competitive in those days than, say, during the Vietnam War. The Korean War veterans had shown they could lead people in combat and survive. When you've had a bayonet stuck in your breastbone and earned the Silver Star, they advance you. Jim and I had superior grades but not that little edge the Army was looking for. I wasn't too disappointed. Jim had a different ego though. He took it hard.

ALYCE   In the middle of February I went into labor. I called Jim but he said he couldn't get out of training to take me to the hospital. So a girl-friend of mine, Elaine Moss, took me to the hospital. Throughout labor I thought about how Jim wouldn't pick a girl's name. He wasn't going to have a girl. He was having a son. When I came out of the anesthetic and found out I had a daughter, I went into hysterics.

Alyce said you wouldn't pick out a girl's name.
Jimmy only. [*Laughing*]

"He wasn't having a girl. He was having a son."
That's right. But I loved all my girls. So, what the hell.

ALYCE   I socialized with the other wives. We had coffees and teas. Anything I could do to help his God Almighty career. I was totally dependent on him. For everything. When Jim finally graduated, his parents came down for the ceremony. By tradition the wife pins on one of the lieutenant bars. His mother the other. His old man wasn't too happy about that.

OFFICER FITNESS REPORT REMARKS

20 November 1958
Lt. Thompson, young, newly commissioned officer, is willing to accept responsibility, is extremely interested in his work and performs his assigned tasks with energy and enthusiasm. These traits, coupled with his desire to instruct, enable him to achieve dependable results in his assigned tasks.
Maj. David T. Oliver, Rating Officer

Lt. Thompson is young and inexperienced. He has a bright, quick mind and works with energy and enthusiasm. . . . He is quick to jump to conclusions and will take a strong stand on something he has not thought out.

Lt. Col. Boyd L. Brown, Endorsing Officer

8 September 1959

This officer is a quick learner and once mistakes are brought to his attention he is capable of taking corrective action. He is inclined to be remiss in his supervisory duties. He seldom checks up on his subordinates to see if they are carrying out his instructions adequately. This undesirable trait should disappear with additional experience.

Maj. David T. Oliver, Rating Officer

Lt. Thompson has a bright quick mind and very retentive memory. He is eager to impress his associates but will jump to conclusions and take a strong stand on something he has not thought out. He cannot be depended upon to exercise the best judgment in absence of orders.

Lt. Col. Boyd L. Brown, Endorsing Officer

15 December 1959

An eager young officer whose enthusiasm tends to seek responsibility beyond his capability. He learns easily and with additional experience will broaden and become even more of an asset to the Army.

Maj. Loren R. Lester, Rating Officer

This officer from the standpoint of technical proficiency is relatively inexperienced. He tends to over emphasize events and happenings. He seeks responsibility and often gets out of channels unknowingly. He should receive an assignment as a platoon leader as soon as possible.

Maj. David T. Oliver, Endorsing Officer

ALYCE   Pam was six months old when Jim went to Ranger school at Benning. He was gone half the time. I got pregnant again and he got orders to Korea for a thirteen-month tour. I began to get fed up with the Army. Jim was to leave in June and the baby was due in September. I asked him to hold off until the baby was born. No, he said, he had to go. It was three months he'd have behind him.

OFFICER FITNESS REPORT REMARKS (IN SOUTH KOREA)

30 November 1960

This officer has a fine understanding of small unit tactics and is capable of making sound recommendations. His efforts greatly enhanced this unit's tactical capability.

Capt. Anthony F. Matta, Rating Officer

His company has developed superior spirit and morale during its short existence for which Lt. Thompson deserves his share of credit.

Lt. Col. H. M. Bowlby Jr., Endorsing Officer

31 March 1961

Lt. Thompson has a great deal of energy and uses it to the benefit of his unit. He has profited greatly by his experience with a rifle company in Korea. His experience and training qualify him ideally for further duty with the infantry battle group.

Capt. Anthony F. Matta, Rating Officer

I consider him outstanding in every respect. He is an especially capable instructor. His instructions to the machine gun sections in this battle group produced outstanding results.

Col. Randolph C. Dickens, Reviewing Officer

ALYCE   Jim did well in Korea. When he came back we moved to Fort Bragg. Laura was ten months old by then. She would have nothing to do with her father. The two of them never got along. I went to the hairdresser's once and left him in charge. When I returned he had put Laura in her walker in the kitchen behind the swinging doors. She was just screaming. Jim said she'd been touching things and crying. He couldn't stand to listen to her. But the sun rose and set on Pam.

When Jim began work as a recruiter I got pregnant again. The baby was due in May. When my pains got a minute apart Jim took me to the hospital. But then they just up and quit. The doctor sent me back home, told me to walk and I would be back soon. Well, I walked for the next two weeks. I was in agony. I couldn't sit. I couldn't lay down. Jim said he had to go on a recruiting trip. "Jim," I said, "why won't you wait until after the baby is born?" No. He had to go.

My mother came down. On the 24th we were up all day and into that night. Walking and in pain. The hospital told her, "If you can't time the pains don't bring her in." Some I had a minute or two apart, then I would go a half hour without any. Finally, Mama said, "I don't give a damn what they say. If they won't take you there, I'll take you to a civilian hospital."

She checked me in at a quarter after eleven. Ruth was born at three minutes to one. And she almost died. The cord was wrapped around her neck. She was nearly black when she came out. All the time I'd been pushing, the cord had been getting tighter and tighter. They had to do extensive work on her, then put her in an incubator. Jim showed up the next day with my mother on his arm and a daiquiri hidden in his coat. Too bad I was laid up, he said. Him and Mama were going to a party. And they did. They had themselves an absolute ball. Of course he sent flowers and candy. He always did something big.

By this time his drinking was getting the better of me. They had a happy hour on post. It's a horrible tradition. Every Tuesday and Thursday night he'd come home smashed. One morning when he left for work I said, "I'm putting the kids to bed early. So come home. We'll have a couple of drinks and a nice dinner." But it was happy hour night. I called to tell him dinner was ready. "I'll be there," he said. "I'll be there, I'll be there, I'll be there." By nine o'clock the dinner was ruined. I thought, if he's there having himself a few, I'll have myself a few. Over the next hour I drank six old-fashioneds. By the time he got home I was feeling no pain. He got angry.

"Don't you ever do that."

"Why not?" I said. "If you can do it at a bar, why can't I do it here?"

8 ■ SPECIAL FORCES

Part of the mystique of Army Special Forces is that its ranks are filled with hard-nosed volunteers only. That wasn't true in the early 1960s, when the Army couldn't get enough volunteers to expand Special Forces units at an acceptable pace for the broad range of new missions ordered by President John F. Kennedy.[*] A young Army officer, Donald Goulet, witnessed how that involuntary expansion of the "Green Berets" changed the course of Jim Thompson's career. Nathan Vail and George Maloney, career Army officers from that era, also came to know Thompson, as well as the pressures that swept him into Special Forces and, before long, into a country few Americans knew, called Vietnam.

DONALD GOULET   After Jim returned from Korea in August 1961 the Army made him a recruiting officer at Fort Bragg. He led a team around to basic training centers to get volunteers for the 101st Airborne at Fort Campbell and 82nd Airborne at Bragg. I worked in the adjutant general shop. I found Jim very supportive, the more senior lieutenant looking out for the young buck.

Bragg, in the early sixties before Vietnam heated up, was a very warm, pleasant atmosphere. I saw Jim at social gatherings. He and Alyce would invite me and the other young bachelors over for dinner. They were a fine

---

[*] A powerful advocate of Special Forces for use in counterinsurgency operations, Kennedy authorized the distinctive headgear in the fall of 1961. He also expanded military and economic aid to Vietnam.

couple. With their three little girls the household was a lot of fun. Within a year, however, I was in Germany and Jim wound up with the 7th Special Forces Group. He was *not* a volunteer.

How did you end up in Special Forces, Jim?
In recruiting. Fine. Good. Let it alone. But Green Berets come. Pull me out. "What's this, goddammit? No!" Call up. [*Holding an imaginary telephone*] No dice. Call up higher. No dice. Green Beret it is.

DONALD GOULET   Jim's reluctance toward SF was perfectly normal. Special Forces had a lot of older captains and majors, guys who had knocked around a long time. They were guys you could count on in the clutch but who might otherwise be unacceptable. Special Forces was not what an officer wanted for career progression.

NATHAN VAIL   Soldiers aiming for the upper ranks stayed in the conventional Army. Officers serving on selection boards had traveled that route themselves and were not likely to endorse a clandestine offshoot. Special Forces were seen as "snake eaters," almost demented in a professional way. Mysterious, exciting, and adventurous but in many ways antiestablishment. They showed a flamboyancy that career officers weren't caught up in. But when not enough officers volunteered after Kennedy ordered Special Forces expanded in 1961, more were detailed there. Many did one tour and got out as quickly as possible.

GEORGE MALONEY   I looked on Special Forces as an interesting assignment, uniquely designed for its times. But the stigma was very real. Even in World War II there was plenty of resentment toward elite units. Following Kennedy's order, however, Special Forces went from a few hundred soldiers to several thousand in a very short time. It literally grew tenfold. When you go from x to 10x you lose some professionalism. Many NCOs went from corporal and sergeant to officer candidates and became Special Forces team leaders.

SAM DEACON   I got my call in August '62. They wanted senior first lieutenants or brand-new captains with some combat training and troop experience. My commander was asked to provide volunteers. "No volunteers," he said, "but I've got one who needs to go!" As a reserve officer I could only stay on active duty as long as they needed infantry officers. So when the call came I figured to do a year or two in SF, gain infantry-like credit, and leave. My first set of orders was to a language institute in Washington, D.C., to study Lingala. That's where I met Jim Thompson.

We shared an apartment with other officers attending the institute. Whenever we sat down together Jim was the first to speak and last to stop.

Part politician, part showman. A song-and-dance man. The unspoken rule was never to discuss women, religion, or politics. And Jim made sure we kept it. But we talked a lot about the Army and, in subtle ways, Jim tried to teach us how to be better officers. He made little teaching points like he was still an instructor. Some thought they were useful. Some didn't. One of our captain friends and two lieutenants who had already served in Europe and Korea, the three of them only tolerated Jim. My attitude was to keep an open mind.

As we prepared to graduate that December we heard 1st Special Forces Group was expanding for Vietnam. In fact the Vietnam mission was escalating to the point they might have to start running teams from the 5th and 7th Groups at Bragg. But we still had another six months training ahead of us.

———

ALYCE   I'd gotten Pam a dollhouse for Christmas that year. Like most every toy then it had to be assembled. But on Christmas Eve, Jim went drinking. I used to dread that night. Jim had it in his head that on Christmas Eve you went out and got drunk. This time when he came home he passed out on the couch. I stayed up until after three o'clock putting the dollhouse together. Jim woke up about five and started in on me. He had wanted to put that toy together.

"You were passed out drunk," I said. "I didn't know if you were going to wake up in time." One thing led to another and I said, "Maybe I should go pack."

"You go ahead," he said. "But the kids stay."

Then he told me something I'll never forget. He said, the Army was his first love, his children were his second, his parents his third love, and his brother was his fourth. I fell behind his brother Danny. Danny! I've never forgotten that. Things changed for me right then and there. But I thought, They're my kids, he won't let me take them, so I'll stick it out.

Alyce said every Christmas Eve you spent drinking with the boys.
No. No. No.

She said the two of you had a fight Christmas Eve, 1962, after you went drinking. There was a dollhouse that needed to be put together.
I made it myself. [*Laughing*]

You woke up and were very upset. . . .
Dollhouse . . . my own self.

Alyce said during the fight you said the Army came first, your children second, your parents third, and your brother fourth. Then Alyce.

No. Army comes first, okay. Second, Alyce. Third, our children.

SAM DEACON   When I got to Bragg and discovered the enlisted men were better than average, I knew Special Forces was the place to be if you wanted to soldier. There was pride and esprit. The emphasis wasn't so much on strength or combat skills as mental endurance and getting things done. The most rugged training occurred the last two weeks of the officer course, in the swamps of Georgia. That was followed by a four-week course on counterinsurgency where we got the overall picture of using Special Forces.

ALYCE   The ceremony where they got their berets was on a Saturday morning. I couldn't go, one of the kids was sick. So I was doing a load of wash when Jim walked in the front door wearing that green thing. "Oh, now you've got your green beanie," I said. God, that was the wrong thing to say! "It's not a beanie. It's a symbol of respect and it's something to be proud of!" He ranted and raved. I never called it a beanie again, not in front of him anyway. But as I sat there, looking at his ears sticking out, with this green thing on his head, it looked so damn funny. [*Alyce laughs so hard her eyes fill with tears.*] The only time he looked funnier was when the Army got the notion to let them wear shorts. Shorts, long-sleeve shirts, socks and shoes. Some of those old men with their knobby knees sticking out. That was terrible!

ROBERT SIRONEN   I couldn't imagine Jim a Green Beret.

BOB KEYES   I was surprised. Jim was . . . how the hell can I say this? Jimmy was a good friend but I had the impression he was a little bit effeminate. Not wimpy but he was a mother's son rather than his father's son. A hell of a lot softer than, say, his brother Danny.

GEORGE MALONEY   Most Special Forces troops going to Vietnam were sent first to Okinawa, where we had a grandiose training camp. I was deputy commander there in the early sixties. We had jungles and natives and gave our soldiers an intense, meaningful indoctrination. Returning teams were debriefed thoroughly and used as instructors before new teams went into the same areas. It was the difference between a quick start and wasting half your tour learning names and faces. If a team was going to Khe Sanh, for example, where the natives are from the Bru tribe of Montagnards, we said, "Here are three hundred words of Bru you've got to know." Okinawa teams knew what they were getting themselves into. And we picked the best people. Bragg teams were different. They had none of the intense orientation needed for a tour in Vietnam. And, boy, it made a difference. Like day and night.

WILLIAM EVANS-SMITH   At Bragg, where I commanded 7th Special Forces Group (Airborne), our assets were diluted by the shift in focus to Vietnam. There were just not enough soldiers to go around. We could not teach a language as obscure as the Montagnards spoke. It was almost humanly impossible in the time allowed.

SAM DEACON   June of '63 we completed individual training at Bragg and were formed into teams. Suddenly we had to be reoriented from Africa to Vietnam. The extra language training wasn't much. Still, everyone's goal was to get on an A-team. I got orders to be team executive officer. Jim Thompson would be in charge

––––––––

ALYCE   After the hell I went through giving birth to Ruthie I didn't plan to have more children. In fact, if Pam had been a boy I probably wouldn't have had any more. If Laura had been a boy I would never have had Ruth. After three girls, Jim was resigned to the fact he wasn't going to have a son. That summer he went on a two-month training stint somewhere. In August I took the kids to New Jersey to spend time with Mother. I got a terrible craving for ice cream. I couldn't get enough of it. Mama began kidding me that I was pregnant. She made me so mad. One day I said, "If you say that one more time, I'm packing up these kids and going home." She did. And I did. When I got back to Bragg I got a doctor's opinion. Sure enough I was pregnant. I told Jim when he came home. That's when he told me he was going to Vietnam. "I'm scheduled to go in December."

"Jim, God Almighty," I said, "you haven't been with me for any of the three births!" In OCS he wasn't five miles away and couldn't get out. Laura was born when he was in Korea. He was on a recruiting trip when Ruthie came. I wanted him with me this time. And Vietnam was voluntary. "Postpone it!" I said. "Go next June. Be here for one of the kids!"

"No," he said. "I've got to go."

That was the story of our life after Jim entered service. Always gone. He lived and breathed the Army. I was hurt. Hurt bad.

Alyce begged you not to go to Vietnam?

Alyce was crying, yeah. But, Army comes first. All my friends too. Army comes first.

GEORGE MALONEY   It was extraordinary that a man would be away for the birth of all four children. But if someone trains to be a fireman, he wants to go to the fire. When your country is in a war, a professional soldier should be there. Vietnam was where the action was. Everyone wanted to get that experience. Every day, captains and sergeants came up to me and said, "Sir, I would really like to go if anybody gets sick or changes their minds." Some volunteered for any job specialty we needed over there.

3 September 1963

Letter of Commendation
To Captain Floyd J. Thompson
Company A, 7th Special Forces Group
Fort Bragg, North Carolina

From 11 July through 16 August 1963 you distinguished yourself as operations officer of detachment B-3. For two weeks of Joint Exercise "Swift Strike III" you were responsible not only to organize and train the guerrilla band and supervise the remainder of the staff. Your calm and mature judgment had a steadying effect on the entire detachment. In the face of unusual operating conditions you displayed the flexibility, imagination, initiative and drive so vital to a Special Forces officer. It has been a distinct pleasure to serve with an officer of your caliber and I would be most happy to serve with you again in any capacity. Your performance of duty during Exercise Swift Strike III reflects great credit upon yourself, Special Forces and the U.S. Army.

William F. Murley
Major
Artillery, Commanding

9 ▪ ORDERS

FRANK ROSE That summer we began training for Vietnam.

HERBERT HOFF Each team had ten enlisted and two officers.

FRANK ROSE The educated Vietnamese all spoke French, so half the team studied French and half Vietnamese. It was no more than survival language training. This was followed by tactical training and cross-training within the team.

HERBERT HOFF We studied weapons, operations, medical, the whole works. Everybody knew everything about each other's job and specialty.

SAM DEACON Jim and I reviewed the team personnel records. First there was Herb Hoff, our team sergeant, an administrative type.

HERBERT HOFF I had been a C-team administrator and was promoted into an operational position.* I didn't go through Special Forces training.

SAM DEACON Rose had extremely good operations experience. Our two medics, Nelson Smith and Doc Blais, were probably the best medics in the whole group. We trusted them with our lives. Weapons men Eddie Trent and Max Jones were extremely knowledgeable on straight weapon applications but they had a lot to learn about operations. Engineers Carr and Hannah were demolition people and now needed to learn how to build bridges, dig wells, and build a trench line.

FRANK ROSE I'd been in the Army eleven years when Captain Thomp-

---

* A Special Forces company was composed of an administrative and operations detachment C, which commanded three operational detachments Bs, each of which commanded four A-teams, the basic twelve-man unit of the Special Forces.

son became my first Special Forces CO. Everything was different in SF. We became more familiar than we would with an infantry CO.

EDDIE TRENT   The captain became one of the guys. If something came up, he was right in the middle of it. When there's only twelve on the team you do that.

NELSON SMITH   He was an excellent officer. Highly motivated. Got along well with the troops. That's important in Special Forces. They isolated us for a long period to see how well we got along. Morale was high during training.

LINDSAY CARR   There was nothing but super people on that team and I thought I was one of 'em. I was very impressed with Captain Jim. During one field problem we switched off carrying medical gear, communication gear, demolition gear. The captain held his own, shared the load. He took his turn pitching wood, cooking the food. The unwritten law in SF was work as a team.

HERBERT HOFF   Among team members, I probably got along best with Captain Thompson. I was team sergeant and we were tight. He knew what he was doing.

OFFICER FITNESS REPORT REMARKS

21 September 1963

Captain Thompson's performance in Special Forces Operational Detachment B-3 has been superior. Due to his sound judgment and knowledge of tactics he planned operations against enemy units and installations that were accomplished with minimum losses to Special Forces and guerrilla personnel during Exercise Swift Strike III. Capt. Thompson constantly strives to better himself in both performance on the job and his education. He adapts readily to the hardships of living under field conditions.

Capt. Robert N. McNatt, Rating Officer

Captain Thompson is a creative and imaginative officer. He volunteered for many assignments during Swift Strike III beyond the scope of his regularly assigned duties. He possesses the qualities of leadership required of a Special Forces Officer.

Maj. William F. Murley, Endorsing Officer

HERBERT HOFF   In November '63 we were watching a medical cross-training film in the post theater when an officer came in and announced Kennedy had been shot.

LINDSAY CARR   I was in demolition class. During a slide presentation an instructor says, "Hey, listen up." We spent the rest of the day with our ears pinned to that radio.

HERBERT HOFF   That evening we went ahead with a scheduled team party at my house. It was tough to party, though, and watch that on television.

LINDSAY CARR   I was in better shape than anyone on the team. The team jock. But put rucksacks on our backs and Rose ran me into the ground. Some people can walk with weight on their backs for miles. Frank Rose was one of 'em.

SAM DEACON   Rose came to me periodically during training to complain about Jim. One day Rose asked me how I thought the team was shaping up. I turned the question around, asked him what he thought. Rose said he had doubts about Jim's leadership.

FRANK ROSE   There were problems. There were people on the team who should not have been there. They did not have the training or background. They were not in the shape they should have been to go into a situation like Vietnam. During that big push to expand Special Forces, many got through who shouldn't have been there. I'm not talking about Nelson Smith. He was crackerjack. Jim Oller was crackerjack. Doc Blais. Max Jones was a good weapons man, and so was Shorty Trent. Carr and Hannah. I would go out on operations with any of those guys, anytime. But we needed a good team sergeant to keep everything straight and under control. Hoff was trained in administration. And I thought Captain Thompson was wishy-washy. I can't give you specifics. But when you're training for raids and ambushes and your officer issues orders with details missing, details that might mean the difference between success and failure, you begin to feel the guy doesn't know what he's talking about. You lose confidence. I don't know if he thought he knew more than he did, or he was trying to bluff his way through because he was the "man." But a Special Forces officer has to have natural leadership ability. He has to be decisive without being a hardass and using his rank. He has to command respect without having to fall back on rank. I didn't think he had those qualities.

EDDIE TRENT   Did you hear about the pigs? I remember so well because it almost cost me my marriage.

LINDSAY CARR   Before taking a field trip one day, we decided to purchase some chow. We knew ahead of time where our base camp was going to be, so we bought all this food, stashed it in the boonies, and built pens to keep pigs and chickens. This would be our subsistence rather than C rations. In SF you improvised.

EDDIE TRENT   We went to this farmer Thanksgiving morning and bought a couple of pigs. One red, one white. But in taking them back to camp both got away. We spent hours chasing 'em. It was about four in the afternoon before we caught the first one.

LINDSAY CARR   We decided to Article 15 the pig right there. We cooked him that night.

EDDIE TRENT   About two or three days later the white one came back. We promised to barbecue him when we got back from Vietnam.

––––––––

SAM DEACON   Jim thought exposing me to certain situations would help build my confidence. It was starting to work. As a lieutenant I was comfortable being executive officer on the team, second in charge. But during training, after I got promoted to captain, I began to feel I made a wrong decision, that perhaps I should have stayed back and waited to get my own team. I had hoped that attitude wasn't interfering with my job. I had to catch myself not to override Jim's decisions. Sometimes I would just be quiet.

EDDIE TRENT   During mission training we spent two or three weeks out in a simulated camp. They sent us into the drop zone, our Vietnamese counterparts met us, and we established a perimeter to make everything tight. Well, the B-team commander comes along and said he didn't think we had enough area encompassed. This major jumped all over Captain Thompson. Things started getting bumfuzzled.

SAM DEACON   It was obvious sometimes that we were going in the wrong direction. Everyone else would be going north and suddenly our team turned east. But we were making a decision, see. And that was Jim's philosophy. When something had to be done, we should act, he said, even if it was wrong. If it's wrong, he said, you can find out later and change it. You can always correct it. I disagreed with him. Jim was a quick enough thinker to stay with a situation and even get ahead of it. But he wouldn't hear all of the information team members were giving us.

No, we weren't the perfect A-team and maybe never would be. There was always a little question in the back of our minds. We had shortcomings and failures. But Jim would always stand up for us.

OFFICER FITNESS REPORT REMARKS

26 December 1963

This officer performed his duties as detachment commander in a superior manner. During garrison training and duty Captain Thompson's unit continually showed signs of tremendous progress and ability to meet situations with sound understanding, professional competence and willingness. He demanded, and received from his subordinates, outstanding instruction. Once in field training situations he became aware of many shortcomings of his people and attempted to overcome these by himself. He did not demand from them the same professionalism and overlooked obvious mistakes. He was more concerned with his men's welfare than with their ability to assist in the accomplishment of his mission. When confronted with a problem he reacts hastily and not logically. He needs more infantry troop duty. His loyalty to his subordinates overshadows their competence. Owing to pre-mission training for Vietnam, this officer was unable to attend off-duty classes to improve his formal education. However, he plans to enroll in extension courses while on duty in Vietnam.

Maj. Richard D. Reish, Rating Officer

GEORGE MALONEY   With a report like that, I'm surprised he made it to Vietnam. Somebody had some reservations.

FRANK ROSE   Each team member was encouraged while training to write to his counterpart on the team in Vietnam to get as much information as possible. The team there could send back all the information it had about the Vietnamese camp commander, the terrain, what the enemy situation was. We should have had that before we left. We didn't.

LINDSAY CARR   I don't think anybody was in personal contact with his counterpart prior to going over, other than Jim. In fact, it wasn't until we were almost through with our mission training that we found out we were going to Khe Sanh. Just before we left, Jim got a letter and some pictures from the team leader he would replace.

SAM DEACON   The information wasn't thorough. They mentioned some problems between U.S. Special Forces and Vietnamese Special Forces. Nothing specific. We knew the camp physically was in bad shape and that there was camp construction going on. We also knew it was difficult getting the Vietnamese camp commander and the other elements there to do the construction required. But not until we got in-country and up to our camp did we realize what a tenuous situation we were entering.

LINDSAY CARR   We had finished our final field problem and were waiting until after the Christmas holiday to leave when Captain Thompson called us in individually for a talk.

FRANK ROSE   He wanted to interview everyone on the team to find out if we had any bitches.

LINDSAY CARR   Captain Thompson said, "Are you sure you want to go as a member of this team? If you want to back out you can, but tell us now."

FRANK ROSE   You have to have one of two things on a Special Forces team—a good captain or a good team sergeant. We lacked both. So when Captain Thompson asked if I had any bitches, I told him the team sergeant didn't know his job. I said Sergeant Hoff does not know anything about running operations but somehow, maybe through politics, he made it onto the team.

There was talk the team might be split in half, so Captain Thompson said, "I'll take Sergeant Hoff with me to take care of that. You go with the XO." Normally, the team sergeant would go with the more junior officer. But Captain Thompson said he personally had enough tactical knowledge to take care of operational duties while Hoff handled administration. But we didn't need an administrative sergeant on an A-team.

LINDSAY CARR   In that final interview, Captain Thompson made a comment I'll never forget. He said, "If I'm ever captured I'm going to keep one round in my weapon for me. I will never be captured alive." I thought that was a very bold statement. I considered it sort of a pep talk, the point being I should foresee eventualities and ask myself how I would handle them. But until the captain made that remark I didn't recall discussing the possibility of becoming a prisoner.

10 ■ GONE AGAIN

NELSON SMITH   The entire mission was classified. We could not tell our families what part of Vietnam we were going to or what we would be doing. We left December 26, 1963.

SAM DEACON   We formed up that morning in the company area. Our detachment got all of our gear together and loaded it on trucks. Then we boarded buses for the airfield.

———

ALYCE   Jim was running late. He had to stop at the post office to pick up cards and stamps. When he got to where he was supposed to meet his group, they'd already left for the airport. We had to hightail it down there. The airplane motors were going when we arrived.

———

SAM DEACON   We wondered where Jim was. When he finally showed he was perturbed about something. I never asked what.

———

ALYCE   I don't remember if he kissed me and the kids goodbye. I just remember him jumping out of that car 'cause the plane was taking off.

TINA CARR   We all said later he should have missed it.

ALYCE   As I watched them fly out of sight I was hurt. I thought, Here I am again. A woman, alone, with three kids. That's hard to take. I made up my mind there would be some changes when he got back in June. I didn't know what but something had to give.

Vietnam was expected to be over in no time at all. And nobody even knew where that was. Like Mama. I told her where Jim went. She said, "Where the hell's that?" I said, "I don't know."

December 26, 1963

My Darling:

All three of our little dolls are in bed now. All three exhausted. I went over to Jane Deacon's after leaving you at Pope and the girls played outside. It was such a beautiful day. Did you find out why the bus left so early? Must have been a reason.

Of course, you haven't even been gone 24 hours, Darling, and we all miss you terribly. Pam kept me very busy this evening. We finished playing Cootie and then we cut out paper dolls. Laura won the Cootie game and Pam came in second. We'll continue this letter tomorrow evening. It should be quite long by the time you receive it.

All my love,
Always,
Alyce

ALYCE   I wrote Jim every night. I'd think about what went on from the time I got up in the morning, to keep him up on the kids mainly, so he wouldn't miss much of them growing up.

———

NELSON SMITH   In Saigon I felt we had stepped into the 1890s. No modern technology. Transportation was bicycle. Streets were crowded but with very few Americans.

HERBERT HOFF   There were only about eight thousand U.S. troops in the whole country.

GEORGE MALONEY   Once in-country the A-teams flew up to Da Nang, my headquarters for the B-team. There soldiers got a little orientation before flying out to their camps. Mission-type orders. "Here's your camp, train your Vietnamese, develop their offensive capabilities, get out on patrol, clear this area and at the same time develop the infrastructure. Keep working on your airfields, keep clearing the jungles, build your roads, get your sick-call people out to the villages, and start developing some loyalty with the natives." And as B-team commander, I told them, "Every day I'm going to be out there on your ass."

FRANK ROSE   Each team member got briefed by their counterpart on the B-team. The intelligence sergeant talked to the B-team intelligence sergeant, the operations sergeant to his B-team operations sergeant, and so on. We wanted all the latest information before we went up on site. When you're on a team that will sit in the farthestmost corner of South Vietnam, near the Laotian and North Vietnamese borders, you have but-terflies. They issued us our weapons. We zeroed the sights and fired to make sure they were okay. We were to bring only personal weapons to the camp—M-2 carbines and .45 pistols. All the bigger weapons were on site.

                                                                New Year's Eve
Dearest:
What a day this has been. It is raining and freezing as fast as it hits. I bet a lot of people will change their minds and stay home tonight. When we got up this a.m., it was 50 degrees in our bedroom and 59 in the living room. Bob came over to check the furnace and the filter was filthy. He changed it and now the bedroom is 62 and the living room 68. The wind is blowing directly at the front of our place. I've got newspapers stuffed around the heater room door. . . .

    I miss you Darling. I know if you were here we'd be getting dressed right now and either going out or having people in. Next year we'll have a double blast. What do you say. . . .

LINDSAY CARR   New Year's Day we got into Khe Sanh.

FRANK ROSE   We arrived in a C-123. A couple members of the other team met us. Whenever a plane approached they had to take a detail and secure the runway. They met us with a World War II three-quarter-ton jeep with a machine gun mount, and an old deuce-and-a-half truck.

SAM DEACON   The airfield was half dirt, half steel planking. A few mor-tar rounds had already hit it because some sections were bent. I thought, Well, we're in a combat zone now. But I didn't have much time to look around. I was concerned about the equipment getting off the aircraft and aboard the truck. My first surprise was that the airfield sat three or four kilometers from camp.

GEORGE MALONEY   The airfield could be reached by only two roads, both subject to mining and sniper fire. That plantation road was called Ambush Valley.

FRANK ROSE   From airport to camp was jungle, a deserted run on a dirt road.

SAM DEACON   We went down to Highway 9 and then west for a while before turning up another hill, through the camp gate, and into the American compound. The gate looked like it was ready to fall off.

GEORGE MALONEY   The camp was built around an old French fort that had fallen to the Vietminh during the revolt against the French. There were quarters for the Special Forces teams, both Vietnamese and U.S., a command post, a mess hall, Nung quarters,* a shower and laundry, supply room, ammo bunker, the VN commander's quarters and mess, a range house and carpentry shop and a dispensary on one rise of a hill. Slightly north and down the hill was the rifle range. To the south were the troop mess and motor pool and west of that troop billets with the artillery battalion command post. The camp's main gate was five hundred meters above the village.

SAM DEACON   As soon as we arrived, I started looking around to see what we'd gotten ourselves into. I stuck my head into the team barracks and the weapons pit. They had one machine gun and one eighty-millimeter mortar. Then I walked along the camp perimeter. Two thousand feet above us was a mountain peak that left us within mortar range. This was a dangerous spot.

It was almost dark by the time I got my stuff out of the middle of the compound and stuck it in a bunk. Our first mission that night was to protect ourselves. We wouldn't rely on anybody else, not the Montagnards nor the South Vietnamese. We ran a guard check, ran a perimeter check, tested the radio, checked ammo supplies, and tried to fix a bed as best we could inside the hooch.

GEORGE MALONEY   Most A-teams had a couple of days to cross-brief each other. The new team would be introduced to anyone important in the area, including the Vietnamese commander, the village chief, French plantation owners. After three or four days the team being relieved would fly back to Da Nang.

SAM DEACON   No one from the other team stayed even a day with us.

FRANK ROSE   For some reason they were overdue getting out. And the weather was so erratic you never knew from one day to the next if a plane could get in. So they didn't brief us on much. They did introduce us to our Vietnamese counterparts. But clearly that team was happy to be getting out.

LINDSAY CARR   They figured they'd pushed their luck far enough.

---

* Nung tribesmen, native to the highlands of North Vietnam, were excellent soldiers with years of combat experience in Indochina. In the early sixties, U.S. Special Forces teams in northern South Vietnam hired them to serve as camp security forces.

Happy New Year Darling!

Well, we didn't freeze today. It warmed up a little and the wind wasn't as bad. Boy, the electric blanket and my flannel nightshirt sure came in handy last night. I'd been froze otherwise. And you should see the shape of me in the nightshirt.

Honey, the girls have all been so good at bedtime. No fooling around. It is amazing. I say, "Come on, bedtime" and off we go. I stagger them one-half hour apart, Ruth at 7, Laura 7:30 and Pam at 8. Well, one week gone by already. About 25 more to go. . . .

> All my love,
> Always,
> Alyce

Part III

WAR AND DREAMS

1964–1973

11 ■ IN-COUNTRY

G EORGE MALONEY   The dominant ethnic group in Vietnam came from China thousands of years ago and settled in two large concentrations, one in the Red River delta area with the capital at Hanoi, the other in the Mekong River delta with the capital at Saigon. But the inland and highland areas of Vietnam were inhabited primarily by natives who lived there for thousands of years before the Chinese arrived. The French called these native people Montagnards or "mountaineers." Slowly they were pushed farther away from the coast and deeper into the hills. Similar to American Indians, they lived in tribes of different languages, customs, and ethnic heritage. Some were very primitive.[*]

When the United States initiated support to the Republic of Vietnam in 1954, these two groups, the lowlanders and the Montagnards, each hostile to the other, needed to be addressed. The lowlanders, or Vietnamese, formed the bulk of the population and held all positions of government. A conventional U.S. Army advisory group developed their military capabilities. The Montagnards occupied key mountain and jungle areas from which any guerrilla war would be based. Responsibility for neutralizing them, a political mission, was assigned to the Central Intelligence Agency. And U.S. Special Forces was the CIA's action agency. A key mission was to give this large third force of Montagnards the means and will to stay out of

---

[*] Colonel Maloney's comments here are drawn from both interviews with the author and from briefing materials he provided to Special Forces teams sent to South Vietnam in the early sixties.

the Viet Cong fold and, where possible, to bring them into the government fold.

So there were two wars in Vietnam in 1964 when Jim Thompson arrived. Along the coast, large conventional Vietnamese units, supported by U.S. advisers, fought to protect the cities and surrounding farms. They got ninety percent of media attention. Along the border, smaller units fought largely unnoticed battles, with whatever assistance the Montagnards could provide, to interdict the endless VC resupply effort that sustained communist coastal units.

Khe Sanh, where Thompson's team was assigned, was the northernmost Special Forces camp in South Vietnam. About twelve kilometers from the Laotian border, the camp was established in 1962 to intercept supply routes that ran from Laos to the coast. Our patrols tried to keep the VC guerrilla bands on the move by hitting suspected support areas and ambushing trails, water points, and villages where they were getting support. By forcing the Viet Cong off roads and trails and into the trackless jungles, we reduced the tonnage they could move and forced them to provide armed escorts to carrying parties and use troops as scouts and guides. We never stopped the flow of arms, ammo, food supplies, and medicine. When we moved into an area, they moved out, shifting to alternate routes. But each time they changed areas they had to rebuild their trail infrastructure of way stations, porters, water sources, goods caches, rest areas, and medical aid stations.

U.S. Special Forces A-teams like Thompson's had twelve men, two of everything. Two officers, a commander and deputy; two medics; two weapons specialists; two communicators; two operations personnel; and two intelligence men. This allowed them to break into two teams if they had to. Also at each camp was a hodgepodge of workers, laborers, mechanics, contractors, soldiers, mercenaries, interpreters, officers, Montagnards, Nungs, pimps, cardsharks. The camps were like the boom towns of the Klondike. Some residents were patriots, some criminals. All were selfish; all were tough. Only the hardy survived. There was no law except camp regulations, and they were only as effective as the commander.

Many Vietnamese military had had French training, particularly the senior officers. By and large they were quite effective. They had been fighting the Vietminh for years and some since they were thirteen or fourteen, all during the late forties and early fifties. When our Special Forces units first went over in an advisory capacity in the late fifties, we trained Vietnamese Ranger units and special units, the cream of what was available. They developed dozens of Ranger companies. As each company graduated, they were farmed out to different provinces to act as an elite strike force.

Gradually, in a series of minor battles, these companies lost two or three veterans each day. Over the years the net effect was the so-called combat elite, a trained nucleus of what should have been Vietnam's military leadership, was dissipated. By the time we got there in the early sixties, we had far less than the elite.

The Vietnamese we dealt with weren't up to the standard of those killed or wounded over the years. Some of the best wound up in different NCO academies and officer candidate schools. But there are a finite number of militarily-capable people in any society. In America, where everyone is basically healthy and reasonably well educated, the pool encompasses just about all young men. In a society like Vietnam, they had so many uneducated people, so many Montagnards, that U.S. forces had no alternative except to get involved in a bigger way.

By 1964 the VN were down to where they were rounding up young men for military service by raiding street corners. They drove up with a bunch of trucks and literally grabbed every man of military age they could. When a plane arrived at our camps, out might come one hundred replacements but also some of the most surly dissidents there could be. These "Saigon Cowboys" made up a very large percentage of VN troops who came to us in the remote camps. They didn't know where they were or even which way to run if they tried to flee. They were ninety kilometers or more from the coast. They had to be cleaned up, clothed, trained. When I say "trained," I'm talking about a very delicate problem here. We certainly didn't offer a rifle to a guy who had just been dragooned. We had to do psychological preparation. Eventually we reached a point where the man wanted to serve, or at least seemed willing to serve. At that point you handed him a rifle. Initially we had an NCO stand behind them with the understanding that if they even looked like they were going to turn guns on anybody, he was to pop them.

The Viet Cong recognized the importance of dividing the South Vietnamese and the Montagnards. They used every ploy and propaganda trick imaginable to stir up trouble between the two groups. Communists had a relationship with the Montagnards dating back to the late 1930s, when they began to organize tribes to fight against the French colonialists. Some areas were completely under Viet Cong control. An important mission at Camp Khe Sanh was maintaining a friendly relationship with the surrounding Bru tribe. Unfortunately, we did not have as great a success as did the Viet Cong, who used terror. They forced Montagnards to serve as bearers in their carrying parties. To ensure the men remained responsive, VC kept families as hostages at jungle way stations.

Bru tribesmen around Khe Sanh were semi-savages in loincloths, less developed than some other tribes. Some of their leaders were polished enough to know the social amenities and play host in a manner that convinced us they were civilized. In the next moment they'd lead a sacrifice or take part in a tribal rite that went back to the cave man. For prolonged field duty, however, they had no superior. We used Montagnards as scouts on patrol, to look for signs we were getting close to VC or were vulnerable. They moved quickly and traveled light, with no food, no water, no supplies. In some cases, barefoot. They drank river water or cut a piece of bamboo, flipped it up, and drank the water inside. Bru ate off the land— peanuts, fruits. When they slept they didn't need a poncho and a sleeping bag. They'd crawl up next to a tree and nap for a couple of hours.

The whole question of allegiance, however, hinged on who could supply security and show evidence of eventual victory. In early 1964, in I Corps, the Vietnamese government could not supply security except in the immediate vicinity of our camps. Nor could it offer evidence of eventual victory. As a result it lost the people and most of the land.

We Americans were advisers only. We did not command the Vietnamese. Our leverage was the money, the materials, the military expertise we supplied. We were anxious not to appear to be colonialists telling them what to do. And they were very anxious to maintain their independence. This was their country, their armies, their mission, and their enemies.

12 ▪ CAMP KHE SANH

GEORGE MALONEY   Around Khe Sanh is some of the highest, most rugged country in South Vietnam. Several thousand feet above sea level. Every morning you appreciate a sweater. By noon you're in the blazing tropics. In winter it's a cold, wet, dreary place shrouded in rain and fog, with extremely limited visibility. The jungle is wild, largely uninhabitable, and very rugged.

FRANK ROSE   It's beautiful there really. Mountainous with triple-canopy jungle. Elephant grass nine or ten feet tall. All kinds of wildlife—wild hogs, tigers, lots of water buffalo, elephant, cobra. Fruits grow wild, especially around the old Montagnard villages. Papayas. Bananas.

GEORGE MALONEY   Thompson's Special Forces camp was remote except for a little strip on either side of Highway 9 running from the coast out to Laos. There were villages, both Vietnamese and Montagnard, and huge French-owned peanut and rubber plantations that had been there for more than one hundred years. There were farms for corn and manioc. Fruit orchards. Tobacco was a huge product. Plantations were one reason Montagnards had such a carefree existence. They walked up and helped themselves. Even after a field had been harvested, residuals were enough to keep Montagnards alive. Streams around were loaded with fish, some of pretty good size. This was before soldiers started throwing hand grenades into them and cleaned them out.

FRANK ROSE   We felt green the first time we entered camp, which was farther north than any other in South Vietnam. We felt on our own and didn't know exactly what was going on.

SAM DEACON   No one told us we'd be sitting in a little triangular French fort that the Vietminh had overrun years ago. No one told us we'd be looking up at a mountain ridge two thousand feet above us and within mortar range. That's when we started getting homesick and wondering how we'd keep ourselves alive.

FRANK ROSE   Besides twelve Americans, we had eight Vietnamese Special Forces troops and about twenty Chinese Nungs who served as our bodyguards. Otherwise we recruited from the local villages—and didn't know who we could trust.

GEORGE MALONEY   Security was complicated by all manner of local people working in or around the camp. It was never possible to be sure the innocent farmboy wasn't a VC agent. There was a large company of Bru, about two hundred. Likable, friendly people but completely without skills. It took hours to teach them to use a shovel, to fill a sandbag, to use an ax or a saw. In the end we taught only the young.

Besides the Bru there were two Vietnamese companies, mostly draftees. We gave them surplus U.S. equipment, mainly carbines. Smaller weapons but very effective. Our soldiers carried the M-1 rifle, which had more stopping power but was too large for the Oriental man.

———

ALYCE   Back home, team wives stuck together. We had coffees or teas to keep up with the news. So-and-so wrote me today and said such-and-such. We discussed newsy things that our husbands wrote home. We supported one another.

January 3, 1964

Hi Honey:

It was a beautiful day. The girls (all three) are in the kitchen eating popcorn. They wanted that as their treat tonight. I called the wives today. Mrs. Hoff, Rose, Oller and Smith. We are having our first coffee here next Tuesday morning. Ruth finally cut her first tooth. Thank goodness. Boy, she is really drooling. Her front has been soaked all day. Just like she had dumped a glass of water down the front of herself. . . . After Laura went to bed tonight Pam asked me how many more babies we were going to have. She said she'd like three. Heaven forbid. It really tickled her when I said "what!" She giggled and giggled. . . .

All my love,
Always,
Alyce

GEORGE MALONEY   Major Art Drurey, my predecessor as B-team commander, had been concerned about Camp Khe Sanh. He told Jim to get
started on fortification. Because there had been plans to shift the camp
to the airport, little had been done to improve it before Jim got there. The
Nung hut was a rat-infested hovel. The Vietnamese troop messes were
standup affairs. Ammo storage was subject to pilferage or sabotage.
Defensive positions were designed to withstand no more than small-
arms fire. The VC had gotten mortars, so the camp needed overhead
cover.

SAM DEACON   Our attitude was, "We're the team. We've trained
together. Everybody knows his job. Now get it done." Within our first
twenty-four hours everyone identified what they had to do and set about
doing it.

NELSON SMITH   We worked around the clock, either on operations or
improving the camp.

SAM DEACON   Each day that passed we branched out, trying to cover the
next point in our minds or written plan. Everybody took inventory and
told me what supplies they needed. Jones, Trent, and I took a jeep down
Highway 9, ninety kilometers, to the coast at Quang Tri to visit with Military Assistance Command, Vietnam [MACV] advisers and pick up supplies. These guys didn't believe we went all that way ourselves. When we
saw their reaction we said, "Somebody's holding out on us." We didn't
realize what a dangerous situation we were in. None of us did.

GEORGE MALONEY   Every day these camps had to have work parties out
cutting jungle, filling sandbags. Every day they had to get a little stronger,
a little better defended.

FRANK ROSE   We had two perimeters. Inside the second slept our team,
Vietnamese Special Forces, and the Nungs. We closed that up at night so
none of the local strike force could get up there. We knew a large percentage of them were Viet Cong. Ten percent was average. We found VC
among our interpreters when we got more sophisticated using polygraphs.
But everything was sloppy and ragged at the camp when we arrived. On
the perimeter the elephant grass had grown up through the barbed wire. If
somebody wanted to attack they could sneak up to within twenty feet.

GEORGE MALONEY   A continuing job in every camp was to prepare the
battlefield, to push the jungle far enough back that snipers couldn't fire
right in. Teams had to burn the brush off but it was so water-laden they
had to cut and dry it first.

SAM DEACON   Jim had trouble getting the Vietnamese commander to
take charge of the clearing team. There were old mines still out there laid

by the French. We had no idea where some of them were. We didn't even
have a diagram of those laid by Americans.

FRANK ROSE   There was no intelligence sergeant on the team we
replaced. No intelligence nets had been set up in the villages. We needed
to recruit agents who had access to VC territory. We paid them to recruit
others and gather information about enemy locations, movements, and
VC sympathizers in the villages. Eventually we were running agents in all
the Bru villages, two or three cells with two or three people in each cell.
Getting the same information from different agents was how we verified
it. I used to pay them in old French coins. The Bru took the silver to make
bracelets for their babies' arms.

　　Bru strike forces were not capable fighters. Imagine trying to take
somebody unacquainted with anything modern and teach him to use these
weapons. Often, when the VC heard we were forming a strike force, they
sent people to be recruited and trained. As soon as they'd get weapons
they'd desert.

SAM DEACON   We had no idea what North Vietnamese or VC strength
was in our area. We did know it was a transit point for supplies. If nobody
bothered them, they would continue to pass nearby, not bothering to
attack except as a training exercise. Why wipe us out if they could regularly sneak supplies out of our camp.

January 4, 1964

Hi Darling:

Your first letter arrived today and I was so happy I was almost in tears. You
are so far away. . . . Tonight was shampoo night. I did it around five and
then had supper because Walt Disney is presenting Dumbo tonight and I
knew the girls would want to see it. . . . I got ambitious this morning and
cleaned out the hassock. I've got to find some way to get these magazines
out of here. Our Readers' Digest book came today. I plan on starting that
tonight. Looks like some real good stories in it. You'll have plenty of reading to catch up on when you get home. . . .

EDDIE TRENT   We had trouble right from the start with the South Vietnamese soldiers.

FRANK ROSE   Captain Thompson had to deal with the camp commander, a son of a bitch.

SAM DEACON   Jim pushed him to send a patrol out but it was difficult
working through an interpreter. Our Vietnamese wasn't good, making it
tough to tactfully convince him to organize a patrol.

FRANK ROSE   Diem was in power until shortly before we got to Vietnam and Vietnamese Special Forces were his hatchet men. A sergeant or even a corporal would frighten a regular ARVN officer. Still, I didn't buy Captain Thompson's approach. He was always trying to butter up the Vietnamese commander, saying "Why don't we do this" or "We ought to go out on patrol." He should have said, "I want a patrol out tomorrow morning." Period.

LINDSAY CARR When two Australians landed in camp, one of them, Rick Rooney, walked over to Jim and said, "I speak fluent Vietnamese." Jim said, "I appreciate that. Please keep your mouth shut 'cause I want to know what's going on."

EDDIE TRENT At the next meeting Rooney heard the VN say to each other, "We don't need these damn Americans around." When Rick told Thompson, we got up and left to show them we understood the insult.

NELSON SMITH We couldn't speak Bru either, and they were the people we really needed to talk with.

SAM DEACON We sent Montagnards out with a coloring book showing pictures of weapons. They were to circle the picture if they saw Viet Cong holding such weapons. We had them put a circle around each one they saw because they didn't grasp numbers.

January 5, 1964

My Darling:

I'm kind of down today. I was okay until my Mom called me. Instead of coming down for a month she'll be down on the 22nd of March and will only stay two weeks. If the baby is early or even on time, I'm going to be S.O.L. I know everyone says "Don't worry, we'll help." But half of them are just saying that. God, I wish your Mom could come down. At least for a week. The one when I'm due. But wishing won't get me anywhere. If it did do any good, you'd be home from my wishing. . . .

GEORGE MALONEY After I returned to Vietnam in January '64 I started around to my camps. When I first visited Jim's camp, I was horrified. I took one look and said to myself, My God, this place could not stand a determined assault. And yet here it was, the closest camp to the enemy. It sat right below the DMZ, farthest away from Da Nang and reinforcements. If attacked, nobody could get to them till daylight the next day. The very lightly constructed bamboo structures would have burned in a minute. Certainly they wouldn't stop a machine gun.

I don't mean Jim's team wasn't doing things to improve the situation. But I was stunned by the relative lack of defenses at the most remote Special Forces camp in Vietnam. I knew the fort had fallen when the French had it. I made sure they knew. "Hey," I said, "Vietnamese units in the vicinity may not come to help you. If the attack comes at night, they may do nothing until morning." But there was a general feeling not to put a lot of effort into fortifying a camp they would be moving soon to the airport. I said, "Hey, you may never make it to the airfield. You're liable to be killed in your tent between now and then."

The Nung bodyguards all slept in the same elongated grass hut and could be wiped out with a single incendiary grenade. The camp had no artillery. It had a few machine guns but they were behind bamboo fortifications. They weren't ready to fight for their lives. Every team's first mission is to see that its own members survive. We weren't asking anybody to die over there.

January 6, 1964

My dearest Jim:

Your letter with your address arrived today. I immediately went to the post office and mailed off the letter I've been writing since you left plus some other things. I guess you've gotten it by now. After I mailed it I realized in my rush, I'd failed to sign it.

Enclosed is a picture of you that Pam drew. After she colored the hair red, she asked me what color your hair was. Consequently the brown on top of it. She wrote out D A D D Y by herself. I also discovered she knows her numbers by sight now. She was putting cards in numerical order. . . .

Please find out if any of the wives (other than myself and Jane) have birthdays while you all are gone. Jane and I thought we'd send them a card. Also if you have a minute, drop your Mom a line before the 28th. That's her birthday. . . . The girls send all their love. . . .

GEORGE MALONEY I met Jim after he'd been at Khe Sanh several weeks. He was the most eager, conscientious, anxious-to-please guy who ever came to Vietnam. Every time I talked to him it was obvious he wanted to make his mark. But he was totally inexperienced. He didn't know much about the area, about the VC, about the command or the Montagnards.

SAM DEACON We thought we had been trained the best we could be. But as the weeks went by we kept saying, "How come we didn't know about this?" We hadn't gotten current information. We didn't have knowledge of the country. At Bragg we hadn't had access to former teams' operational summaries. It was not until the first Bragg teams started returning that newer teams left for Vietnam with good information on what worked and what didn't.

GEORGE MALONEY Of all the teams I saw over the years, visiting the four corps areas of South Vietnam, this Khe Sanh team was in the lowest ten percent in knowledge and experience. I was more troubled by the lack of training. Nobody would have had combat experience unless they fought in Korea fourteen years before and everyone seemed so young. Sergeant Rose was the oldest, probably in his early thirties. Among Special Forces officers I quickly could tell who had a college degree. They picked things up faster. They learned quicker. They were more aware of the big picture. I didn't have to spell out details. Jim was not in that category. He was not a well-educated man. He was conscientious, eager, but not a big-picture man. It was obvious I wasn't going to be able in words to give him a sense of what it was we were trying to create up there. So I took him to see some other camps where we had some very innovative, very imaginative guys.

SAM DEACON No, Jim wasn't the kind of hard charger Maloney talks about: the Charlie Beckwiths, the Roger Dolans, the Larry Andersons. That wasn't Jim.

EDDIE TRENT Okay, he never attacked a machine-gun nest with guns blazing. But he took care of us. I had three and a half tours in Vietnam and had team leaders a lot worse.

January 7, 1964

My darling:

Another day gone by. About 167 more to go.

We had our A-31 coffee today. Real nice. Only four of us. Jane, Mrs. Hoff, Mrs. Rose and myself. We're getting together next Sunday afternoon at Mrs. Hoff's to make brownies for the team. She insisted on having it there, as her kitchen is bigger. . . .

Ruth took a tumble off one of the girl's chairs tonight and busted her bottom lip and chipped one of her teeth. The tooth isn't loose though, thank goodness. Laura has been an absolute demon this afternoon and tonight. That child can find more things to do than any three. She teased the life out of Pam today. Pam finally belted her a good one. . . .

GEORGE MALONEY I spent quite a bit of time trying to get Jim to visualize things that could happen to him. "Jim," I said, "what do you think you would most need if your camp was attacked tonight? If you only had x number of hours before an attack you knew was coming, what else would you want? More defense? Get the radios hooked up with the outside world? Think about it." Had poor Jim been subject to an attack in the first three months, he'd have been hurting. I don't think that thought ever crossed his mind unless I brought it up. Ninety percent of the time, when

I raised certain issues, I saw he hadn't given it consideration. I was drawing a blank.

Take the road that linked the camp to the airport. We had vehicles ripping along that every day, running out to deliver mail, to meet every plane that came and get the aircrew. How difficult would it have been for the Viet Cong to put a road mine out there? All these things Jim noted and started to go on.

January 8, 1964

My darling:

I went to the hospital today for a check-up. I weigh 127 lbs. Gained 4 lbs. . . . The doctor said the baby is fine. Good strong heart beat. Also I can continue bowling. Said anything I wanted to do. I have to go back in three weeks and then every two weeks. Now when the baby kicks my whole stomach bounces. . . .

GEORGE MALONEY   I took Jim to the camp at Kham Duc and stopped at A Shau on the way back. After that, certain little things were done at Khe Sanh but never on the massive scale needed or that had been done in the other camps. In stature alone Jim was not the most imposing military figure. He did not have a dominating personality. While the whole team impressed me as being the least knowledgeable over there, many of them were fine soldiers. Rose was as capable and conscientious a soldier as you would want, and the most military of the team. Well-built, very gung ho. I was impressed. Hoff was an impressive soldier too. Blais was always out doing something with the Vietnamese too.

January 10, 1964

My darling,

Jerry Lee called the other day. He and Edith have another daughter. Born last Friday. They are disappointed, of course. Hadn't even picked a girl's name out. Sound familiar?

Laura had a box of CrackerJacks today. She didn't finish her box. I asked her why and she said she was saving it for Daddy. They'll be pretty stale come June. . . .

GEORGE MALONEY   Our Special Forces teams split their effort between camp development and area development. The local Vietnamese and Bru worked harder on camp projects when they knew we would work hard on village projects. But we were careful to take on only those jobs the people wanted. There was an unending requirement for welfare services in Montagnard communities—a complete lack of health and sanitation knowledge, no schools or public installations. Their livelihood was hunting for the men and farming for the women, and both were denied them under wartime conditions.

Camp Khe Sanh assisted 239 villages with either aid, protection, training, or medical care. Throughout rural Vietnam there was an absolute absence of doctors. So the skills of the Special Forces medics represented an enormous improvement over any other alternative.

NELSON SMITH   We had a twenty-bed hospital to take care of troops in the camp and ran sick call in outlying areas.

GEORGE MALONEY   These extraordinary men undertook all manner of medical emergencies and won lasting appreciation. The most prevalent ailments were skin diseases, tuberculosis, venereal disease, and diet deficiencies. Medical aid was our greatest friend-maker. Sick call visits were unannounced and on an irregular but frequent schedule. This helped to prevent the VC from setting up an ambush.

January 13, 1964

My darling:

At this moment Mitch Miller's group is singing "Miss You Since You Went Away Dear." I'm just about in tears. The words are just what is in my heart. . . .

GEORGE MALONEY   In the Bru tribe, as is true throughout the Orient, women did the hardest and dirtiest jobs. They ran the shops, did the farming, and raised the children. They held the families together. Each camp had from twenty to forty Bru women who shared the hardships. Some were related to camp members; some came by invitation; some just showed up; some had no other homes. All were put on the payroll and all worked from dawn till dark, seven days a week. All played some role in camp defense. They were pioneer women.

FRANK ROSE   We hired Montagnards to clear the elephant grass from the barbwire. One day a woman stepped on a mine and nearly blew her foot off. Smitty amputated. Then the Montagnards took her back to the village. When we tried to care for her the Montagnards declined. They had a witch doctor doing his thing and he had her believing she was going to die. Eventually she did.

January 14, 1964

My darling,

Today was very happy. I received your letter of the 9th and 10th. . . .Thank goodness the minefield blew the way it did. Don't the mountain people have any way of making a monetary income? It is such a shame. I guess getting the rice is really great to them.

Did you notice in the picture that no matter where you sit, Pam still seems to look right at you? . . .

All my love,
Always,
Alyce

13 ▪ PATROLS

NELSON SMITH The team we replaced said enemy activity was not bad. The only time we were going to have problems was at the border with Laos. Go down there, they said, and you get in trouble.

SAM DEACON We discovered the South Vietnamese ran patrols only during daylight hours. At dark they didn't want to put anyone outside the camp. They assured us they were putting listening posts beyond the wire at night. But walking the perimeter in daylight we found no evidence they'd been out there.

FRANK ROSE The VC got around us easy enough. Major infiltration routes moved south of us into the southern part of I Corps and into II Corps. There was activity too at the border, six or seven kilometers away.

GEORGE MALONEY It was tempting to neglect training and operations while developing an impregnable camp. Many a team lost the entire area while they were hardening what became their prisons. The only way to defend against guerrillas was through continuous, aggressive patrolling, having ten, fifteen, twenty percent of your troops out at all times and another patrol ready to go. Fatigue, casualties, and lack of incentives made this very difficult. Very often the Vietnamese commanders wouldn't send patrols into areas of known VC activity.

SAM DEACON It took a full week for us to get a company-size operation out of camp. Jim, Frank Rose, Jones, Oller, and Smith went from our team with four Vietnamese Special Forces and half of the irregular defense group, fifty to seventy-five men. They were gone three or four days, mov-

ing southwest toward the river, then swinging around south and back up
north to camp. They found a lot of punji stakes, got a good assessment of
the area, found trails.

January 15, 1964

My darling:

Today we start the 150-day count down. Went over to Mrs. Hoff's this
morning. Made brownies for the team. Everyone showed up but Mrs.
Oller. We had an enjoyable time. . . .

Enclosed is a star Pam made in school today. She wants you to have it.
Said, "It's a little lopsided but that's okay, huh, Mom?" I'm tired tonight.
Pam woke up about three this morning and went to the bathroom. Got
back in bed and preceded to cry because she couldn't get back to sleep.
This woke Laura so I wound up with the two of them in bed with me,
both wide awake. . . .

All my love,
Always
Alyce

GEORGE MALONEY   Once on patrol with Vietnamese forces, the U.S.
team assumed as much control as they wished. Leadership was the primary
deficiency among Vietnamese and the principal contribution of our Special Forces. But it might take six months between the time a bunch of raw
Vietnamese recruits arrived and the time you felt comfortable they would
make a good account of themselves in a fight. The typical Viet Cong guerrilla, on the other hand, was highly motivated. One of the inescapable
impressions of extensive, close combat with both the Viet Cong and the
South Vietnamese was the superiority of the Viet Cong's will to fight.
They fought exceptionally well, even when faced with terrible odds. All
bravery is never on one side of the war. Many derided the Viet Cong performance and made a convincing case they fought only because of duress.
But in I Corps in 1964, with the smell of victory getting stronger, the Viet
Cong repeatedly outfought the Vietnamese. Allied wins were invariably
the result of U.S. and Nung and Australian efforts. Left to their own, the
Vietnamese in I Corps would have collapsed before Christmas that year.

16 January 64

My darling:

Today was gorgeous outside. Temperature in the upper 40's, but not real
cold. All the snow melted except right in front where the sun never hits.
Laura was out all day and Pam all afternoon.

General Westmoreland is leaving next week for Vietnam. He has only
been here since July. The paper said he'll serve there in a new post as
deputy to Gen. Hawkins, commander U.S. Forces there. You know he is
only 49? Pretty young to be a general. I filled the gas tank yesterday. . . .

GEORGE MALONEY   We tried to have two Americans on every patrol so
no American was ever alone. Generally you needed at least two skills—a
medic to take care of the wounded because we never let a Vietnamese
work on an American, and a radio operator to find out where you were
and what was going on. We spent the first couple patrols in an area where
we didn't expect trouble, to give our troops a break-in period, to teach
them how to cross rivers and streams safely in a teamlike operation, how
to bring back the wounded. The biggest thing was how to use a map so
they knew where they were. That was absolutely essential. In the jungle, if
you want artillery support or an air strike, you have to know where you
are.

FRANK ROSE   On every patrol we had contact with the enemy. We went
out for two or three days, usually to the river along the border, and got
fired on. There were all kinds of punji traps. They had them for miles
and miles on or along the side of trails. They planted them in elephant
grass at the same angle the grass grew so we could run into them when
fired upon. Consequently we seldom traveled on trails. We went across
country.

January 17, 1964

My darling:

Joe got in at 7 this morning and brought your letter. It is a wonderful letter Darling. Made me feel so much more at ease. I'm glad conditions over
there are better than you expected. Hope you can get a new shower and
"john." Also hope you don't have too much of a waiting line after coffee in
the morning. Have you gotten your linens as yet? If not, what are you
using? Is it as hot there as it was in Nha Trang?

Joe had been sitting in Saigon since Saturday waiting for a plane. They
had one all set but got bumped for 60 Vietnam students. He said the
Americans almost went downtown and tore it apart they were so angry. . . .

Honey, I just looked at the calendar and the baby is due in 8 and a half
weeks. And in almost 10 weeks, half your tour will be up. As far as the girls
forgetting who their Daddy is, not a chance. They tell your pictures goodnight every night and also in their prayers they say, "Please keep our
Daddy safe." The two older ones keep asking when you'll be home. They
miss you very much. . . .

HERBERT HOFF   Captain Thompson talked about Alyce and the kids all the time. He talked about wanting a boy and about the children he had. He was a good family man.

19 January 64

My darling:
When I spoke to your Mom yesterday she was quite worried about you after the seven getting killed Thursday and Friday over there. I told her not to worry, that you weren't in the vicinity of those casualties. I hope I set her mind at ease a little. . . .

LINDSAY CARR   We didn't patrol constantly. I was out on three or four. Herb Hoff and Jim were on no more than two.

FRANK ROSE   I only remember one patrol Captain Thompson went on. The information I got back was he couldn't keep up with the Montagnards.

EDDIE TRENT   Captain Thompson didn't shirk his duties. He went out on as many patrols as I did.

LINDSAY CARR   It was the first time for anyone of us in a combat situation. The times I went out I was scared shitless. Things happened that I look back on now and chuckle. But at the time you only thanked God you were still alive.

GEORGE MALONEY   Officers have to inspire troops to expose themselves to fire. Even more difficult, they have to get them to kill somebody. Most Americans are so civilized, thank God, the thought of killing somebody is anathema. Most eighteen-, nineteen-year-olds don't want to kill anybody. And to take these nice young kids, highly civilized, and throw them in against some of these savage bastards we had to contend with, who thought nothing of life, who had seen death and physical beatings as a matter of course, and to ask these kids to kill or be killed . . . well, that was a real challenge. That was the hardest thing I've ever had to do in my life.

FRANK ROSE   We respected Captain Thompson because he wore his bars, not because of his leadership. I didn't trust his judgment. When there is doubt in your mind about the leader, you tend to question everything, to hesitate at following orders. I'm trying to explain how a person felt in such a situation. Some people you fall in behind and you know, when he says "Do," you're going to do it. Not because he wears bars but he has ability. If he doesn't, it's soon known by everybody under him.

January 20, 1964

My darling,

Tonight was Bingo night. Jane won a chrome canister set similar to ours. Very nice. She got a cake server with hers instead of a bread box. I came close but no luck. . . .

GEORGE MALONEY   Let me tell you of a small incident that came up when I spent a night at Camp Khe Sanh. It was my first visit. I spent most of my time with the American team, telling them the background of the camp, my great concern for their vulnerability. They seemed less cognizant than other teams that they were in a serious, bitter war with an enemy that could kick their butts.

The Vietnamese in camp had caught some VC who were extraordinarily well equipped. That night I heard screaming from the Vietnamese headquarters. I asked some of our team members if they heard it. They said they did and that they had heard it before. It was probably the Vietnamese working over a prisoner, they said. I was very upset. I put on my holster and hat, took an Australian warrant officer with me who spoke Vietnamese, and walked across the compound. And I'll be damned if that isn't exactly what I found. They had a Vietnamese prisoner with his hands tied behind him and were hitting him with bamboo switches across the back and face and head. Each time they'd hit the guy he let out a moan and holler. He was getting the hell knocked out of him with a half-dozen people interrogating him.

I stepped in, took the camp commander outside, and gave him a lecture. We could all become prisoners, I said, and that was the last thing we'd like happen to us. The best way to get something out of people was to treat them kindly. I said everybody in the valley will think less of you for beating up a prisoner.

This commander went back in, cut the bonds of the prisoner, and we cleaned him up. I went back and told the team I wanted them to get off their butts when they heard someone being abused. I stressed this could happen to them. Jim fully recognized the way it should be. He was just so new he didn't know what he could do and couldn't do.

January 22, 1964

My darling,

Joe got his footlocker and brought over the hats you gave him. The girls look real cute. Mine fits also and I couldn't be happier with it. It is just what I wanted. . . .

The coffee at Mrs. Rossi's was very enjoyable. Major Rossi came and talked to us for a while. He is making up new rosters and plans a newsletter once a month. Also he said if we have any magazines we think you would like to have to bring them to the company and they'll send them over postage free with the other company mail. Also said the 7th is having a formal the 5th of February and extended all of us an invitation to go as his and Mrs. Rossi's guests. That is very nice of him. Jane and I are considering going. Back to the magazines, are there any you would like? Your Army Times or News & World Report? Let me know. . . .

TINA CARR   It was my first experience being close to an officer's wife and Alyce was very nice. When you're a spec 5's wife and an officer's wife is so friendly, it makes you feel good. She cared about all of us.

January 22, 1964

Dear Mom & Dad:

Sorry I haven't written sooner but I just have not had a chance. I have been busier than a one-armed paperhanger. I can't tell you much about what I am doing but I assure you you will not find me among the statistics coming out of Vietnam.

I will have to send you some pictures of this place otherwise you would not believe it. The countryside is beautiful. I think it is classed as subtropics. Just down the road is a coffee plantation owned by a wealthy Frenchman. Banana trees grow right in our compound. In nearby jungles, oranges, lemons and grapefruit grow in abundance.

The little Montainards (pronounced Mountain Yards), meaning Hill People, are forever bringing me all sorts of "goodies" from the patrols. These little brown people are extremely friendly and eager to please. They get a big kick out of us "huge" Americans. They also have a good sense of humor. Somewhat different from ours but very keen never the less. After a long hot patrol, carrying twice the equipment as I, they will climb that last mountain and grin as I struggle up it.

All Americans are forbidden to eat local foods for fear of disease, however if you refuse they are broken-hearted. I'm sure you have heard me say I'll try anything once. This has led me to many interesting experiments in the gourmet department. Already I have dined on everything from rice and fish, a staple of their diet, to 100-year-old eggs. That may sound revolting but actually they are delicious. I also have sampled some of the local booze. Mostly made of rice or local fruit. Some is real good but real potent. Even after eating all this I have not gotten sick. I guess my constitution is hardier than most.

Getting along with these people is perhaps the most important part of the job. Therefore I will go to almost any length to do so. I spend a great deal of time in the local villages. My medics treat their sick as well as our own. We distribute rice to keep them from starving. These people are so poor many do not even have clothes. To this end I employ about 100 laborers to work around the camp simply to provide work for them. They work for three kilos (a little more than three quarts) of rice per day. This is good for both of us. They can work and gain self respect and I get a lot of work done thus freeing my troops for combat operations.

By the way, I can't run down to the corner drug store and get a birthday card so this will have to do. "Happy Birthday Mom!!!" I wish you many more of them.

Right now I am sitting outside my building watching the sun go down over the hills. The sight is beautiful. All is so peaceful and serene you would hardly know there is a war going on except for the troops walking guard. As I said, the sun is going down and, as we don't have the luxury of electricity all the time, I will have to close.

Love,
Jim

14 ■ FRIENDLY FIRE

GEORGE MALONEY I was getting very nervous about when Jim's team was going to wing into action. By my fourth visit, his people still were walking around without weapons, carrying cans of beer. I had to convince them they could get knocked off up there.

LINDSAY CARR I drank more in Vietnam than I did in the States. But Jim made it a policy we would not be drunk in camp. Drink all you want, he said, but no one will be drunk. I drank about a case of beer a day, but spaced throughout the day so I was never drunk.

HERBERT HOFF We had beer and whiskey. But remember there was no recreation. Leave the camp at night and you could get killed.

January 23, 1964

My Darling:

Today was beautiful all the way around. Weather-wise it was almost 70. Bowling-wise, my high was 164. Mail-wise (and this I liked the most) a beautiful letter from you, honey. . . .

Quite a coincidence you instructed Capt. Giai at Benning. I certainly do remember that party. Linda does also. That's one we're not likely to forget. You and Bob had a ball eating shrimp. . . .

All my love,
Always,
Alyce

EDDIE TRENT We had a radio operator we couldn't trust.

LINDSAY CARR   One night he almost caused me to blow Eddie Trent away. It was this guy's turn on guard. Everyone else hit the rack. Our communication shack was in the same building where we slept. This guy had gone over to the Vietnamese Special Force communication shack and used their radio with the call sign of our patrol. He was horsing around, not thinking about the consequences. When he called I was dead asleep. Eddie Trent heard it, woke up, rolled out of his rack, and ran down the corridor to answer the call. I felt someone running by me and grabbed my .45 from underneath my pillow. I rolled over and started to point it at Trent. He turned the corner and went out of sight, or I might have shot him. Captain Jim decided to boot this sergeant out of camp.

January 24, 1964

My darling:

Mrs. Hoff was over for a little while this afternoon. She told me Mrs. Rose was worried because she hadn't heard from Sgt. Rose in almost two weeks. So I called Mrs. Rose and told her about the weather and why no mail was getting out. . . . So far I haven't heard a word around post about that sergeant. I know it must have hurt you deeply to do it but you had no choice. No more said. Subject is forgotten. . . .

———

January 24, 1964

Dear Mom & Dad:

This will be a short one as it is now past midnight and I am beat. I just finished up my shift on guard. My last letter is still here because we have not seen a plane for quite a while. Planes are our only means of getting stuff in or out so we just have to wait on one.

   The main reason I am writing so soon after the last letter is to ask one hell of a big favor. I just got a letter from Alyce and she told me her mother will not be able to come down for the entire month as she had planned. . . . As you know, the baby is due on the 18th. Of course our friends have offered to help and Alyce can hire a woman for a week. But she doesn't feel right about it and neither do I. I know March is probably your busiest time but do you think you could get away for the week of 15–22 March? Alyce would feel much better knowing the children are with you and I would certainly be greatly relieved both knowing the girls were with you and Alyce would not have that additional worry while she is having the baby. . . . I feel so helpless being this far way. Seems I have a habit of being away when Alyce needs me the most.

   If you can make it I would be happy to pay for the plane fare. That

would be the least I could do. Once again, if you can't make it we can
manage OK. Until I hear from you then, be good, stay in good health

Love,
Jim

GEORGE MALONEY   There were several more incidents at the camp that
were negative but none I would associate with Jim personally. The first
was the unfortunate self-inflicted wound to Nelson Smith, a black
sergeant who accidentally shot himself in the foot.

NELSON SMITH   Three or four of us were sitting around talking in the
team dining area. I had a gun in my holster, a .45, and a round in chamber.
When I jumped up, the hammer hit the back of the chair and went off.

GEORGE MALONEY   Smith was evacuated to the hospital at Da Nang. I
was angry. For a professional soldier, who is supposed to be handling guns
all the time, to let it go off is terrible. To let it hit him is worse. Smith
stayed in Da Nang until he could walk and then he went back to camp.
There he shuffled around in sandals for I don't know how long. Several
times I visited the camp. He was still shuffling around with a can of beer in
his hand and house slippers on. I thought, How long before he is up and
charging again? We lost his effectiveness for the better part of a month. I
told Smith this could be the most productive and fruitful tour of his career
and to hang in there. Make everyone understand it was an accident.

Jan 25th, 1964

Dear Jimmy:
I guess by the time you receive this the news of Aunt Helma's passing is
known to you. Through calling Ruth, Alyce was informed as I had. The
family was well pleased with the thought that she ordered a basket of flowers through her mother. . . .

We were wondering. When it is 8 a.m. where you are, what day and
time is it here at the same time? We still talk about your Christmas visit
with us and what good sports you all were to sleep on the floor. It was a
good thing it wasn't freezing cold. It was like old times in Bergenfield
when you used to help me shopping in Dover store. Thank you for all
your help in your own quiet way. Nothing was said if I had enough money,
and I didn't say anything, as you said.

So far I have received quite a few cards and two among them came
from your children and Alyce and you. They never forget us at anytime. I
wish we could be near her, but then I know you understand our circumstances, which at the present is beyond our control. . . .

Guess I had better close, wishing you health, success in all you and your men do. May God safely keep you and guard you and always may you trust in him.

Love,
Mom

Hi ya, Jim, how's things where you are   all is well here at present it is snowing now just a slight flurry. I went to the dentist last week had two teeth ext. I feel better. the package you spoke of when you were here came two days later   we sure are very happy and proud of it. all is so natural and nice we shall keep it always always always. well it is near that time of day so I will say so long for now and do better next time. take care of your self at all times don't forget what I said
so long Jim

Love and affection
Dad

————

January 26, 1964

My Darling:
I just put Laura and Ruth to bed. Pam is watching *The Wizard of Oz* for the 3rd or 4th time. . . . She just came over by me. The Wicked Witch was chasing Dorothy. Pam said, "Mom move over. This is scary. Oh, Brother."

Well, honey, our 5th week separated is gone. Only about 20 more to go. Miss you so very much and love you so much. . . .

GEORGE MALONEY   The second incident that disturbed me enormously was a VC night attack on a local village below Khe Sanh. They knocked the hell out the garrison, scattered it and captured every damn thing in the camp. Didn't leave a toothpick. Mortar and machine-gun rounds, food, lanterns, flashlights, and all the rest. And then organized the villagers to be their carrying party. A brazen thing to do. They had them head out toward the Co Co Va Mountains, a known VC stronghold where there are caves. The Vietnamese security force should have had radio communication with the camp at Khe Sanh or certainly back to Vietnamese headquarters. Word came back to Da Nang that an attack was taking place. I immediately changed my schedule to get up there. What angered me was the VC operation went on until roughly noon. By one-thirty a Vietnamese reinforcing unit moved down Route 9 and took the village back.

When I got to our camp I found everyone quite secure. I started to ask what role the Special Forces team had played. I was told they immediately increased security around the camp and doubled the guard. But not a single soldier left to go down to the fight, which went on all night. Nobody had done anything to interrupt the rape of the village. This was a terrible disappointment to me. It was just inconceivable, like being at the police station, hearing a robbery, and closing the police doors. Our men could have at least coordinated air strikes up there to interfere with this march to the jungle. We should have urged the Vietnamese camp commander to move troops down there, and go with them. Instead, nothing was done.

Had this been any of my other commanders they would have welcomed the opportunity to move out and take the pressure off. There were five companies on that hill. One or two would have been enough. Certainly they would have prevented a large-scale evacuation of the goods. We lost face with the locals.

In fairness to Jim, I had never gone over with him what to do in case of an attack on another camp or village. The different camps had operational orders as to how to handle attacks on their own camp and how to get all kinds of support. But this would have called for a little initiative.

After the attack, Jim and I discussed it. I let him know a more forceful, dynamic reaction would have been in order. He said he didn't feel he could have pushed the Vietnamese to the point of action. Thompson and his young executive officer, Deacon, were so brand-new I couldn't chew them out. But let me say this: every damn Special Forces man on that team felt very guilty the next day that they hadn't done more.

FRANK ROSE   Everybody wished they could have done more. But if I remember the situation right, there was nothing more we could do. I'm sure we increased our security, with a unit that close being attacked. But there was no way we were going to get those Vietnamese to go across the border to reinforce a Laotian battalion. No way we could have gotten that Vietnamese commander to do it. An ARVN* battalion stationed between us and the border did very little except maintain communication. The most we could have done was to go to the border with a patrol. There was no combat air support then. No medevac. Nothing.

Later on in the war we could call in an air strike. But in January 1964 the only air support we had were the Vietnamese in old World War II propeller-driven aircraft we gave them.

January 29, 1964

My Darling:
Went to the doctor today. Everything is just fine. . . . Only gained ¼ lb. Weigh 127¼ lbs. My Mom called last night to let me know she had sent

---

* Army of the Republic of South Vietnam.

the cradle. Also said she spoke to her boss about coming down. He said not until after the 21st. So guess she'll be down sometime on the 22nd of March. Sure hope the baby is late. . . .

Just heard over the news there is an outbreak of Cholera in V.N. Any near you? God, I hope not. . . .

GEORGE MALONEY   The incident with Jim's executive officer was not Jim's fault either. But what an uproar.

SAM DEACON   My feeling about that day is part embarrassment, part shame, and a lot of "What the heck happened?"

An Air Force C-123 came in on a resupply mission. The shipment was all on rollers. We'd roll it out of the plane and onto the ground where we could get it packed up in trucks and moved out of the way.

GEORGE MALONEY   At these isolated airfields the Air Force was not anxious to sit any longer than it absolutely had to. Planes touched down, supplies were off-loaded, planes took off. They never shut engines down because a mortar round could knock out a multimillion-dollar plane.

SAM DEACON   The captain and copilot stayed in the cockpit, so we were dealing with the enlisted crew chief and his assistant. They were saying, "Come on, y'all, get this stuff off."

GEORGE MALONEY   This guy Deacon apparently was hot-tempered or out of sorts, and he got into a rhubarb with the Air Force NCO.

SAM DEACON   I said, "You guys aren't doing too bad for a pigs-and-rice run." The term wasn't derogatory. Everybody used "pigs-and-rice run" to mean resupply deliveries. The crew chief said something like "You ground-pounders never see it in the right perspective." We were kidding each other, that's all. Nobody got mad. I didn't see them getting upset and I certainly wasn't.

We had left our mail back at the camp. They said they would only wait so long, and we sent someone to get it. When the aircraft was unloaded we said, "Are you sure you can't wait a few minutes longer?" They said no. Okay, get it the next time. That was my feeling. I don't get mad about something like that. And I don't remember anyone else getting hot. We got back out of the way and they taxied down to get in position for takeoff.

I was sittin' in the jeep and had the butt of the shotgun resting in my lap, my fingers around the trigger guard. I knew the gun, a Remington pump, had a hair trigger. If we dropped it, it would go off, but it was the only shotgun we had. I carried it for safety. We didn't have a way to secure it in camp and didn't want it to disappear. I said, "I'm just going to give them a big wave as they take off." The aircraft was on a roll. So about when it got to us I started waving and the damn shotgun went off.

GEORGE MALONEY   What I heard was that Deacon frantically hollered for them to stop and then let loose with a shotgun at the door.

SAM DEACON   I had my fingers on the outside of the trigger guard! I couldn't believe it fired. I turned around and looked back at whoever was there as if to say, "What happened?"

GEORGE MALONEY   The NCO hit the floor of the plane and wasn't hit. Later he gave this amazing testimony. He said he couldn't believe the idiot would do that. All around the door were pellet holes.

EDDIE TRENT   One pellet hit the seat someone was sitting in. Another went between the crew chief's legs. Back at camp we got a call that they were receiving fire. They said the aircraft had received two hits.

SAM DEACON   We looked back at the aircraft and they fired a red flare, which signaled they had received fire. They made one turn around. I put the shotgun down and began crossing my arms to wave it off. I knew the gun had gone off but it hit in front of me, off the apron. But that apron was harder than concrete. The shell hit the ground and went up. Their crew chief was standing by the door with his foot up against the bulkhead. He didn't know what had happened. I waved to give them the okay so they went ahead and left. When I got back to camp Jim said, "Hey, you hit an airplane." They'd already sent a radio message back from the B-team in Da Nang. I told Jim it went off accidentally. We decided right then we should get rid of the damn shotgun, cut it up in pieces or whatever.

GEORGE MALONEY   The Air Force was livid. The plane sergeant said he saw the gun raised, saw the belch, and hit the floor. The first report I got was a scream from the senior Air Force man that an Army guy had fired at his aircraft. A message was sent back to headquarters. They could no more believe it than I could. I wanted my deputy to talk to this guy to see if he had cracked.

SAM DEACON   We sent a message down trying to explain what had happened. But the next message back wasn't "Will you please send him . . ." It was "He will report to . . ." And it was "bags and baggage." I was going home.

January 30, 1964
144 D.T.G. (more or less)

My Darling:

Well, I see in the news tonight that V.N. is in a mess again. A new coup took over today. How will that affect you honey? I remember how the one in November really fowled Joe up getting home. I hope and pray it won't affect you too much. Please let me know if you can. . . .

GEORGE MALONEY   Deacon said the shotgun discharged accidentally. The only witness was the man in the doorway.

SAM DEACON   I was feeling very bad. Embarrassed, shocked, angry at myself. I don't recall any lengthy discussion with Jim about it. But I thought he should have stuck up for me more. He said he didn't have any other choice. The B-team XO told him either I had to go home or the whole team would.

At Da Nang I told them what happened. But I was shunned. No one would talk to me. I don't know if they were told not to or were afraid to. I caught a ride out to the gate, went downtown, and got a room at the Grand Terrene Hotel. I spent the night there by myself and did a lot of thinking. Like "What the heck is happening?" It was a mistake, an accident, but nobody believes me. They were trying to build it into something. That night I decided I would go back to the B-team XO and say, "I'm saying it was an accident. You're not believing me. Is there another place I can be transferred to, another team?"

But the next morning the XO confronted me. "What's the matter?" he said. "You couldn't leave the women alone?"

"Wait a minute," I said. "I went downtown to be by myself and I was by myself! Now, if you know anything different, I want to see the proof. Otherwise don't make that statement!" Then I shut my mouth because it was clear something else was going on. They were looking to charge me, or to charge Jim, or the team. All minds were made up.

GEORGE MALONEY   The next thing we knew Deacon was on his way back to Bragg. He was lucky to get out of there without being court-martialed. The Air Force was adamant they wanted him and there was all sorts of talk about paying for the damage.

SAM DEACON   On the way back I'm saying to myself, "Why didn't Jim say anything?" He didn't say if he tried to get me put on another team or if he tried to find out what happened at the airfield. It wasn't like him not to stand up for someone on the team.

NELSON SMITH   We were all upset when Deacon detached. We'd trained so long together. Jim had relied on him a great deal. In Special Forces everybody has a job. This left a great burden.

15 ▪ FINAL LETTERS

February 3, 1964

My Darling:

I could have hugged the mailman today. He brought two letters from you.
. . . I also sit and dream of time gone by and time to come. I long to have
you hold me and me hold you. So much at times it hurts. We both feel the
same. I'm proud that after 10½ years of marriage, Darling, we still feel that
way. So many people don't. But we do and I couldn't be happier about it. . . .

You mentioned making all kinds of plans when you get home. Let me
in on some of them, okay? . . .

> All my love,
> Always,
> Alyce

February 12, 1964

My Darling:

What is going on pray tell? Sam called Jane last night. He was at Travis.
All he said to Jane was he "goofed." Is it serious honey? What about a
replacement? Please let me know what it is all about. Your story. Okay?
I'm upset over the whole thing. Jane is a wreck, and will be until she gets
the whole story. . . . I love and miss you so very much darling. The girls
send love and kisses. . . .

SAM DEACON   I told my wife what happened. Alyce wanted to know why
was I back. I said, "Well, I made a mistake. I got a reprimand and was sent

home." Then I tried to talk about the team. I know I was visibly upset. I felt I let the team down.

February 14, 1964

My Darling:

Happy Valentines Day. I hope my card and the girls' got there on time. . . . Sam, Jane and young Mark came over for a while last night. Said to tell you he got to speak to Colonel E.S. before the papers from Saigon arrived. Outside of that, and the fact he "goofed," it's all I know. . . .

February 17, 1964

My Darling:

Well, one month from today our little one is due. I'm getting anxious. . . . The new mess hall sounds great. Hope the party is a smash. Have a drink for me, Honey. . . . Sam still won't tell me anything except he hurt his back. I've got more sense than to believe that. . . . I'm sure the girls would love to have a little something from their Daddy. Especially Laura, Honey. She misses you something awful. Every night she asks when Daddy will be home. Pam misses you also but when I tell Pam four more months she understands. Laura still has no evaluation of time. . . .

———

Feb. 17, 1964

Dear Mom & Dad:

I got your letter of the 5th today and I feel much better. I also got a letter from Alyce telling me you planned to be there for her. She feels much relieved, as she was worried she might have to go early. She said, "The only thing in this world that could make me feel any better is that you (that's me) would be home."

Alyce has told me many times, Mom, that you and she became very close while I was in Korea. We have made many wonderful friends at Fort Bragg but nothing is the same as having your own family around you at a time like this. . . . Life is pretty much the same here. We just celebrated the Vietnamese New Year. It's much the same as we celebrate it but they throw Christmas and the 4th of July in for good measure. They have big parties, give presents, lots of firecrackers and they go New Year calling and make all kinds of wishes. When they paid their call on me I gave them a drink and made a toast to the New Year. They wished me riches, a promotion to major and a boy next month. . . .

Love,
Jim

—————

February 20, 1964

My Darling:

Your letter of the 16th brightened up my whole day. . . . The bar you remodeled sounds grand. Don't forget to send pictures. I started making lists of liquor companies to write to. Plan to give a few to the other wives. Can't guarantee anything but never can tell. . . .

Saw Joe Schwar today. Showed him the picture of the mess hall. He could see much improvement. Also told him about the bar. He said, "What's he trying to do, make it into a club?" . . .

February 25, 1964

My Darling:

Jane doesn't seem to have too much to say now that Sam is back. She is a sky-diving widow again. . . . I got the addresses of some liquor companies today. Our next Wives meeting is Monday so will take the list and see if some wives will give me a hand writing to them. I thought I'd call some of the beer distributors downtown and see what they would offer to send you. . . .

February 27, 1964

Dear Jimmy:

To be able to go south for even a week means a great deal to me as I am fed up with this place. Maybe when I get back I will feel better. Just hope I can get to Alyce before the baby comes and also hope to be able to see it before I have to leave for him. . . . To ---- with this job. I just don't care. My children come first. I feel if you are serving our country for all races, creed or color, there isn't anybody to stop me. I think my thickheaded German blood pressure is going up.

As to Alyce and I becoming so close, I have watched her so much since she spent time with us when you were in Korea, and I have come to the conclusion there aren't many like her anymore. She seems to think along the same lines I do and that wherever she can spare a penny she will do it. The main thing in life is one must not forget we have a God in heaven who loves us and will make everything possible if it is His will. I live on this everyday and believe me, Jimmy, without this belief, Life wouldn't be worthwhile. You know what I mean.

I can imagine that New Year's celebration was something out of this world and that you will remember for a long time. It is also nice to know how differently people live besides our way. It just goes to show their

wishes for someone else are no different than ours. It was very nice of
them to hope the baby will be a boy and hope you won't have to disap-
point them.

It is time for me to close this letter as I want to get one in the mail for
Alyce as she gets lonesome for mail. So I will say "Good Morning" and
hope all is well with you and fellow workers.

Love
Mom and Dad

Dear Jim all is well in Freedom this a.m. hope all is well with you. Mom
is counting the days until she can be with Alyce. A pleasure she has never
had to be with her daughterinlaw at a time like this all's well that ends
well. with love and most sincere wishes from   Dad

March 12, 1964

My Darling:
Today has been one of those days I should have stayed in bed. All three
girls woke up "deaf in one ear and can't hear out of the other." It's bad
enough when one misbehaves but all three is too much. I'd have done better talking to the wall.

I cleaned out the cereal cabinet this morning and Ruth and Laura
dumped cereal all over the floor. Pam started whining because we were
having soup for lunch. She wound up eating it though. I told her that was
what we had for lunch and if she didn't want it, well, that was it until supper. . . . Then the mailman came and no letter from you. . . .

March 14, 1964

My Darling:
Mom arrived safe and sound and a little tired. She had a good trip. It certainly is good having her here. The girls haven't stopped talking. Especially Pam. She is telling her all about school. . . . We had a nice supper.
Mom enjoyed it. I guess more so being she didn't have to cook it. Steak,
fries and salad. While I washed the girls hair and bathed them, Mom did
the dishes. . . .

Dear Jimmy, Surprised? Alyce thought I would like to write you a few
lines. Had a very pleasant flight down here. The whole family was there to
meet me and I feel just fine and hope to enjoy myself very much. I will go
home on Sunday 22nd. Wish it could be longer. Left Daddy in good hands
with canned beans, spaghetti, raviolis, Dinty Moore Stew, plus eggs and

pancake flour. He says he will eat out of the pots. This is all for now and please don't worry about anything.

Love,
Mom

March 16, 1964

My Darling:

Sam still hasn't told me why he was sent back. Please tell me. . . . So far nothing on the liquor companies. They aren't as generous as you'd think. The beer companies flatly refused. . . . In every letter you say that by the time I get it the baby will probably be here. But here I sit as pregnant as ever. . . . The girls send their love to their Daddy. . . .

16 ▪ CAPTURE

JIM THOMPSON   On the afternoon of March 26 we got word an aircraft, an L-19 Birddog, was coming in from B Detachment. Anytime we got an aircraft in we used it for reconnaissance with whatever fuel the pilot could spare.

FRANK ROSE   Flying recon missions was my job, but I wasn't there. I was sent to Da Nang to get supplies. Once there, we normally stayed for three days' R&R if the weather allowed. By late March everybody had taken R&R except me and Blais. Anyone else on the team could have flown that recon mission. But Captain Thompson, being team leader, decided to take it.

JIM THOMPSON   We had new information on enemy locations and installations.

DONALD GOULET   When Jim and I were lieutenants at Bragg we both knew Sam Kinchloe. He also turned up an infantry officer in Vietnam. That day in March of '64 it was Kinchloe who got off the aircraft so Jim could get on.

SAMUEL KINCHLOE   I made monthly pay runs to all the A-team detachments. Khe Sanh was mountainous, very rugged, very dense. Thompson and his team sergeant, Herb Hoff, had driven up to the airstrip in a jeep. I got out. Thompson got aboard. The plane only held the pilot and one passenger.

DONALD GOULET   That was the last any of us saw of Jim Thompson for a long, long time.

———

JIM THOMPSON   We took off around thirteen-thirty and essentially flew down the Tchepone River. We were committed to flight minimums, an altitude no lower than fifteen hundred feet. That was high enough to keep us out of range of small-arms fire. We were flying a little below that when I noticed what I thought was a footbridge. I told the pilot to circle around and down. We violated flight minimums but we wanted to have a good look. If we stayed high enough to be safe, we couldn't see what was on the ground. We had to take a chance once in a while.

As we flew below the ridgeline we were hit by small-arms fire. I presumed an automatic weapon. I received one round across my cheek. I thought the pilot was hit but I wasn't sure. A very brief instant passed between the time we were hit and the crash. That's how low we were. The plane exploded on impact.

———

SAMUEL KINCHLOE   Later that afternoon the weather set in. Clouds covered the valley and the mountaintops. They came in quickly at that time of year. When the plane failed to return I assumed it went to Da Nang rather than try to land at Khe Sanh. By six that evening it was turning dark. We were weathered in for the night. Hoff called Da Nang to see if the aircraft had returned. It hadn't.

———

JIM THOMPSON   I would regain consciousness for a few minutes and pass out again. I recall looking around, seeing the aircraft. The engine was gone, torn off on impact. There was no sign of the pilot, Captain Whitesides. My first impulse was to get away because I knew the VC would be coming in. My second thought was to stay near the aircraft for rescue ships. In fact I had no option. I couldn't move. I couldn't even crawl. I thought my back was broken.

VC guerrillas found the crash. I regained consciousness when one of them grabbed my hand. He had a knife and was about to slice my finger off to get my birthstone ring, a ruby. I got the ring off myself and handed it to him. They'd already stripped me of weapons and everything I had in my pockets. The next thing I recall it was dark. I was tied to a litter and being carried down the mountain. When I regained consciousness, that night or the next, I was tied spread-eagle to the floor of a Montagnard hut.

———

FRANK ROSE   Blais and I were in a safe house in Da Nang when the sergeant major for B-team got us. "Your captain went down in a plane," he said. "Get your stuff together. You're going back up there."

17 ■ MISSING

ALYCE   I was ten days overdue on the 27th of March when at five in the morning there was a knock on the door. A chaplain was standing there. He didn't have to open his mouth. I knew something had happened. I screamed for my mother and went into labor.

PAM   I remember the voices that night, and finding my mother on the porch steps outside with my grandmother. I put my arms around her.

ALYCE   About nine o'clock the telegraph office called my neighbor asking her to please get over to my house. I was going to get some bad news. "She already knows," she said.

MRS ALYCE J THOMPSON

DONT PHONE REPORT DELIVER 11-A SUNCHON FT BRAGG

THE SECRETARY OF THE ARMY HAS ASKED ME TO EXPRESS HIS DEEP REGRET THAT YOUR HUSBAND, CAPTAIN FLOYD J THOMPSON, HAS BEEN MISSING IN VIETNAM SINCE 26 MARCH 1964. HE WAS AN OBSERVER ABOARD A MILITARY AIRCRAFT ON A RECONNAISSANCE MISSION. THE PLANE DID NOT RETURN AT ITS SCHEDULED TIME OF 4:15 PM 26 MARCH. SEARCH EFFORTS HAVE BEEN DELAYED UNTIL 27 MARCH BECAUSE OF BAD WEATHER. YOU WILL BE ADVISED PROMPTLY WHEN FURTHER INFORMATION IS RECEIVED. A REPRESENTATIVE OF THE COM-

MANDING GENERAL THIRD US ARMY WILL CONTACT YOU PERSONALLY
TO OFFER ASSISTANCE. HIS PARENTS ARE BEING NOTIFIED.
J C LAMBERT
MAJOR GENERAL USA
THE ADJUTANT GENERAL

SAM DEACON   I felt empty when I heard. They called me at home, told me to come in. I was to be Alyce's survival assistance officer, the guy there to pick up the pieces after the chaplain leaves. Alyce was in shock. It was a big blur, like a dream.

ALYCE   Sam went all to pieces too, blaming himself, saying, "Maybe it would have been me in that plane instead of him."

SAM DEACON   I did blame myself. The anger I'd felt earlier turned into frustration at not being there to help look for Jim. There wasn't enough information to conclude he was dead. They couldn't even find the aircraft. I felt if I'd have been there maybe I could have found it.

LEA HOFF   Alyce called crying to say Jim was missing. But she said she hadn't lost hope. She knew he was going to be found.

ALYCE   Mother took me to the hospital. It was Good Friday, and the day of the big Alaskan earthquake. While in labor I kept asking if the nurses had heard anything. About six o'clock that evening young Jim was born. I'd been given a saddle block, so back in my room I had to lay flat on my back for eight hours to avoid a bad headache. The nurse brought in a bouquet of red roses. Eleven blooms and one stem. There was a card from Jim in his handwriting. "How can this be?" I screamed. Later I learned Jim had arranged with a friend to have flowers delivered when the baby came. The florist said he'd sent over twelve roses. But that eleven-rose bouquet hurt me the most the day little Jim was born.

Easter Sunday all the churches sent me white lilies off their altars. My room looked like a funeral parlor. I lay awake at night. Every time the phone rang in the maternity ward I got up to ask if it was word about Jim. A real bad time.

———

FRANK ROSE   For three days I tapped all my intelligence sources to see if we could find out anything.

SAMUEL KINCHLOE   Army and Air Force planes together conducted an air search. Three to five aircraft up at any one time for the next four or five days. But it was only intermittently clear. The amount of daylight, especially in low-lying areas, was very limited.

FRANK ROSE It was an intense search operation, with planes and helicopters. We had some sightings from Montagnards, but in that jungle, trying to find a recon plane was like looking for that needle in a haystack.

———

ALYCE   Back then babies weren't brought to the mother. Mama went down to the nursery at feeding time. The kids were lined up and the mother checked the number on her band against the number on the baby's leg and arm. I didn't have to. All I had to do was look at the ears. He was the spitting image of his father.

———

JIM THOMPSON   Those first several days I was moved from place to place on a stretcher. About the fourth day I met the first VC cadre, dressed in gray uniform, hat, and sandals. He spoke a little French and we were able to communicate haltingly. He put a bandage on the burn on my leg but had little equipment or medication. The nearby village, long since destroyed, was now a VC hideaway. They tried to feed me but I couldn't take food. I was in horrendous pain.

Within a week I began to regain my senses but my mind was in turmoil. A thousand things running through it. Alyce was due to deliver. I was anxious over what would come first—the baby or news I had gone down. I had many irons in the fire at camp. My executive officer had gone back to the States a short time before I crashed. I was concerned over who was going to take my place, whether all our operational and tactical plans would be carried out. I had thought myself indispensable. Then there was my own safety. As each day went by I kept thinking they're about to lower the boom.

———

GEORGE MALONEY   Because no American had seen the plane go down, we were totally dependent on Montagnard witnesses. We located the two Australian warrant officers again. One was a Montagnard linguist, which was very rare. He went to Khe Sanh and learned Jim's plane was seen smoking and losing altitude at a very precipitous angle, toward the Co Co Va Mountains, which run parallel to the Laos border but are still inside South Vietnam. The significance, of course, was the plane wasn't heading for Route 9. Why not, if the pilot were conscious?

Montagnards were incapable of giving us a precise definition of speed or even the general direction they saw it come from or saw it go. The Australian figured a general search area by laying out sticks and stones for them. Montagnards said they had been along the river on the valley floor and lost sight of the plane when it went over the mountains. I was horrified when I realized the enormous area we needed to search. About sixteen to twenty square miles. The Vietnamese Special Forces groups at Khe Sanh would never be able to cover it. It would take the better part of a day just to work their way from the valley floor to the peak of the mountains. The terrain was so rugged. A battalion of Vietnamese Rangers were flown up from Da Nang and the next morning started off. We helicoptered as many as we could to different squares of the map. The Air Force was very helpful, getting every plane not involved in a mission to search the valley. We looked for some sign of penetration in the jungle's canopy. Trees there grew to enormous heights, between one hundred fifty and one hundred seventy feet. A secondary growth came below that level, maybe to within fifty feet, and then there was undergrowth. So it was possible the plane crashed through the upper canopy and got hung up in the second canopy, neither visible from the air or the ground.

We offered a reward for information about the two Americans. We dropped leaflets printed in Vietnamese on one side and, for Montagnards, graphic depictions on the other. We indicated we would give some fabulous reward for any information that led to the plane's location. We dropped leaflets by the tens of thousands over remote villages, every area we knew Montagnards were living, and up and down the spring bed occupied by Vietnamese. We wanted everybody to know we were looking for these guys.

FRANK ROSE   Jim Oller and I scoured the area with the Ranger battalion. I wished I'd been in that plane. I had more experience, more time in the jungle, than any man on the team. More experience with the Montagnards. I knew my way around because I had flown on these recon missions so often. Of course, I never knew what actually happened or what kind of condition Captain Thompson was in after the crash. It might not have made any difference who was aboard.

GEORGE MALONEY   I had Kinchloe take over the team temporarily.

SAMUEL KINCHLOE   Jim's Vietnamese counterpart found out I was in charge and wanted to impress on me the inadequacy of camp defenses. He wanted fewer offensive operations. Morale was not too good on the team. They had problems with quality of personnel, professionalism, getting the job done, ability to train and assist the Vietnamese. The Deacon incident reflected a lack of discipline. Leadership wasn't strong. There was over-familiarity between the NCOs and officers. From the number of operations they had conducted and the results, it seemed that not much was being accomplished. I never believed in body counts but I looked for other signs of performance, like number of patrols, number of enemy contacts, number of weapons recovered. This detachment wasn't performing as well as others. And this was the most northern team, so the enemy was out there. All of that fell on Jim Thompson.

———

JIM THOMPSON   About two weeks after the crash a VC medic showed up and looked at the burn on my leg and bullet wound across my face. My right eye had some internal hemorrhaging. The big injury was my back. I had such pain I couldn't stand. This medic looked at me and said there's nothing wrong. For the infected burn on my leg he pulled out a syringe. It was so cruddy I refused to let him give me a shot. He finally went away without doing anything. The next day a doctor went to work on the leg wound and did a reasonably good job. Two heavy men sat on me as they cut away the decayed flesh, then gave me some penicillin.

FROM THE *Observer*,[*] APRIL 4, 1964

MISSING L-19 CREW IDENTIFIED HERE

The two American officers reported missing in Quang Tri Province since last Thursday, when their L-19 failed to return to Khe Sanh Special Forces camp after a two-hour reconnaissance mission, were identified as USAF Capt. Richard L. Whitesides (Stockton, Calif.), the pilot, and Army Capt. Floyd J. Thompson (Ft. Bragg, N.C.), the observer.

The search for the missing plane is still in progress with 18 fixed wing aircraft including L-19s, T-28s and C-123s checking the general area of the L-19's flight. As of Monday, 188 sorties totaling some 300 hours had been flown in search operations. Poor visibility, bad weather and the mountainous terrain continue to hamper the search operations. . . .

Two H-34 helicopters are on stand-by for medical evacuation and 12 other H-34s are on alert to fly troops to secure the area when the missing plane is located.

GEORGE MALONEY   We pulled the Rangers out after eight days. Jim's team and other Special Forces units in the area continued the search for as long as they remained in Vietnam.

FRANK ROSE   We spent thirty days on jungle patrol looking for him.

GEORGE MALONEY   With the seasons, we knew vegetation might

[*] Military newspaper for U.S. Forces in Vietnam.

change, so every patrol that went out was told an additional mission was to find any sign of the crash. None of us ever found anything. The plane had disappeared like it had gone off the earth. We found no wreckage. Not a piece of handkerchief nor a piece of torn uniform. Nothing. We presumed the plane was caught in the trees where it couldn't be seen. The Army classifies soldiers as missing in action when they don't know what happened. But in my heart, having flown over the area and knowing how desolate and rugged it was, and having walked on the ground with the Rangers, I concluded he was gone.

Months later I wrote a final fitness report. In light of the fact I thought Jim was dead, the report was devoid of criticism. I wrote Alyce a nice letter too but never got a reply. Years later, when I learned Jim was alive, it came as a stunning surprise.

———

ALYCE   When I got home I fell into a deep depression. I couldn't sleep. I couldn't eat. I saw my life deteriorating. I had depended on Jim so much. Mother stayed for three weeks and went home. When I couldn't handle things she came back down.

SAM DEACON   I visited Alyce often to see what she needed. I explained her benefits and what she could expect from the Army. We had daily contact. Alyce tried to stay busy. But when we talked, questions always surfaced and she wept.

ALYCE   I wanted word, one way or the other. I needed information. Not knowing what happened to Jim was so terrible. The Army said I would hear momentarily. The plane would be found or he would come walking in.

The kooks started calling. I had the John Birch Society wanting me to join. "Get a lifetime membership for only two hundred and fifty dollars," they said. Retired general Edwin Walker called from Texas, wanting me to help impeach President Johnson because he had sent my husband to Vietnam.

SAM DEACON   After a while I felt Alyce was relying on me like she had Jim. It was like I had two families. It wore me down. I had gotten too close. I couldn't be objective. I was asking the Army the same questions Alyce did: Why haven't we heard anything? Why aren't they doing more? Why haven't we been told? I felt like a relative, not an assistance officer. So I asked to be relieved.

ALYCE   The Special Forces commander and his wife, Colonel and Mrs. Mattice, couldn't have been kinder. She was special. Even bought baby Jim a gift. Any social activity on post I not only was invited to but the Mattices made sure a single guy escorted me. Dinner, dance, cocktail party, what-ever, those people made sure I came.

Still things turned from bad to worse. At Pam's graduation from kindergarten, walking down cement steps, my high heel caught in a crack and I fell, scraping my shin from the knee down. When I got home my leg was so swollen it cut off circulation to my foot. Mama took me to the hospital. For several nights, when the baby woke up, I couldn't walk down the stairs to feed him. I sat on my fanny and bumped down. Then bumped my fanny back up.

One day the post minister came over. "Well," he said, "just remember God is up there in his place." And I thought, Bullshit. I prayed to him before and what good did it do me? I quit going to church. I didn't want nothing to do with it. Here I was stuck in this house with four kids and didn't know if my husband was dead or alive.

———

JIM THOMPSON   I was taken from village to village in the weeks follow-ing my capture. They made no attempt to interrogate me or to treat me like a prisoner. I couldn't walk, so they weren't worried about an escape. They were solicitous of my welfare. One day a cadre did show up who spoke broken English. He handed me a piece of paper, a message to cap-tured prisoners from the National Liberation Front. It said they had a very humane and lenient policy toward prisoners of war. Prisoners were never maltreated or humiliated or tortured and they always received plenty of food and medical care. About this time they had elections in North Vietnam. They brought a radio down and advised me to listen to broadcasts over Radio Hanoi describing the election results and the activ-ities of the National Assembly. It was all capped off with a speech by Ho Chi Minh. I was absolutely amazed they had the gall to present this as democracy. Even to the most uninformed observer it was a mockery of freedom, a mockery of democracy. Yes, everybody was free to run—if selected by the party. And everybody was free to vote—but the choice was the party representative or no one.

———

SAM DEACON   My wife, Jane, and I still stopped by to see Alyce occa-sionally. We'd take her to functions on post. But then Jane thought we might not be helping her. She felt Alyce would begin to resent us or feel we were interfering in her life. So Jane decided if Alyce needed something she would call.

ALYCE   My mother stayed two months until I got back on my feet. Then

she had to get back. They wouldn't hold her job open any longer. That's
when Jim's parents came down. I thought it would be just for a little while.
But it went on and on and on.

———

JIM THOMPSON   I was in mental anguish over my family, particularly
what had happened to my wife and baby. I worried too about my work in
Khe Sanh and my own safety. Each day was a living torment waiting for
something to happen. I couldn't understand why they weren't questioning
me. When was it going to start? When were they going to put the pressure on? Before my capture I had heard of all kinds of atrocities at the
hands of the communists. I was as tense as an overwound spring.

One morning I woke up and I felt as if something were wrong. No, not
wrong, but just very different. It took me a while to realize what it was
because I hadn't experienced it for so long. But I woke up . . . at peace. I
had complete peace of mind and in my heart. I knew the baby had been
born. I knew it was a boy. I knew both Alyce and the child were doing fine.
And I knew I would survive.

Many people will gibe at something like this. But there's only one place
this could have come from. There was no doubt in my mind this was the
work of the Good Lord.

———

ALYCE   I knew nothing—nothing—about what happened to Jim. I still
didn't know where the hell he was assigned over there until his boss at
Bragg, Major Rossi, came for a visit. I had played bridge with his wife and
told her I didn't know anything. She sent her husband over the next day.
"This is top secret," he said. "Don't tell anybody I showed it to you." And
he pulled out a map of Vietnam and pointed to where Jim's team was and
where his plane went down. But I had to keep my mouth shut. At that time
in the war, if your husband went to Vietnam, it was very hush-hush. A
secret mission to a secret land. We didn't even talk to people in the 82nd
Airborne about Special Forces. And if your husband turned up missing, oh
my God, we didn't talk about that either.

———

JIM THOMPSON   I made three escape attempts within the first month of
capture. Frankly, they were hardly worthy of the title "escape attempts." I
was held in a small village on the Laos side of the Tchepone River. I had
been on the Vietnamese side on foot patrol and flown over this area.
There's a very distinct loop in the river, so I knew where I was. Twenty-

five kilometers from my own camp. I knew this might be my best chance of escape. The guards were not regular troops but Montagnards. Most were young and inexperienced. Security was not tight. Problem was I was barely able to walk.

The village was a hundred yards back from the river. During the day they moved me down to a small lean-to on the riverbank. They had one guard posted, a young fellow, eighteen or nineteen. About the second day there the guard decided to take a swim. I saw him in the river, not watching me closely. I got up and started walking. The jungle was thick just a few steps from the lean-to, so I immediately was hidden from him. I got perhaps fifty yards when I ran into another guard coming down the trail. I don't believe he knew I was trying to escape. Only that I was wandering around. But he carried a gun and that was enough for me. Through sign language I indicated I had left camp to relieve myself. He nodded and smiled and marched me back.

Two or three days later the same opportunity presented itself. I assumed other guards had come down from an outpost to the north, so I headed south along the river. I got a little farther, about a hundred yards, but again ran into an outpost and turned around.

On May 9, 1964, Australian warrant officer Rick Rooney interrogated an eighteen-year-old Viet Cong defector, Tran Say, from the Thua Tien Province of South Vietnam. That same day Rooney filed the following report with U.S. authorities.

On the night of 26 March, at approximately 2000 hours, a group of about 20 VC entered the village of Trach Huu, assembled the villagers and forced Tran Say to follow them. After three days march, they arrived at a VC training center that goes under the name of B6. It comprises 40 men who are accommodated in one large house. Tran Say was given six weeks of intensive political and military training. After completion, he was issued a Thompson submarine gun and 100 rounds of ammunition.

The mission of this training center is to recruit and train reinforcements for nearby VC units. Their secondary mission is to carry out limited activity against hamlets in the Pho Trach area.

Tran Say's first operational mission was to attack his own village. It was not his belief that innocent women and children should be killed, thus at the first opportunity he slipped away from his squad and surrendered to ARVN [Army of the Republic of Vietnam].

Approximately three nights after being established in this training center, Tran Say was present when his company commander and platoon leader, during a conversation, mentioned that a recent VC success was the shooting down of a small aircraft to the North. The VC had shot the plane down but did not see where it came to earth. A Montagnard friendly to the VC found the aircraft and accompanied the VC to the location. In the aircraft were two Americans, one dead and the other slightly wounded. The VC recovered a .45 pistol only. The wounded American, it was said, would be indoctrinated and on completion would be returned.

Personnel Impression: After five hours of questioning Tran Say, I had him repeat the conversation between the company commander and the platoon leader several times. Each time the story did not differ. . . .

He cannot read a map but after a little instruction he was able to point out the general location of the training camp. He does not have any idea where the aircraft came down except that it was very far to the North. I consider the story bears a great degree of truth.

R. E. Rooney, WO2
Australian Intelligence Corps

MAY 21 1964

WESTERN UNION TELEGRAM
MRS ALYCE THOMPSON DONT PHONE REPORT DELIVERY
11-A SUNCHON FORT BRAGG
REPORT HAS BEEN RECEIVED FROM THE US COMMANDER IN VIETNAM THAT A DEFECTOR FROM THE VIET CONG HAS STATED THAT AT THE END OF MARCH 1964 THE VIET CONG HIT AND DOWNED ONE AMERICAN AIRCRAFT APPROXIMATELY 29 MILES WEST OF HUE, REPUBLIC OF VIET-NAM. THERE WERE TWO AMERICANS IN THE AIRCRAFT. ONE AMERI-CAN WAS KILLED AND ONE WAS WOUNDED AND TAKEN AWAY BY THE VIET CONG. PRESENT LOCATION OF WOUNDED AMERICAN UNKNOWN. THE STATEMENT BY THE VIET CONG DEFECTOR CANNOT BE CONFIRMED BY UNITED STATES OFFICIALS. HOWEVER, THE TIME AND PLACE HE MENTIONED INDICATES THAT THIS MAY BE THE INCIDENT IN WHICH YOUR HUSBAND CAPTAIN FLOYD J THOMPSON WAS INVOLVED.

A CONCENTRATED SEARCH OF THE AREA HAS BEEN INITIATED AND LEAFLETS OFFERING A REWARD ARE BEING DROPPED. IF ADDITIONAL INFORMATION IS RECEIVED YOU WILL BE PROMPTLY ADVISED.

J C LAMBERT
MAJOR GENERAL USA
THE ADJUTANT GENERAL

ALYCE   They said Captain Whitesides, the pilot, was killed. The Air Force declared him dead within six months. Jim was listed as missing in action.

————

JIM THOMPSON   After another move, I was held in a small hut in a mountain village. These guards stayed directly outside the door. The huts were on stilts, six to eight feet off the ground. Guards removed the ladder at night to keep me in. I had a fire inside; they sat by a fire outside and watched my open door. One night I awoke and couldn't see any guard out there. I had to relieve myself. I was supposed to call the guard and he would bring the ladder. But there wasn't any in sight. Their fire had died down. I presumed they had gone to sleep somewhere.

I had a walking stick and used it to lower myself out of the hut. On the ground no one was in sight. I took off, this time heading west toward Laos. Directly behind the house was an open field and I came upon a trail and walked alongside it. I got about five hundred yards when again I ran into a guard. I indicated again that I was going to relieve myself. He nodded and smiled and let me do my business, then sent me back to the hooch. These young Montagnards either didn't realize what they were to do or didn't realize what I was trying to do. They didn't appear angry or hostile. I don't think they ever reported these incidents to the Vietnamese commander.

————

ALYCE   Three months after Jim turned up missing, Colonel Mattice got orders to a new assignment and wished me well. Things changed under the new commander and his wife. I got word back she considered me a wet blanket, someone she didn't want around. I would get no more invitations to post functions. I bothered her. More men were training and leaving for six-month increments. With my husband already missing she didn't want that spoiling her parties. The others might think, "God, this could happen to me!"

SAM DEACON   As months went by Jane and I made fewer functions on post so we saw Alyce less and less. Like a woman whose husband dies, Alyce began to feel like a fifth wheel.

TINA CARR   I felt so sorry for her. She was in a position like no one else had been. She had no one to share things with. Alone with all those children. I mean, what status did she have? She had been an officer's wife and then . . . she was nothing.

LEA HOFF   Alyce kept saying, "Nobody can tell me anything." She didn't know how long she would receive his Army income. She didn't know if she belonged on post.

ALYCE   I continued to write to Jim every day. Then all of the letters came back in one fell swoop. They told me not to bother writing anymore. It was just more work for them sending it back.

TINA CARR   Alyce didn't get much comfort from the military. Later on, as more men were captured, wives could come together for strength. But she had no one. On top of that, Special Forces wives had been taught to shut up. Teams went together and came back together and wives formed into small groups to wait. But soon Alyce had no team.

HERBERT HOFF   In June the rest of us came back, without Alyce's husband. That was sad.

LINDSAY CARR   We held a team barbecue and invited Alyce.

TINA CARR   They had that pig left over from the field trip before they left, which they'd promised to Article 15. And they did. But it was difficult planning that party with the captain missing.

LINDSAY CARR   There was a bottle of champagne left over. We didn't pop it, though. Herb and his wife, Lea, said they would hang on to it for when Jim returned.

JEAN LEDBETTER   I found it prestigious being married to a Green Beret officer. In the summer of '64, the Vietnam War had been going on about a year. My husband had been in fourteen years and his assignment to Vietnam was his first combat action. Finally he was using all his training. Secrecy was key in these assignments to Vietnam. Missions were classified. By the time my husband, Tom, was over there, Bragg had set up a small Vietnamese village, with huts and all. Special Forces wives were invited to see what they were doing. Tom was assigned to the farthest-northwest section of Vietnam, near Laos, in a camp with primitive people, bare-breasted women and men who only wore G-strings. That June I had gone to visit my mother in Florida. At two o'clock one morning, my brother woke me up to say a colonel was at the door. They had sent one of my husband's good friends along, too, an officer from company at Benning. He said Tom was missing. They had a plane waiting to fly me back to Bragg. I left our daughters with Mother and Dad.

They said Tom, his corporal, and a medic were on patrol with Montagnards when they were ambushed. They found a lot of bodies but no Americans. Survivors said Tom had been shot in the stomach and probably died of his wound. But they couldn't be sure. They hoped he had been captured. Until they knew more they would carry him as missing. Officially they were presumed captured June 16, 1964. And we wives were in limbo. After a few weeks I got back Tom's footlocker with his personal belongings.

Then I began to get a form letter every month saying there was no news. A colonel came by to say, "I'm sorry. But we don't know anything." Different men from the company stopped by and said they knew Tom so they had hope. Today I feel they did this in part to keep me quiet. They said not to speak to newspapers. "Come and tell us first." I was interviewed by the *Charlotte Observer* with the survivor assistance officer right there. The newspaper wanted to see what life was like when you're waiting. I could tell them. It was bad.

ALYCE   I heard there was this woman, with three little girls, who was going off the deep end since her husband was reported missing. She had told several people she was going to do herself in. The chaplain asked if I would talk to her.

JEAN LEDBETTER   Alyce called to say she was in the same predicament, that we should get together. We lived two miles apart, so I went right over. When I got there I was the one who felt pity. Alyce had just had a baby. She had all these other little kids. Her in-laws were there. The house was a mess. Letters piled all around. The same ones I was getting: "Sorry to inform you that we don't know anything." She had sandy, shoulder-length hair, glasses, and was very thin. Pleasant to look at although not beautiful. But real sweet and real thoughtful.

We compared notes: where our husbands were assigned; what we and our kids were going through; what we were going to do. We were a shoulder for each other. Her neighbors were real nice for a time, she said, then started to drift away. As with a death in the family, after a while you have nobody.

ALYCE   Finally we had somebody to talk to. Jean and I were the same age. Each had three girls. We became best of friends. It was nothing for me to call Jean at two o'clock in the morning and bawl my head off. Jean did the same.

JEAN LEDBETTER   We called each other when we had dreams of people running through the jungle or when we'd have premonitions. There were times when Alyce said we weren't going to make it. We talked of suicide. But then we said, "No way. Not with these kids." Yet when you're twenty-eight and missing your husband, especially in the military, it is rough. Every night we'd see husbands coming home. We'd tell each other how good it would be to get away from that. A life that was gone for us.

I was in limbo; Alyce was worse off. They told her they thought Jim was still alive. A friend of Tom's, a major, told me from the beginning not to get my hopes up. "I want you to realize he will not be coming back," he said. "Don't let them let you believe he's alive." One night a sergeant from my husband's company came to my house. "I would want my wife to know," he said. "There is no hope." He said Tom had been wounded and infection sets in so fast over there. Then he'd only survive if not beaten or starved. They were a vicious group over there, he said. They took the men they killed and hung them by their feet, then split their stomachs open so they deteriorated faster. The sergeant said he heard this had happened to Tom. I used to have nightmares about it.

Not only was my situation different but Alyce and I had come from two completely different backgrounds. I'm from the South; Alyce was raised in northern New Jersey. She had a difficult childhood; I grew up comfortable. Alyce was never independent. I was. She had no responsibility to make decisions before Jim left. So she had to be led. Finally, while I had had a happy marriage, Alyce talked about Jim in a less positive way. He had a drinking problem and Alyce had felt used.

Every time I visited those first several weeks, Alyce was in her nightgown. She felt she had to stay by the phone for somebody to call. And with all those kids, that poor girl worked herself to death. By the time she washed, cleaned, and took care of them, she looked haggard. Gradually, however, she gained momentum, took responsibility for herself. She had to be strong and show the kids they were okay, they were going to make it. Within a couple of months Alyce was back on her feet. We started doing things together to get out of the house.

ALYCE   One night we went to the movies to see *The Pink Panther* and almost died laughing. We saw James Bond together. We'd go shopping and on picnics with our families.

JEAN LEDBETTER   Jim's parents were quiet, distant, very unusual. They were drab people. Not a couple I could carry on a conversation with. In fact his father left the room when I came over. Jim's mother was like an old German lady. Wore plain, homemade dresses with little flowers on them. The two of them drove Alyce nuts. They couldn't stand for her to leave the house and leave them with the children. The phone was going to ring, they said. It was going to be Jim. We almost wanted to stay home ourselves waiting for the phone to ring. But Alyce started dressing up, making herself more presentable. Officer wives typically dress more swanky. Alyce didn't look like an officer's wife. Still, we went to the club for dinner, took the kids to movies, or went to bingo. And as soon as we'd get back Alyce would ask if anybody called.

18 ■ CONFINEMENT

JIM THOMPSON I was moved to a camp in Thua Thien Province, in the northwestern corner of South Vietnam, sometime in late spring of 1964. I could walk by then, for a few hours at any rate. They took every precaution to keep me hidden from the civilian population, insisting I wear a big hat with mosquito netting. They had no prisoner-of-war camps in this area, so one had been set up to receive me. It was still under construction when I got there.

My captors introduced themselves as members of the major staff of the central committee of the National Liberation Front. I didn't know what National Liberation Front meant. All I knew was "VC." They told me they were not interrogators. They were teachers. They came to teach a course in political education. They realized I was not an "imperialist aggressor" but a man who had been duped into following imperialist ways. The Vietnamese people had no desire to keep me long. They wanted to educate me, to tell me the truth. Once I understood I would be released.

They began with the history of Vietnam, going back some five thousand years and moving forward through the Mongol invasions and various other conflicts. They told me what a grand and glorious tradition the Vietnamese people had fighting for independence and freedom.

The communists handle prisoners of war completely different than we do and, I confess, I was unprepared. The lectures lasted four to eight hours a day. Occasionally they stuck in gentle probing questions but never applied real pressure. As soon as I understood their side of the war I would be allowed to go. They lectured and then asked me to comment. What did

I think about the Trung sisters?* The Mongol invaders? The Chinese invasions? On into the French colonial period. They began to get aggravated when I refused to discuss these things. "This has nothing to do with the war effort," they said. "This is history." They asked about my family, where I was born and where I was educated. They were interested in my political status and affiliations. My economic status. When I refused to answer they drifted back to this history lesson. I didn't understand until much later that these people were masters. A cardinal principle of interrogation is to get the guy talking. About anything. Silence thwarts all efforts to gain insight into what a prisoner thinks. But you can learn a lot if you get him to talk, even from what subjects he avoids.

Normally when my team went out on patrol we left notebooks and any personal effects in camp. But I had had my wallet with me when captured. It had a copy of my orders and my itinerary. From the time I left the States, I had jotted down notes on the back of my orders. So they knew who I was, when I got to Vietnam, the names of people in my detachment. They knew our mission. They knew when I was scheduled to leave Vietnam.

My interrogators spoke excellent English. One was from Hanoi and apparently had studied under an English teacher there. He had a British accent. The other was from Nha Trang in South Vietnam. He spoke excellent French, too. Both were in their early thirties. About six weeks into my interrogation, they got off the gentle approach, the history thing, and began to apply pressure. Sessions got longer and more demanding. They began to do things to make my life miserable. Before this I had had plenty of sleep and sufficient food and tobacco. Medicine, too. Now they reduced all these things. They'd say, "You're a very intelligent man. You're a very reasonable person. As soon as you see the truth you'll realize what you must do. That is, give us any information we want. Answer all our questions. Do everything you're told. We will never force you to accept our viewpoint or to change your ideas. We'll just explain. Once you see the truth you'll know what to do. Then you'll go home."

They combined this message with a technique of altering the pressure. If you put pressure on somebody and hold it, he can learn to live with it. But alternating a hard day with an easy day, a hard day with an easy day, causes mental pressure to build. Initially they demanded that I tell them everything they wanted to know—make political statements, propaganda broadcasts, write letters. Eventually they reduced these demands.

* Trung Trac and Trung Nhi were proclaimed co-queens of Vietnam in A.D. 39 after leading an army that drove Chinese occupation forces from territory stretching from Hue into southern China. They became revered symbols of Vietnamese resistance.

My strength at this point was much diminished. I was still in a great deal of back pain. Just being obliged to sit during interrogation was pure torture. An upright position was excruciating. Malaria had begun to set in for the third time since my capture. My stomach couldn't accept their food. I had dysentery. I was fed mostly a rice gruel, the only thing I could get down. My normal weight, one hundred seventy-seven, was down thirty pounds. Weak and getting weaker. The pressures and threats of torture increased. I knew that the sooner I escaped, the better chance I would have. I felt if I didn't get away soon I was going to cash it in.

On the 21st of July [1964] I awoke at dawn when we usually had our breakfast. For some reason, they hadn't called me for interrogation. So I went back to sleep. I was exhausted and in pain. When I woke again in midmorning, I saw the guard outside my hut asleep with a submachine gun cradled in his arms. I was the only prisoner but had fifteen guards. So I knew I wouldn't be able to shoot my way out. My only chance was to sneak out. I put on my boots, which I still had, and eased on around to the latrine out back. I was supposed to ask permission to leave the hut but thought if the guard caught me all he'd do is holler and chase me back in.

I had crossed the area to the north to get to this camp, so I knew it was VC-controlled. South was the Ashua Valley, infested with VC. Vietnam is only thirty miles wide from the Lao border to the ocean in this part of the country. Though I had no map or compass and knew no trails, I knew if I kept going east I'd eventually make the coast. Assuming three miles a day through mountainous jungle, I would make it in ten to fifteen days. Then, I figured that they'd come to the same conclusion, so I would travel north one day and then east.

It was a desperate sudden attempt to get away rather than any cold, calculated thing. I thought my chances pretty slim but off I went. I got a fifteen- or twenty-minute head start before I heard an uproar. But the jungle was so thick they couldn't follow without dogs. I spent the rest of the day going across country, strictly up and down. I tried to find a spot where I could survey the terrain and get a fix on my position. I found a banana tree and stuffed my pockets. I ate one or two but wasn't much interested in food. I heard distant voices, people searching through jungle. But as thick at it was, they would have to get right on top of me to find me.

I felt good. If I was able to survive two or three days I figured my chances excellent on this fourth escape attempt to make the coast. The farther I got, the larger the search area and the more men they would need to find me. Late in the afternoon I came out on the crest of a hill and looked down. Below was a river I recognized. I had to cross to go east. I decided to approach the river but stay in the brush until night. It needed to be dark before I'd dare cross. I moved to the bank undetected. The river was thirty yards wide but shallow. Now I really was feeling good. I knew I had not covered much terrain but the longer I stayed gone the better my chances.

For the next hour or two I waited, looked and listened. I never heard the sound of other men. I was free. Even the air seemed different, just breathing without a guard over my shoulder. Of course, everybody likes to play the hero. I had visions of a big beer bust at the club at Da Nang. I would call home and tell my wife I was all right. I would find out I had a son. I thought what a relief it would be to hear Alyce's voice. Then I'd get back to where the VC had held me and clean their clock. I knew where the bastards were. I planned a coordinated operation, with both Special Forces and regular ARVN troops. A large heliborne assault. Hard intelligence was a tough thing to come by in 1964. Here I was with a headful of good stuff and dying to use it. I knew now how the VC operated, how they brought in supplies, how they forced Montagnards to support them.

At dusk, hearing nothing, I moved from behind the brush toward the river. As I got knee-deep in the river, the bank on the other side erupted. Twenty-five or thirty Montagnards stood up at once. They lit torches as more began coming out of the jungle. They seemed afraid to approach me, but soon there were hundreds of them, from bearded old men to little kids. I tried to get away, moving farther up the sandbank, but I only attracted more people. They followed along the opposite bank, whooping and hollering. I couldn't go back into the jungle. Behind me was only a large field. I had no cover. Finally a VC came out, grabbed a weapon, and fired into the water in front me. That was the end of that. I suddenly was completely exhausted, physically and mentally. A hundred people flocked around me. As I was brought back to camp, I was hoping some of them would get the word out that I was there.

It only took thirty minutes on the trail to return to my hut. That was disheartening. This time the VC commander took a rather dim view of the escape. He had lost face. I was tied hand and foot. He began hitting my face with his fists, wilder and wilder. Then he grabbed a stick and began using that. He left me unconscious in the mud. Sometime later the two interrogators came along with the political officer and revived me. They were almost apologetic. "How are you? We're sorry this happened but you broke camp regulations. He was very angry." They sent me down to the creek to bathe and made the guards light a fire. They gave me dry clothes and a bowl of soup. Then they took me out to the shack and began an all-night interrogation.

It started out mild, but they soon were threatening to shoot me. They said any person who attempts escape can be shot. They had guards lined up, ready, but would give me an opportunity to atone for my sins. I was so drained. It was all downhill from that night on. Subsequent interrogation sessions got longer and more pressure was applied. Their policy of leniency, they said, was towards those with good attitudes, those of good-will. Reasonable people. If I was a stubborn diehard then I was not a rea-sonable man. I was a "brass hat" then, not some misinformed citizen. Their policy toward this type of person was considerably different than toward most American soldiers. I was an imperialist aggressor rather than an average citizen. Requiring harsher treatment. There were lightly veiled threats of torture.

Many of their questions were impossible to answer for anybody not on the general staff. How many U.S. aircraft in Vietnam? How many ships in the Seventh Fleet? How many aircraft in the Fifteenth Air Force? How many airfields? How many radios, of what type and what frequency used? They'd start some sessions with no pressure at all, nice and solicitous. Then short periods of pressure being nasty. And longer periods being nice. Then gradually the pattern reversed. Pressure was applied for longer and longer periods, off for shorter and shorter periods. Maybe a week of solid pressure and then a day off. Each time they came back with renewed force and veiled threats of physical torture, even of death.

Finally they said it was too late to offer information. They showed me a large map, three feet square, obviously done by somebody in our camp or somebody who had spent a great deal of time observing it. All the trenches and machine-gun positions were plotted. "We no longer need anything you might tell us. Now what we want is a statement about the treatment you have received. And that you understand now that Vietnam is for the Vietnamese. Americans should go home."

So their goal all along had been a statement. The pressure now got as high as it could without killing me. I had lost forty to fifty pounds in three months. It was an effort to put one foot in front of the other. If I was down on my knees, or squatting to work on a fire, it took me minutes to get back up. I had to move very, very slowly or I'd pass out. And I did. Frequently. One night I fell into the fire, knocking the cook pot over, my body sprawl-ing across the coals. The guard pulled me out. It's difficult to recreate this atmosphere. I knew what they were doing to me but I couldn't minimize the effect. They knew my wife had been expecting a baby from correspon-dence found in my pockets when I was captured. "How do you think your wife feels?" they asked. "Having a baby and not knowing whether you're dead or alive?" They said they still had some prisoners from the French war, people not fit to return to their families. Some had been executed because they weren't fit to live. They threatened to execute me. They threatened to contact my family through unnamed organizations in the States.

It was the second or third week in August now and they had been working on me since June. All they wanted was a lousy statement. They had this whole camp set up for me. They had all these guards. They had these interrogators. All for the statement. So they wrote out a statement saying I had been treated well, that I'd been provided various necessities of life, received excellent medical care, never been mistreated, humiliated, or tortured. The NLF, it said, was not a bunch of bloodthirsty rebels but organized, well disciplined, and fighting for their country's freedom. Vietnam should be left for the Vietnamese.

I'll never forget that damn thing. They placed a small desk in front of me in the interrogation hooch and on top of that the statement, another piece of paper, and a pen. I sat there with pen in hand as they shouted at me to write. Then they listed the reasons I should write, why I would be forced to write it. I refused. But I had to sit there and hold the pen. Then they altered their approach, from trying to convince me I should write to cajoling me. Then trying to force me to write it. On and on and on. Periodically they hit me with bamboo. Not hard enough to knock me unconscious or to break the skin. Just enough to hurt. They kept at it for eight, ten, twelve hours a day. Maybe four hours at a time, knock off for lunch and then back in the afternoon and again at night. I would lose touch with reality. An hour would go by and I would have no memory of what transpired. It faded out and back in. I'd realize he was saying something entirely different from the last thing that registered. When I finally signed the thing, the statement, it was as if I were standing to the side, watching myself do it. As soon as I signed it, the pressure stopped. They sent me back to my hooch. The next day they brought me back and told me to rewrite it in my own handwriting and sign it. Which I did. They put a microphone in front of me and said, "Read it."

And I read it.

19 ■ HAROLD

JEAN LEDBETTER   One day Alyce suggested we go bowling. I didn't know how but we went to relax. The pins became the enemy and we threw as hard as we could, drilling them down. It sounds crazy but we tried to kill them as though we were fighting the VC ourselves.

ALYCE   Throwing at those pins got rid of a lot of tension. Jean and I belonged to two leagues—a daytime league with Special Forces wives and a women's league at night. We practiced for our tournaments. Didn't want none of this 120 crap. My biggest game was 286. I was good. The main bowling alley by Bragg's PX was busy at night with league play but they kept another one at the other end of the post, used mostly by GIs. Harold ran that one.

JEAN LEDBETTER   I was with Alyce when she met Harold. He was a great person, somebody we could talk to. The most understanding person I ever met.

ALYCE   He came over to us one night and said, "Look, instead of you gals sitting here waiting for lanes, why don't you call me before you come. I'll tell you how long it will be."

JEAN LEDBETTER   Harold was a sergeant, a quartermaster. Always in khakis. We never had had much association with enlisted people before. "I hope nobody says anything about that," I told Alyce. But Harold said he'd teach us how to bowl. And he was a good-looking man.

ALYCE   I'd call and say, "Harold, this is Alyce. You got any lanes open?" He'd say, "Not right now, but I will have one. Come down in a half hour." He'd hold it for us.

JEAN LEDBETTER   The two of them hit it off. After that we always went late and to the same alley. Alyce started fixing herself up, trying to look even better. She started putting on makeup and making plans. "Let's go bowling, 'cause Harold's going to be there," she'd say.

ALYCE   Harold was a friend. That's all it started out to be. Just a friend, and we got close. He was a very caring person. Wouldn't hurt a fly.

JEAN LEDBETTER   Harold sympathized with us and had sympathy for soldiers missing and killed and those coming back wounded. Harold had a boy and a girl himself and brought them to the alley. Real nice kids. Harold and wife had divorced and he had custody.

ALYCE   Harold had gone up one weekend, told them he was taking Lucy and her brother Keith on a picnic, and then took them across the state line. Lucy, his daughter, was petrified her mother would take her back but evidently she didn't want to.

FRED KILEY   After signing that statement Jim got very depressed. He told me about it years later while I was preparing the official Defense Department history of our POWs in Vietnam. One thing Jim didn't have that American aviators held in the main camps up north had was peer support. The pilots were very tough guys. Their motto was "The big four and nothing more." Name, rank, serial number, and date of birth. After they had been tortured and made to say something, or to sign something, they were tremendously depressed too. It couldn't happen to them but it did. Yet they had that tremendous peer support. As soon as a pilot was brought back to his cell, having given a statement, he communicated with the others, either through the walls, through a note, any method they were using. Pretty soon everybody told everybody everything. A man who went off to a "quiz" reported back on the subject, on who had been there, on what he had said. When a guy was depressed about having said something, his companions picked him up. These guys had tremendous mental health when they came home, which they wouldn't have had if they had been truly isolated all those years. Jim Thompson never had that.

Besides that, captivity in the South was miserable. Deaths ran as high as forty percent in some camps. Conditions were terrible; there was no leadership. Captives suffered more being on the run half the time. They ate what their captors could spare. Sometimes that meant nothing. They died of malnutrition, beriberi, dysentery, fevers. Guys became so weak a spider bite might kill them. Thompson's situation was particularly remarkable. There were no other U.S. prisoners the first several years he was held around the DMZ and Laos. The question is not why he was isolated but why he was kept alive. The answer is that statement. After he made it, the world knew he was alive. Once a man's name was in the system in Hanoi, whoever was in charge of that prisoner knew he'd better keep him alive. Those statements kept alive men who otherwise might have been killed.

———

JIM THOMPSON   On the 18th of August, the two interrogators came down to my hut. They asked how many days I thought I had been there. I said eighty-five. "We believe," one of them said, "this is the longest you will stay in one camp."

"Do you mean I will be released in eighty-five days?" I asked. All along they had been telling me that as soon as I "understood" I would be returned to my family. They nodded and smiled and said something to the effect, "For sure, within six months."

I thought, What in hell are these people up to now? They've gotten what they want. There's no reason to lie to me anymore. I figured they wouldn't say this now, after the interrogation was over, unless they meant it. I wanted to believe. I wanted to believe the war was over and I was going home. Before my capture they had released three prisoners I knew of, two NCOs and one civilian. I thought about this on the way to the next camp, a few hours' walk away.

As I feared, however, here they demanded additional statements, but the skilled interrogators were gone. This camp commander's English was not good. He demanded I write another statement. I refused. He worked at it about a week, but without torture or extreme pressure. Then he gave up. I never heard more of him.

But my physical condition was poor and deteriorating. I still suffered from the injured back and now from malaria. The guards had it too. During my first two years as a prisoner I counted twenty-two attacks of the disease.

———

JEAN LEDBETTER   Three or four months after we met, Alyce began dating Harold. At first we never discussed her getting romantically involved. But I could feel it. And so could others. Somebody made some comment about her seeing Harold. "They don't want me to do this and do that. They want me to stay home and do nothing," she said.

ALYCE   Harold called one night and asked if I wanted to go to a movie. I said yes. After that he asked me out to dinner. This was all off post. I didn't flaunt it. One thing just led to another.

———

JIM THOMPSON   At this camp I spent most of my time in a bamboo hut, six foot square, with absolutely nothing to do. Occasionally I had some work, like splitting firewood to carry it back to the camp. But no one spoke English and I was left completely to my own devices. A guard sat out front. If I had to leave I asked permission. I could go down to the creek and wash or go to the latrine. If I needed wood, the guard handed me an ax and told me to go cut it. Otherwise, I was left alone with nothing to occupy my time. No reading material. Nothing to write with. Nothing to pass the time except to sit and think.

————

JEAN LEDBETTER   Alyce wrote a letter to her congressman. She said she wanted to know why she was left in limbo. The Army hadn't told us anything except "We are sorry to inform you your husband is still missing."

5 Oct. 1964

Dear Mr. Osmers:*
I am writing you concerning my husband, Capt. Floyd J. Thompson, who has been missing in Viet Nam since the 26th of March 1964. I am beginning to wonder what the State Department is doing to find my husband. I have been pacified constantly with people telling me how dense the jungle is over there and I couldn't possibly imagine it unless I saw it for myself. But a person just cannot vanish into thin air.

It has crossed my mind that possibly, and I mean possibly, my husband might be in Laos. Is there any way this could be checked out? As far as I know, no one has checked into this. But my husband's Special Forces Camp was so close to the Laotian border and the flight plan they were to follow came close to it also. There is the chance the plane flew over into Laos unintentionally and that this is the reason the plane and my husband and the pilot have not been found as yet in Viet Nam. It has been over six months. Is there any way at all this could be checked out? I know the Pathet Lao have at times let the American Embassy in Laos know when they are holding prisoners. I hate to keep bothering you but I know of no one else to turn to.

Sincerely,
Mrs. F. J. Thompson

23 Oct 64

Dear Mr. Osmers:
As Mrs. Thompson was advised by the Adjutant General's office, a statement from a Viet Cong defector indicated an American aircraft with two

* Representative Frank C. Osmers, Jr., then a New Jersey Republican.

persons aboard was hit and downed in the Republic of Vietnam. The time and place coincide with the flight plan of the plane on which Captain Thompson was reported missing. One American was reportedly killed in the crash and one was wounded and taken away by the Viet Cong.

According to reports from search parties, the terrain varies from mountainous with heavy undergrowth and double canopy of trees to rolling hills with elephant grass six to fifteen feet high. Concentrated aerial and ground searches have failed to produce any material evidence of the plane or its personnel. Our military commanders in the field recruit civilians who are familiar with the area to assist in searching all areas adjacent to the proposed route of our missing aircraft. This effort has proven futile. There have been no reports that any of our military personnel are missing in Laos or that any have been detained by that government. . . .

I realize how anxiously Mrs. Thompson is waiting for some encouraging information and you may be assured she will be notified upon the receipt of any additional information.

> Sincerely,
> F. W. Boye, Jr.
> Major General
> Chief of Legislative Liaison

JIM THOMPSON   I invented all manner of things to pass the time. One favorite pastime was building houses. My wife's stepfather was a building contractor, and I had helped him from time to time. I had worked for a roofing and siding man too. I knew enough to come up with some reasonable designs. I started off remodeling houses that I had lived in, then designing and building new ones. It's amazing how the mind works. I would dwell for days on insignificant details. Everything in the plan had to be absolutely perfect. I computed the number of board feet of lumber and the exact number of bricks I needed. All the fixtures, the electrical wiring, the plumbing. Everything was as accurate as possible, although they were based on cost estimates twenty years old. I did all this in my head, just for something to do, but it became important. I had to be accurate down to the penny. Otherwise it would have been a complete waste of time.

––––––

ALYCE   Jim's father wouldn't accept the fact that he was missing. He felt Jim went over there to spy for the United States, that the government was carrying him MIA as cover. We couldn't get the facts through his head. Ben was very peculiar. I couldn't continue living the way we were. I had three girls sleeping in a small bedroom and Jimmy in the crib in my room.

Ben and Elizabeth were in the other bedroom. It was getting to be too much. I got no money from his parents. I was feeding them and housing them, which I didn't mind. But I had to do everything for them. The car I had, a two-door Pontiac, was breaking down and it was impossible to fit everybody in.

———

JIM THOMPSON   About the fifth house I designed was our dreamhouse. I didn't know if I could ever afford to build it. It had five bedrooms. The master bedroom had a walk-in dressing room. Twin bathrooms, mine just a stall shower. A man's bathroom. My wife's bathroom had a tub and built-in vanity. There was a boy's room—I knew with certainty I had a son now. His room had a bathroom. The hall bathroom would be for the three girls. There was an L-shaped living room with space for a grand piano, a dining room, and large kitchen. There was an informal dining area off the kitchen. A full-size basement with game room and bar. A workshop plus a big, two-car garage.

I planned quite a few innovations in the house. Usually basements were so low you had to duck to get under the beams. But for very little additional cost you can put in plenty of headroom. It's a matter of two, three additional courses of block around the base. Cheap considering the value. I-beam construction in the basement was unusual but it eliminates the Lally columns so you have full use of the basement. It's much more versatile. Also, a lot of people didn't realize that for the price of hardwood flooring, you can put in a plywood base and have wall-to-wall carpeting installed. I wanted almost no woodwork framing around windows and doors. It costs a fortune yet you cover it with curtains and drapes. With metal lathing used for plaster you can have beautiful square framing of windows. I planned to have central air conditioning. I also planned an underground shooting gallery, a twenty-five-meter thing, going underground out in the backyard. It's possible with modern sound engineering to build it so it doesn't disturb the whole house or the neighbors. And it's quite safe. I thought this all up in 1964.

FROM HANOI VNA INTERNATIONAL SERVICE, NOVEMBER 4, 1964

HANOI HANNAH: "Since the South Vietnam National Liberation Front maintains a lenient policy toward all prisoners of war, prisoners of war are not maltreated, humiliated, tortured," said Special Forces Captain Floyd James Thompson, now detained in a front-controlled area of South Vietnam.

Floyd James Thompson, captain in the U.S. Army Special Forces, was captured by the patriotic guerillas in Quang Tri Province when his L-19 plane, manned by Richard Whitesides was shot down on March 26 last.

In a recorded statement broadcast recently by Liberation Radio, organ of the Liberation Front, he said:

I was taken prisoner of war by the South Vietnam National Liberation Front. Since I was taken prisoner I have received the best of medical care, have been well treated, and every effort has been expended to maintain my health. I have not lost any weight. I have been given a mosquito net, blanket, hammock, extra clothes and anti-malaria pills regularly. I have been fed as well as possible. I have never been maltreated, humiliated or tortured in any way. Tobacco is provided for my use regularly and I enjoy it very much.

In the area under control of the South Vietnam National Liberation Front, I have never seen any active terror used. On the contrary, the atti-tude of both Liberation Army men and the civilians toward each other is friendly. It shows mutual respect, and the attitude of the population is not the attitude of terrorized people. Their attitude toward me is always kind and considerate. The behavior of the liberation soldiers, both regular army and guerrilla, shows that they are not members of loose rebel bands but that they belong to a national front whose structure and degree of organization far surpass anything I had imagined before my captivity. They are well-disciplined, well-behaved men dedicated to their cause: that is, to fight for freedom and independence for their country. One cannot help but admire them for being willing to endure the hardship and depri-vation of the guerrilla fighter.

It is remarkable under these circumstances that they can be kind and considerate toward a prisoner of war and have as cheerful a past time as playing a homemade instrument and singing in the evening. The goals of the South Vietnam National Liberation Front are to achieve peace, free-dom, independence, democracy and neutrality for their country. These goals certainly enjoy widespread support among the South Vietnamese people.

I think the solution to the problem in South Vietnam is to call a cease-fire, withdraw all U.S. forces from South Vietnam, and let the South Viet-namese people settle their own affairs themselves by peaceful means. In the end it is the majority of the South Vietnamese people who will decide on their own future, their own government and their own way of life. As the South Vietnamese National Liberation Front maintains a lenient pol-icy toward all prisoners of war, prisoners are not maltreated, humiliated or tortured. This policy embodies the highest ideals of mankind and is certainly a very humane policy.

HANOI HANNAH: You have just listened to a recorded tape of U.S. Special Forces Captain Floyd James Thompson giving his impressions about the South Vietnamese National Liberation Front and filled with interest for American servicemen in South Vietnam. This broadcast is on the air daily at 1415 hours, except Sunday. Until the next broadcast, this is your announcer Tu Hun signing off from Hanoi.

ALYCE   Seven or eight months after Jim's disappearance I got a call from a neighbor who happened to be listening to a radio station out of New York. She said, "I just heard a recording by Jim."

JEAN LEDBETTER   Alyce called me, really excited. Jim was alive, she said, but that's all she knew. I went over. The parents seemed thrilled.

FROM THE *Fayetteville Observer*, NOVEMBER 5, 1964

PENTAGON DOUBTS BRAGG OFFICER MADE PROPAGANDA PITCH OVER RADIO HANOI

TOKYO (UPI)—A broadcast by Communist North Viet Nam's Radio claimed today that a U.S. Army Special Forces officer made a statement in which he allegedly said the South Vietnamese people support the aims of the Viet Cong rebels.

Capt. Floyd James Thompson allegedly made the statement originally in a broadcast over the Red Viet Cong Radio in South Vietnam. U.S. authorities in Saigon, however, moved immediately to cast doubt on the validity of the alleged statement. An Army spokesman said military monitoring services had not detected any such broadcast in South Vietnam. Capt. Thompson's alleged statement was similar to those made by other U.S. prisoners of the Communists in Southeast Asia.

The statements are not made under duress. Usually the prisoner is given the choice of a message loaded with propaganda and telling his family he is safe, or no message at all. . . .

ALYCE   When that recording came out and the story hit the paper, I had people writing letters and postcards, some praising the Lord and some saying, "He's dead. He got just what he deserved."

I called the ABC affiliate in North Carolina and they couldn't tell me anything about the statement. So I called the New York radio station.

They sent me a copy of the broadcast on a tape reel. But I had no way of listening to it. Through Special Forces I tried to find the right machine. I don't know whether, conveniently, they didn't have one or what. But I never got to listen to that tape. I still don't know what's on it. It was supposedly a bunch of propaganda.

FROM THE *Fayetteville Observer*, NOVEMBER 5, 1964

SHE'S ON CLOUD NINE AT HEARING HE'S SAFE

Radio Hanoi today quoted a Ft. Bragg officer as saying that the South Viet-namese people support Viet Cong goals. The officer's wife, Mrs. Floyd James Thompson of Ft. Bragg, said she was "on cloud nine" this morning after hear-ing that her husband, who was shot down last March, is still alive. She said she was not disturbed by his statement because she understood the circum-stances under which it was made.

"I've been praying for this for seven months," Mrs. Thompson said, "and now my prayers have been answered. Before, I didn't know whether he was alive or not.

"It's kind of hard when your oldest kid keeps asking, 'When will Daddy come home?' and you don't know whether he's alive or not. This morning I told Pam her daddy isn't lost any more, that he will be coming home. She kind of smiled. I don't think she really understood."

Capt. and Mrs. Thompson have been living for three years at 11-A Sun-chon St., Hammond Hill, Ft. Bragg. Their four children are Pam 6½, Laura 4, Ruth 2½ and Jimmy, their seven-month-old son who was born March 27, the day after his father's plane was shot down in Quang Tri Province, South Viet Nam. While at Ft. Bragg, Capt. Thompson served with C Co., 7th Special Forces Group. He is a 31-year-old native of Bergenfield, N.J.

Mrs. Thompson said she had not seen the statement which Communist Viet Nam's Radio Hanoi attributed to her husband. In this alleged statement, Capt. Thompson was quoted as saying the South Vietnamese people support Viet Cong goals. Viet Cong prisoners generally are given a chance to make a statement loaded with propaganda telling his family he is safe, or no mes-sage at all. Mrs. Thompson said her husband probably chose to make this statement "because he knows I'm a worrywart. I used to worry if he went to jump and came in minutes late."

TINA CARR   Some people said he gave more information than he should have. That was awful. Things were played up too much.

GEORGE MALONEY   Jim didn't admit to atrocities. He didn't say Americans had been told to come over to Vietnam to rape the women and napalm villages. The first part is just an accurate statement; the second is a glorified statement of the Viet Cong. Anybody would recognize it as a self-serving statement forced on him, something written by the enemy. In the hands of the enemy you take whatever measures you need to survive. It's easy to say you would not make a statement. But the VC would as soon cut your balls off as look at you. Everyone has the right to seek his own survival, short of acting to the detriment of other prisoners. All of us have to ask what would we do in that situation. I had a wife and four lovely kids and paramount in my mind throughout every day I was in Vietnam was to get my ass back to them. I wanted to do a good job but if faced with the truth that this day I would be killed I wouldn't have gotten out of bed.

My own war wounds were relatively minor but enough to scare the hell out of me. People I admired greatly, when they realized they were going to die—and some were so seriously wounded they could feel life ebbing from them—they went right back to God and motherhood. I mean pretty tough sergeants. They wanted their mothers. Under a situation then where a man is a prisoner and isolated, he can lose all hope. The only thing that may have benefited Jim was he was over there such a short time he really didn't have a chance to know combat. He didn't lose any team members. He had a relatively quiet tour, free of brutality, before capture. Several other teams by then were in some brutal patrols, under fire for twenty-five days at a time, day and night, worried sick as to whether they would get out alive. Some teams had horrendous experiences. Later on it was almost beyond our capability to tell a wife what her husband had been through.

November 6, 1964

Dear Alyce,

We have received word that Jimmy is alive, even though a prisoner. I know how much you must be rejoicing in this answer to your prayers. You never once have doubted he was alive. I want you to know that our prayers are continuing in Old North Church that Jimmy may be kept safe and brought home to his loved ones sometime in the near future.

While we are far away we want you to know that we think of you constantly and uphold you before God in your need. If your plans have not been changed by this word about Jimmy we look forward to seeing you at Thanksgiving time.

Sincerely,
Albert H. Van Dyke
Minister, Old North Reformed Church
Dumont, N.J.

ALYCE   I got my hopes up real high. If he was alive and coming back, we could talk about our problems. I wanted him back and to get things straightened out. But after a few weeks my hopes soured. The Army refused to acknowledge the broadcast. They told me nobody from the Army had heard it and they could not say for sure it was Jim.

FROM THE *Bergen Record*, NOVEMBER 19, 1964

U.S. DOUBTS OFFICER MADE PRO-RED TALK
(special to The Record)

SAIGON—United States military authorities today cast doubt on a reported North Vietnamese broadcast stating a captured Army Special Forces officer, formerly from Bergenfield, N.J., had said the South Vietnamese people supported the Communist Viet Cong goals.

A military spokesman said Saigon monitoring services had not picked up any broadcast statement attributed to U.S. Army Captain Floyd James Thompson. . . .

Rev. Dr. Albert H. Van Dyke, pastor of Old North Reformed Church in Dumont, where three of the Thompson children were baptized, said the family had heard no word that Thompson was alive. Parishioners of the Dumont church, where the Thompsons are still listed as members, had been praying for his safe return. His wife, said Dr. Van Dyke, had a strong faith that the captain was still alive. . . .

TINA CARR   On post Alyce and the kids became outcasts. They were suffering. The oldest daughter, Pam, particularly. The other kids teased her that her father had said things that were not with U.S. policy. Alyce was upset about how they talked to her child. Some told Pam her father was dead. Little kids hear grown-ups talking. They made it ugly for that little girl.

PAM   I never had another friend after that. Parents kept their kids away from me. We were isolated.

TINA CARR   People wondered why Alyce was still living on post. There was talk that she had an enlisted friend too. I didn't pay much attention to it.

JEAN LEDBETTER   After Christmas and New Year, when Alyce was real involved with Harold, she would call to talk. Occasionally we went out to the officers' club or to play bingo. We won a bottle of champagne on New Year's 1965. Alyce and I drank it all and got tipsy. We felt real sorry for ourselves, drinking and crying, lonely and sad.

15 January 1965

Mrs. Alyce D. Thompson
11-A Sunchon
Fort Bragg, North Carolina

Dear Mrs. Thompson:

I am writing again concerning your husband, Captain Floyd J. Thompson, who has been missing in Vietnam since 26 March 1964.

As I mentioned in my last letter, efforts were being made to determine the validity of the report that your husband had recorded a statement which was broadcast by the Viet Cong. Unfortunately, all attempts so far have been unsuccessful. As far as can be learned, the purported broadcast by the Viet Cong was not recorded by any United States agency. Due to the time lapse it is now unlikely that any more information can be obtained concerning the alleged broadcast.

I regret that more definite information could not be obtained. Let me assure you, however, that efforts are continuing in behalf of our service members who are missing and you will be promptly advised if any additional information is received concerning your husband.

> Sincerely yours,
> J. C. Lambert
> Major General, USA
> The Adjutant General

SAM DEACON   I was often gone from Bragg, but my wife heard rumors about Alyce. The two of them weren't overly friendly anyway but Jane chose at that point to totally disassociate herself. I told her that was wrong.

"Well," my wife said, "she shouldn't have put herself in a position to have those rumors begin."

JEAN LEDBETTER   After she took up with Harold, Alyce and I sort of faded off. She'd take her kids over to his house for supper.

ALYCE   I had decided that, with Jim's parents, the apartment on post was too small. So I went house-hunting. The Army said it would be perfectly all right.

TINA CARR   Alyce had tried to buy a house herself but they wouldn't sell her one, alone. She couldn't say how long she would receive Jim's pay to cover the mortgage. And if you've got four children, well . . .

ALYCE   I was going to get a job, but what about the kids? Elizabeth said, "Don't worry. Get your job. I'll take care of the kids and Ben can handle the grass and the yard."

So I got a job and finally got the loan. The house we picked wasn't finished yet but it had been framed out. Four bedrooms. About thirty-two thousand dollars. It had a nice backyard and I got to pick out colors. When Ben came out to see it, he said how we could put up a fence and wouldn't have to worry about the kids. I put a thousand dollars down, paid closing costs, signed the papers.

PAM   I had even tied a little ribbon around the trees we wanted to save. They would clear the rest of the lot.

ALYCE   Two days before we were to move in, Ben came down that morning and said, "You'll be moving into your house in a couple of days. We're not moving with you. We're leaving."

My mouth dropped open.

"When?"

"In a couple of weeks," he said.

"Why?"

"I want to go back to New Jersey."

"Well, why the hell did you let me go through all of this?" I said. "Picking out the colors for decoration. Going down to the lot, tying trees that we wanted left, making plans, building up my dreams. And now you tell me it's not going through."

I called the bank and stopped the loan. I got hold of the realtor and got my money back. I should have lost it but he felt sorry for me. Then Ben stayed and stayed. One day I said, "Hey, you told me you was going back to New Jersey. When the hell are you going?"

"Would tomorrow morning suit ya?" he said.

"That's just fine. Go pack your bags and get the hell out!"

They left the following morning. I kissed Elizabeth goodbye. We both cried. She didn't want to go; I didn't want her to go. "I have to go," she said. "He's my husband."

JEAN LEDBETTER   I suppose Jim's parents had gotten wind that Alyce was seeing Harold. This is probably why they became so cold and sadistic. They knew what she was doing. When they left it was like a load off Alyce's head. They'd driven her nuts long enough. Then Alyce said the heck with everybody. It was Harold who gave her love and understanding. That's what she needed.

ALYCE   Neighbors saw Harold coming and going but I didn't mind. I was mainly afraid some bigwig would kick me off post. One neighbor stuck his nose in. He told me to quit going out and quit running around, and this and that. I told him where to shove it. As close a friend as he and his wife were supposed to be, they never once invited us over to watch TV or for dinner. Put yourself in my place. I was twenty-nine, at the peak of life, with four kids. Yet I was expected to sit in a goddamn rocking chair with a prayer book and wait. For my own sanity and for the sake of my kids, I wasn't going to do that. I started to realize I had to fight for my kids, and for myself. Finally I said, "Hey, you can do it. You can tell somebody to go to hell if you want to. You don't have to have your husband do it for you."

20 ■ MASSACHUSETTS

J EAN LEDBETTER   Let's face it, Alyce and Harold were doing wrong, living like that. I used to tell Alyce, "This isn't right. You should at least wait until you know whether Jim is dead or alive."

"I've never been loved by anyone until now," she said. It was like they both lit up when together. When with Harold, Alyce was a different person. He brought out all the good in her.

ALYCE   It was a physical thing at first. That, and my loneliness. But I thought I was in love.

JEAN LEDBETTER   Other women told me I shouldn't associate with her. Nobody could understand what Alyce was going through, what we were going through.

15 Feb 1965

Dear Mrs. Thompson:

Although United States officials are still making every reasonable effort in behalf of the Americans missing or detained in Vietnam, there has been no new information since I last wrote to you. Army officials continue to hope that the status and whereabouts of your husband can soon be determined.

It is hoped that the fortitude with which you have so far borne the anxiety and uncertainty will continue to sustain you. If any additional information is received you will be immediately notified. My continuing sympathy is with you.

> Sincerely yours,
> J. C. Lambert
> Major General, USA
> The Adjutant General

ALYCE   I got the same letter once a month. It got so I had it memorized. It was a joke, a waste of a stamp.

JEAN LEDBETTER   Looking back at that war, I can understand why so many are so bitter. It was like nobody cared. A so-what type of thing. People in the commissary would point to us and say her husband has been missing for so many months or so many years. We were a pair in another boat. Eventually, however, our numbers grew.

On 31 March 65, the Adjutant General informed Mrs. Thompson that, under provisions of the Missing Persons Act, a member of the Army may be carried on the rolls in a missing status as long as there is a reasonable doubt as to whether he is living or deceased; that the law further provides a review and determination of his status should be made after he has been missing 12 months; that all information concerning her husband has been carefully reviewed; and that an official determination continuing him in the status of missing had been made 27 March 65.

The Adjutant General further stated that the Missing Persons Act further provided pay and allowances to be credited to a missing person's account, also that payment of authorized allotments were to be continued during the absence of such persons in a missing status.

> —from the Army's Thompson family case file

ALYCE   When I heard Jim's pilot was believed dead, I begged the Army to give me that man's name and number so I could call his wife. I called her in April of '65. I said my husband is MIA and I'm sorry your husband was killed. She was very bitter. She got left with a little boy, a toddler. The conversation was real short. Maybe she thought I called to gloat. I just let it go.

JIM THOMPSON   The Christmas Gospel according to St. Luke is the best version. I had memorized it as a youngster and could still remember most passages verbatim. No one appreciates the wonderful freedom of religion and of worship until it's denied to him. All too often Sunday mornings we do other things rather than go to church. But when the right to worship is denied you, it hurts deeply. To compensate while a prisoner, at least in my own mind, I designed and built a little chapel. I called it our Chapel in the Sky. I pictured a small rustic chapel sitting on a cloud. It had stained-glass windows, very large ones behind the altar. The inside was knotty pine and natural-finished oak. There was a red rug on the floor, red upholstered cushions on the benches. The chapel had an organ and a small choir. The altar had a simple cross, similar to the one in my home-town church. Not a whole lot different from many small chapels. Fifteen people would fill it. Every Sunday morning at this Chapel in the Sky I met my wife and children and we attended worship service together. This con-tact with my family was a major factor in maintaining my sanity.

———

ALYCE   Jean learned one day they had killed her husband. They dragged his body through a camp and took photographs of it.

JEAN LEDBETTER   Tom was legally declared dead. We held a funeral. Everyone was there. The Army put me through all these ceremonies. Green Beret. A plaque. Then, suddenly, I was all alone. They would allow me to live on post one year. After that, they said, I had to find someplace else. I only planned to stay until school was finished. The Army would help me pack. The kids and I would return to Florida.

ALYCE   "It's horrible to say," Jean told me, "but my ordeal is over. I can start my life again." Her heart went out to me.

JEAN LEDBETTER   Alyce could have stayed in quarters but Harold got reassigned. He left Bragg even before I did. One day at her kitchen table, Alyce said she wanted to go to Massachusetts to start a new life with Harold.

"The kids like him and he likes the kids," she said.

She was tired of all the snooping and all the gossip and resentment. Everywhere she turned people were down on her.

"With you getting ready to leave, Jean," she said, "Harold is all I have."

ALYCE   My mother was totally against my plan and very angry. But then, Mom was starting a new life for herself too. She was sporting an engage-ment ring and happy-go-lucky. Yet she said I was doing wrong. You've got to understand. Jean was leaving me. The in-laws had left and tore up my plans about the house and getting a job for myself. Mother was becoming involved with another man. Every day I saw husbands come home at night to their families and me sitting there like a bump on the log. A fifth wheel. I wasn't invited to more parties. Old neighbors all got reassigned and new ones didn't know my situation. The Army didn't want me on post. My being there meant bad things happened over in that little country.

When Harold said, "I'm going to Massachusetts," it was the last straw. "I'm going too," I said.

JEAN LEDBETTER   I understood. "If you can get up in the morning and accept it, then do it," I said. "It's your life."

ALYCE   I told the kids we were moving. They were young enough I didn't have to explain nothing. I told the Army I had to get away and told my neighbors the same thing.

                                                            5 May 1965
Dear Mrs. Thompson:

There has still been no additional information received concerning your husband, Captain Floyd J. Thompson, since I last wrote to you.

At all levels within the military establishment, we are deeply concerned over the welfare of our service members whose whereabouts are unknown, and fully realize the distress felt by their loved ones. The Departments of Defense and State, through diplomatic channels, as well as the International Committee of the Red Cross, are still exploring every possible means to obtain definite information regarding the status of these personnel.

It is most regrettable that no information has been received which would relieve your anxiety.

                                        Sincerely yours,
                                        J. C. Lambert
                                        Major General, USA
                                        The Adjutant General

JIM THOMPSON   I had the benefit of a very good Christian education as a youngster. From that faith I drew strength. It was this faith, and a belief in what we were doing as soldiers, that kept me alive. What we were doing was very necessary. We were protecting not only my own family but the families of all free men.

When seen through the eyes of a prisoner of war, the 23rd Psalm takes on an entirely new meaning. When we speak of the Valley of Shadows, when we speak of green pastures, when we say, 'Preparing a table before me in the presence of mine enemies,' from the point of view of a prisoner it is a real inspiration. For me it took on a meaning I had never dreamed of before. I recited it in my Sunday worship service every week.

30 June '65

Maj. Gen. J. C. Lambert, U.S.A.
The Adjutant General
Hdq., Dept. of Army
Washington D.C.

Dear Sir:
Please be advised that as of the date of this letter, my residence is the new address shown for Hudson, Mass.

I would appreciate any correspondence from you concerning my husband, Capt. Floyd J. Thompson, who has been missing in action in Vietnam since 26 March 64, coming to the above address.

Sincerely,
Alyce J. Thompson

SAM DEACON   When I came back to Bragg from an assignment in mid-1965, no one knew where Alyce had gone. I heard rumors she left for Fort Devens to live with an E-5. I was surprised. I had seen Alyce take charge of herself. It seemed to me she could have stayed independent.

———

ALYCE   Harold would be a father image for my kids and I would be a mother image for his. That's the way we explained it to ourselves. I needed somebody, he needed somebody, and there we were. So much had happened in the year since Jim was lost. Maybe if it had been scattered over more time I wouldn't have gone to Massachusetts. I don't know. Unless you can go through something like that, you have no idea how horrible it is. I know what I did sounds terrible. But I did it to maintain my sanity and to give the kids a routine life.

21 ■ A NEW LIFE

Thompson's routine at Camp "Delta" from August 1964 to November 1965 was marked by boredom. [Thompson gave each camp a letter designation, so this was his fourth.] He received two meals a day, at dawn and in the evening. Meals generally were the same, morning and evening, largely because they had to eat what was available in the area. Thompson did some work, splitting wood, and he was encouraged to exercise. He was detained in a bamboo hut. The VC guard slept in a hut nearby. Three Montagnards sat by a fire near Thompson's hut apparently with instructions to wake VC guards if anything happened. At no time was Thompson restrained by anything other than the walls of his hut and the surveillance of his guards. But there was no opportunity to escape.

—from Army Intelligence debriefing report

JIM THOMPSON   I developed a new and very sincere respect for people who closet themselves away for the sake of meditation. Monks in a monastery, for example, are experiencing life on a much higher plane than the average person can conceive. They are able to almost divorce the mind from the needs of the body. Their work, their thoughts, take them away from the needs of the flesh. They closet themselves for weeks, oblivious to food, sleep, or anything else. A similar phenomenon occurred to me. In solitary I was divorced from the necessities of everyday life. My food was handed to me. I had a place to sleep. I was completely closeted from reality. And completely free to think.

For months on end I was almost undisturbed. The subconscious started coming closer and closer to the surface of my mind. When realities of everyday life are removed, things deep down inside begin to come out. I was able to do some free, creative thinking.

Everybody has their own sense of values, of right and wrong, morals, ethics. These things constitute a person's philosophy of life. Yet few people stop to think it out, to put it into words. It's just there. You grow up with it. It develops as you mature. In prison I had an opportunity to think about these things and to come up with a genuine sense of values. In some instances it upsets a sense of values. In other cases, it crystallizes them.

Things came out of my subconscious I'd long forgotten. I could remember the names of all my grammar school teachers, from kindergarten on. Passages too from the Bible we memorized as children. I remembered almost the entire order of worship from church services. Even parts the pastor normally reads, I could quote verbatim. I incorporated this into the Sunday church service in our Chapel in the Sky. Many songs I had sung as a youngster took on an entirely new meaning to me as a prisoner of war.

––––––––

LAURA   I had no memories of my real father. It was Harold who came into our lives when I was very small. I remember riding in a big station wagon for a long trip.

PAM   I had been my dad's favorite before he left for Vietnam, so I remembered him going to work, helping us take a bath, getting us ready for school. Fond memories. My only lasting impression of his appearance was that he was tall.

About the time we moved to Massachusetts I was keeping to myself a lot. My best friend in North Carolina had gotten transferred. I didn't have another. I've never made friends easily. I started reading a lot and became interested in school.

ALYCE   We adjusted well to the new house. Harold's daughter Lucy, a teenager, was growing up fast. The two of us took care of the girls. Pam enjoyed having an older sister. Lucy was like a mother hen. She loved having all those little ones around. She was good as gold with those kids and loved little Jimmy to death. I could relax there. My kids were in brand-new schools. I found a doctor I loved and who the kids loved. I tried to be a good housewife and make friends with the neighbors. Nobody knew Harold's past and nobody knew mine.

JEAN LEDBETTER   Everyone thought they were married. Alyce wanted it that way. She even wore a gold band. I addressed letters to Alyce using Harold's last name.

ALYCE   I had my own checking account. I paid for the kids' clothes. Once in a while, like when tax time came, Harold might be a little short. I either put a little towards the tax bill or the house payments. I bought some of our food. I paid some of the rent. I helped out with utility bills because we were living in his house. If we had a very cold winter and the gas bill was sky-high, I might pay that. Otherwise, the money mainly went for the kids.

LAURA   We called Harold "Dad."

PAM   I never saw him as a substitute for my real father. He wanted to be, but I didn't see him that way. Mama didn't either. She wore his ring and used his name but that was just to keep people from asking unnecessary questions. I knew they weren't married. They liked each other. They hugged each other. But I just tolerated him. We stayed out of each other's way.

4 August 1965

Colonel G. R. McLaughlin
Adjutant General
XIII Corps, United States Army
Fort Devens, Mass. 01433

Dear Colonel McLaughlin:
Enclosed is the tape we discussed on the telephone. We have kept Mrs. Thompson informed of whatever meager information we have received on her husband. I have not played this tape but it is supposed to be a broadcast allegedly made by Captain Floyd J. Thompson whose wife resides at the following address.

Please advise Mrs. Thompson we would like her to verify whether she recognizes the voice as her husband. She should also be advised that though the broadcast was taped 13 July, this does not necessarily mean it was a live broadcast from Hanoi but that, more than likely, it is a repeat of the tape which had previously been broadcast over Radio Hanoi.

Should she verify this tape as her husband's voice, she may retain the tape. A report of her reaction will be appreciated.

Sincerely yours,
V. G. Johnson
Lieutenant Colonel, AGC
Chief Casualty Branch

ALYCE   By summer of '65, I thought the Army soon would declare Jim dead and Harold and I could marry, start a life. A legitimate life. But that

August, they called about that tape. A year earlier, they had said they couldn't identify whose voice it was, so they could not say Jim was no longer missing. So I figured he was dead, killed like the pilot. I really did. Now they were coming by with the tape. Wanted me to listen and identify a voice I had not heard in almost two years. But they came, and I sat and I listened.

10 August 1965

Lt. Col. V. G. Johnson
Chief, Casualty Branch
Office of the Adjutant General
Washington, D.C.

Dear Colonel Johnson:
I made personal contact with Mrs. Thompson at 1045 hours, 9 August 1965, at her residence, in Hudson, Massachusetts. The tape was played several times in Mrs. Thompson's presence.

During the first playing she stated that, certainly, the first part sounded like her husband but that the second part did not. During the latter half, at the second playing, Mrs. Thompson asked her seven-year-old daughter (without providing her any information) if she knew who was talking. After a moment's hesitation the child replied, "Daddy."

Mrs. Thompson asked her if she was certain. Her daughter then asked if it was her uncle's voice (her father's brother). After the third playing, Mrs. Thompson stated emphatically that it was a tape of her husband's voice. She stated her husband had a distinct way of drawing in air through his teeth when talking that she could discern on the tape.

A few minutes lapsed between the playing of the tape and my departure during which Mrs. Thompson talked in general terms of personal financial problems, medical care for the children, etc. Just before my departure she voluntarily altered her statement concerning the tape saying that, "while I believe the voice to be my husband's I cannot be absolutely positive."

Sincerely,
C. L. Wilson, Jr.
Major, AGC
Chief, Reserve Personnel Division

ALYCE   Pam was excited, hearing her daddy. I wondered what would happen next. Harold and I decided to take it one day at a time. But they were tough days. My worst fear was that I would be found out and my kids would get hurt.

2 September 1965

Dear Mrs. Thompson:

As you were able to identify your husband's voice on the tape recording which was provided you, it is apparent he is being held by the Viet Cong. Therefore, the Department of the Army has changed his status from that of "missing" to "detained in a foreign country against his will," effective 1 September 1965.

I wish to emphasize this change of status is merely a technical change in the missing persons category under which he will be listed on Army records. I know how much it means to you to have further reassurances that your husband survived the aircraft crash and is apparently in good health. You can rest assured that if any further reports are received concerning Floyd you will be promptly advised.

Sincerely yours,
J. C. Lambert
Major General, USA
The Adjutant General

ALYCE   Why didn't they let me hear the tape in '64? Why hadn't they brought it to me before then? I felt my world ready to crumble down around my ears.

22 ■ SETTLING IN

One night in November 1965, Thompson walked a short distance from Camp Delta to Camp Echo, escorted by six Viet Cong guards. Camp Echo consisted of three bamboo huts with thatched roofs. This semi-permanent camp was next to a stream. It was so overgrown near the camp it was almost impossible to exercise.

On one occasion when Thompson and the guards were out in an open field, some U.S. planes flew very low overhead. Had he had some sort of device to signal with, they would probably have seen him since he could clearly see the faces of the pilots. He could make no effort to wave his arms or signal in some other manner since a guard nearby cocked his weapon when Thompson saw the aircraft.

In June 1966, the entire camp left hurriedly one day and stayed in a village a short way off. They remained there about two days and then returned. Thompson saw C-ration cans upon their return and surmised that his captors had known of an upcoming operation in their area. He had no information as to how they may have known of this.

—from Army Intelligence debriefing report

ALYCE   I still got a letter every month: "We are writing concerning your husband, Captain Floyd James Thompson. Sorry to report we have no further word on his status. If we hear anything we will let you know immediately. Sincerely."

Every month. As far as I was concerned, Jim was still missing. That tape might have been made the day after he was captured. He could still be dead. That's what I went with.

We became a fairly happy family. Kids going to school. Me keeping house. Taking care of the yard and garden. We had a big house but not enough money to make it fancy. I did the cooking, the ironing and cleaning. I had rose bushes. We'd have dinner, watch TV, and go to bed.

Once in a while we'd drive down to Pennsylvania to pick apples for pies at Aunt Willa and Uncle Marty's farm. They came up quite a bit, too. I was friendly with neighbors, especially Sheila next door. I told them my husband was dead. If they questioned me further I said I didn't want to talk about it. I knew I wasn't leading a normal life. I was living in hell. A private hell.

25 March 1966

Dear Mrs. Thompson:

I am enclosing a copy of a recent Associated Press news item you may have already read. The story refers to the alleged channel for delivery of mail to those being held by the North Vietnamese. Inasmuch as your husband was detained in South Vietnam, it must be assumed he is still in the South. There has been no word of any American prisoners in South Vietnam being moved to North Vietnam. Therefore, even if the news story proves factual, the channel mentioned would not be appropriate for mail addressed to him. . . .

Sincerely yours,
J. C. Lambert
Major General, USA
The Adjutant General

JEAN LEDBETTER   In the summer of 1966, my girls and I drove up from Florida to visit Alyce and Harold. They had a big, beautiful two-story colonial with four bedrooms, a great big living room, a kitchen, and a basement. A nice neighborhood with a lot of new homes. There were eight of them altogether and they were having it hard.

Jimmy was starting to walk and was a holy terror. Alyce was always washing and cooking and cleaning. They had a lot of furniture, both Harold's and hers, but they needed a new car.

"I would give anything," Alyce said, "to have a little extra money."

Then she showed me a stack of Jim's savings bonds she couldn't cash.

Overall, though, they were happy. For Alyce, it was like the family she never had. Harold was open, friendly, sincere. The type of guy you felt you'd known all your life. Alyce had always been a lonely person. Brilliant in her way—she played the piano and typed like a whiz—but very lonely. In Massachusetts, though, they seemed like the happiest family you ever saw.

When we got a quiet moment to ourselves, Alyce and I talked about what she would do if Jim came back. "I really don't know," she said. "But I love Harold. I'd stay with him."

On 19 September 1966, the commanding officer, Boston Army Base, informed the commanding general First Army that Mrs. Thompson had been visited to review any unsolved problems. She stated there were no problems at the time. She did say that on several occasions the procedure of receiving her allotment check around the 13th of the month did not help her in meeting bills due before the 15th.

—from family assistance officer case file

PAM   I was happy in Massachusetts. I liked the area. I made a few friends.

LAURA   Our house was gorgeous, with an out-of-ground pool. Nice furnishings. The master bedroom was beautiful, with thick carpet, a brass lamp.

PAM   We had a big backyard. In winter we could ice skate near the woods when a drainage pipe backed up and made a makeshift pond.

LAURA   It ran like a normal household, with Harold acting as husband. He was pleasant but kept very much to himself. Put food on the table. That was about it.

ALYCE   Harold paid more attention to my younger ones, Ruth and Jimmy, than to Pam and Laura.

LAURA   He didn't bother too much with us kids. He didn't even bother too much with his own kids. He never hesitated to get the belt out when we were bad. But it was always proper. Harold never abused us. No father-daughter chats either, though. Picking us up, holding our hands, he did none of that. He wasn't affectionate. It wasn't an affectionate family.

ALYCE   I gave my kids presents to make up for the lack of close relationships. Maybe I overdid it. Maybe I spoiled them rotten.

LAURA   My mother was always more into the men in her life than into her children. We weren't neglected, but she and Harold put their money and effort into material things rather than family activities. Report cards were important, but my mother had no interest in PTA meetings or my drama classes. She wouldn't come to an open house at school. When I wanted to join Brownies it cost too much. Things that mean a lot to a child. But we got our share of material things.

PAM   Harold wouldn't talk about my father. If we mentioned him he said, "Shut up. I don't want to talk about it." Mama only talked about him if Harold wasn't around.

My first fight with Harold was over my father. I asked Mama if I could have a picture of Daddy. Harold took a fit. He didn't want pictures of "that man" in the house. I got mad. That night Mama gave me a photo. She said I could keep it in my drawer somewhere.

ALYCE   Yeah, my older kids asked about him. Pam especially missed him. She knew he was missing in action. That's all I could tell her. I didn't know anything else. The younger ones didn't ask. Jimmy and Ruthie had no idea who he was.

LAURA   I never even dreamed about my dad. I had no pictures. No contact with his relatives. Nothing.

———

JIM THOMPSON   November 1966 began my worst stretch in South Vietnam. I had been moved to a new camp in a rain forest where they had, for the first time, a full-time political officer and camp commander. The political officer could only be described as a sadist. He took delight in making another man miserable. Until this camp, guards had been decent. They turned hostile under this political officer and my living conditions turned extremely poor.

My food ration was reduced. When I asked for more, or tried to convince them I wasn't getting enough, the camp commander laughed. He took delight in standing before me belching, or throwing rice on the ground for the chickens, then looking at me with a smile.

I could see into the kitchen where they prepared the meals. I could see them killing pigs, chickens, ducks for themselves. But a scrap of meat never showed up in my food. I got only rice and a boiled vegetable. They let my share sit on the ground where I could see it get cold while they ate. My weight fell close to a hundred pounds.

The hut they built for me wasn't fit for a dog. It was cut into the side of a steep bank at ground level next to a creek bed. I was surrounded constantly by a sea of mud on which mist and fog lay. The sides of the hut were a latticework of palm. It rained all the time. I never had enough clothing. No blanket. The roof leaked and they refused to fix it. I wasn't permitted a fire. My guards had a warm dry place, twenty feet higher and always a good fire, for which they forced me to cut wood.

Nobody spoke English well enough to attempt indoctrination or interrogation. But they went out of their way to make me miserable. Sometimes they gave me tobacco, sometimes not. Before this, I had a set ration.

They said they didn't have tobacco, then blew smoke in my face. The camp commander relished denying me things, forcing me to live as squalid as was possible.

On 17 November 1966, Mrs. Thompson, in a letter to the Adjutant General, stated that her husband's status had been changed from "missing" to "detained in a foreign country against his will" and in a more recent letter the Army had referred to Captain Thompson as a "prisoner." She wanted to know when and how such a change occurred. She further stated that she had listened to the tape from Fort Devens, and the voice at the beginning was her husband but it seemed to change. She requested that the Adjutant General not release her name or address to anyone, not for her sake but for her four children, as it had been quite hard on the two oldest girls. She said she had been living in a personal hell for almost three years.

—from family assistance officer case file

ALYCE   I was afraid they were going to release news bulletins that Jim was alive. Then our lives would collapse.

On 26 January 1967, Mrs. Thompson was advised that it was an administrative determination to use the term "prisoner" as opposed to "detainee." This word was not a change in Captain Thompson's status, only a change in terminology. She was also informed that her request for anonymity for the sake of the children was fully appreciated and news release agencies had been apprised of her desires.

—from family assistance officer case file

23 ■ NORTH VIETNAM

JIM THOMPSON   I tasted meat about five times my last eight months in South Vietnam. Christmas '66, the Lunar New Year, the Tet celebration—on these occasions I had the taste of meat, some skin off a pig or its feet. When the cadre came to pick me up for the trip north, he had a fit. I was too weak to travel. Rather than start north, he ordered meals with meat and condensed milk to build up my strength. We finally left for North Vietnam on the 21st of July in '67.

It was twenty days of walking the Ho Chi Minh Trail, moving from camp to camp. Four to six hours between stopovers. Trail camps were well equipped. They had medics and good supplies. A great communication system, both telegraph and radio, hooked camps together. Wherever we stopped the cadre checked in with the camp commander, who immediately sent a medic over. He must have told them, "We've got to fatten this guy up." I had extra groceries all along the trail and good medical attention for the first time in years. After two and a half weeks we got on a vehicle to continue north, traveling by night. We saw American aircraft frequently and all kinds of bomb craters. The road in many places had been torn up and patched. We saw bombing, too, close enough to feel. Volunteer youth brigades repaired the roads as soon as they were bombed. They built new roads, too, using primitive equipment, hands and hand-made wheelbarrows and explosives to bust up stone for the roadbeds. Their ingenuity, their ability to do this in the jungle with little equipment, was amazing to see.

Thompson completed the move north on 20 August 1967. No other prisoners of war accompanied him. No one joined him along the way. The new camp was a large village of about 200 buildings. Thompson was confined in a bamboo hut with thatched roofing and a dirt floor. He was fed two meals a day and not allowed outside his cell except for interrogation or indoctrination. Thompson was tortured at this camp.

—from Army Intelligence debriefing report

JIM THOMPSON   I was put into a small cell in the middle of a large village, a place built as a civilian prison. I was the only prisoner. My bed was a board, ten inches wide, atop two bricks. The cell was infested with flies, mosquitoes, and all manner of crawling things. I had no mosquito netting. I was handcuffed, placed in leg irons, and blindfolded. And left to lay on this board. I was fed an extremely reduced diet. Periodically I was taken into an office at the end of the building where an interrogator began with a lecture. He told me I was a criminal, not a prisoner of war. I deserved to be shot for untold crimes against the Vietnamese people. He wasn't after a statement. He wasn't after information. All the hell that guy wanted was for me to read some stuff from a propaganda magazine printed in English. He was rather crude and inexperienced. I believed he wanted me to read aloud so he could improve his English. But I also figured he had a tape recorder hidden someplace. I refused. That sadistic devil tortured me every day for two weeks.

He had the guard tie my elbows behind my back until they touched. It can't be done unless extreme force is applied. They attached a rope to my elbows and threw it over a ceiling beam and hoisted me up. This forced my arms back even farther, causing excruciating pain on my breastbone. I felt my chest would split open.

Thankfully I'd contracted dysentery and was extremely weak. Every time they tortured me, I'd pass out. They'd about get started and I'd be unconscious. As soon as they put pressure on the ropes, I lost consciousness. I'd be revived and they'd start again. This went on for days. Finally he got disgusted and tried hanging me by my thumbs. That didn't work either. Then he forced me to stay on my knees for long periods, trying to find some method of discomfort I could withstand without passing out. But I was so weak none of it lasted long. Sometimes only minutes. Sometimes an hour or so. They'd do other crude stuff, like have the guards slap me around.

After two weeks of this, the camp commander called me into his office and said, "Do you know what day tomorrow is?"

"Yeah, it's Tuesday."

"No," he said. "Do you know what the date is?"

"Yeah, it's the 2nd of September."

"What does this day mean to you?"

I thought for a while. It didn't mean a daggoned thing. He had an officer with him and both grew incensed. I sat there like a dunce, without the faintest idea what they were talking about. He finally exploded, "The whole world knows this date! It's a pity you have been a prisoner so long, you have gone through so much reeducation, and you still do not know the significance of this date!"

I couldn't figure out what the devil he was driving at. Turned out September 2, 1945, was the day Ho Chi Minh declared North Vietnam's independence. I couldn't have cared less. And that got me on their list.

On the evening of 1 September, escorted by six North Vietnamese Army guards, Thompson was bound by his wrists, tied to a guard in front and another to his rear and walked for about three hours. When they reached a river, Thompson and his guards boarded a sampan. Thompson was bound to the floor by his wrists and was unable to see out. They traveled north for the remainder of the night. The next morning they walked another three hours to arrive at a new camp. Camp India, nicknamed Bao Cao, consisted of six buildings constructed of wooden planks and covering an area of about 45,000 square feet.

—From Army Intelligence debriefing report

JIM THOMPSON   I was put into a horizontal cage maybe two feet wide, two feet high, and five feet long. There I was kept for four months, chained hand and feet. The leg irons were a nasty device, a U-bolt with a rusted rod through the back, much too small for American legs. Every time they put the thing on it took a chunk of flesh. This cage sat in the back room of a house, in complete darkness. They had a bamboo wall around it so I saw nothing. I was not let out for exercise. For ten minutes a day I could use the latrine and wash up. Then they'd stick me back in and put the leg irons back on.

About an hour each day I was taken out to sit at a long table. He demanded a statement similar to the one I had made years earlier—saying I was well treated and had never been tortured and I was receiving excellent care, that we should leave and let the Vietnamese people settle their own affairs. It was the same technique as before, with a variety of ridiculous excuses to punish me, all designed to soften me up. He shoved paper and pen across the table and said, "Now you must write!" When I refused he launched into a lecture.

One day he tried to reason with me, explaining that their cause was just and ours was unjust. They were fighting for their freedom; we were the aggressors. They wanted only independence; we were trying to subjugate them. We were neocolonialists trying to turn Vietnam into a base for further aggression; they were defending their inalienable rights to self-determination. They said I was a criminal, not a prisoner of war.

"You have come to massacre the Vietnamese people. We have every right to kill you. It is only because of our humane policy that we permit you to live. By stubbornly refusing to do as you are told, you take advantage of the humane and lenient policy of the National Liberation Front. If you continue to do so we have no choice but to punish you. You must remember there are still Frenchmen in our prisons who did not reform their minds. They lack goodwill. They are hostile toward our people. We can keep you in prison forever too. You will never see your family again. You can be executed because some people do not deserve to live."

They even threatened my family if I did not comply.

"We have contacts in the United States, people who will see your family and who will take action against them."

Usually lectures lasted about an hour. Then the interrogator went away, leaving instructions that I sit at the table with pencil in hand until I wrote. From time to time the guard told me in Vietnamese I must write. Occasionally some new face came in and acted like all innocence.

"Oh, what are you doing here? Why are you sitting here? You're supposed to be writing, I see. You really should. You're foolish to resist. Why don't you just write? No problem."

Another one would come in with threats.

"You are stubborn, and obstinate."

One cajoled, the other threatened. And then the first guy came back and said, "You mean you haven't written yet? You must write!"

This would last all day, into the night. They'd bring a lamp and force me to sit there for hours at night. Once they threatened to withhold food until I wrote. Normally they fed me around four in the afternoon. This particular day, the interrogator ordered the guards not to bring food until I wrote. It was about eight or nine o'clock, well after dark, when they finally brought food. They about threw it at me. Then they put me back in the cage.

On 25 November 1967 Mrs. Thompson was informed that the post office, State and Defense Departments, with help from the armed forces, had developed a plan to send Christmas packages to prisoners. She was asked to send her package not later than 5 December 1967. Captain Thompson's parents

were informed of this plan on 28 November 1967 and asked to refrain from
sending a separate package since only one package per family was permitted.

—from family assistance officer case file

ALYCE   Families of the missing were given a list of stuff we could send at
Christmastime. Vitamins, toothpaste, toothbrushes, dental floss, underwear, handkerchiefs, and candy. For a time I sent packages. I had to go
down to the post office, to the postmaster. He looked at everything. It had
to be a certain weight, not the least bit over. That meant not wrapping
anything. I put all the supplies I could in there, as best I could. I sent four
packages altogether, addressed to Jim in care of the North Vietnamese.
Others got packages through. Mine always came back.

———

JIM THOMPSON   One day, while I was still in the cage, they brought in a
couple of officials. They took the irons off and told me I must bow to
them, salute and show respect. Because I refused, I was starved and denied
water for three days.

On the evening of the third day they dragged me out of the cage,
knocked me to my knees, and beat me with fists and clubs, like a policeman's billyclub. They put a length of gauze tape around my throat as a
garrote to strangle me. All the time they shouted and yelled in Vietnamese. They were telling me I was very stubborn and belligerent.

Then the camp commander gave me a lesson on how to bow to the
Vietnamese cadre. He kicked me in the belly and, grabbing a handful of
hair, banged my head on the dirt floor. He did this repeatedly until I
passed out. I'd be revived and he'd do it again. He kept repeating the
process for two hours. I passed out ten or twelve times. From then on, I
was obliged to bow anytime one of them approached the cage, even
though it wasn't big enough to sit up in.

After three days of starvation, of being worked over, an interrogator
showed up. He was short, even by Vietnamese standards. He had curly
hair, rather stocky. In his early thirties. He spoke with a strong British
accent. And was cocky. Americans, in his view, were an inferior race. Like
dirt under his feet.

"You have already lost the war. We were the victors," he said.
Extremely sarcastic, heavy-handed, very domineering, and rather crude.
He never tried to persuade. It was strictly the hard approach. He'd open a
conversation like this:

"The contents of our forthcoming statement will be . . ."

I started shaking my head.

He said, "You will make a statement."

"I will not."

"You will! I have the power to do whatever is necessary to force you to make a statement."

"I refuse."

He began with threats—of reducing my meager rations, of applying more torture, of doing whatever he felt necessary.

"Your life is in my hands." That was one of his favorite expressions. "And I can do whatever I feel is necessary. And if you refuse to cooperate you will be killed."

Then he trotted out that same old argument.

"If you do as you are told, you will be well treated, you will be released and allowed to go home." At which point I started to laugh. He got angry.

"Why are you laughing?"

Over the years I had learned to keep my big mouth shut, but it was time to tell him off.

"You don't expect me to believe that shit after all these years, do you?" I said.

That was the wrong thing to say. I got a two-hour harangue on being polite.

"Imperialist aggressors! Extremely barbarous people! Encroaching upon the sovereignty of the Vietnamese people! Taking away their inalienable rights!"

This was to soften me for a written statement. They even threatened to make their own statement and put my name on it. They said I had already been in prison nearly four years and my voice will have changed. People won't recognize it. They would put my name to all manner of radical anti-war statements and antigovernment statements. It would be better for me to make a milder statement, one that would be my own. I refused. So I stayed in the cage.

24 ■ CHRISTMAS '67

RUTH   After a few years in Massachusetts I did see the photo of my father that Pam had. It showed him sitting with his three little girls, all of us blond and in yellow dresses. Still I never thought a lot about him, because Harold was there. Harold completed the family. We weren't close, but he took care of us. We had a pool in summer and a hill for sledding in winter. We had children our own age to run around with.

ALYCE   Harold wanted a home, peace and quiet, a good meal on the table, and a happy home life. That's all. He was good as gold with young Jim. They built model airplanes and would fly 'em. He'd take him on trips to the dump. I remember little Jim next to Harold on the front seat of the truck, a blond crewcut, standing up like a little soldier. Harold would take him fishing. They'd play ball. He took him to the barber. He'd say, "Come on, young man. We want to get a haircut." It was Harold who showed him how to ride his first two-wheeler. Things a man's supposed to do with a little boy. Without Harold, little Jim wouldn't have had that.

JIM JR.   I thought he was my father. Called him "Dad." They didn't let me know no different. He disciplined me. He raised me. I didn't ask no questions and none of my family ever talked about another man. I guess Mama figured why tell me if she didn't know he was alive or dead.

ALYCE   Harold's own son was a teenager by then and gave him a lot of trouble. Keith didn't like me. He had gotten a lot of attention from his father until me and mine came. Then some of that was taken away.

———

JIM THOMPSON   I was moved from the cage to a walled cell two days before Christmas '67. My weight had dropped below a hundred pounds. I developed digestive disorders. My stomach refused to accept food. When your system shuts down so far, instead of being hungry you lose your appetite and go down faster.

For a Christmas present in the new building they took my chains off. The cell was three feet wide, six feet long, and six feet high—the size of a palace compared to the cage. At least I could stand and pace a bit. It had solid board walls, floor, and ceiling and a thatch roof. I couldn't see out. The cell was dug in, about four and a half feet below ground, with just the roof protruding above ground. Still, it was luxury to move a little, to have the chains off my hands and feet. They even permitted a Christmas tree of sorts, a branch of a pine tree I decorated with some scraps of paper they gave me. When I got it finished the thing looked so pathetic I cried.

I thought a great deal about Christmas while in prison. It had always been a very precious time for my wife and me. When we were first married, we started a kind of a Christmas Eve tradition. We would decorate the tree, get the gifts ready, pour ourselves a drink, sit back, and look at it. And reflect on our blessings. We carried on this tradition from our first Christmas together. Even after the children arrived, especially after the children arrived. Later on it was expanded to include a bottle of champagne and usually a grilled steak.

So thoughts of Christmas in prison always went back to Christmas Eves at home and how precious they were. My heart was not on my troubles; my heart was always at home on Christmas Eve. It was by far the most difficult time of the year for me. I thought about how Alyce would be celebrating Christmas, having to do it by herself. It would have been real easy for me to give in to melancholy, but I thought of all my poor wife had to do on her own, knowing that in her heart she felt as badly as I did but she couldn't show it. She had to keep up a good front for the sake of the children. My prayers were with her during this time, that she would have the strength to see it through and do up Christmas as it should be for the children.

I pictured happy scenes of Christmas day, when the youngsters came down, and the tree and the gifts and the happy faces as they opened their gifts. This picture was easy to take. The toughest part was remembering Christmas Eve when Alyce and I would be so close, thinking back over the year and counting our blessings. I closed my eyes and relived the last Christmas at home. I had left for Vietnam the next day so the last vivid memories of my home were of Christmas. I could recall it in minute detail. The gifts I put together for the children. All the memories took an hour to recall. A bicycle for Pam. A Flintstone car for Laura, one of these things in a large box with directions. Nut A and bolt B, washer C. I recall the instructions that came with it. A little packet of directions on how to put this thing together. The title was "When All Else Fails, Read This." I finally put this confounded thing together and had fun doing it. Ruth was just a baby, so her toys were some small things.

When I counted my blessings that Christmas Eve, I remembered all the things that had transpired that year. The standard of living we were able to maintain. Alyce and I both came from rather poor families, me in particular. We were now able to lead a real good life. We looked at the tree and at the gifts. Our material blessings were certainly there. But most important were our spiritual blessings. The love we felt for each other. Three wonderful children. Knowing the fourth was on the way, hoping it would be a boy. Knowing we had a good life, I had a good career and was doing something I believed in. Feeling as though the world was our oyster. We were happy.

And I tried to keep in my mind the true meaning of Christmas, to take it away from the commercial and think of the real meaning. [*Jim's voice cracks and he begins to cry.*] Excuse me. So this Christmas, of 1967, was more memorable than others in prison. Guards down south didn't recognize or celebrate Christmas. The day came and went like any other. I was alone with my thoughts and torn between two emotions. One, to slip into melancholy and feel sorry for myself and my family. It's real easy to do. But I thought, I expect my wife to be strong, to be able to carry it through and to make a good Christmas for herself and for the children. How can I be weak?

I found comfort in the true spirit of Christmas. I felt very close to my family [*voice breaking again*], almost as if I were with them. Certainly I was in spirit. I went through all the most popular Christmas carols. Not out loud, of course, because the guards were there. But in my mind. Our little chapel in the sky was all decorated for Christmas. Pine boughs and holly and candles. We had a special candlelight service. In my hometown church they turned the lights out before midnight on Christmas Eve and from candles on the altar would light the candles of everybody in the front of the church. Those folks would turn around, pass the light back, and eventually everybody would be holding a candle. The recessional hymn, as the choir leaves the loft, would be entirely by candlelight. The closing hymn that last Christmas Eve was "Hark the Herald Angels Sing."

The guards put out a good meal that day, the first I'd had since I'd been captured. Broiled chicken, some pork with sweet and sour sauce, which was excellent. Some peanuts, a salad, which apparently is only served on a holiday. And there was some good rice instead of the poor-quality rice they normally fed us. Finally, a shot of rum and some candy. The rum came in one of these little teacups. Orange rum made in Hanoi. Good stuff too.

I ate as much as I could, then I promptly vomited.

In early January 1968 Thompson executed a propaganda statement similar to the one they had gotten from him in 1964.

—from Army Intelligence debriefing report

25 ▪ BAO CAO

ALYCE   I never did make amends with my mother over leaving
with Harold. But she visited once in a while or we went down to see
her in New Jersey. She was always cold toward Harold. Jim had
showered me with gifts—a fur coat, fancy TVs and stereos and furniture.
All the things money can buy. Harold couldn't do that, so Mom felt I lowered myself.

"You had such a good life with Jim and you gave it all up," she said.

On 3 February, 1968, Mrs. Alyce Thompson wrote the Adjutant General saying she had sent a package to Capt. Thompson before the 3 December mailing deadline and had not received word that it reached her husband; that
she had not given the address to any one of her relatives nor friends; that she
did not know if her husband's parents received the address because she was
not in contact with them; that it soon would be four years since her husband
had been a captive; that the only word she knew confirming his capture was
a tape recording she could partially identify. She said the past four years had
been a personal hell for her and her children.

—from family assistance officer case file

ALYCE   The kids didn't know. It was my hell alone, really. Only Pam knew
he was missing, that Harold and I weren't married. It didn't seem to
bother her. She never said anything. I sent packages mainly to find out if
he was alive.

JIM THOMPSON   That winter of '68 was cold but the goddamn political officer took delight in seeing me miserable. A guard felt sorry for me and gave me an extra blanket. I used it for about two weeks during the coldest part of the winter, then the political officer found out and took it away. It was so cold and damp that when he said, "Give me back the blanket," I saw his breath.

One night I got so cold I wrapped myself in my mosquito net. Another guard came by and insisted I hang it back up. When I refused he clubbed me with his rifle butt until I hung the damn thing up again.

My digestive disorder continued. I was unable to eat even the meager ration they gave me. I was going downhill.

In a single month, February 1968, the U.S. prisoner-of-war population captured in South Vietnam tripled, from twenty-three still held to more than seventy, when Viet Cong and North Vietnamese Army regulars launched a massive offensive against U.S. and ARVN forces throughout South Vietnam.[*] Almost 4,000 U.S. servicemen, 5,000 South Vietnamese soldiers, and 59,000 North Vietnamese and Viet Cong died in the two-month Tet Offensive. In Hue, Communist forces slaughtered 2,800 locals and captured small groups of U.S. soldiers and civilians who would later meet Jim Thompson. They included Navy Department civilians Larry Stark and Lew Meyer, Voice of America technician Chuck Willis, Army Intelligence sergeant Don Rander, and defense contract engineer Cloden "Speed" Adkins. The Tet Offensive, which began as a simultaneous attack on more than a hundred cities and towns, stunned Americans and influenced President Lyndon Johnson not to run for reelection that year.

LARRY STARK   I was working temporarily for the Navy's industrial relations department in Hue. They had only one person. When he had some problems, I was called up from Da Nang.

LEW MEYER   I was a fireman on an inspection tour of Hue. It was getting toward the Tet New Year and all transportation had stopped. Stores were closed. I was on the road, hitchhiking to try to catch an airplane back to Da Nang, when Larry Stark offered me a ride and a stayover in Hue. Turned out to be a very long stayover.

SPEED ADKINS   The Army didn't want to call up reservists for Vietnam, so civilians like us took care of all engineering except that done by the combat engineer units. I was supply chief for Pacific Architects and Engi-

* Prisoner statistics from *Honor Bound: The History of American Prisoners of War, 1961–1973*, by Stuart I. Rochester and Frederick Kiley, 1998, Historical Office of the Secretary of Defense.

neers, Inc. We maintained equipment, built buildings and roads. I was in Hue with an inspection team checking logistics.

LEW MEYER   The Tet celebration began with Fourth-of-July-like fireworks. We went out on the rooftop to watch and saw ARVN soldiers firing their weapons in the air. We hoped they'd stop, because they were wasting ammunition. It was dangerous, too. Spent rounds continued to rain down, so we went to bed. Early the next morning an American guard woke me, handed me a .30-06 rifle, and told me to shoot. I looked down in the street and saw long columns of uniforms, pith helmets and knapsacks, on both sides of the road, going from left to right. It looked like a parade. But these were North Vietnamese marching into Hue. I told the guard to keep quiet and get back from the window. Firefights erupted in different parts of the city and spread. The enemy had a hit list for certain parts of the city. We figured our area was third on the list. Those of us in the industrial relations section were joined by Army Intelligence people next door.

DON RANDER   There were five of us military intelligence types living in a villa next door.

LARRY STARK   We held out for a couple of days. Lost a couple of people, one military, one civilian. We all got wounded to various degrees. My wounds were minor. Lew Meyer lost hearing in one ear when they dropped a mortar on our roof.

LEW MEYER   We drew more fire from our own forces than we did from the NVA. All heavy stuff—the strafing, the rockets, the tanks. We had wounded ready to evacuate when U.S. tanks came down the road firing. One fired a ninety millimeter. I saw the roof of the building behind me disintegrate. Fortunately our building was so close the tanks couldn't cut a round that short. The shells went through the walls without exploding.

DON RANDER   By the next morning the North Vietnamese had overrun the city. We were cut off from Americans in the Hue compound.

SPEED ADKINS   North Vietnamese commanded the operation, but it was VC who captured us. They took us at dusk on the 31st of January after practically mortaring the house down on our heads. I was captured with another Pacific Architects and Engineers man, Alex Henderson, our installation manager at Pu Ba. Capture came very close to my fifty-second birthday.

LEW MEYER   The VC obviously had a specific mission and led us away quickly. We carried the severely wounded, including one man who was strapped to a door with a couple of belts. They told us to leave him at a church along the way. They put us for a time in the shower room of a building. Our first prison cell. Douglas AD Skyraiders, flown by the South

Vietnamese, dropped bombs all around us. The next day when a chopper came by, randomly saturating the area with machine-gun fire, we began moving.

SPEED ADKINS   They took us through the city to its northern limit. We crossed a river. Occasionally as we marched the battalion commander hit us in the belly or on the legs with a tree limb. About eight or ten of us hopped this way out of the city.

DON RANDER   That began a two-month journey north by foot and by truck. Our group arrived at a camp we called Bao Cao on the night of April 12, Good Friday. This was our first organized camp. We were put in a long wooden building with cells facing each other, a small walkway down the center. The cells were six feet long by six feet high and three feet wide. They had hard wooden floors with thin reed mats to sleep on. They gave us a mosquito net and a blanket. Our diet was rice, twice a day, and some kind of soup or vegetable. Usually squash. We were allowed to relieve ourselves in a crude hole they had out back. Interrogations began here. Sessions lasted a day or two but were spaced ten days or so apart.

————

JIM THOMPSON   They moved me that spring to another building, this one above ground. It was warmer and drier and by then the weather had improved, which eased conditions considerably. I had extreme pain shooting through my hands and feet. I thought it was rheumatism but found out later it's caused by malnutrition. My joints were swollen. My weight stayed well below a hundred pounds.

There were nine wooden cells in this building, but I was the only prisoner. One day I went out to the latrine for some daylight and I spotted other prisoners across the field. For the first time in nearly four years I caught a glimpse of other Americans. I could see them working with tools, clearing the field, cultivating vegetables. I couldn't communicate. The guards said I was kept separate because I had a particularly bad attitude. Special security was necessary because I had escaped repeatedly. Sure. My last escape attempt had been three years before.

As more Americans arrived at Bao Cao, space became a problem and the plan to keep Thompson separated from other prisoners had to change. By the middle of April, he had his first American neighbors. James DiBernardo, a Marine officer, had been running the Armed Forces Television and Radio station in Hue when captured on February 3, 1968. On the trail north he fell in with other POWs, including Army warrant officer Mike O`Connor, copilot of a helicopter gunship in the 1st Cavalry Division that was shot

down north of Hue on February 4, and Roy "Dick" Ziegler, another warrant officer and helo pilot, shot down and captured on February 8. Air
Force captain Edward W. Leonard, Jr., reached Bao Cao several weeks later.

JAMES DIBERNARDO   They had smashed my glasses, so I was virtually
blind. We were brought into camp at night. The first building had a
thatched roof and was partially sunken, I supposed, to protect against
enemy bombardment. Cells were back to back, four on one side and three
on the other.

I saw Jim Thompson for the first time through a crack in my door. He
was outside, sitting on his haunches, sweeping out the area. Just a gray
head and jump boots, which on him looked like size fifteen. He was
sweeping the floor in a duck walk, like a baseball catcher. It seemed the
only way he could walk. He wore manila-and-blue-striped pajamas, different from ours, which were black.

Without my glasses I couldn't tell what he looked like. Later, when we
moved to another building, we were allowed to go to a creek together to
bathe. That's when I got my first good look at him. My God, I thought.

MIKE O'CONNOR   The guards left the top half of our cell doors open
about fifteen minutes a day. We could sit on our leg stocks and look out.
When open, the door blocked our view of the next cell. But one day I
looked through the crack near the hinge and saw the guy next door. He
was standing right next to me. This guy is dead, I thought. As part of some
cruel joke, I thought, they had stuck a corpse up against the door. Then I
realized he was moving. He looked like something out of Auschwitz. I
remembered seeing a picture in *Life* magazine years earlier of those World
War II prisoners. This guy looked like them. I didn't know how he stood
up, how he breathed, how he did anything. His features were so distorted.

Later when we could wash up together, I could literally see his entire
skeleton and the balls of his joints around his knees and elbows. Ninety-
nine persons out of a hundred would have thought he was dead. His stomach was completely wrapped under his ribcage.

But it shocked me at first to see someone in his condition still moving.
Incredible. Until then I had been feeling sorry for myself. I'd lost about
sixty pounds and was down to about one hundred twenty. But after seeing
Thompson I thought I was in pretty good shape. As both of us looked
straight ahead out of our closetlike cells I asked him his name.

"Jim Thompson—Special Forces," he said. Then he told me his capture date. I was shocked. I said to myself, My God, all the things that have
happened in the last four years!

I told Jim what I knew about the war and home. The guards would have beaten us if they caught us talking, so the best we did was pass basic information. I could tell he enjoyed the conversations. That we talked at considerable risk indicated how important they were to him.

DICK ZIEGLER I had only been at Bao Cao a matter of days when I heard another American outside my cell talking to a guard. Loud enough for us to hear, he said he was Jim Thompson and had been shot down in March 1964. I did some quick figuring and thought, My God! Am I going to look like that in four years? I started to cry, he looked so emaciated. Eyes sunk way back in his head, cheekbones sticking out. A big head on a bony frame. A skeleton with hair. He had no muscle whatsoever. He scared me to death. I understood then what was waiting for me.

Later when we bathed together I noticed he had no ass, just two calluses. I cried again. Seeing him made me lose all hope that we would be home anytime soon.

JAMES DIBERNARDO When I found out how long he'd been a prisoner, I thought, I'd rather be dead. His condition wasn't encouraging. On top of that he would have these screaming nightmares in the middle of the night. Scared us to death!

MIKE O'CONNOR As the days passed I heard Thompson scratching on the side of the wall next to me. One day I asked him what he was doing.

"Standing up," he said.

Standing up. It took him half an hour to stand. His entire constitution. Every day I heard him stand up. Talk about a gutsy guy. I don't know anybody else who could have lived through the stuff he did.

One day he saw me outside the cell. Jim said, "You guys still look healthy!" I was down to one hundred twenty pounds.

Jim said he was concerned about his children, upset because he wasn't there to see them grow up. One kid, he said, was born while he was in captivity. He was concerned too about what his wife was going through. This was common among prisoners. You know what you're going through but can't imagine what it's like for your family. I could see the strain on Jim's face when he spoke of his family but I never heard him give up hope. He never was going to give up.

As Thompson entered his fifth year in captivity, the Army not only withheld his name from published lists of prisoners of war but, on multiple occasions, denied him promotion. We can speculate on why. Thompson lacked any formal education beyond high school. Fitness reports before capture didn't show a consistent level of excellence. Assignment to Special Forces put Thompson outside a traditional career path for an infantry officer. And even if he was still alive, his training and experience stood four years behind that of his peers.

24 April 1968

To: Chief, Casualty Division
From: Chief Promotion Branch

1. Captain Floyd J. Thompson has been reported as captured in Vietnam since 26 March 1964. He was considered for temporary promotion to major by an Army Standby Advisory Board which adjourned on 24 January 1968. . . . He was not selected for promotion to the higher grade. He was also considered for temporary promotion to major by an Army Standby Advisory Board which adjourned on 29 February 1968. . . . He was found fully qualified but not best qualified and was not recommended for promotion to the higher grade.

2. Captain Thompson was also considered for temporary promotion to major by the regularly constituted selection board which adjourned 6 January 1968. . . . He was not recommended for promotion by this board.

3. Notification of his promotion status has not been sent to Captain Thompson in view of his captured status.

E. W. Froll
Major, AGC

DICK ZIEGLER   I could only lie catty-corner in my cell, and the ceiling was so low I couldn't stand straight. We had a bamboo tube to urinate in, and periodically they let us out to take a dump. We used a pit dug in the ground. It had sticks across it for support. We squatted over the pit and did our business. I was scared to death I was going to fall in. All the little trees around this pit were leaf-free because they didn't have any toilet paper.

MIKE O'CONNOR   Food was a watery rice gruel served twice a day. About twenty percent was actually rat turds. It was the same stuff they fed the animals.

DICK ZIEGLER   Sometimes they took us out at night and marched us to a village where they loaded us up with rice and bundles of clothes and supplies, then marched us back to camp. They used us as pack animals, but it was the only exercise we got. Jim Thompson was in no condition to go along. He couldn't lift ten pounds.

30 April 1968

Dear Mrs. Thompson:
The lack of information concerning Floyd has, I know, been of much concern to you. I assure you, however, our efforts to obtain additional information concerning captured Army personnel are never ending. The recent

events with respect to peace negotiations between the President and the Hanoi authorities have, I am sure, been encouraging to you as well as all other Americans. It is hoped that these peace overtures will bring about a settlement, or agreement, which will pave the way to the release of our personnel who are being held prisoner.

I would like to take this opportunity to inform you of how you may avail yourself to travel aboard military transport aircraft in the Continental United States on a space available basis for humanitarian reasons. This mode of free transportation is granted to the wives of missing or captured personnel and this entitlement is extended to you as long as your husband remains in that status. Unfortunately, we are not permitted to extend this privilege to children. . . .

May the faith and hope which has sustained you in the past continue in the days that follow.

Sincerely,
Kenneth G. Wickham
Major General, USA
The Adjutant General

MIKE O'CONNOR   We went through extensive interrogation. During these sessions they forced us to sit on sawhorses. I did this once eighteen days straight. Blood from the blisters on my rear soaked through my pajamas.

Jim was spared this. They knew he couldn't have lived through it. By that time he had gone through a lot worse.

They were group sessions with at least four North Vietnamese, believed to be civilians, who spoke on such subjects as the illegality of the U.S. position in Vietnam, the winning position of the North Vietnamese and how certain they were of victory. The sessions lasted two or three hours a day, not every day. They also heard tape recordings of Doctor Spock and other Americans which were anti-war in nature.

—from Army Intelligence debriefing report

DICK ZIEGLER   Solitary confinement was very difficult for me. Some people, like Jim Thompson, could survive solitary for years. I didn't cope well. I was very depressed, very sorry for myself. I cried myself to sleep and cried myself awake. Once I got out of solitary, had I ever been put back, I might have gone bonkers. I discovered I liked people.

In a cell, without anything to do, we just thought and we watched. I'd feed rice to the ants. I'd watch one go off and he'd bring back a friend. I did anything to entertain myself.

JIM THOMPSON   In this camp they made a real big thing of being polite and courteous. That's why we gave it that name, Bao Cao. That's Vietnamese for "Report!" We used Bao Cao to ask permission to go to the latrine, to go pick up our food, to go to wash. It was a means to humiliate us. We heard "Bao Cao" all day long.

MIKE O'CONNOR   Jim wasn't defiant in a way that he told the guards to go to hell. But he argued with them. They wanted him to see the error of his ways and he threw it right back at them. "There have been a lot of errors made, some of them right here in this camp," he said. He was cantankerous. He never gave in.

DICK ZIEGLER   Once every three days they took us down the river to bathe. There we could speak to each other a little.

JAMES DIBERNARDO   Jim was reluctant to speak. He said, "Guys, let's cut the chatter. This is the best I've had it in years." He kept conversations short.

MIKE O'CONNOR   We didn't have shit cans at this camp that needed emptying and through which information could be passed. Not like the aviators. So it was hard to communicate. A tap code was impossible on the wood walls because the noise could carry right to the command post. Jim told us to hang in there and gave us words of encouragement. But given the camp structure and his condition, that was all he could do. Still, he was a model for everybody. Leading by example.

JAMES DIBERNARDO   Our inspiration came from the fact Jim had endured this for more than four years. That alone said so much about the man.

On 2 June 1968 Mrs. Thompson, in a letter to the Adjutant General, said that on June 1 she received a package she had sent to Captain Thompson on or about 17 June 1967. There were notations in French she did not understand but one she did which said "refused." She noted that the Adjutant General, in his letter of 25 November 1967, advised that if packages were returned, not to open them but let the postal inspectors do it. With all the writing on the package she thought it best to send it to him and have him get officials to open it. She lived in such a small town, she said, word would get from one person to the other. If so, it would have a bad effect on her children. She asked that when the inspection was completed the contents should be destroyed with the exception of the pictures of the children which she wanted returned. She said she would appreciate that not a bit of publicity get out about the package being returned. She felt this was her concern and no one else's business.

—from family assistance officer case file

ALYCE   God, I didn't even want to look at that package. Who knows what they'd done to it. If the Army suspected I was living with someone they never said anything to me.

———

EDWARD LEONARD   I was the last one to reach Bao Cao and saw Thompson only briefly. There was a mystique about him. I can't explain it. No one knew much about him and apparently the guards didn't want him to mix too much with the rest of us. We all had active imaginations. For me, he was the ghost of Christmases to come. He looked to be in his late seventies rather than early thirties. And that's how he appeared to a bunch of people who were themselves starving.

JAMES DIBERNARDO   They brought us all together periodically for indoctrination sessions. During one of these Jim went into convulsions.

MIKE O'CONNOR   A couple of us were told to carry him back to his cell. We didn't see him move.

JIM THOMPSON   I suffered what the North Vietnamese thought was a heart attack. Actually, it was heart seizure brought on by malnutrition. A medic, I was told, gave me some adrenaline through a needle in the chest and kept me quiet for a couple of days. They also gave me a few vitamin pills. The aftereffects of such a seizure are similar to those of a heart attack. It felt like I had lead in my arms and legs. That moment was the nadir of my physical condition. I knew I was in bad shape. But I also knew I was going to make it.

EDWARD LEONARD   A few days later we saw Jim very briefly. They had us out of our cages. The guards came walking up with Jim. We had a couple minutes to talk but he wasn't coherent. He didn't seem to hear or understand us. Then they led him off.

JAMES DIBERNARDO   On the night of July 3, 1968, they came to Jim's cell and took him away. That was the last time we saw him.

MIKE O'CONNOR   I thought he finally had passed away. We'd ask the guard where he had been taken. "Don't ask," he said.

EDWARD LEONARD   With Jim in such pathetic health, I never expected him to survive. A few days later they took the rest of us to a camp fifteen miles southwest of Hanoi.

26 ■ CAMP K-77

From 3 July 1968 to 7 July 1968, Thompson and two other Army officers, Colonel Ben Purcell and Captain Ted Gostas, were moved to another camp. Thompson was told he was being moved because of his poor health. The three American officers were accompanied by five North Vietnamese Army guards and one medic. The first two nights they walked; during the day they rested at unidentified villages. When they weren't walking they traveled by truck, blindfolded.

—from Army Intelligence debriefing report

BEN PURCELL   There actually were fifteen Americans in our group, but three of us were kept a hundred yards behind the rest—Thompson, Gostas, and me. We walked all night. At dawn the second day they put the rest of the group in an abandoned schoolhouse and the three of us in a bamboo thicket. We weren't supposed to talk. After about three hours, with American ingenuity, we figured out a way to communicate.

JIM THOMPSON   I got in one short conversation with Purcell.

BEN PURCELL   We shared the experience of not trusting each other, and didn't want to open our hearts to someone under those circumstances. Jim was quiet in spirit, too. He said he'd been a prisoner more than four years.

JIM THOMPSON   Purcell was surprised. He said, "How the hell have you stood it so long?"

BEN PURCELL   He looked haggard. Very thin, very tired. But he clearly was a fine trooper. Hard as nails.

JIM THOMPSON   I was interested in what had gone on in the war since

'64. In five minutes Purcell brought me up to date on major developments. He indicated that U.S. forces thought we had it pretty well wrapped up until Tet. Then all hell broke loose.

Purcell had been with the logistics command in Hue, so he was able to tell me about the buildup of forces. What troubled me was he confirmed the antiwar feelings I'd been hearing about.

LARRY STARK   As they moved us civilians together as a group we noticed this guy trailing along behind us under separate guard. I didn't know he was there until someone said, "Who the hell is that guy? Boy, he's in bad shape."

He wore faded pajamas and had a pair of jungle boots draped around his neck. He was so weak he barely managed to carry himself, let alone the boots. When he came closer we volunteered to carry them for him, along with a little pack he had. We weren't in such great shape ourselves but much better off than this guy. We had to stop several times for him to catch up and rest.

LEW MEYER   Mostly they kept him isolated from the rest of us. They had a couple of guards on him, just this skinny figure, dark and shuffling. I never looked him in the face. I didn't want to.

LARRY STARK   The guy wouldn't say a word. Obviously he knew we were Americans but he didn't know what sort of Americans. He was suspicious, like we might be spies there to get him to talk. We tried not to mention his condition. He was skin and bones. Hollowed eyes. Big black circles around them, the way a person looks when they've been ill for a long time. This was Jim Thompson.

DON RANDER   I caught my first glimpse of Jim as he was coming off the back of a canvas-covered truck. He looked like death warmed over.

JIM THOMPSON   We arrived on the outskirts of Hanoi in the early morning hours of July 7, 1968.

LARRY STARK   There we were separated again and put into solitary.

BEN PURCELL   I called this camp K-77.

———

ALYCE   As the war heated up, so did the protests. It made me mad, seeing these creeps demonstrating. Moving to Canada to get away from the draft. Here my stepbrother, Red, went over and got killed in Vietnam in '68. It hit me hard. He had eighteen and a half years in the Marines and five kids at home. Three weeks there and he got killed. I called his wife, Wanda, but she hung up on me. She knew my situation and considered me a tramp. My mother probably talked to her.

———

LEW MEYER   K-77 was an old monastery. Larry Stark pointed that out. The monk cells became our cells.

LARRY STARK   The camp had various names—K-77, Camp Huey, Skid Row.

SPEED ADKINS   The Japanese had used this place as a prison during World War II. Then the French used it during colonial days.

JIM THOMPSON   Cells were masonry and iron bars. There was a solid Dutch door with bars on the top half. Each cell was six foot square, half of it taken up by a plank bed.

DON RANDER   I was in number seven, Jim in five, and Lew Meyer in three.

LEW MEYER   We faced a courtyard but cells were also back-to-back. Only every other cell had an American, so on all three sides of us were non-English-speaking prisoners. When they tapped through the wall it was garbage. I couldn't decipher it. Of course, I had ear damage anyway. I'd walk around my bed, looking down at it. I was scared of it. I had seen what lying down meant. Instead I began exercising.

JIM THOMPSON   The guards patrolled constantly. Anytime they moved someone through the courtyard, they closed our doors so we couldn't see who it was.

LARRY STARK   Life is so much better when you're with somebody. The Vietnamese knew that. Depriving us of any association with other Americans was a form of mental torture. And, hell, they did it with malice. They knew we wanted to talk and the only person they'd provide was the interrogator. The only reading material they'd provide was propaganda.

At daybreak they'd open the doors so we could see out through the steel bars. A little while later they let us out, one at a time, to go wash our face and empty our bucket at the end of the cellblock. We had two minutes to get down there and get back.

LEW MEYER   I saw Jim Thompson when we were both let out of our cells at the same time by mistake. He had asked to get his clothes off the line as I was coming out. When we saw each other we both jumped back in our cells.

DON RANDER   In the evening we'd walk down again to one end of the building to wash. I'd start singing, making up words to songs with whatever message I wanted to convey. Jim couldn't pass my cell because the wash stand was in the other direction. I passed him, though. I didn't know his name but I knew he was there. I'd sing, "I'm from Baltimore and my wife and kids are . . ." This had several purposes. First, it was nice to hear each other. Second, if any one of us got out we could say who else was in there. Also it was encouraging. Hearing the others picked me up. More than that, we were getting something over on the enemy.

LARRY STARK   Even as temperatures rose beyond one hundred we weren't allowed to wash more often. During one period I wasn't allowed to fully bathe for nineteen days. We picked up fungus and other unwelcome residents in our crotch. It was awful. The more we scratched, the more it spread. We had periods of dysentery too. Every two or three months the bugs built up in our intestines to the point where the only way to get rid of them was nature's way. A complete clear-out.

DON RANDER   I have never been as hot or as cold as I was there in North Vietnam. I mean bone-chilling cold. It seemed like once a month I came down with a fever. I used to call it my period. I don't know whether I was having sympathy with my wife or what, but once a month, sure as shit, I woke up with a low-grade temperature, feeling sick as a dog. I'd start sniffling, sneezing. The fever wouldn't break until I made myself sweat. I'd cover up, run or walk around a lot. I didn't want to lie down. That scared me. I knew they weren't going to give me anything.

LEW MEYER   All our wounds had stopped bleeding on the way up the trail. But because it was dark in solitary I couldn't see that wounds on my face still ran with pus. Light came in only if they opened the top half of the Dutch door. Pus ran from my cheek and dropped into my rice and my soup. I learned later to hold everything to the left as I ate or I'd have to throw it away.

DON RANDER   We had a ration of two cigarettes a day. We'd get a haircut once a month. And once every ten days they'd give us a razor blade to shave. Each blade had been used by ten to fifteen people by the time it reached us. We couldn't have cut butter with it.

JIM THOMPSON   The food improved. They had bread in this camp, instead of rice, and boiled a vegetable with a ration of meat in it. We called it a hangnail but it was meat. Several months after we were there they started feeding us three meals a day instead of two. The morning meal had an extra chunk of bread.

LARRY STARK   In the afternoon we were let out for our second meal. We brought along our pot or bowl or can and one of the trustees dished out food and a small loaf of bread. We picked it up and came back to our cells.

DON RANDER   The bakery had to be somewhere nearby. Sometimes the bread was even hot. It was a French loaf, very doughy, very heavy. We found things in it we didn't want, like insects, rat turds, and rocks.

LARRY STARK   Some sesame seeds had legs. But if we started to pick them out we'd end up with half a loaf, so we decided to eat them. We weren't getting much protein anyway. We were fed a spinach-like vegetable called manioc found in swampy areas or around irrigation ditches.

Tasted good until we had it in one form or another twice a day for six months.

DON RANDER   Despite everything we went through, there was occasional humor. One time Jim said he was constipated. He yelled and screamed for them to give him something. Pills didn't work, so they decided to give him an enema. They fixed up some soapy water in a large white porcelain cup, made a hole in it, fitted a rubber hose in there, and put a douche thing on the end.

We saw them bring this contraption across the courtyard, holding this large thing at one end. [*Laughing*] I heard Jim yell, "Oh my God! You expect me to stick that thing up my ass?"

We used some rough language with the guards. I was more afraid of jets bombing us than I was of them. At some point I decided they weren't going to kill me. If anything, I would die of disease or from our own bombs. I guess Jim had that same feeling.

LEW MEYER   They still put us through intensive interrogation. To start each session we were supposed to bow. Then they asked if we had any complaints or needs. It didn't take us too long to figure out nothing was going to be done anyway. They provided a cigarette or a cup of tea, then tried to get us talking. I acted kind of cocky.

One day, July 27, 1968, they asked me what day it was. I said, "My brother's birthday." They asked me to go back to my cell and reaffirm my mind. So I did. I sat there and sat there. The next time they called me out was September. They didn't even offer me a chair. They asked me how far away the window was on my right. I told them. They said go back. What was that about, I wondered. Well, I went back to my cell and was lying in my rack with the mosquito net down, thinking about distances. I'm thinking I'm in a twelve-by-eight-foot room, a monster of a place. A good cell with a window up top for a breeze. I can do exercise, jumping jacks, and I said, "This is great." But then I stretched out my feet. My toes touch the wall. I stretched out my arms and my hands touch. I'm not in a twelve-foot cell! I thought. All my perceptions had changed.

DON RANDER   Jim was too weak to endure more torture. The rest of us got some. Well, I hesitate to use the word "torture" because, compared to what others went through, it was nothing. I was beaten with fists. Had my legs in stocks for extended periods. I was made to kneel on a rough surface for eight to ten hours at a time. My training as an altar boy came in handy, but frankly, it wasn't adequate.

27 ▪ ROOMMATES

DON RANDER On March 31, 1969, they told us, "Tomorrow you're moving in with roommates." I wondered if they knew about April Fools' Day. I didn't believe them until the next day when they put us in rooms with four cots.

LARRY STARK Lew joined me in a new cell, and Chuck Willis. The last one to come in was Jim Thompson. He still had his boots with him.

My God, we said to ourselves, what did they do to this guy?

He looked awful. He weighed not much more than one hundred pounds. Had a terrible wound on his calf. His hair had gone white and he was so bent he would have passed for sixty. We exchanged basic information about who we were, but Jim was very reserved. We asked what unit he was with. He'd only say he was an Army captain. More or less name, rank, and serial number.

We asked about family. Forget it. He was happy to be with us but was so suspicious of his cellmates that the experience had an edge on it.

JIM THOMPSON I had been in solitary for five years and five days. It was the greatest thing in the world to meet other Americans.

LEW MEYER At first we thought this move might be the next step to being released. But then Jim told us he'd been there five years. That set us back.

JIM THOMPSON I was shocked to find my cellmates were civilians. I hadn't even considered that there might be civilians involved in the war.

LARRY STARK Gradually we gained Jim's confidence. His reservations wore down.

"When I saw you guys," he said, "I thought you were spies put here to get me to talk."

For one, we were in so much better shape than he was. But the sad thing was he missed that elation he should have felt upon meeting his first Americans.

DON RANDER   I believe the move saved Jim's life. I don't think he could have withstood isolation any longer. He had slipped into a bad case of lethargy. He was at a very low ebb, mentally and physically. But once he had cellmates he started to pick himself up. He felt he needed to set an example. Like, "I'm a captain in the United States Army. I'm a Green Beret. I've got to show them. I've got to take pride in myself." His back began to stiffen.

LARRY STARK   Jim was proud of being Green Beret. He never bragged about it but was reservedly proud.

DON RANDER   We weren't suppose to communicate with guys in the other cells, but we could hear Thompson's group over there. One day when we were out washing up, Jim and his cellmates were on the other side of the wall doing the same. By talking among ourselves they heard us and we heard them. Larry, Lew, and Chuck had been captured in Hue and moved north with us. We didn't know this Thompson. There were two in captivity now. Dennis was an Army sergeant, also Special Forces. So I said across the wall, "I'm confused. There are a couple of Thompsons. What's your name?"

"Captain," he said.

That rubbed me the wrong way. Obviously Jim found out I was enlisted.

"Yeah," I said. "Okay."

JIM THOMPSON   After recounting our personal trials, discussion in our cell turned to the war, things back home, new developments, new inventions, space exploration. Cars. Electronics. Chuck Willis, an electronics engineer, told us about developments in radio and in telephone systems. Direct dialing for long distance had been getting off the ground when I left. It was now nationwide. They filled me in on changes in lifestyles— men's hairstylists; miniskirts; topless waitresses.

LEW MEYER   Larry, Chuck, and Jim talked and talked and talked. Jim exhausted himself. I've never been much of a talker. I had a ruptured eardrum anyway. But Jim was shocked at some of the news. The Gulf of Tonkin incident. Capture of the USS *Pueblo*. Until then Jim had only heard the North's side of all this. Guards told us about the riots after Martin Luther King was shot and how Bobby Kennedy had been shot. We only heard sports stories, for example, if bleachers collapsed. But now we talked among ourselves about everything. The braless look, and go-gos. Remote-control TV. The civil rights movement.

LARRY STARK   Jim didn't believe the way we said people in the States were reacting to the war. He couldn't accept it or understand.

JIM THOMPSON   It was discouraging to hear about antiwar activities. I had dismissed what the interrogators told me as propaganda, as garbage. Coming from fellow Americans it was hard to take. The worst part was them confirming prominent people, responsible citizens, participated in antiwar efforts. I could understand the radical element, people who are against anything and everything. But when I heard of congressmen, senators, educators, professional people who had taken an antiwar stand—college professors and presidents, religious leaders—I couldn't conceive of it. They seemed completely ignorant of communist motives, their goals and the cold hard facts. The stated goal to dominate the world. People didn't believe that one day we'd have to fight on our own shores if we didn't do it in Vietnam. How could intelligent people miss the truth in this?

LEW MEYER   Our first night as roommates, Jim and I happened to bunk next to each other. In the morning I got up and started my daily routine, beginning with push-ups. I'd been exercising since my capture. Jim looked down at me from his bunk, jumped up screaming "Airborne," and fell flat on his face. He couldn't even catch himself to do a single push-up. He strained and strained and was shocked at his condition. He began to cry. It shook me up, enough so I stopped my routine, telling him I was finished.

JIM THOMPSON   My health was extremely poor after a long period of malnutrition and after what I thought was a heart attack and continuing digestive problems. But I figured I was either going to cash it in doing nothing, or cash it in trying. I wanted to build myself back up. Lew Meyer was my physical and moral support. He's one hell of a fine man. A real soldier. With his encouragement I forced myself to eat more and started mild exercises.

LEW MEYER   Jim and I would get up early. We tried to be considerate of the others. I already had an exercise program but ignored that and asked Jim about different routines. Most of them I knew but I wanted him to believe he was teaching me.

JIM THOMPSON   At first I could do almost nothing. Deep-breathing exercises made me dizzy. I was afraid to press too hard because of the heart attack. After about a month I tried to do push-ups and again I couldn't. So I stuck with the deep-breathing and limbering-up exercises, bending and stretching. Progress was slow. I got tired very quickly and dizzy to the point of passing out. I couldn't wring the water out of my clothes after I washed them.

LEW MEYER   Jim was not athletic. He didn't know anything about football or baseball. Frankly he didn't seem like the kind of guy to go Ranger or Green Beret. All he was was guts and heart.

JIM THOMPSON   Gradually I moved to the easiest exercises of the Army's daily dozen, touching my toes, some knee bends and side benders and trunk twisters. Loosening up muscles a little bit.

LEW MEYER   There was no way we could do push-ups or other exercises together. Jim would have tried to top me. So we paced ourselves. We worked up a plan that within six months we would be doing the full daily-dozen routine. The first several of the daily dozen were warm-up exercises. Then one heel down, the other out, jumping back and forth. This was number four or five. By then we were working. Push-ups became a piece of cake. Over time we worked up to about sixty one-arm push-ups. We always went through commands as though Jim were drilling a whole battalion in cadence, "One-one, one-two, one-three . . . Assume the position!" Jim called it out. He practiced what he had learned in OCS. Willis and Larry looked at us as two fools. As time passed, though, they saw how it improved Jim's health.

After our morning routine we made our bedroll and swept the floor. Larry would be getting up about then. Chuck Willis's signal to rise was when he heard the doors rattling in the next cellblock. We waited for our breakfast, a piece of bread about half the size of a hotdog roll and lump of sugar. We sat on the bed and ate. Afterwards, we checked the bed for any grains of sugar that fell off, wet our fingers, and picked them up. We finished every morsel. Our first real meal of the day came about eleven. A bowl of soup, sometimes cucumber or pumpkin or, if we were lucky, potato, and a teacup of rice. Then another minimal meal in the evening. Surviving each day was the important thing.

CHUCK WILLIS   I told Jim he ought to slow down with the exercises, considering the nourishment he was getting.

LEW MEYER   Chuck thought by the time we got out of there they'd have a pill he could take to stay in shape. He was very fortunate to be able to stay in condition doing so little. Chuck was forty-three but born a little old man. "Woe is me." I used to get up every morning and say, "Good morning, sun." He was always negative. But he could see what good the exercise did Jim. It wasn't too long before Jim was saying, "Let's get at it," as if we had a full day planned.

While we built toward a full exercise routine, I was getting soft waiting for Jim. So I'd do more on my own in the evening or early in the morning while Jim was sleeping. I did isometrics. I had to be discreet and he never caught me.

Jim's birthday was in early July, three weeks before mine. When it came that year, 1969, he was taken out by the guards. He came back later with a few cookies, which he gave to us. I got called out too on my birthday under the same leniency policy. "We hope you spend the next one with your family," the camp commander said. Then, looking at my infected wound, he asked what was wrong with my face.

"Shrapnel," I said.

He didn't understand. "Spell it."

I did. He looked it up, came back, and said, "Wounded!" I was sent back to my cell, and a medic came to remove the metal from my face. That was fine. But a short time later they took me out and worked me over. "You said you were not wounded!" I missed out on my next two birthday celebrations. Didn't have the right attitude.

———

ALYCE   In 1969 we added on to the house. We made our dining room into a den, made the kitchen six feet bigger, and put in a big family room with fireplace and a garage. It was my idea. I figured I'd be there the rest of my life.

LAURA   Mom had told me my father was dead, and for years and years that's what I believed. Pam, though, began to talk about Dad. She remembered how he had taken us out to lunch as little girls and did things a father does with his daughters. She described a very kind, warm-hearted person and said how much she missed him. It helped her to talk about him.

RUTH   Pam said how great he was, how she and him used to wrestle on the floor with Mama until Mama got pregnant and couldn't play that game anymore. So Dad and her played it alone.

ALYCE   The Army set Jim's allotment aside each month. When it reached ten thousand dollars they started giving me his full salary less money each month for two fifty-dollar savings bonds. A lot of shit was raised later about me slurping his money. But no matter where I lived I would have had to raise my children. They needed food. They needed clothing. They needed a car. I did too. We couldn't stay in a cocoon. I'd go to Fort Devens to see the family assistance officer when I had a problem. Go or call him. I asked him never to stop by. That would have bothered me. I was nervous enough every time I went up there. But I wasn't worried about the Army stopping the allotments. They couldn't do that to me as long as I had those kids.

PAM   I never thought about the Vietnam War growing up. I never picked up the paper except for the funny pages. I only knew Mama was fighting the Army to get more money for us. She said much of it was money she couldn't get to without going through miles of red tape.

———————

LARRY STARK   Jim never talked about being unlucky. Not once.

LEW MEYER   We didn't hear about the torture for a while. When we did, some tales he didn't finish. He'd get tears in his eyes.

LARRY STARK   He did mention the rope trick where they made it feel like his arms were being pulled from their sockets. That's the way he described it. He also made some reference to a bamboo cage.

DON RANDER   If he expressed any resentment it was always toward the Vietnamese, not the Army nor U.S. policy. When he spoke of his captivity it wasn't bragging either, like, "Look how tough I am." It was in the form of a lesson.

"Here are the things that happened to me," he said. "You should watch out for this."

LARRY STARK   Jim didn't dwell on this stuff. Never did. We would ask him. He would tell us. He told us about the time he had endured all this torture so they wouldn't get camp information and then they came to him and said, "We would like to show you something." They had a table covered with a sheet. They pulled off the sheet and he saw an exact replica of his camp at Khe Sanh. Obviously it was a blast in the ass.

LEW MEYER   Everything Jim had done up to this point was unwitnessed, unconfirmed. A couple of prisoners said, "He could say anything he wanted to about those escape attempts and what he went through. Who would know?"

I didn't have to be convinced. Jim was a soldier. His mind functioned like a soldier's mind. It was his duty to escape. He'd done it several times. He'd do it again.

LARRY STARK   It wasn't long after we came together in the cell that we were awakened in the middle of the night by this horrendous scream. A blood-curdling scream. It kept going on and on and on. At first I thought it was the guy next to me, Willis. But it was Thompson. Then I remembered how when we were in solitary we'd hear a guy screaming in the night.

LEW MEYER   I thought, So this was the raving maniac from down the hall.

LARRY STARK   Such an awful sound! My word! It took four or five minutes to wake him. The guards came around and said, "No good! No good!"

"Yeah," we said, "and if you hadn't tortured him so badly he wouldn't be like this."

The nightmares came on a recurring basis. It seemed just when we had forgotten about them, and were enjoying a sound sleep, all of a sudden, "Yeeeaaah!"

Jim told me once that a headless man was chasing him and would catch up to him. He'd wake up in a sweat. One time he was so hoarse from screaming he couldn't talk for a few days.

SPEED ADKINS   It sounded like someone in mortal pain. He talked about having been held so long in that cage. That would have been enough to drive anyone crazy.

LEW MEYER   "Stop! No! No!" he'd scream and would cry out in pain in Vietnamese. Sometimes, lying in the bunk next to him, I heard him picking up steam and could catch him before he got into it. I'd grab him and pin him down when I came out of my own sleep. Often, by the time I'd reach him, he would have pulled the mosquito netting down and gotten himself wrapped up in his blanket. Then Jim and I would walk the floor for half an hour, not talking about it, just getting him calmed down. I'd say, "You're safe now. You're safe."

There'd be no light in the cell. Only the shadow of the bars in the moonlight. I'd put my arm on his shoulder and we would walk. Occasionally I'd feel him breaking up again or fighting it. He couldn't control himself. He'd have to have a couple of cigarettes before he could go back to sleep. He scared the hell out of me many nights. It disrupted the whole camp. In time we learned Jim would have the nightmares when we'd talk about certain subjects during the day.

30 August 1969

Dear Mrs. Thompson:

I would like to inform you of the possibility of increased publicity concerning the treatment of personnel held prisoner by the enemy. As you know the Secretary of Defense has expressed deep concern as to the status of the 1,325 U.S. servicemen who are listed as prisoners or missing in action. He has assured all families that these men will not be forgotten by the United States government.

On August 4, three U.S. servicemen who were prisoners in North Vietnam returned to the United States. While the U.S. is pleased these three men have been returned, we cannot be content with propaganda-planned releases of a few men at infrequent intervals. It is the belief of the Department of Defense that the American public should continue to be aware of Hanoi's intransigent attitude regarding prisoner matters.

It is possible that in coming weeks you may be receiving information through the news media concerning the treatment of U.S. prisoners held by North Vietnam. Some of this information may be distressing. Please understand, however, that any such statements are made with clear recognition that our first responsibility is to improve the welfare of our U.S. servicemen held prisoner in Southeast Asia. You can be assured the Department of Defense will continue to give this matter its closest attention.

Kenneth G. Wickham
Major General, USA
The Adjutant General

ALYCE   Aunt Willa and Uncle Marty liked Harold and invited us down to their farm in Pennsylvania. They had a pool. In summer, the kids could swim all day or walk down the dirt road and not worry about somebody picking them up. Willa and Marty and Harold and I would play canasta every night. We'd go down in the fall, too, to pick our own apples.

At home, for social life, we'd get together with Harold's brother and his wife and four other couples, mostly neighbors of theirs. We went to dinner and dancing every two months or so.

————

LARRY STARK   Jim maintained a posture of realistic resistance. No cooperation but no sense getting ourselves into trouble. He concluded the serious torture was over unless we brought it on ourselves. After a while we learned how far we could go. We got prison moxie.

LEW MEYER   Jim showed leadership. A few days after we were put together they took him out to talk to another POW who had withdrawn, staying in a corner of his cell and not responding to anyone. This young Marine had been captured shortly after he got to Vietnam. He refused to shave or get a haircut or leave solitary. Jim assured him everything would be all right and got him moved into communal living.

Jim was amazingly sharp, with a unique ability to assess a situation. I saw it in the way he responded to the guards. Always careful not to talk about military subjects. One day in September of '69, the guards turned up all wearing black armbands. Jim said Ho Chi Minh must have died. The guards asked us later how we knew.

DON RANDER   Jim knew if we were going to have any organization he was going to have to take charge as senior military man there.

LARRY STARK   Jim wanted to lead but was frustrated that he wasn't accepted in that role by many civilians in camp. In fact, Lew was the sole exception. Many others were older than Jim and nonmilitary. They questioned whether they came under his chain of command.

DON RANDER   The civilians didn't rebel to the point where they got nasty. But there was no way in hell Jim was going to get an organization going.

LEW MEYER   There were several categories of civilians. Federal workers, contractors, construction workers, foreign workers. Hardly a military situation. But there was never any question in my mind who was in charge. In the battle in Hue there had been no leadership. I knew somebody had to step up if we were going to survive the camp.

LARRY STARK   Lew, a very likable guy, had spent time in the military. He knew what the rest of us did not know, which was that Jim really was in charge as senior military man. That applied to everybody, not just military. I found that out later. Lew knew it from the first.

DON RANDER   It was fortunate for everybody that Jim didn't push it. It wouldn't have worked and he would have been ostracized. One or two people he didn't get along with at all.

LARRY STARK   If we had all been military it would have worked very well. Jim would be a great guy to be alongside on the battlefield. Totally reliable and knowledgeable. I had no doubt he'd risk his life for me. I tried to conform to the Code of Conduct and discussed it with Jim. He was very reasonable. He advised us on communist interrogation techniques. Some of us didn't realize telling them anything gave them important information they could piece together.

SPEED ADKINS   Some fellow Americans cooperated with the Vietnamese. A couple of them collaborated. I told one cellmate things about my life, like that I had retired from the Army as a major in '63 after twenty-five years active duty, that I was in the Pacific in World War II and in Korea in that war. At Fort Bliss, I said, I went into missiles. Soon this cellmate was being pulled out for interrogation practically every day. Each time, they give him two cigarettes. I didn't pay a whole lot of attention. Later they came and got me. I began three days of interrogation. I saw Russians in the area. All of the questions were on missiles. I insisted I hadn't been a missile officer, just an artillery commander. But boy they gave me hell. The old police deal, with one screaming and slamming or hitting, the other being real nice. They had maps galore and asked me questions as though they were taking them from a book. When I got back to my cell I confronted this guy. I said, "The interrogation was on a subject only you and I know about."

"I didn't tell them anything about you!"

"Don't give me that bullshit," I said. "If you open your mouth again about me I'll kill ya." That afternoon they took him from the cell. He never came in again.

LARRY STARK   We wouldn't exclude Jim's advice but we tried to think things out ourselves. We philosophized over what they were really trying to get at.

LEW MEYER Jim thought some guys believed the propaganda we received. He'd say, "How can you form that opinion based on news from the North Vietnamese? Consider the source!"

DON RANDER He came across as very militaristic, very right-wing, a strong personality and a strong commander. He loved command. He could be intolerant of another person's weaknesses, another person's likes or dislikes. One time he made me very resentful as a black. An interrogator had passed our cells with a radio. Hanoi Hannah from time to time played American music, and this time it was Aretha Franklin singing in her inevitable way. The Vietnamese said it was good American music. That was what I used to listen to. I mean that's "The Lady." But Jim was very quick and inconsiderate to remark, with me standing there, "You call that music! I wouldn't call that music. . . ." Blah, blah, blah. Very strong language. I was hurt. Lew picked up on my resentment and defended me because I was only a staff sergeant and Jim was a captain. "Hey, Jim, you shouldn't be like that," he said. Jim never did apologize, even after he realized he had stepped on my feelings.

13 October 1969

Dear Mrs. Thompson:

My office has received inquiries from several congressmen requesting the names and addresses of the families of Army personnel who are missing and captured. It is Department of Defense policy not to release your name and address to anyone without your knowledge and consent. In order to reply to these inquiries, I would like to ask that you complete the attached form indicating your decision concerning the release of your name to members of Congress.

You may have noticed in the news media that some individuals have formed organizations of wives and families of missing and captured persons. One such organization is the National League of Families of American Prisoners in Southeast Asia. Mrs. Sybil Stockdale, wife of a Navy officer who is a prisoner in North Vietnam, is the national coordinator and has asked that information of this organization be provided to you. As I stated above, we will not release your name and address without your consent. I am, however, providing the address for this organization in the event you desire to obtain information. . . .

Kenneth G. Wickham
Major General, USA
The Adjutant General

ALYCE   The National League of Families tried to get me involved. I told
them I wasn't interested. Granted, they did good work. But there was no
way I could pack up and leave my four kids to go roving all over the country. They did the job and that was fine.

GAIL MEYER   I did get involved in the League and stayed very involved
through the years. In time it helped me adjust to my limbo situation, the
trial of not knowing what happened to Lew. I went back to school to work
on a psychology degree. In time my life became pretty fulfilling again.

———

DON RANDER   Even POWs had light moments. One dreary day they
allowed us to take a bath. Russ Page, myself, Larry Stark, and Jim were all
out in a little courtyard. Everybody was down that day, for one reason or
another. I felt the mood and started making up words to the song "Ahab
the Arab." Jim had never heard it so he didn't know what I was singing.
But I made up more words as I went along. Here I was buck-ass naked,
twirling my towel around. Clowning, dancing, moving. Jim couldn't get
over this. He started laughing. Said something about the show. I said,
"Yeah, Masta, you know all us black boys can sing and dance!" That
floored everybody.

10 November 1969

Dear Mrs. Thompson:

Recent news reports concerning the announcement that North Vietnam
plans to provide information on captured American servicemen through
groups opposed to American participation in the Vietnam war have
prompted inquiries from many families concerning a recommended course
of action they might follow. In general I can say that we do not desire to
impede the flow of information concerning our captured or missing personnel if the enemy chooses to provide it in this manner. To do so would
only deny to you important information concerning your loved ones.
However, we do not endorse these groups, nor do we appreciate their use
by the North Vietnamese or Viet Cong to further political objectives,
especially at your expense. When I consider the anxiety and suffering
imposed on you in recent years as a direct result of the intransigent North
Vietnamese and Viet Cong policy on prisoner matters, it becomes obvious
that this most recent action is a propaganda ploy, most probably prompted
by world-wide public condemnation of their previous prisoner policies. . . .

To our knowledge no information concerning the status of any servicemen has been provided at the present time. . . .

We will continue to make every effort to obtain the release and the safe return of your loved one. I join in your prayers that these efforts will soon succeed.

> Kenneth G. Wickham
> Major General, USA
> The Adjutant General

LEW MEYER   Life in the cell wasn't all exercise for Jim and me. After the first full meal of the day, the whole camp went into a siesta period. I usually laid back and did some mental exercises or, in winter, just got under the blanket and kept warm. As Jim got stronger he taught us to play bridge and we had tournaments.

DON RANDER   We made cards. Later they gave us some. A new deck about once a year, whether they needed changing or not. Can you imagine what they looked like? Cards were in constant use during daylight hours. If not bridge, solitaire. Twelve hours a day.

LEW MEYER   I made a cribbage board using a nail and a piece of wood. My fingers hurt today just thinking about it. We also got reading material each day.

DON RANDER   I read a Hemingway book and six or seven Émile Zola novels, in French. I had had French in high school and spent two years in France. I wasn't fluent but I got propaganda papers that used both French and English and made a dictionary. After remembering my syntax, I was able to read Zola pretty well.

LEW MEYER   I did a lot of mathematics and fire department hydraulics. I made a slide rule using my bed slats. Five and a half feet long and pretty accurate but we didn't have much to run it against. In the cell on our right was Rander, Art Balagot, and two Filipinos. On our left were Gary Daves and one other. We occasionally talked to them over the wall. Eventually the guards opened the gates between our courtyards, and once in a while Daves, who was a teacher, came in and held classes. He helped me on the slide rule.

Our tool to work wood was a loose nail. When guards would inspect, I'd stick the nail back in its hole. We used it and a piece of wire to drill a hole into the cell behind us which held four other civilians—Alex Henderson, Bob Olsen, Tom Rush, and Russell Page. That took a week. We hid the work not only from the guards but, for a time, from Willis. It scared the hell out of him when we not only made contact with the other side but started passing notes. That was breaking a camp regulation. Fortunately Willis never brought it up during our monthly "criticism/self-criticism" sessions with the interrogators. Interrogators asked, "What have you done? What rules have you violated?" Some prisoners actually criticized themselves. If Willis broke a regulation [*laughing*] he'd tell them about it. Then he'd get a smoke. When it got around to me I'd say, "I am not aware of any camp regulations I broke that you are aware of." No one laughed because it would have gotten me in trouble. They never made progress with Jim either. He used the sessions to ask for books.

DON RANDER   We got three cigarettes a day. Later they upped it to four. But when we'd go out to interrogation sessions, we'd steal paper, tear the cigarette down, loosen the tobacco, and reroll it. Almost like a reefer. That way we got five of six smokes out of one cigarette. But *Reader's Digest* pages don't smoke too well.

LEW MEYER   During five years in solitary Jim probably relived everything he had done in his lifetime. I only spent one year like that and met again everyone I had ever known, thought about a lot of people I would eventually meet, and visited places I would eventually see. Sounds screwy, I know. But weird things happened in there. We often couldn't tell fact from fantasy. For instance, I could almost transport myself from the cell to a wining-and-dining atmosphere.

But I came to believe Jim was reliving a lot of things that weren't going happen when he got back. He was not facing reality. He talked of a dream car, a Pontiac convertible, and a dream house. Alyce could do no wrong. Nor could his mother, whom he described as almost a saint. His father didn't make out too well. But Jim began carrying on these conversations like we weren't there. Willis would lay back and signal us, like "Here goes Jim again."

CHUCK WILLIS   He'd get on these long-winded stories about him and Alyce and Coney Island and riding the rides and she was his high school sweetheart.

LEW MEYER   He'd remember Alyce's birthday and their wedding anniversary and the kids' birthdays. We'd all celebrate each other's important days. Jim talked about his life back to OCS and earlier. How he'd almost been a juvenile delinquent. How he was a draftee rather than a volunteer. He dreamed of becoming a regular officer rather than reserve. But he was concerned he didn't have enough time as a commanding officer to make rank.

DON RANDER   Jim wanted to be a general someday. That was really wishful thinking, because you had to be extremely lucky or from the old boys' club at West Point.

LEW MEYER   I'd nod while Jim told his stories but I felt he was letting himself in for a big letdown. Everybody needed a pipe dream, but no one's dreams were as detailed as Jim's. He repeated them so many times they became real for him and for him alone.

CHUCK WILLIS　Jim had too strict a military view of everything. He stuck to name, rank, and serial number like a fanatic. He was working out a way to escape. I was for that, I said. But I reserved the right to determine whether it was safe. He said, "You'll do it because it will be an order." He got upset once when Larry said our interrogators were only doing their job, that he didn't hold it against them.

LARRY STARK　We hadn't gone through what Jim had in solitary. We didn't have that great animosity toward the guards. I felt we could accomplish the mission without antagonizing them. We didn't need to give information but we didn't have to rub their noses in it.

DON RANDER　Jim was tough toward the Vietnamese. He wanted to set an example for us.

LEW MEYER　There was one interrogator Jim would have loved to get his hands on. A former torturer. Most of us were stretched out on our beds one afternoon when this guy walked by and Jim went for him. The guy stepped back, out of reach, and walked on. I grabbed Jim and tried to calm him. He broke down. He didn't have to tell me what the guy did. We could tell from his nighttime screams. Jim never forgot what monsters they could be.

JIM THOMPSON　Stark and Willis had doubts about U.S. involvement in Vietnam. They weren't antiwar; I don't mean that. They weren't collaborators. But they weren't firm in their determination, their loyalty. They weren't absolutely sure what they were doing there. They were beginning to question. Some things the VC told them made them doubt the legitimacy of our presence in Vietnam. Doubt the legality of it. Doubt the right and wrong of the war.

LARRY STARK　Jim was unwavering. For example, he said the United States would never stop giving aid to Vietnam. We just would never do it. He could not picture it in his mind where we would ever do it. But we had heard about the Church Amendment,* and we told him about the protesters back home. He wouldn't believe it. He almost thought we were spies because our attitude was so different than his. Our attitude was different because during the five years he spent in solitary, we were exposed to what was going on in the States. When Jim was captured people didn't even know what Vietnam was about. He could never imagine these things at home. He gave the benefit of the doubt to the U.S. military and wrote off as propaganda a great deal of information.

　　Willis and Jim didn't get along, partly because Chuck was a casual guy and Jim was precise. In a close relationship it can create real problems. Jim

---

* The 1970 Cooper-Church Amendment prohibited Nixon from using ground troops in Cambodia. These were the first Congresionally imposed limits on presidential power in wartime.

prided himself on precision, on mathematics. Chuck was always ballpark. Ten percent off was good enough. Jim liked to get within one tenth of one percent.

DON RANDER   Larry had a what-are-we-doing-in-this-country attitude. And if Larry has an idea, he'll tell you about it and say he's right. Jim didn't like it. But he had far more animosity toward others in the camp who didn't respect the country's position.

LEW MEYER   Antimilitary feelings began to develop among some in camp. At one point Willis called Jim a warmonger. Jim wasn't like that. He wouldn't abide warmongers in uniform because the enemy shoots real bullets.

JIM THOMPSON   Lew once summed it up beautifully. He said, "I don't see how a person like that can stand confinement because knowing it's all worthwhile is the only thing that makes it bearable." This portrays Lew's attitude, his character. He's a completely selfless man, a guy who denies himself all to give you the shirt off his back. Completely loyal. Thinks nothing of himself. It's all for country. Lew was quiet, not one to get into political arguments. Not even an articulate man. But when he did come out with a comment, it was loaded. Really loaded. He's very deep, very profound, extremely dedicated American. One of the finest men I've ever met in my life. Heart and mind a soldier.

LEW MEYER   I found it ironic that Jim was the only one in the group who had been ordered over to Vietnam. The rest of us were volunteers. Willis in fact had just extended his tour before capture. One minute he complained about being in Vietnam and the next he'd mention the benefits and the reasons he'd extended. Jim never let his personal hardship interfere with his support for the U.S. position. In his weakest moments he was always sharp, always able to understand what the North Vietnamese were trying to do.

JIM THOMPSON   When you're cooped up in a small place without escape valves, you make every effort to avoid confrontation or hard feelings. But over the course of some months little things got bottled up inside. Gradually it built and built and finally there came an explosion. Sometime after Christmas of '69 the four of us in the cell had a terrific argument. It nearly came to blows. Lew and I against the other two. We couldn't tolerate their attitude anymore. It began as a flap over pictures the interrogator showed us of an antiwar demonstration. One of the others said, "Good, maybe it'll get us out of here."

CHUCK WILLIS   I had to threaten Thompson with a bed slat. He got nasty. Jim wasn't big but I'd hate to tangle with him. He was a Green Beret. When I got the slat he got in a jujitsu stance. I said, "Look fella, I've had a little training too and know something about it."

LEW MEYER   I don't remember that. I either would have laughed or I'd have dropped Willis myself. But Jim was very vocal. The three of them got into heated arguments. I was fortunate, I guess, that I lost my hearing. And I played it up. It was bad enough hearing that stuff from the other side of the bars. I mean, basing comments on what *Pravda* said. I couldn't understand that. To get a laugh I just said, "Watch out or Jim will have another one of his nightmares."

JIM THOMPSON   It had gotten to the point where if the four of us were confined in that cell much longer, it was going to lead to violence. Lew and I were tired of listening to it. We had requested, without telling each other, to be put back in solitary. Now that's a disgrace, to prefer solitary to the company of other Americans. But both Lew and I found their attitude absolutely intolerable. No regard for the cause, no regard for what was right or wrong. Just get me out. Thinking of nothing but one's own skin and losing sight of the fact that we were Americans fighting for the freedom of an oppressed people and, indirectly, for our own way of life. It was "Get me out!" Lew and I held back as long as we could. We didn't want our guards to know we couldn't get along. But we had to do something or it was going to lead to bloodshed.

LARRY STARK   Our personalities didn't fit together well. I was, to some degree, like Willis. Never precise or accurate enough. I like to think I'm a little better now. Jim, though, was down the line with everything while in prison. And he was within his right to take the positions he did.

JIM THOMPSON   We made it appear to the guards that the four of us were parting amicably. We rehearsed. Finally, just after Christmas in '69, they put Lew and me in the cell next door. We shook hands with Larry and Willis as we left.

28 ■ SHAPING UP

Food at K-77 was greatly improved. Besides bread with his meals, for the first time Thompson also had meat, about 100 grams a week. He was fed twice a day and on rare occasions was allowed to exercise outside. Work was voluntary. There was no reward for work and no punishment for not working but it allowed one to get outside so Thompson did weeding chores, rolled coal balls and performed general maintenance duties.

—from Army Intelligence debriefing report

DON RANDER By 1970, the guards allowed us to get together once or twice a week with Jim, Lew, and the others. When we got such freedom we were tenacious holding on to it. If they allowed us something once, we never let them forget it. Together we talked mostly about food and families. About our kids all the time. Jim was very proud of his daughters. We speculated on his fourth child. He was sure it was a boy. We teased him that he got another girl.

We talked about our pasts, what we did on certain occasions. "Well, today is Andrew's birthday," I'd say, or "I remember three years ago I took my wife to a nice club. . . ." We provided details because we were telling a story and the other guys wanted to listen to occupy time. But discussions always turned to food. Always food.

Jim talked about his boyhood near New York and how he worked for the A&P. He talked about Alyce. I could tell he was in love. Nobody spoke about the possibility that wives were fooling around. But there was a realization that, hey, x number of years is a long time, maybe my wife doesn't know I'm alive, maybe the Army's declared me dead. The feeling was that a wife might have to get on with her life.

3 November 1970

Subject: Reconsideration for Promotion
To: Secretariat for Department of Army Selection Boards

1. Captain Floyd J. Thompson was considered and not recommended for promotion to major by the following boards: 30 March 1966; 29 May 1967; 6 January 1968; 30 August 1968; 3 July 1969.

2. The following action constitutes a material change in subject officer's records as reviewed by the above boards:

Officer was reported missing on 26 March 1964. His status subsequently was changed to "detained in a foreign country against his will." Army regulations then in effect required that an Officer Efficiency Report be submitted when the rated officer was missing. . . . Consequently a delayed OER [attached] has been prepared for the period 27 December 1963 to 26 March 1964 and was placed in his file on 2 November 1970.

3. Recommend that this case be referred to the Army Standby Advisory Board for reconsideration for promotion.

Donald S. Aines
Colonel
Adjutant General Corps

DELAYED OFFICER EFFICIENCY REPORT

Captain Thompson was in every way an exemplary officer. He planned, advised and personally accompanied extensive combat operations in an area known to be an enemy base area in western Quang Tri Province. His leadership of his detachment, his relations with his Vietnamese counterpart and his administration of the Khe Sanh camp were all outstanding. His personal conduct was above reproach and set a high standard for his subordinates. He was personally forceful, active and aggressive in meeting the challenges of his difficult assignment. His professional competence, imagination and ingenuity were remarkable. His last known act was to make an air reconnaissance over an area of known enemy concentration; typically, he wanted to inform himself so that he could properly plan combat operations. His aircraft was shot down on that mission and he has been missing since that time. Captain Thompson demonstrated that he was thoroughly capable of combat operations with a battalion-sized force. I feel strongly that his per-

formance in this assignment shows that he was capable of superior performance in two grades higher than his present rank.

George A. Maloney, Colonel, Inf.

Co D, 1st Special Forces Gp (Abn)

1st SF, Det B-420, Commanding

GEORGE MALONEY   If you think a guy is dead, there's no point saying anything adverse about him. This fitness report was to complete a record. Any man in combat I ever lost I had to write a report on him and I would say something like that.

———

JIM THOMPSON   Lew and I got along beautifully in a cell by ourselves. With his help, I made considerable progress regaining my health. I built myself up to where I could go through a full exercise program. With thought of escape always on my mind, I was determined that, should the opportunity present itself, I would be in shape to go. In time I could do the full twelve repetitions of the Army's daily dozen without pausing. Plus I could do fifty to one hundred sit-ups and up to eighty-seven push-ups, the most I'd ever done. It was the same program followed by our airborne troops.

LEW MEYER   We started to modify the daily dozen. Push-ups not only had to be done with a straight back and touching chin and chest, but we turned our palms in, rather than out, to call on different muscles. Then we started doing elevated push-ups, inclined push-ups with one foot in the air and shifting weight. Jim called them Ranger push-ups. We came up with one we called fireman push-ups. We competed against each other. I'd say, "Fireman have to be tough." He'd say, "Rangers have to be tougher."

JIM THOMPSON   We'd put our bunks together and run around the cell. At first I had trouble with my feet. Nutritional deficiencies left them swollen and painful and the nerves damaged. When the pain stopped, my feet stayed numb like I'd been out in the cold too long. They tended to curl and cramp up. The morning after my first run I couldn't get out of bed. But steady Lew started his morning by massaging my feet until they limbered up a bit. Then we trotted around the room. It took two months to work out the stiffness to where I could start building up my wind. Eventually we had running contests. We got to the point where we ran for well over an hour. Not real fast but enough to work up a good solid sweat. By the end of 1970 we were doing a full exercise program for the active-duty airborne soldier.

On 24 January 1971, Mrs. Thompson said she did not want to be "both-ered" by anyone unless actual news of her husband was received; she did not want to participate in any POW or survivor program; she did not want her or her husband's name released for any reason and that she was presently trying to have her husband pronounced legally dead in civilian courts.

—from family assistance officer case file

ALYCE   They kept pestering me on the phone, wanting to know how things were going. Did I have any questions? It got to be a pain in the ass. I told them to leave me alone. I was pretty well disgusted with the Army. I was trying to have Jim declared dead so I could get on with my life. I didn't know if I would marry Harold but I wanted to be free to start over. The problem was Jim was not missing any longer. He was a POW. And you cannot have a POW declared dead. I didn't know that. Army officials said even if the other POWs came back it would still not be proof Jim was dead.

I went to a private lawyer and he told me the same thing. I wanted a private lawyer because they've got that thing to remain silent. Yeah, attor-ney-client relationship. I told this lawyer I was living with somebody and wanted to get on with my life. He got a book out and looked it up but said, "Can't do it." Yet the Army hadn't shown me any actual proof Jim was alive, other than the tape recording. And I had only identified part of that tape. That's all they were going on.

"You mean this could go on for fifty years?" I asked my lawyer.

"Yeah," he said. I cried outside his office.

Meanwhile, publicity on POWs was building. I got a damn ulcer. My blood pressure went sky-high. Harold and I discussed the possibility that if anything came out in the press about us we'd have to move out of the neighborhood, out of state probably. He thought as a chef he could get a job anywhere. Other POW wives started that crap about going over to Paris during the peace talks. That irritated me. Those peace talks had been going on for months over what shape the table was going to be. But these wives got together and wanted to fly over there. I just didn't want to get into it.

4 February 1971

Dear Mrs. Thompson:

I wish to advise you that your husband was promoted to the grade of major.

I am enclosing a copy of the promotion order. Army financial records are being changed to reflect this promotion, and proper adjustment will be made so that his pay and allowances accrue to his account at the rate established for the new grade.

Our government policy of phasing down our military commitment in South Vietnam has caused concern for our missing and captured personnel. Be assured these men will not be forgotten. . . . The status of our missing and captured personnel must be resolved before any peace agreement can be concluded. There recently has been a large amount of publicity focused on the plight of American prisoners, and public involvement in this area has increased considerably. These efforts in publicizing the fact that the Viet Cong and Hanoi officials refuse to adhere to the terms of the Geneva Convention have brought an awareness of the situation to people around the world. We believe this is having an effect. . . .

Kenneth G. Wickham
Major General, USA
The Adjutant General

LEW MEYER   It was the South Vietnamese who first got Jim and me talking about escape. At K-77, five or six South Vietnamese Rangers were packed into a cell opposite us. One day a couple of them strolled over during siesta time, after picking a couple of locks including the gate between our two compounds. While they talked with Jim, I served as lookout, standing on my rack and peeking through a ventilation opening by the ceiling. The Vietnamese had closer American neighbors, but they knew Jim was a Green Beret. One said he had gone to school in the States. They asked if we were willing to escape with them. All of them had training in escape and evasion and contacts in Hanoi who could get us down to Haiphong. But quite a bit of money was needed to get to the harbor and bundle us out. They didn't believe their contacts would do it for Vietnamese alone. If they had a couple of "round eyes" with them their chances would improve. They asked us to think about it and said they would be back.

By the time those Vietnamese prisoners returned to their cells, however, others had learned of their visit. One American POW knew an escape plan was in the mill. When a guard went by, he asked to go to interrogation. That was the last we heard from the South Vietnamese. The guards closed some inner doors in the compound after that. Jim knew Morse code and tried a couple of tappings on our back wall but they were gone.

For Jim and me, however, the torch was lit. Now, we thought, there might be people out there to help us. That day we started training to run long distances. The question we asked ourselves: "How far can we go?"

On 11 March 1971, Mrs. Thompson was asked on behalf of the National League of Families of American Prisoners and Missing in Southeast Asia for permission to use Captain Thompson's name in certain post offices to draw the public's attention to the fact he had been in a captured status going on eight years. Mrs. Thompson replied, "His name will be released to no one and if it is there will be hell to pay."

—from family assistance officer case file

ALYCE   I was desperate. All hell was gonna break loose. They were putting POWs' names on envelopes before the bracelet shit came out. I requested his name not be put on any bracelets either.

———

ALBERT VAN DYKE   By the time I became pastor of the Old North Reformed Church in Dumont, in 1958, Jim was in the Army. We ran something in the church bulletin recognizing his commission. The three girls had all been baptized at Old North.

　　After his plane was lost, none of us believed Jim was dead. He was on our prayer list throughout his captivity. One thing bothered me greatly, however. As the years passed, another man, also held captive quite a while, got a lot more recognition than Jim. Magazine profiles. Television reports. Yet by our records Jim was a captive longer. I called the Pentagon, quite exasperated that no information was coming out on Jim Thompson. Someone wasn't doing right by him.

TED JOHANSSON   As deputy adjutant general at Fort Devens, I had responsibility for family support officers throughout New England. Generally I didn't get involved in family service matters but only made sure the programs ran properly. One day in 1971, I got a call from the Pentagon. In our area, they said, was the family of the longest-held POW. There had been a recent change in her family assistance officer and Mrs. Thompson was upset. I got the assignment instead. At the same time a congressman had inserted a list of POWs into the *Congressional Record*.

On 15 March 1971, Captain Theodore W. Johansson, replacement Family Service and Assistance Officer at Fort Devens, told Mrs. Thompson in a letter that he was sending her a page from the Congressional Record. She had requested that it be sent rather than delivered personally. Johansson said her desire for complete anonymity was understood. He also understood her wish that her husband's name not be used or released in any way except for official purposes. He reassured her that the request to use her husband's name by the National League of Families of American Prisoners and Missing in Southeast Asia on envelopes had been turned down and her wishes would be respected; that her wishes that her name or her children's names or whereabouts not be released from either Fort Devens or the Department of the Army would be completely respected; that the Office of Information of DA and its counterpart in DoD had been contacted and they understood her wishes in not releasing her husband's name. But it was further stated that because her husband's name had appeared on the page of the attached Congressional Record, it was now a matter of public record and the information could be used by anyone for any purpose, specifically representatives of the news media.

—from family assistance officer case file

TED JOHANSSON   I was worried about the list and needed to let Alyce know she might be getting publicity. Our initial meeting was in her car, in a neutral place. She insisted on it. But she had my home phone number and we talked extensively anytime she had a problem. I tried to make her life more comfortable and worry-free. I never did go to her home. We met sometimes at the Devens officers' club, sometimes on the side of the road. I didn't think anything of it, except that she was interested in privacy for her children. I'm not a suspicious person by nature.

FROM THE Associated Press, MARCH 22, 1971

CAPTIVE 7 YEARS, CAPTAIN SYMBOLIC OF POW ISSUE

WASHINGTON (AP)—Seven years ago this week Army Capt. Floyd J. Thompson was captured by the Viet Cong. Today he is symbolic of the whole prisoner-of-war issue.

The public knows nothing about Thompson except these simple facts. The Pentagon won't say anything about him, in keeping with its POW policy, and his family carefully avoids notice.

He has been captive, by the records, longer than any other American serviceman taken prisoner of war in the history of this country. Although others were captured earlier in Vietnam, the Pentagon says they have gained their freedom or been killed.

Thompson was captured in South Vietnam on March 26, 1964. The Army won't say why it thinks he is captive. No mail or other communication from Thompson ever has been received. In many respects it is almost as if he didn't exist. And for many this describes the plight of the POWs. Some of their wives and mothers, fathers and children work to keep the issue, and the men, alive. This week they are observing a "National Week of Concern for Prisoners of War and Missing in Action."

Special church services were held in many communities Sunday. Proclamations were being issued from the White House to city hall. They will fly the flag at half staff all week. . . .

DON RANDER   Jogging, push-ups, pull-ups. Jim and Lew exercised a lot, mostly in the morning so they could go out then and wash up. Jim did very well for the condition he was in. But I thought they both exercised excessively. Still they had their program and became fast friends. They kept close track of their distances by taking ordinary steps during their runs—perhaps thirty inches—and calculating the number of laps. "Today I ran twelve kilometers," one of them would say. With the diet we had, they couldn't maintain that. The PT was as much of a time-passer as it was a defense mechanism, as it was a morale booster, as it was part of Jim's macho image. Green Beret. Frankly, if he had cut it in half it would have done him more physical good. But that's his way. Jim can be too enthusiastic when he believes this direction is the way to go.

LEW MEYER   We thought we might be able to hit one hundred kilometers. So one day that's what I did. Jim stayed awake a full day, counting laps and changing the straps on my "Ho Chi Minh slippers." Our sandals were pieces of tire tread, with straps made from strips of inner tube. If while exercising a strap broke we kicked the sandals off and continued barefoot. But we started that morning aiming to perfect our Ho Chi Minh repair. Our threading tool was a piece of bamboo, later a piece of tin. We used it to push the bands of inner tube through the cut in the sole. We'd pull out the old straps and put in the new. We had collected bad straps from the other cells or traded for straps they'd thrown away. We started to stockpile. We decided our first provisions for escape were extra straps and running extra kilometers.

That morning I set out to run twenty kilometers with sandals and two kilometers barefoot to see how long we could run on the bottoms of our feet. We knew we needed calluses. I swore I'd never let my feet go soft again after our march north, seeing the misery people went through. Take boots off GIs and you almost had them tied up.

After reaching my objective that morning I wasn't winded and decided to keep going. I went on and on and on. It got dark. The guard kept coming to look at us. It went past midnight. Then the sun was coming up.

When I saw that, I knew one hundred kilometers—sixty miles—was feasible. I was hurting but I got to thinking if sixty miles were possible why not one hundred miles. At some point I just gave up. I looked for some excuse and went to bed. I'd been running for twenty-four hours when I quit.

DON RANDER   Lew toned down his workout when blood appeared in his urine. He blamed it on all the pounding on concrete.

On the night of 21 June 1971 Thompson and thirteen other POWs in his group were moved from Camp Juliet (K-77) to Camp India (Rockpile) by truck and arrived the same night. No reason was given for this move. Seven North Vietnamese guards, including the political officer, accompanied them. They traveled south through Phu Ly.

—from Army Intelligence debriefing report

29 ■ ROCKPILE

DON RANDER They moved Jim, Lew, and a dozen others by truck to a military installation about sixty-five kilometers south of Hanoi. The rest of us stayed at K-77.

JIM THOMPSON The new prison, an annex to a larger one, was built specifically to accommodate us. Construction was completed just as we arrived.

SPEED ADKINS It had a gate on only one of four sides. Nearby was a military school, three or four large buildings for classrooms. The other housed North Vietnamese soldiers and their women. The school commandant was also stockade commander.

JIM THOMPSON Our building inside the compound was large, built of brick with barred windows and shutters. It had four rooms for all of us to use. We had free access to all spaces, a considerable improvement in living conditions. Two rooms were bunkrooms, about twelve feet by twenty, with seven men sleeping in each room.

LEW MEYER On each side of the bunkrooms was raised flooring for sleeping, almost like a stage. We rolled our rice mat out and that was our bunk. They told us where to sleep. Jim was placed in the other bunkroom.

JIM THOMPSON Three men slept side by side on one platform, four on the other, in each room.

LARRY STARK Three sleeping was comfortable; four was not, so we switched off. We put our clothes in a bundle and used it for a pillow.

JIM THOMPSON We had a dining room with tables and stools. For the first time in seven years I could sit at a table to eat a meal. We also had a separate latrine. No real plumbing, just a tank of water, but it was a vast improvement from a pot in the corner of a six-by-six-foot room. Here we could take a bath and wash dishes.

LARRY STARK   We thought it was the best prison in Vietnam. Some guys worried it meant they planned to keep us a long time.

JIM THOMPSON   Our building stood in the middle of a courtyard, maybe one hundred twenty-five feet long by sixty feet wide. The courtyard was surrounded by a sixteen-foot solid stone wall.

LEW MEYER   A monster of a wall. It was a yard wide at the base, maybe two feet at the top.

JIM THOMPSON   We nicknamed the camp Rockpile.

SPEED ADKINS   I had never met Thompson before Rockpile, although I'd heard his name. I knew he had been imprisoned in the South and was the longest-held among us. Most civilians felt as I did, that Jim had been through a hell of a lot and was a little shaky.

LARRY STARK   Jim and one enlisted Marine, Frank Cius, now were the only military people in our compound.

JIM THOMPSON   Of the twelve civilians, three were foreign nationals, two Filipinos working for Voice of America and a Canadian. Among the nine other civilians, six were employed by Pacific Architects and Engineers. Construction workers and mechanics primarily. We got along, but only with effort. We had group meetings where we concluded everybody had to try to get along. We couldn't act as individuals. We had to think about the group's welfare. It was real hard to instill such a feeling in these people. With military only we would have had a disciplined group, an organized group. These people resisted any form of discipline or leadership. The only time they'd be willing to listen was when the chips were down, when things got a little tough.

SPEED ADKINS   Jim had it in his head he was supposed to take charge. Most of the civilians resented that, including me. I thought it ridiculous. "Jim," I said, "you have no authority here. These are civilians. If you were in a military prison, yeah, you'd be able to give orders. But not here."

LEW MEYER   Speed Adkins contributed a lot to that attitude among the civilians. He was a retired major. Ex-artillery. Army regulars like Speed, of course, never really retire, so Speed could have spoken as the senior responsible officer. But he wouldn't step forward. When we were first captured, there were other officers like that. One in particular could have been a leader but he was just the opposite. Yet here was Jim, a guy who almost died and came back to life, someone who wanted to speak for his men, only to find they didn't want him. It was not like Jim wanted them to fall out every morning for inspection. There were no privileges to go with command here, only responsibility.

LARRY STARK   Jim was ready to lead—to advise if asked, to take command if we would allow him. But because Jim was so rigid regarding what information we should give and to what extent we could cooperate, some didn't want to go along. I respected Jim for his attitude and demeanor and military bearing. Throughout confinement he maintained his decorum and presence as an officer. Everyone, even those not particularly fond of Jim, agreed with that. He was consistent and persistent. He taught us all to play bridge, a big contribution to our sanity. And though very serious most of the time, he had a good sense of humor. He could even produce a genuine horse laugh once in a while. But we had an election and decided I would represent the civilians; Jim would represent the military. Jim was uneasy with that but went along and took his responsibility very seriously. He did his absolute best to convince the camp commander to improve our conditions. I respected Jim, and not because he was the longest-held or because he had been tortured. This was a guy who consistently rose above all that. He tried to take as much control as this motley group of bastard civilians would let him. And we had a few fights. But the guy's judgment was good in almost all cases. If there was a negative it was that Jim made snap decisions. I'm the other way around. The whole thing would be resolved before I decided to do something.

Lew Meyer was the only civilian who said, "Jim is in charge." Lew was a shining example of what we all should have been. Outstanding in every way.

LEW MEYER   The others said Larry would speak for them. I only recognized Jim as in charge. They could take a vote. So what. They could vote what time they thought the guards were going to open the doors the next day but that wasn't going to get the doors opened.

LARRY STARK   The division of leadership, with me speaking for all the civilians except Lew, didn't make Jim happy. There were some words over it. He said he was the leader and was going to do whatever was within the realm of reason to lead. But you can only lead if you have followers.

SPEED ADKINS   It was after the vote that Jim started giving Frank Cius, the only other serviceman there, a hard time. Frank had been in a Marine helicopter, a rescue unit, when shot down. Everyone else in his crew died.

LARRY STARK   Frank said one guy died in his arms.

SPEED ADKINS   The kid had spent a year in the city jail in Hanoi with murderers and everything else. That's why he was a little rocky. Jim got so serious with Frank I was afraid the kid was going to do something to him,

or that Jim would drive the kid over the brink. He kept ordering him
around. Jumping all over him. It was getting to Frank. I caught him loosening the bars of his door. He looked like he was going off his rocker.

LARRY STARK   The situation was very difficult. Jim cut Frank all the
slack he could. That was the best way. Any other way would have
destroyed the harmony of the camp.

Indoctrination at Rockpile took the form of newspapers and magazines which
were constantly available. Reading material included daily transcripts of
Radio Hanoi, books on Russia and China, Russian and Chinese magazines,
a newspaper from Cuba and party line material from such authors as Marx,
Lenin and Mao as well as Ho Chi Minh.

—from Army Intelligence debriefing report

SPEED ADKINS   There were hills behind our prison and on one side. We
were on a main bombing route into Hanoi. We'd hear the B-52s coming
in and antiaircraft guns responding. There was a lot of action.

LEW MEYER   Jim and I said, "Maybe we'll be bombed and the wall will
get knocked down." If so, we planned to take advantage.

JIM THOMPSON   Soon after we got to Rockpile, Lew and I realized
security was lax and the possibility of escape pretty good.

LEW MEYER   We were in there two months when they let us out of our
building to start exercising. We began working on a volleyball court. We
raked and moved rocks. We also began making a circular path walking
around the building.

JIM THOMPSON   The building itself was secure but the guards were not
alert. Five or six were assigned to our compound. A hundred yards away
was the provincial prison holding Vietnamese criminals and civil offend-
ers.

LEW MEYER   After a while I approached Jim and said, "I can get over that
wall."

"Okay," he said. "We'll get together." That was the moment we started
making our plans.

30 ■ ESCAPE

JIM THOMPSON   Lew and I kept our plans in complete secrecy. It was not a matter of distrusting anyone, just a good security precaution. The fewer people who knew, the fewer possibilities of it being compromised.

LEW MEYER   Firemen are professionals at forcible entry with minimal damage. I showed Jim how we could take off the big doors inside our cellblock and, by turning them over, have a ladder.

JIM THOMPSON   They were regular wooden doors between our bunkrooms and the dining area, but they had Z-shaped pleats as reinforcements that made excellent rungs. They could be lifted off their hinges without removing a bolt.

LEW MEYER   By placing the doors on tables or on stools, it would be a piece of cake to get over the wall.

JIM THOMPSON   I wanted Lew to go with me because he's heart and soul a soldier. He respected my authority, unquestionably so. He supported me in all the work I was trying to do to get these people organized and get something going. Lew was my staunch ally and exerted considerable influence over the others.

LEW MEYER   We talked about escape daily in our courtyard walks.

JIM THOMPSON   The guards let us out for exercise once in the morning and once in the afternoon, and frequently they left us alone in the compound, which shows how lax they were.

LEW MEYER   As we passed each other we'd mention a couple of things about the plan and keep walking. We made it a point to keep apart but we began making a list of what we needed. At the top were straps for our sandals and strap tools. We found some nails in the courtyard. We used them to make some tools, including fishhooks. We started stealing old socks from guys, unraveling them, and making rope. We took old clothing, layered it, and made a backpack.

JIM THOMPSON   We feigned illness to acquire medicines—Mercurochrome, aspirin, sulfa, some fungus medicine and eye medicine. Occasionally when someone was sick they brought soup in a small pot. We managed to hold on to one of these. They weren't checking us very closely. I swiped a box of matches on my birthday, July 8th. They had a custom of giving us a little birthday party. The guards called the prisoner out, the camp commander came down with goodies, like cookies or fruit or a pack of Vietnamese cigarettes. The whole thing took five or ten minutes. We'd bring the goodies back and divide them among the others. At my little ceremony the camp commander pushed a package of cigarettes and wooden safety matches across to me. While he was talking with the guards I slipped the matches into my pocket.

We had a piece of metal brought back from outside and honed it down on the cement floor into a homemade knife. Alex Henderson was a mechanic, so they called him out to help overhaul the camp motorcycle. I saw them working on it one day on the way to interrogation. There was an odd conglomeration of tools, including a machete. When the interrogator wasn't looking I indicated to Henderson that I wanted it. He hid it under some leaves. When they put the tools away it wasn't missed. The following day he hid the machete under his clothes and brought it into the compound. Later Lew and I stuck it in the bamboo of the rafters. That was the most valuable piece of equipment we collected.

LEW MEYER   Alex also gave us some idea of the terrain outside. Otherwise we didn't know what we would find. We'd been brought in at night. I began using Bob Olsen as a human weight for exercising. He stood on my hands and I'd use him to do presses. One day I lifted him up on my shoulders near the water tower and asked him to look over the wall and tell me what was there. He panicked and said it was against camp regulations.

Jim approached Candido "Pop" Badu, one of the Filipinos, to ask if he wanted to escape with us. I knew and approved of this contact. Pop said he couldn't possibly go, with his fellow countryman Art Balagot in poor health. Pop thought Art might die of loneliness. Then Jim approached Olsen, because he could speak Vietnamese. Jim hadn't said anything about that beforehand, but he was calling the shots. Olsen elected not to go. The prospect scared the hell out of him.

We planned to go September 12, 1971, exactly ninety days before my wife Gail's birthday. We gave ourselves that long to get to a friendly phone and call her. We also decided instead of heading toward the coast, a logical direction, we'd go inland through the mountains to Laos.

JIM THOMPSON   The only other choice was to head east, try to steal a boat, and get to friendly shipping. I elected Laos. The border couldn't possibly be guarded too closely. I was sure we could slip through. And we knew about where we were. If we went southwest we would hit Route 7, a large road I was sure to recognize, and using it reach Long Chang, the South Vietnamese Special Forces base in Laos, about one hundred miles away.

LEW MEYER   We figured they'd search in the other direction. We compared it to scaling a steep cliff. They'd expect us to take the stairs. Instead we would tackle the cliff face. That's the only way, Jim said. "Sweat saves blood." The longer we could hold up after our escape, the better our chances. In two to three weeks, if they didn't detect us, the search would probably be called off.

JIM THOMPSON   I told Lew, very frankly, that our chances were not good. I felt he should understand this. We had no accurate map, just a pen-and-ink sketch. No compass. Only a machete for survival. And we were in the center of North Vietnam. But we agreed a slim chance was better than none. I also told Lew we were letting ourselves in for severe punishment if recaptured. There was a good possibility we'd be killed. He accepted this. Lew was with me one hundred percent, knowing it could mean pure misery or death.

LEW MEYER   If caught, we expected to be shot. But there was no fear. It wasn't reckless. I was certain it was going to work. A few days before the 12th we started collecting bread. It was the only food we could carry. That and a little bag of salt.

LARRY STARK   Bunking next to Lew I noticed he was making a pack out of his clothes and was saving bread, as though getting ready to head over the wall. So I asked him about it. He said I was right and he'd appreciate it if I helped put provisions aside. Giving up part of my bread ration wasn't hard, the stuff was so bad. Lew and I would share one loaf, put the other into the kitty.

LEW MEYER   I've always been a good judge of character and thought awhile before I approached anybody to ask about giving up their rations. I approached Speed Adkins because here was one guy not fit enough to escape. But when I asked him to save some bread he immediately jumped on me. "No," he said. "And you better not be planning an escape 'cause it will foul me up."

SPEED ADKINS   I'd been working on my own plan. At the front of the prison yard the ground had a depression. I figured that one day, as the others went back inside, I could lay down in that depression and not be seen. Our guards didn't count heads. There was a water tank at the end of the building, which they filled through a manhole on top. After hiding in the depression until the guards left, I could climb into the tank and stay until dark. When the guard entered the compound next morning, I would slip out the open gate. I was getting ready to pull it off when Lew asked me to save them food.

LEW MEYER   I told Speed, "You know the rules. If there's going to be an escape you have to clear it with the senior responsible officer. You have to clear it with Jim." Well, Speed wouldn't even play cards with Jim. He wouldn't do anything with any group Jim was in.

SPEED ADKINS   I stayed away from people I disliked. Still, I went to Jim and said, "I hear you guys are planning an escape."

LEW MEYER   For the first time since we entered the camp the two of them walked around the courtyard together so they could talk. I'm sure the sight startled the other guys.

JIM THOMPSON   I told Adkins no, he couldn't go with us. His physical condition was poor and he wanted to go a different direction, toward the coast. He argued that once we left, security would be tightened and he'd miss his chance. He insisted on going. We finally agreed I'd take him over the wall. But once away from the prison, we'd go our separate ways.

LEW MEYER   Jim said he had no choice. "We'd better get somebody here as a witness to the agreement," I said. So we got Stark.

LARRY STARK   Thompson told Speed he was not in good enough shape, that they had a better chance without him. So outside the wall they'd go different directions.

LEW MEYER   Jim didn't have anything against Speed, except he was close to sixty and wheezed from respiratory problems.

LARRY STARK   If asked, I wouldn't have included Speed. It not only hurt their chances but our ability to cover for them. If too many left, the guards would know in a minute. Lew and Jim had both been exercising. They were in good shape. Both had military backgrounds. They had a good shot at escape. My job was to give them all the support I could. I wasn't privy to their plans beyond the wall. The less I knew the less I could tell if tortured. The possibility of being tortured or mistreated, well, that was part of the deal. I had no problem with it. Those of us who knew they were going just hoped for the best. For one thing, none of us had communicated yet with home. Some of us questioned whether anybody knew we were alive. Jim and Lew could tell them we were.

LEW MEYER   We wanted rain to cover our movement but hoped to get out before the monsoons began. The day before we were to go, Jim and I retrieved the machete. We were set. Then on the morning of the 12th [September 12, 1971] they never opened our compound door. For two weeks straight it was torrential rains and heavy flooding. We watched snakes driven from the jungle slither up the wall. Rats came into our building and bunked with us. Water even reached our cell before it receded. The bread we had stockpiled started getting mold. When we began switching it for fresher bread, some guys complained, so we stopped. We figured the less that others were involved, the easier it would go down for them when we were gone.

Finally, on the 1st of October, the guard unlocked the cellblock. I watched him walk away, following his every step back toward the guard shack. Then I ran into the bunkroom. Russ Page and Tom Rushton watched as I jumped up on the bunk. Nobody had ever stepped on a bed before. I turned my pillow into a backpack, threw it over my shoulder, and off I went. They were stunned.

LARRY STARK   This was about two in the afternoon. Lew and Frank Cius, the Marine corporal, took the doors separating the bunkroom from the dining area off their hinges and ran them out of the building toward the back wall.

LEW MEYER   Someone already had a table near the wall and a chair on top of the table. Jim had coordinated everything. The guards couldn't see any of this from their shack.

JIM THOMPSON   Larry posted himself out front to watch the gate so we were safe inside. We knew a guard was outside the wall somewhere making his rounds, but we had no way to time his movement.

LEW MEYER   For all we knew there could have been barracks on the other side. Once on top, though, I saw only jungle below. I was feeling confident. Then a strap on Jim's sandal broke as he climbed up the door. Cius, of all people, took off his sandal and put it on Jim's foot.

LARRY STARK   It was an amazing sight. Frank didn't like Jim, yet he was the first to grab a door and, when Thompson lost his sandal, to help him make good his escape.

LEW MEYER   Our concern now was what kind of landing we would have, particularly Speed. I'd taken judo, so I could fall and roll. Still, even I hesitated, trying to find a clearing from that height before I jumped. I was up there longer than I wanted to be, but there was no turning back. Below us were rocks and brush. I looked back into the compound at Tom Rushton. He gave a thumbs-up, saluted, and I went over. Speed hung on, then dropped.

SPEED ADKINS   All around was broken rock holding back the jungle for the narrow path the guard used. We dropped fourteen or fifteen feet but were lucky.

LEW MEYER   We landed in shrubs. If we ever touched the ground I don't remember. We found ourselves walking on top of vines over thick jungle underbrush. The nearest guard tower wasn't manned. No shots were fired. No sirens sounded. We just kept going. The escape had gone like clockwork.

————

LARRY STARK   While I occupied the guards, the others brought everything back inside, rehung the doors, and continued on as before. Some guys were in shock. One was bug-eyed.

"Man, what's goin' on?" he said. "What do we do now?"

"Just cool it," I said. "Cool it. They're gone."

"But what the hell is going on?"

"Meyer and Jim and Adkins are trying to make it."

"Well, what do we do when the guards find out?"

And the inevitable question: "Should we tell the guards?"

"No, we shouldn't tell the guards," I said.

"But when they find out they're going to beat the hell out of us!"

"Let's just see how long we can cover for 'em. See what happens. And when the first guard asks we say we didn't know anything about it. The first thing we knew they were headed over the wall." Some of us thought they wouldn't be gone the night without being detected.

————

JIM THOMPSON   Foliage was so thick it took three or four hours to go the first hundred yards. It was impenetrable. We clawed over and through the brush. The machete would have made too much noise. Every damned bush, every leaf it seemed, had thorns. Our hands and feet got scratched bad.

LEW MEYER   Thorns cut into our clothes and flesh. There was no trail, no path. Just vines and limbs. We went on this way, walking on top of brush, switching leads, for several hours.

JIM THOMPSON   Finally beyond the jungle was a large, open, swampy area. It was there, having gotten through the thickest stuff together, that we separated. Lew and I headed west, Adkins toward the coast.

LEW MEYER   Speed wanted to get to a rail line, but he was already complaining about an ankle he hurt on the drop to the rocks.

————

LARRY STARK   The guards had gotten so slack we didn't have a daily roll call. That afternoon we spread out through our building in an effort to confuse the guards as to our number. Covering for three missing guys out of fourteen wasn't easy. Adkins and Meyers had both slept next to me and taken one mosquito net with them. We spread the remaining net to its fullest to cover two spots. Lew had made a dummy of some clothes. We put it down on his mat. For Adkins we gathered a bunch of clothes to look like someone was there.

We were praying for them, as the weather turned atrocious.

JIM THOMPSON   Just after dark we ran again into thick stuff. My original plan was to avoid trails and head straight across country, but the foliage was so thick our plans needed to change. We had to move faster to put greater distance between us and the prison.

LEW MEYER   We used a few trails but mostly it was thick, mountainous jungle. We entered a farmer's shed at one point to keep out of the rain.

JIM THOMPSON   I decided we should wait until morning to continue. We were wearing ourselves out, wasting strength and making little progress. We had passed a trail on the other side of the ridge. I wasn't too sure where it went, but by morning we decided to try it. As we came up to the crest of the hill and looked down, we found ourselves staring into the main camp—only a few hundred yards from our prison compound.

LEW MEYER   We had circled around. Gone a long way and ended up not far from where we started.

JIM THOMPSON   It had taken all afternoon, beating through the foliage, to reach a point only a fifteen-minute walk on the trail. With daylight upon us, we holed up in a small cave just off the trail, figuring the best thing we could do was wait until dark, then try to get around camp and start off in a westerly direction.

SPEED ADKINS   I tried two or three ways to get to a road but kept bogging down in the jungle. The only way to a road was back through camp. I had to go through in daytime because they put dogs there at night. That afternoon I moved down the hill and up to the compound. I could see soldiers from the camp school outside on break. I sat there deciding what to do. All at once a bell rang and they went inside. I said, "If I'm ever going to get through, I've got to do it now."

I walked past all the buildings, then houses used by the camp's permanent staff and their families. I could see the compound's main gate open and trucks moving through it with supplies. On the other side, the road went downhill. If I could get through that gate I could hide out until evening and work my way down the road. I was loping past the last building when the door opened. The camp commander stood there, mouth wide open. I stopped. I knew I couldn't get far enough away now, and would get killed trying.

"What are you doing here?" he asked.

"Trying to get the hell away!"

He motioned for me to come inside. He made some tea, gave me a cigarette, and went out.

LARRY STARK   Guards came and said the camp commander was coming so get cleaned up. They said he's bringing something special. The guys were nervous. What the hell were they going to do to us? What followed actually was the funniest thing I ever saw. The interpreter came down first, opened the door to our building, and found us all standing side by side. He had a strange expression on his face like "Gee, it doesn't look like everybody's here." He looked some more.

"Where's Thompson?"

"Anybody know where Jim is?" we asked ourselves.

"Anybody see Jim?" It was comical.

"Maybe he's in the shower room there."

"No, not in here."

Then he counts heads.

"Where's Meyer?" he asked.

"Anybody see Lew?"

This guy takes off and literally runs right out of his blue sandals. Right out of them. The camp commander at this moment is coming through the gate. Told that Thompson and Meyer are missing, he immediately turns and races toward the military base. In a few moments the interpreter is back, and he's pissed.

"Where did they go?"

We're playing dumb as hell.

"We just found them gone," we said. "They probably went over the wall."

He counts heads again.

"One, two, three . . . eleven. Who is missing? Where's Adkins?"

Bang. Out the door again.

SPEED ADKINS   The camp commander found three gone. He only had one. That's when all the turmoil started. They sent trucks down the highway. Soldiers started beating the bushes. By that time they had me in a room off the guard shack in leg irons and handcuffs.

LARRY STARK   We knew that whole scene had embarrassed the camp commander. Everybody worried now what he would do.

JIM THOMPSON   I had left a note with the men telling them that as soon as the escape was detected there would be an investigation and likely some reprisals. I told them to give any information asked for, and to deny any prior knowledge of the escape or of providing assistance.

LARRY STARK   I was appointed spokesman. No one, I said, should make up any stories. "If you don't know anything, say you don't know anything. What can be a better story than that?"

The rest of us were on our own. When asked about the escape, I said, "Yeah, I knew they were gone. I think it's great." That blew their minds.

"Oh no," they said. "Very bad."

"It's not bad," I said. "You're in the military. You know you're supposed to try to escape. They're doing what military men are obliged to do. Hell, they didn't kill anybody! They just left!"

The feeling among prisoners was mixed. Most felt like me that it was fantastic. Some were miffed that they weren't told. Some remarked about being left behind. But it was understood only a certain number could leave or the escape would have been immediately discovered.

LEW MEYER   We heard sirens. Then we saw troops moving out of the compound in our direction. Word spread quickly. Later, when I heard Speed had walked back into the compound in broad daylight, I wasn't surprised. I didn't give him much credit.

JIM THOMPSON   We could see the search parties with dogs. Fortunately it was raining.

LEW MEYER   We heard them set up generators like a command post in the field. When the dogs came sniffing around, Jim and I were lying together in the small cave. They got so close we found ourselves staring at a soldier's fist holding a leash. The dog was two feet from us with Jim and I frozen on a little ledge of rock. As we had hoped, the rain protected us. We looked at each other and the party continued on.

LARRY STARK   Speed looked like he had been through a meat grinder with all these cuts on his legs. We never thought we'd see Jim and Lew again. They had either escaped or taken a risk that would kill them.

———

JIM THOMPSON   On the second night we moved out.

LEW MEYER   With most of the soldiers now behind us or to our right, moving through camp seemed the safest direction. We infiltrated the larger prison compound.

JIM THOMPSON   The back of the main prison came up to the trees. We passed a couple of buildings and could see Vietnamese prisoners inside. We didn't know whether they were North Vietnamese civilians or South Vietnamese prisoners of war. Moving off to one side, we went a good distance but were only about halfway through the camp before we stopped to study movements. There seemed to be twenty-five to thirty buildings. Up ahead we saw more guards with dogs and knew we'd never make it through the camp. We decided to go back the way we came and try a different route. We had no intelligence on the area, no idea what we were going to run into in any direction. It was trial and error. And now they knew we were out there somewhere.

LEW MEYER   Our plan to avoid all people changed. Hiding beside the prison compound, Jim decided to make contact.

JIM THOMPSON   There might be South Vietnamese inside. I decided to see if I could spring them to help guide us out of there. It was a valid chance that the prisoners would be friendly and would want to escape. I saw a man alone in the latrine at the end of the building. Jungle brush went right up to the barred window. I got his attention. We spoke. He was extremely friendly. Stuck his hand between the bars and shook mine. Wished us luck. I indicated we could help him out of there. Only one guard was on duty. We could kill him and get the prison open and let these people out. He shook his head no. He wouldn't go with us. But he wished us luck.

We got on our way again. Now Lew and I really started to move out, this time back up the trail we came down, a saddle between two hills. We were halfway up this trail when all hell broke loose. Guards, dogs, cadre. Everyone came out.

LEW MEYER   We were running up the hill when we came under small-arms fire. We saw the slugs hitting the dirt ahead of us.

JIM THOMPSON   A couple bursts of automatic fire and we knew escape now was impossible. There were twenty of them within fifty yards of us. All of them armed. We had nothing. I had told Lew that if recaptured, any plans we had made would be worthless so don't hold back during interrogation. The only thing we didn't want to tell them was where we got our equipment, how we came up with the machete and the knife.

LEW MEYER   I threw the machete off the trail.

JIM THOMPSON   We pitched the knife and all our equipment into the brush. You could throw something six feet into that foliage and never find it. The only things we still had as they approached were extra clothes and bread.

LEW MEYER   Jim and I shook hands and agreed we gave it a good try. The shooting continued for a time after. Soldiers firing on the run. Finally they saw we had stopped. They surrounded us. An officer came up with pistol in hand. He pushed the soldiers back and said, "Come with me."

JIM THOMPSON   I will say this much for the Vietnamese: they picked a damn good place to build a prison. There was one access road. The only other way out was with a bulldozer or an army wielding machetes.

They separated Lew and me, brought us back to the main prison and put us in wristlocks, nasty little devices shaped like a figure eight that splits down the middle. They clanked them tight.

LEW MEYER   A little later I heard shots and knew what had happened. In a while they brought in a bowl of rice. I let it sit. The guard came back in later and said, "Why don't you eat?"

"Why should I eat and get shot like Thompson?"

No, he said, that was a signal calling the guards back in.

I thought: I've died and now somehow survived. Any additional day I live from this point on would be icing on the cake. I took my food and ate it.

JIM THOMPSON   What impressed me about our escape attempt was that with a little boldness we found we could get away with most anything. We were inside the compound for over an hour without being detected. Observing the guards and the dogs. Looking for a pattern in their movements, trying to find a way to get through. It seemed unbelievable. And this after they knew we were loose. Had I not contacted that prisoner, it's possible we'd have gotten away. Who knows. Afterwards, of course, they questioned us.

"What were you doing? Why did you do it? Which way were you going?"

"I'm not going to tell you."

They tried some pressure but never tortured us, never beat us, never punished us other than keeping us in wristlocks for three nights. Then they put us back with the others. The last time I had escaped, in South Vietnam, I caught hell. This time, nothing. I have no explanation other than this one was a relatively loose-security prison, and times were changing.

LEW MEYER   Jim and I became even closer. Real brothers. In a fire department you train and train so that in an actual emergency you do what you've been trained to do. But until there is an emergency you don't know how the man next to you will respond. There was no question now that Jim and I could rely on each other. To be associated with someone like that—with no fear between us as the bullets hit all around us, shaking hands and knowing we gave it our best shot—well [*voice cracking*], that's someone who's a brother. Any actions Jim Thompson has taken since that day will never change my opinion of him, or my respect for him.

31 ■ PEACE TALKS

J IM THOMPSON   Our escape embarrassed them all, from camp
commander right down the line. That three of us could escape and not
be detected for twenty hours caused some very severe "criticism sessions." [*Laughing*]

LEW MEYER   The guards took more hell than we did. All of them were
replaced.

JIM THOMPSON   Security got tighter for all of us. The policy in camp
was mass punishment. We cost the whole group outside time.

LARRY STARK   We spent the next year inside that building.

SPEED ADKINS   Some guys were pissed.

LARRY STARK   I wasn't angry. And I was proud of the guys, too, the way
they handled the situation. Especially being confined to the building. I
didn't recall anyone saying, "This is because of you guys." Jim's attitude
was always professional. "As a soldier," he said, "escape is something I am
proud to do. As long as I didn't kill anybody. The Geneva Convention
wouldn't support that."

JIM THOMPSON   For three months the guards went out of their way to
make our lives miserable. They held two to three inspections a day. Four
or five times a day they had us line up to count noses. The quality of food
petered off too. Medical attention dropped drastically. Before the escape,
if we asked for something they tried to get it. Now they refused simple
requests for medicine or care.

LARRY STARK   It got bad. All that harassment. Finally we had had
enough. In December 1971 we went on a hunger strike. We knew if we

didn't eat, they'd have problems. They didn't want us to die. During the strike, Thompson got an audience with the camp commander. He told him our complaints, and conditions did improve. But outside exercise time wasn't reinstated for eleven more months.

Almost seven years after Jim Thompson's disappearance, three years after the Army received an eyewitness report that Thompson had survived the plane crash and at least four years of captivity, Army officials shared that information with Alyce.

9 December 1971

Dear Mrs. Thompson:

After a complete review of all prisoner and missing files, both in Vietnam and in our Washington office, additional information concerning Floyd has been found which parallels information previously provided to you in a tape recording. A North Vietnamese doctor captured by our forces in July 1968, who was undergoing routine questioning, stated that he gave medical treatment to an American prisoner of the Viet Cong. The American identified himself as a Captain Thompson. . . .

The doctor further advised that the prisoner had remained in his care for two weeks until he was in good health, at which time he was transferred to an unknown destination. The physical description of the prisoner, as furnished by the doctor, reasonably fitted that of Floyd. Records of all American prisoners and missing personnel were closely screened to determine the individual who most nearly fitted the description. After careful examination of the record it was determined the American prisoner was most probably Major Thompson. . . . It tends to confirm Floyd was in the hands of the enemy at that time. I regret the delay in providing you this additional information.

Sincerely,
Verne L. Bowers
Major General, USA
The Adjutant General

ALYCE   By late 1971, things turned sour between me and Harold. I believed he loved me and loved Ruthie. I didn't know if he loved the other children.

PAM   Mama wanted him to quit bugging me.

ALYCE   No matter what that kid did it was wrong. I accused Harold of bringing me into the home just to raise his kids. Now that they were gone, things were going downhill. I said it was time he paid more attention to Pam, time she had a little importance in life.

LAURA   I liked to walk by myself along the stone walls near our house. Many times on these walks I thought about my dad. Pam had described what he was like. I began to understand what she was talking about, that the man I grew up thinking was my father really wasn't.

JIM JR.   I carried the Thompson name but didn't understand why. One time a friend wanted to call me after school. I told him to look up the number in the book. He tried all the Thompsons. It never clicked with me that my home phone number was under another name. I didn't know anything about my real father.

LAURA   I'd ask my mother, "Where is he?" and "What happened?"

"He was in the war," she said once, "and was bitten by a rattlesnake."

"Where's the grave? Let's go see it."

I wouldn't let up sometimes.

"Why won't you talk about him?"

She always broke off such conversations. Avoided the issue.

"Well, he's dead," she'd say, "and now Harold's your father."

ALYCE   Yeah, I told them he was dead. Because I believed it. I mean, after almost eight years and seeing how the war built up over there, I couldn't see how any human could live through that. I talked to Nick Rowe, an Army captain who had escaped in 1968. I went to several lectures he gave. I read his book, *Five Years to Freedom*. I couldn't see how anybody could live eight years under those conditions. But by early 1972 I was also getting anxious. Things were heating up at the peace conference. I scheduled a visit to Fort Devens and prepared a list of points I was going to bring up.

On 25 February 1972, Mrs. Alyce Thompson visited the chief of the prisoner-of-war/missing-in-action branch to review Major Thompson's file and discuss her personal problems. She said she would like to have "the whole damn thing settled soon." She said she deeply feels her husband is dead and has doubts he ever survived.

Mrs. Thompson said she has a $40,000 home with a swimming pool, a large savings account, everything paid for and she feels financially independent. She has not spoken to her parents-in-law since late '64. She admits to dating whenever she can and looks at herself as being a person rapidly aging, gaining weight and becoming more bitter about life. She said if her husband's status is not determined soon she might not be able to remarry and start a new life.

The reprocessing plan for the POWs was discussed. Mrs. Thompson was asked not to tell her husband "to go to Hell" on the first telephone call after his release. She agreed, but definitely felt she could no longer live as his wife. Mrs. Thompson demanded that no contact be made to her by someone in uniform and that no one expose her case.

—from family assistance officer case file

ALYCE   I just wanted to get things over with, one way or the other. The young part of my life was slipping away. Jim's was too, I know, sitting in that hellhole. But I was aging and gaining weight and if he was declared dead what the hell kind of life was I going to have, an older woman with four kids?

On March 26, 1972, the San Diego *Union*, in its lead editorial, took note of the eighth anniversary of Jim Thompson's imprisonment by the North Vietnamese communists and called it "a blot upon the conscience of the entire civilized world." No American, it said, has "heard from or about him since 1964."

"International rules of conduct, codified in the Geneva Convention on proper treatment of prisoners of war, require that Captain Thompson be accorded many rights, including decent treatment, periodic verification of his condition by neutral observers, and mail and packages at regular intervals. He is also entitled to be sent to the United States if he is either wounded or ill. He has been accorded none of these rights."

The editorial writer surmised that Thompson "and his unhappy family are living in a dark half-world of pain and uncertainty reminiscent of the inhumanity of the Spanish Inquisition."

The newspaper noted that Thompson's plight "is only characteristic of the scar upon our national conscience" resulting from the treatment of U.S. service members missing or held without benefit of humane treatment in Vietnam.

President Richard Nixon established the next seven days as a "National Week of Concern for Prisoners of War and Men Missing in Action." He designated March 26 as a national day of prayer "for the lives and safety of these men."

"The stubbornness of the Communists" at the peace talks in Paris, said the *Union*, "has largely been a product of their appraisal of the American temper. They believe we are weak, divided and irresolute. On this basis, an impressive weeklong expression of American support for the government's policy of insisting upon residual American troops in Vietnam as long as Americans are held prisoner may convince the Communists that there is not going to be any cheap way out of the conflict for them, even at this 11th hour."

LARRY STARK There were great difficulties having fourteen of us cooped up for a year. Thompson showed leadership to help us overcome the situation. He read almost everything that came into camp and tried to guide us as to the real meaning behind the propaganda. Jim read the material only for the five to ten percent that was factual.

JIM THOMPSON Propaganda lectures used antiwar statements attributed to prominent Americans. "This is what the real American people think," they said. "This is what loyal ones feel. You should be loyal to the American people, not to traitors in government."

They showed us an article written by a POW wife in *Life* magazine. Passed it around to everyone in Rockpile. Most disturbing were things she said about goings-on in the prison camps, telling other wives to expect problems with their husbands when they came back. Marital problems. Homosexuality in the prisons. Psychological problems from long confinement. Things that would unnerve families.

One photo they showed us was of Dr. Spock at a rally in Washington. There were others, of Vietnam Veterans Against the War. Looking at the type of people protesting only reinforced our conviction this was a radical element, not the American majority. But the whole antiwar effort was disheartening. By far the most discouraging statements were attributed to the Democratic Party platform during the '72 election. We had received a typewritten sheet of paper—without caption, without signature or authentication—entitled "Proposed Plank of the Democratic Party Platform." It made us sick. Guaranteed amnesty for draft-dodgers. Total pullout from Southeast Asia within ninety days. Something like that could cause someone to crumple up in disgust.

LARRY STARK Jim had a fantastic memory and his analyses proved to be amazingly accurate. He tried to show us how the reading material was designed to demoralize us. He was always thinking of ways to boost morale. He never seemed to be down and was ready to lend support when someone else was feeling low.

JIM THOMPSON Every prisoner I talked with had demanded writing privileges guaranteed by the Geneva Convention. Prisoners have the right to correspond with families. This was never granted to us. We read a report from the Vietnamese News Agency that American pilots somewhere were receiving mail and packages. We demanded that we be permitted to write home. The standard answer was "Conditions are not right" or "It depends on individuals."

I wrote a letter of protest via the camp commander in July '72, demanding that the discrimination against us be stopped and we be granted writing privileges. I addressed it to their officer in charge of prisoners of war. I got no reply. For two months we constantly hit up the interpreter with "Why don't we get an answer?"

"The matter is under consideration."

In September we sent a follow-up letter, worded even stronger. We threatened a prisoner demonstration. They said if we did anything like that it would go badly for us.

SPEED ADKINS   In October 1972, when U.S. and Vietnamese negotiators were talking in Paris, we were allowed out in the courtyard.

JIM THOMPSON   That's when we heard about the peace agreements. Negotiations were almost complete. They were to be signed at the end of the month. Our interpreter fed us information from Voice of America Radio. He never let us hear the broadcasts, so we couldn't be sure what was going on. But this interpreter seemed genuinely interested in my opinion on the progress of the negotiations. It was as though he had been exposed to so much propaganda that U.S. information must be propaganda too.

One morning he called me out. He had heard on Voice of America a Kissinger* announcement that only minor points remained to be worked out to complete the agreement. Kissinger felt it could be done in one more meeting. The interpreter wanted to know if I thought this was true. He was anxious himself for the war to be over. On the 13th of October, 1972, they started putting out some pretty good chow to build us up. I remember the date. It happened to be a Friday and they brought us a big treat, a sweet pudding.

LARRY STARK   We got more bananas and more meat than we ever had before, more than in the whole previous year. Guards became friendlier. The agreements were supposed to be signed on the 20th.

Suddenly things changed. The agreement was bogged down on a few points. Food returned to normal.

JIM THOMPSON   For weeks after that, all we got was communist propaganda on why the agreements weren't signed. But statements by President Nixon only enhanced his stature with me. The United States, he said, would not be stampeded into signing. A month before U.S. elections, the North Vietnamese were making a last-ditch effort to gain concessions.

Dissension arose in our group. One guy who didn't respect Nixon felt he would make concessions to get elected. I maintained the election would have absolutely no bearing on whether the agreements were signed. I

* Henry A. Kissinger, Nixon's top foreign policy adviser.

believed President Nixon was very courageous and wouldn't sell the country short for a few votes. So when peace did not come before the election I was cheered, not crushed. It reinforced my confidence in my president. I felt good that he insisted on an honorable solution. But in our compound, preelection arguments raged.

LEW MEYER McGovern versus Nixon became a heated debate. The week of October 11 is National Fire Prevention Week, so I put one sign up announcing that. And a second sign that said, "Vote for Nixon." Larry claimed that violated the Hatch Act, which barred federal employees from becoming involved in national politics. Gary Daves and some others said, "Hey, you can't do that!" Gary was a very nice person but a socialist and anti–Nixon administration. The sign stayed up.

JIM THOMPSON Election eve we held a straw vote. Nixon won eight to three with three foreign nationals abstaining. The minority felt McGovern would win because of the platform against the war. Next day the interpreter came in and announced Nixon had won. My first question was "By what majority?" He carried forty-nine states.

A cheer went up. I about blasted the roof off. I felt a tremendous weight lift off my shoulders. It justified our belief in the American people. For the first time, American voters had made a clear choice, for President Nixon's peace with honor and against McGovern's peace at any cost. It was a wonderful day, believe me. We felt so lighthearted and happy. The greatest morale boost we'd had since we'd been there. This effectively torpedoed all the propaganda all these years.

Only sixty percent of eligible voters had turned out. Russ Page, a civilian, said, "I guess things can't be so bad in the States. Otherwise, a hell of a lot of more people would have voted."

That was right. Problems back home weren't anywhere near the magnitude our captors would have us believe, or voter turnout would have been much higher. The communists never realized what this did for our morale.

———

LAURA At one point, for some reason, I became convinced my mother knew he was alive. A gut feeling. She had been receiving Dad's wages all those years. It didn't make sense that the Army would keep paying her if they didn't have hope. But why didn't they check on her? Shouldn't the allotments have stopped if she was involved with another man? That's probably why they never got married, I thought, so she could continue to draw the checks.

Suddenly there was talk everywhere about POWs. One day Pam, me, and a girlfriend got out a Ouija board and went out to a field. This day we decided to ask it questions about our father.

PAM   That was too weird. We asked it my parents' anniversary date. Sure, I may have known it, but I'm not real good on dates. The board knew both the date and the year.

Then we asked, "Is he alive?"

It said, "Yes."

We asked if he was coming home.

It said, "Yes."

We freaked out.

————

JIM THOMPSON   The communist definition of democracy is a mockery. The whole concept is to prostitute the cause. I saw this again the weeks after the October agreements fell through. Communists put all the blame on Americans, insisting the North Vietnamese had goodwill and showed the proper attitude while the Americans were obdurate. They accused Americans of defaulting on our word. As tensions built, it was obvious something had to happen. The night of 18 December the massive bombing of Hanoi began.

Though sixty-five kilometers from Hanoi we could hear it—and see it. The sky to the north lit up. There was a steady rumbling and roar all night long. Most of us stayed up all night to watch. Honestly, it was the most beautiful sight I'd seen in all the time I'd been held captive. From time to time fighter-bombers flew over us, and rather close. Some bombs fell near enough to shake us up. One town under attack was only six kilometers away. Instead of ducking for cover, we hung out of the barred window to watch the action. The closer they got, the better we felt.

The entrance to our cell was a large, iron-barred double door. After the evening meal, just before dark, we'd drag our stools over there and wait for the show to start. There were surface-to-air missile sites nearby. We saw SAMs go up, watched them fall, and we cheered. We never saw them hit a plane. Yet the propaganda reports said thousands of planes had been shot down. On the newspaper's front page. "Today the count is four thousand eight hundred and ninety-six." Amusing. They even listed the number of bombs dropped, an impossible figure. There were antiaircraft locations nearby too, so we watched the ack-ack going up. We'd hear the planes, see the ack-ack, see the missiles go up. We tried to determine the planes' tactics. One would come in, draw fire. The rest would blow the hell out of the ack-ack site. And we'd cheer.

Our captors showed no reaction. The guards didn't turn hostile. The interpreter didn't try to condemn the United States. The rest of the camp's cadre said nothing. I got the impression these people were sick of the war and wanted it over. I felt, in their hearts and souls, they wanted their own government to knock it off.

————

LAURA   By late 1972 things got hush-hush in our house. My mother grew very concerned about us talking to anybody. She instructed us not to answer the phone but didn't tell us why. If anyone came up to us we were not to talk to them.

PAM   I hadn't said anything to Mama about Dad returning. But I heard things from friends and knew she was keeping something from us. She was worried and acting real strange.

LAURA   With all the talk about POWs, and with our house being so quiet, we put two and two together. I began to suspect she'd been lying to us all those years. It was an emotional time. I was twelve and so confused. Who was I going to talk to about it? Harold became very quiet. I think he loved us, though not in the same way he loved his own kids.

ALYCE   I was fixin' to leave Harold anyway when the kids got out of school that June [1973]. Mother never believed this but it's the damn truth.

LAURA   I overheard an argument between my mother and grandmother during one of her visits. Grandmother loved my dad. He could do no wrong.

"There shouldn't be any question in your mind," she was telling my mother. "You're crazy." Her point, I learned later, was that if my dad was alive, my mother should return to him.

ALYCE   Aunt Willa and Uncle Marty had come up Christmas of '72. Willa saw I was unhappy. "Come on down," she said. They could put me up in their nice little house in Honesdale until I got a job and got on with my life. We agreed they would come up that summer and help us move. The kids loved to spend summers down there anyway. And I knew I had to get out. Things were going downhill with Harold and everything else.

————

JIM THOMPSON   Initial word on the peace agreement came from a guard. On the 27th of January [1973] he said peace had been achieved.

LARRY STARK   Jim had the same attitude I did: I'm not going to get elated until I'm on my way out of here.

JIM THOMPSON   That afternoon the chief political officer came down from Hanoi. The camp commander then came into the compound and made a big production of announcing the agreements had been signed. He said we would be leaving the following morning so we should pack our things. He told us we could write a letter home, which we immediately did . . . and which our families never received.

The next morning they gave us a big send-off breakfast, the best meal we'd had there. Twelve or fifteen dishes. Vietnamese-style but real good chow. Goose, pork, vegetables with sauces and spices, things we hadn't seen in all the time we'd been captured. Fried potatoes. There was even apricot wine, which was quite good. A real spread. After breakfast they put us all in a land rover.

SPEED ADKINS   We didn't know where we were going. I asked Larry. He didn't know. On the way, they showed us all the damage done by the bombings. There was plenty.

JIM THOMPSON   We saw the effect on railroads and factory districts. Believe me, it was a sight for sore eyes. And some of the population waved to us. American prisoners and they were waving! They seemed so friendly. A few hostile glances but very few. Most people nodded and smiled. As we crossed the river on a ferry, with many pedestrians aboard, they crowded around our vehicles, smiling, wanting to shake hands, offering us cigarettes.

SPEED ADKINS   Some of us almost got killed moving that final leg into Hanoi. We passed through communities where they threw rocks. One gal tried to stick a knife in me. I moved just in time. The guy behind me almost got it. Guards grabbed her and took her away. They wanted us to know how the people really felt.

JIM THOMPSON   They said every Vietnamese family had been touched by the war. I believed this. But I was convinced these people were sick of war. These poor devils had been at it since Ho Chi Minh went south in the thirties. Since then the loss of life had been fantastic.

SPEED ADKINS   We stopped in front of Hoa Lo prison, the Hanoi Hilton. Men had begun arriving from five or six outlying prisons.

32 ■ NO BRACELET

On January 23, 1973, President Nixon told the world in a television address that the United States had reached an agreement in Paris with North Vietnam that would bring "peace with honor" to Southeast Asia. A cease-fire would take effect in three days. Within sixty days, the United States would withdraw its remaining combat force of 23,700 from South Vietnam. The North Vietnamese would release all U.S. prisoners of war. They claimed to hold fewer than six hundred.

America reacted mostly with joy and relief to news that its longest, most divisive foreign war was ending. Many citizens felt only a profound sadness at the cost of the war, in lives and suffering. Some expressed cynicism that U.S. leaders actually believed the peace would last.

The planned return of American POWs quickly became a focal point for the nation's emotional storm over the war. Though these men would not return as victors, they were symbols of sacrifice, of freedom, of years of brutality that fellow Americans could only try to imagine. As U.S. authorities released the official list of returnees, from information finally provided by Hanoi, the nation longed to share in the homecoming and to hear their stories. Most Americans didn't understand that some of the most painful stories of the war were still to be played out.

ALYCE   The call came one morning in January 1973. I don't remember who it was, but he said the list had come out and Jim's name was on it. I was shocked. I really didn't think he was alive. I knew the government was about to release a list of names of returning POWs. It had been on the news. I knew I was going to find out. But when I did I was shocked.

TED JOHANSSON   Normally the Army would have released Jim's name and capitalized on his stature. Instead, a Navy officer, Everett Alvarez, got all the publicity as "longest-held." It seemed strange that the Navy pushed that, and the Army let them. But our main objective was to protect the Thompson family. That was the directive from the Pentagon. "Mrs. Thompson doesn't want publicity. Do what you can to stop any."

ALYCE   My kids were at school when the call came. I immediately called Harold at work and told him. I called my mother too, told her Jim was alive. "I told you that all along," she said.

"Mom, you didn't know," I said. "You didn't know!"

"I felt it in my heart," she said. "I knew. I knew."

"I don't give a shit what anybody feels in their heart!"

Her attitude was almost like "Now, you'll get what you deserved."

When the kids came home I sat them down at the kitchen table.

RUTH   I thought something was wrong as soon as we came in the house. The way she looked. I couldn't tell if she was sad or happy or what. It was wild.

JIM JR.   I was already playin' outside when she told me to come in. Because I was still wantin' to play I really wasn't payin' much attention.

LAURA   My mother said, "You're probably wondering why everything has been hush-hush."

ALYCE   "Your father," I said, "was missing in action. I found out this morning he's alive."

RUTH   "Oh, Mama!" Pam yelled. "I can't believe it! I can't believe it! Is he really coming back?" The two of them held each other and cried and carried on. The rest of us sat there like, "What is going on?" We were in shock. Just sitting there, staring. It was wild.

LAURA   She didn't go into a lot of detail but said she didn't know what to do. She was confused. She told us to help her decide whether to go back with my father or not. "If I decide to go back with him," she said, "you know it will mean we're going to move away."

"What about Dad?" I said, meaning Harold.

"That's the decision," she said. "It's a hard decision."

PAM   I had the only picture of him in the house.

ALYCE   We got the photograph out and showed the other kids.

RUTH   Him sitting there in his uniform with three little blond girls in dresses.

JIM JR.   She showed me this picture and said, "This man is your father." It dumbstruck me. I didn't know what to do. It was like, "Hey, forget him [*pointing in one direction*], that's the one."

It was weird.

RUTH   It blew our minds. Before this I had never thought about him. He wasn't talked about.

ALYCE   Ruth and little Jim didn't say much. Pam cried with joy. She had felt rejected by everybody. Suddenly she had this vision of somebody returning who loved her. Her knight in shining armor.

LAURA   While the two little ones stared at my mom, bewildered, Pam was ecstatic and I got angry. I wanted nothing to do with the decision. I flew into a terrible tantrum. I cried, I screamed, I called her names. I always had a mouth on me anyway. Now I said, "Why did you lie?" My mother tried to calm me down, but I wouldn't let her touch me. I ran to my room. She just let me cry it out. To this day we never have talked about it. The day she told me the truth was the day I stopped believing in her.

JIM JR.   Laura took it hard. I just went outside and played. I mean, what can you say, a nine-year-old boy. I didn't want to listen to nothin' serious like that.

PAM   Little Jim, of course, hadn't been born when my dad left. Ruth had been barely two and Laura four. He wasn't around enough where they could build a relationship with him. But I had. I had been his little princess. When Mama told me he was alive and coming home, I was relieved we finally could talk about him all together as a family. It wasn't a secret between me and my mom anymore.

LAURA   Even before I knew my father I loved him. And I hated my mother from that day forward for not allowing me to know him all those years. I will always hate her for that. She cheated me out of a lot of emotion. Pam was happy, though. She wanted to go back with him. None of us had strong ties to Harold. I appreciated what the man did for us. He did put a roof over our heads. But Pam, well, Pam had been a daddy's girl when little and remembered him the way he was. She was psyched to have that back.

ALYCE   Harold came home from work early. That night he asked what I was going to do. I told him I didn't know. He said he would let me make the decision. But he was going through hell too. Then everything exploded around us. The news hit the papers. Jim's name, our address, everything. Somebody let the word loose in Washington, I guess. God, what a horrible day. Those damn Boston TV stations were knocking at my front door. TV cameramen. I didn't let them in. I didn't answer the door. They took pictures of the front of the house. I wouldn't comment. A reporter from the *Boston Globe* banged on the front door, wanting an interview. I got phone calls from the press. "No comment," I said, and hung up.

The local VFW called me. They were real nasty. They said they couldn't understand somebody behaving like that, that I was nothin' but a whore. They said if I had needed help in any way I could have come to their organization. That was bullshit. They were just trying to get their names in the paper.

The kids respected my wishes and did not answer the door or the telephone. Sheila, my neighbor and best friend, had no idea what my situation had been until all hell broke loose. I called her and asked her to come over. We sat down and I explained it all. She was shocked. She had believed me all those years that Jim was dead and Harold and I were married. She wondered why I hadn't said anything to her before. She said she would have understood. Jan, another neighbor, came over and hugged me. Jan said she had an idea what was going on but it was my own business and she wasn't about to interfere. She and Butch, her husband, both understood and wished me every bit of luck. Sheila and Jan were right there for me. The others turned their backs.

I was more worried about my kids, what was going to be said about them. This was a Catholic neighborhood. They stayed out of school the following day, then went back. I don't know how they handled that. I do know that in the weeks that followed some neighborhood kids weren't allowed to play with them anymore. Their mother was a whore. And with Jim being a POW, they said, "How could you do this?" I wondered what they would have done.

LAURA   Schoolmates can be cruel. With all the publicity about returning POWs, the story got around fast in my junior high. Kids did know Harold wasn't our father. We used the name Thompson. But they had thought our father was dead. Now we got teased. "What are you going to do now, Laura? Which father do you want?" I would come home in tears.

ALYCE   Our lives were in an uproar. My mother and other relatives were calling. I couldn't eat. I couldn't sleep. Everything I feared would happen was happening. And I had nobody to blame but myself. When it's your bed, you lie on it.

LAURA   Some kids at school had started wearing POW-MIA bracelets. Now that I knew my father was alive and coming home, I wanted one too. I told my Mom. She said I couldn't get one. She didn't say that there wasn't one made with his name on it.

Pam saw I was hurting. Her attitude toward me had always been "Oh, get away." About the only time she showed any closeness was when this stuff happened. I had questions she knew I needed answered. She sympathized and answered what she could. Grandmother brought up lots of pictures of my father and the family when we were younger. I had never even seen a baby picture of myself. Now my grandmother wanted us to see what Dad looked like. I noticed my mother's yearbook had a note from Dad, about them getting married right after high school. How they couldn't wait.

A schoolmate had written, "Good luck, Alyce, you've got a great man. You're going to be happy."

33 ■ GOING HOME

JIM THOMPSON   We arrived at Hoa Lo sometime around eleven the morning of the 28th [of January, 1973]. The reception from camp commander and guards was almost cordial. They read us the peace agreements with full protocols and distributed copies. To comply with the terms they were assembling all of us in one prison within a matter of hours.

LARRY STARK   Pilots held in the North and military and civilians captured in the South were brought together for the first time.

JIM THOMPSON   We were restricted to particular areas of the prison but otherwise had a good deal of freedom. Although still isolated from most prisoners, I was reunited with guys I knew from K-77 and saw a few new faces too.

DON MacPHAIL   Like Captain Thompson, I was Special Forces. I'd been held in Cambodia most of my fifty-four months. Thompson, me, and some other new arrivals were put in a room where Air Force colonel Ted Guy was in charge.

MICHAEL O'CONNOR   When new prisoners began arriving in another section, we got names back. One of them was Thompson. I figured that wasn't Jim Thompson. He was dead.

TED GUY   Jim Thompson was skin, bones, and white hair, looking like he might have aged thirty years while held. I had been shot down almost five years before we met. When I learned Thompson's capture date, I was amazed he was still alive.

DON MacPHAIL   It was a big thing for me, after thirty-eight months in solitary, just having other Americans in the room. I'd never heard of Jim Thompson. About the time he got captured, I was graduating from high school. Our first conversation was about Special Forces. The Viet Cong hadn't let many of us live after capture. Jim and I knew a lot of the same people. Guys he had served with had become my instructors before I went to Vietnam. We talked about home and family. Jim clearly missed his family very much.

BEN PURCELL   I finally met Thompson again, after all those years. We had both changed since we met so briefly on the jungle trail in 1968. Our spirits were high.

JIM THOMPSON   We still were kept separate from the pilots. I figured they wanted us on a special diet. I thought I was in good shape until I saw guys who had been in Hanoi on good groceries for a year. I'd forgotten what a healthy man looked like.

DON MacPHAIL   Lots of my buddies had died down south from lack of food or medical treatment. Now at Hoa Lo I felt like I was in a real Hilton. They wanted us to look decent to the Jane Fondas of the world.

JIM THOMPSON   We got food we hadn't seen since our capture. Big plates of canned fish and canned pork fat. Good rice, not the poor-quality stuff they'd been giving us. Good bread. Vegetables. Pepper and spices. Things we'd been longing for for years. There was candy—oh goodness—and fruit!

––––––––

PAUL BLAIR   Word that the POWs were coming home brought the escort program to life. We were to be liaisons between the returning POW and his family, providing one-to-one contact to help bring him back into the mainstream of life in the United Sates. Knowing it would be a difficult period of psychological readjustment, the Army tried to find escorts who had the same rank and similar background as the returnees. I was stationed in Okinawa when they asked for volunteers. Jim Thompson and I were both Special Forces. I had six daughters; he had four children. I was interested in helping get the prisoners of war back, so the base commander tapped me for the program. They didn't give me a lot of family information—only that Alyce was living in Massachusetts and that Jim had a young son whom he had never seen. Other escorts were encouraged to contact their POWs' families.

When I asked to do the same, they said, "Absolutely not!"

It was the first of many decisions I disagreed with.

––––––––

LARRY STARK   Prisoners held all those years at Hoa Lo didn't know Jim Thompson was the longest-held. To them, Alvarez was. But about the first question we asked each other was "When were you captured?" And word soon spread.

EVERETT ALVAREZ   I knew within a couple of months of my shoot-down, in August of 1964, that other Americans had been captured earlier down south. The English version of the Hanoi newspaper even had referred to Jim Thompson. I remember asking the guard eight years earlier, "Where's this guy being held?" The story described Thompson as sitting on a hilltop, looking over a valley, above the jungle, and how beautiful it was. It was propaganda, possibly something he wrote to please them. They had worked hard on all of us to get statements. They got me to apologize for the bombings, for destroying villages and hurting innocent women and children. I don't even remember what all I wrote. They came for a statement, came again and came again.

As the years passed, I remembered Thompson and wondered about him. Other prisoners would tell of guys shot down and captured in Laos, but none had ever showed up in our camp. Many, in fact, didn't survive. I didn't expect Thompson had either. So I became known as the longest-held. I guess it carried some status, both here and at home. I wish I didn't have it but I did.

About the time the bombings stopped, in January 1973, many more prisoners entered the camp, in an area called Little Vegas. We were in Camp Unity, the big courtyard. We made contact with a roomful of brand-new shoot-downs. They, in turn, made contact with another new group. One day they called back.

"Tell Alvarez there's a guy here who's been held longer than him. Name of Thompson."

"I'll be damned," I said.

DON MacPHAIL   Jim Thompson was a man I'd salute no matter what the consequences. You could see what he had endured. You can see torture on a person—in the nose, the eyes, the fingernails and toenails. As an Army soldier among mostly pilots, I felt a little pride when Thompson's name came up. Hell, after nine years he knew the ropes better than anyone. He had an attitude to emulate. If there was only one loaf of bread and a sick man in the room, the sick man got the bread. He was like a psychologist. He could treat me rough and get away with it. Others he treated like they were kids. He got all our spirits up, saying, "We'll be home soon." Some of us had harder attitudes than others toward the communists. Jim was a troublemaker. He'd sit down with a Vietnamese officer and argue point after point and not be intimidated. A tough nut.

JIM THOMPSON   On the 9th of February, 1973, we were moved in with guys I had left years before at Bao Cao—DiBernardo, O'Connor, Leonard, Ziegler. They looked at me as though they were seeing a ghost. We shed an awful lot of tears that day. After being with civilians so long, joining a group of GIs, hearing the slang, was like coming home.

MICHAEL O'CONNOR   Jim was skinny as hell but not the skeleton we knew from Bao Cao. It took me a while to realize it was him. Not one of us who'd seen him five years earlier thought his survival was anything less than a miracle. It took pure guts and determination to live through that.

———

PAUL BLAIR   Everyone was on pins and needles about the ensuing release. The services moved all escorts and medical personnel to Clark Air Base. No one was sure who would be aboard what flight until names of those who boarded in Hanoi were released.

———

DON MacPHAIL   As much as we respected Jim, he was opinionated and could be intolerant. Even in the Hilton, with freedom so near, he had his run-ins.

TED GUY   I had a very difficult time with Jim. He tried to take command. As a lieutenant colonel, I was senior ranking officer in our section. I had an agreement with the pilots that rank on the date of shootdown determined seniority. Jim thought he might have made lieutenant colonel before I did, that he might outrank everyone in our section. He believed strongly in the Code of Conduct and that if you're senior you must take command. A bunch of my guys heard about the argument and, well, it boiled down to this: I had led these guys for four years and they weren't going to accept somebody else. We had had the best camp in Vietnam and were tight by the time Jim showed up. In contrast, I knew there had been some dissension between Jim and people who came up with him. Not many wanted to follow him. In fact, a couple of them came to me and said they did not feel he was fit to command. He was inexperienced in handling people. Frankly, sometimes his mind wasn't engaged before the mouth kicked into gear.

We also disagreed over my policy that there would be no escape attempts. Jim wanted to escape again. It was stupid, really. There was no reason. "Jim," I said, "the goddamn war is over."

BEN PURCELL   Having served longer in prison than the rest of us, Jim was not willing to admit there could be two opinions on a subject. We were all dogmatic. We had been arguing with ourselves for years in solitary and we always won. But with Jim you had to consider all his years of deprivation, maltreatment, threats, pressures. The absence of information. All the years he never heard anything good about America. It takes a special kind of guy to get through that.

———

HERVEY PEEBLES   I was an Air Force captain working at the personnel office there at Clark, part of a purple suit operation—that is, multiservice—for Operation Homecoming.

FRAN PEEBLES CWYNAR   My husband at the time couldn't tell us a whole lot. But he did say that when the men came home we probably wouldn't be able to see them. A big crowd would be too much of a shock.

———

ALYCE   While the whole list of POWs had come out at once, they decided to bring the men back in increments. It was a nervous couple of months. We never knew when Jim would come home. Tension built up as the first group was coming out. "This is it," we thought. But he wasn't in that group.

———

FRAN PEEBLES CWYNAR   When the first aircraft arrived at Clark there were maybe two hundred people to greet them. It was late afternoon. As the plane taxied we couldn't see anyone inside but we waved and cheered and cried. The love and caring was indescribable.

HERVEY PEEBLES   My throat got so tight with emotion, so sore, I couldn't help but cry. When Jeremiah Denton, the first man off that plane, gave his speech, about how proud he was to be able to serve his country, it grabbed our guts.

———

ALYCE   We watched TV as the first ones came off the planes. There were many tears when I saw those men, saw how happy they were to see us. I noticed they said Alvarez was longest held. I made mention of that as we watched the telecast. When the second plane was coming out tension built up again but Jim wasn't on that one either.

FROM THE *Bergen Record*, FEBRUARY 14, 1973

LONGEST HELD POW WAS BORN IN BERGEN
by Sheila Schimpf
Staff Writer

The parents of America's longest-held prisoner of war, bound by a family code of silence, learned yesterday that their son is headed home.

Floyd "Jimmy" Thompson, shot down over South Vietnam March 26, 1964, is scheduled to be released after almost nine years, Pentagon spokesmen said yesterday.

His parents, Mr. and Mrs. Benjamin Thompson, 34 Church St., Lodi, read the same list of names printed in the Record Jan. 30 but saw a Floyd H. Thompson. What they didn't know, and what no one told them, is that a clerical error changed their son's middle initial "J" to "H."

Thompson's parents live on the first floor of an aging apartment building, behind a gray, weather-beaten door. For the nine years that their son has been a prisoner they have shunned publicity. For eight years they have had no contact with their son's wife, Alyce Joan Devries Thompson, who is from New Milford but now lives with their four children in Hudson, Mass. The youngest child, Jimmy, now almost nine, was born the day after his father was captured. The Thompsons had three older children, Pamela, now fifteen, Laura, now twelve, and Ruth, now eleven. Mrs. Thompson could not be reached.

Her mother, Ruth Michels, who still lives in Bergen County, pleaded for her daughter's privacy. Mrs. Michels said her daughter has heard from the Army that Thompson definitely is a prisoner. No one contacted Benjamin Thompson and his wife. Yesterday, when Thompson was told that his son is alive and coming home after nine years, the older Thompson retained the stoic, silent front he has kept up for so long.

"He's welcome here any time," said Thompson, a World War I veteran. "We'll let him do the talking."

Thompson's family had asked the Pentagon not to name him as the longest-held prisoner, but the fact leaked out. The Pentagon had been listing Lt. Cmdr. Everett Alvarez Jr. as the prisoner held longer than all but one. Alvarez, shot down Aug. 5, 1964, four and a half months after Thompson, was among the first prisoners released. . . .

At the Old North Church in Dumont, where Thompson was married and three of his children baptized, the congregation has been praying for his health and safety. They now are praying for a safe homecoming, says the Rev. Albert Van Dyke, pastor.

"Most of my people don't even know who he is," Dr. Van Dyke said. "He's been away from Old North for sixteen years. But when word came that he was captured we started praying for him." The Sunday prayer list at Old North has carried Thompson's name for nine years.

LARRY STARK   My last week in captivity, Jim, Lew Meyer, and several others began a hunger strike. They had been moved to the other side of the prison, where they learned that another guy, the last one captured and held separately, was worried he wouldn't get out. He had been shot down the date the agreement was signed.

BEN PURCELL   I heard this guy whistling "The Streets of Laredo" and said, "Who's that?"

"Lieutenant Commander Phillip Kientzler."

He had been shot down January 27, 1973. They had told him his name had not been turned over to the American delegation in Paris because he wasn't at that time a prisoner. They didn't intend to release him. So we started a hunger strike.

LARRY STARK   That didn't endear them to the authorities.

BEN PURCELL   We were put in isolation. Four days later, however, they pulled us out and the next day they let Kientzler out.

LARRY STARK   Jim was still on the other side of the prison when I left, so I didn't have a chance to say goodbye. I had assumed we would be going home together, or more likely that he would be going first because of his time there. The two of us had never been close, but I had a lot of respect for Jim Thompson. Still do. He was constant, consistent, never flagging in his attitude toward the enemy and toward our country. There was the escape attempt I saw, and the others he made before we met. I thought his behavior over nine years of captivity heroic.

FROM THE *Washington Post*, MARCH 14, 1973

LONGEST-HELD POW IS ON FRIDAY'S LIST
(*from news dispatches*)

The American war prisoner held captive longer than any other U.S. soldier in history is on the list of 32 which the Vietcong said they will free in Hanoi on Friday.

Maj. Floyd J. Thompson of New Milford, N.H. [*sic*] was captured March 26, 1964, in Quangtri Province just below the demilitarized zone. He was serving as a U.S. adviser with South Vietnamese forces. . . .

The circumstances surrounding Thompson's captivity of nearly nine years are shrouded with an aura of mystery that will not be lifted until he returns and tells his story. . . .

LEW MEYER   Days before our release, Jim met another of his former interrogators. This time he shocked me. Rather than attack him, he called him "the teacher" and shook his hand. He said if it wasn't for this guy intervening, he wouldn't have made it.

DON MacPHAIL   Finally one morning, early, Jim, I, and some others were told to dress. They brought us out to where the pilots had been held. We stripped so they could check for contraband, then dressed again. We took a last look at the place, and remembered what had happened to us. That took a lot. They put shackles on a select few. Jim and I both wore handcuffs.

It was a beautiful morning. Honest to God it was. You couldn't ask for anything better. We got on a bus and rode twenty minutes through the city. It looked like one big bomb crater. There was total silence among us when we reached Gia Lam airport. We were like the guy who knew he had won megabucks in the lottery but continued to check the ticket over and over again, a million times, still not being sure the jackpot was his. We saw reporters. We didn't know who they belonged to but they all spoke English. They asked how we felt going home. We were told to be quiet and kept moving. We didn't want to do anything to screw our chances. I still didn't believe I was going home.

They put us into a little holding pen—something like a carport. Gave us a sandwich, just pieces of pork between bread. I don't think any of us ate. We gave them to the guards. About thirty or forty minutes later we looked up and saw such a beautiful sight. An airplane with the American flag on its tail. I got goose bumps from my toes to the top of my head. That airplane circled the field twice before landing. Every one of us prayed with all our hearts it wouldn't crash. There were tears streaming down our faces, but silently. Silently. No big emotional scene. No one dared scream.

———

LONNIE JOHNSON   This was my fifth flight into North Vietnam for Operation Homecoming. When I had returned from my fourth, my boss told me he wanted me to go back the next morning. And this mission would be special. There would be Special Forces released. I had extra berets brought in quickly from Okinawa. I'd served in Special Forces in

Vietnam from '62 through '73. The only years I was not there was '67 and '71. I saw the war from beginning to end. But before this flight I had never heard of Jim Thompson.

———

DON MacPHAIL   After the plane landed, we were taken to the tarmac and one by one reported in to an American Air Force colonel.

"Army sergeant Don MacPhail, sir."

"Welcome home, son," he said.

LONNIE JOHNSON   Every flight out had been almost identical but I'll never forget greeting the first POW aboard this one. I said, "Welcome home." Without saying a word this man walked onto the plane and moved as far forward as he could go. Then he sat down in the far corner seat. As the others boarded I handed this man a photograph and asked if he would autograph it for me. He signed his name and handed it back. Then he grabbed it again and wrote in parentheses, "Every little obstacle touches me." He never said a word, from the time he walked on that aircraft until he got off in the Philippines.

Captain Thompson was the last one to board, though at the time I didn't know who he was. Then a crowd of Vietnamese began pressing in. They seemed curious about what the aircraft looked like inside. All these Vietnamese were standing there as we closed the clamshell door and raised the tailgate of the C-141. One POW looked out the window and spotted a couple of guards he knew.

"Just let me off this aircraft for five minutes."

"No," I said. "It's over."

JIM THOMPSON   I felt like a spring that's been under tension too damn long! Wound too tight. Just numb. I didn't believe it, didn't fully realize what was happening. It took time to sink in. Details from the time I boarded the aircraft are hard to remember. I was in a fog.

TED GUY   When the doors closed we were kind of in shock.

LONNIE JOHNSON   We taxied down the runway. There was a tense moment before liftoff.

DON MacPHAIL   Everyone was silent. Not a damn noise on that aircraft except the engines. I sat next to a civilian named Mike. As I looked past him out the window I saw tears streaming down his face. When the plane finally left the tarmac, that aircraft went crazy! Everybody started scream-ing and yelling, "Thank God!" and "I told you so!" We hugged the nurses.

LONNIE JOHNSON   The men were out of their seats, throwing things, jerking cushions off their seats, just letting it out. I thought a few would break their knuckles beating on the fuselage. Lots of emotions, lots of tears. Such a moving experience.

TED GUY   I'll never forget the feeling as the airplane left the ground. And then again when we saw the coast of Vietnam behind us. Everyone was crying.

JIM THOMPSON   Another cheer went up when the pilot announced we had left North Vietnamese territory. Still the reaction, not only from me but from the entire group, wasn't the violent exuberance I had expected. I mean, yes, we threw pillows and stuff, but . . . it wasn't what I expected. For most of us it just took a long time to sink in, a long time to really, truly believe we were free.

LONNIE JOHNSON   Some of the men were concerned about South Vietnam. Did we win? they asked.

I'd ask them, "What year were you captured?"

When they told me, I'd say, "Well, it's changed a bit."

Some pilots said we should have dropped the bomb on the North. They wouldn't have minded flying that mission.

JIM THOMPSON   The crew welcomed us so warmly. They wanted autographs.

DON MacPHAIL   They gave us each a little ditty bag with chewing gum and cigarettes. Someone even had a *Playboy* magazine. They should have had sixty of 'em. Opening that centerfold . . . well, people nearly fell out of their seats. It was the first time I'd ever seen a beaver shot in a magazine. As we soon would discover, a lot had changed.

TED GUY   I was told to come forward. There the chaplain on board told me my father had died in 1970.

LONNIE JOHNSON   People began getting some news, going through personal changes, or blowing off steam. I posted myself near the kitchen, out of the way. I was standing there when this one guy walked by me. He looked like a little old man, maybe pushing fifty. He had a cigar in his mouth, quite long. I had shaken his hand as he got on the plane but didn't know then he was Special Forces. Now as he passed me he looked up at my beret.

"I've been waiting for one of those for nine years," he said. And introduced himself as Captain Jim Thompson.

"If you wait a few minutes longer, sir," I said, "I will be holding a ceremony and will present you with one."

JIM THOMPSON   Three other Special Forces, enlisted men, were aboard. Johnson called us up to the front of the plane and presented each of us with a beret. That did my heart good. I was very touched.

Colonel Guy learned there would be a crowd at Clark and that he should speak. That's all he was told. He jotted down a few notes. "What do you think?" he asked. I looked them over.

"Sounds good to me."

LONNIE JOHNSON Captain Thompson was a character. Happy. Talkative. As we approached Clark the senior officer aboard told him he couldn't wear his beret off the aircraft.

"The hell I'm not," he said.

——————

JIM JR. I saw him on TV as he stepped off the plane at some Air Force base. My mother set me down in front and said, "That's your father, right there." It was a weird feeling.

——————

SAM DEACON Jane and I were watching as he got off that airplane. I knew it was him [*choking up*] coming through the door. I pointed. "Jane, look! Coming down those stairs!"

I cheered. [*Remembering the scene, Deacon's eyes fill with tears.*] It was total elation. I felt a big weight lifted off my shoulders.

TINA CARR The ears were the first thing we noticed. "There are the ears!" we said.

ROBERT SIRONEN The last time I had seen my childhood friend he was a first lieutenant. Now, there he was on television. He looked so skinny. He looked . . . old. For some reason, they still didn't want no publicity on him being longest-held. They just said, "Major Floyd James Thompson."

——————

HERVEY PEEBLES The atmosphere at the airfield as each plane returned was just nuts. Everyone was thrilled. Just beside themselves. The tarmac was jammed with people.

PAUL BLAIR All the returnees looked skinny. All wore gray prison garb or some sort of North Vietnamese uniform.

JIM THOMPSON General Ogden, an Air Force brigadier, officially received us. The reception was marvelous. Seeing an American in uniform and throwing a salute!

DON MacPHAIL There was a flag at the bottom of the aircraft stairs. I stopped, squared, and saluted. The officer said, "You don't have to do that."

"I think we should, sir. Don't you?"

"Yeah," he said.

My happiest moment, the point at which I fully realized we were home, was when I started saluting that line of American officers. It looked like two million of them and I started saluting. I caught hell from Jim Thompson 'cause I was chewing gum. I had come out of the plane blowing a bubble. He was waiting for me at the end walkway, grabbed me by the ass, and said, "Sergeant, get rid of the goddamn gum!" He meant it. But he was joking too.

LONNIE JOHNSON   It wasn't until after the mission was completed that I learned Major Thompson was the longest-held prisoner in American history. We were thinking Alvarez was. When Alvarez returned, they had a PA system set up for his speech. Thompson gave no speech. When he came off it was just another flight completed. As I stood under the jet's engine, watching the POWs come off, the first man to get on that flight, the one who hadn't said a word the whole trip, came to the plane's door. He stood there as if lost and finally walked down the stairs. An admiral, dressed in his Navy whites, extended his hand. This fellow passed by as though he didn't see him, walked down the carpet, took two steps past the colors, stopped, turned, faced the colors, saluted, and walked on.

DON MacPHAIL   After the speeches somebody started singing "God Bless America." Jim and I looked at each other, put our arms around each other, and that was it. We lost it. I thought, It's all coming out now. Jesus, all the years of not crying, all the years of just taking it.

Part IV

THE WAR
COMES HOME

1973–1980

34 ■ THE FIRST LIE

On March 16, 1973, ten days short of nine years, Jim Thompson's cruel captivity ended. He and thirty-one other prisoners formed the sixth increment, the fourteenth flight, of Operation Homecoming. More than four hundred POWs had been repatriated before Thompson, despite complaints from cellmates that Thompson, dubbed the "old man of the South" by some prisoners, should have been freed with the first group. Some prisoners, including Thompson, suspected the North Vietnamese kept him extra weeks so more decent meals might improve his health and appearance before release.

Alvarez, on the first flight, had been home more than a month when Thompson arrived at Clark. Stories about Thompson surfaced late, after the wave of homecoming stories had crested. Mostly local journalists were interested now in a home-state soldier who had survived a longer captivity than even Alvarez, the long-celebrated naval officer. Some journalists wondered why the Army hadn't touted Thompson's status more. Why let Air Force and Navy pilots grab all the headlines?

Thompson knew nothing of this as he soaked in the joyous pandemonium at Clark that day—the cheering crowds, the red carpet and honor guard, the receiving line of flag officers and dignitaries. He didn't know that through much of his captivity, the Army he so loved had deferred to the demands of Alyce and had declined, during some of his most difficult years, to release his name.

DON MacPHAIL   Inside the terminal at Clark we drank a can of Pabst

Blue Ribbon beer. "Look, Jim," I said, "my brand. They knew I was coming."

Of course, if it had been weasel piss I would have drunk it. We were bombarded with so many things: freedom; hearing English spoken all around us; realizing thousands of people had turned out to see not more than forty POWs. They lined both sides of the road on our way to the base hospital.

Once there, any man with an immediate medical problem was taken where he needed to go. The rest of us were taken to the cafeteria and told we could have anything we wanted. I wanted a can of peanut butter and a big spoon.

HERVEY PEEBLES   The doctors had debated what to feed the returnees but watched in wonder as they ate everything like a horde of locusts. Gastrointestinally speaking, it shouldn't have happened. But the euphoria was so great most returnees said, "The hell with hospital rules."

Some said, "Let's go down to the club and have a drink!"

DON MacPHAIL   We all had basic ailments like jungle rot, intestinal parasites, beriberi scabs, and scars all over our bodies. Many had emotional problems. Those who had had a death in the family were told right away.

DON RANDER   An escort officer greeted each of us, took us where we had to go, taught us how to make a phone call. They even gave us phone numbers and a folder with letters or news about our families.

PAUL BLAIR   I introduced myself to Jim. Told him I would be his shadow, providing him with whatever he might need until he got home. He was happy at first. Then he asked me a question: "Where are my wife and family?"

I hesitated.

"Massachusetts," I said.

"Why in Massachusetts?"

Being a good military man, I said, "I don't know." In that instant I created a gap in our relationship I could never close. Jim suddenly became very withdrawn. He didn't accuse me of lying, but I knew that's what he thought. I had lied. My orders were not to tell him anything about the family. I disagreed with that order. I thought it was wrong to withhold information, regardless of circumstance. But they wanted the chaplain to tell him. It was one of many mistakes made in handling Jim Thompson. The first was not letting me write to Jim's family before he returned. Now I didn't even have a family dossier to give him. And I'd lost his trust.

LONNIE JOHNSON   Many POWs had mail waiting. Greetings from loved ones. Jim's folder had nothing in it except a pay voucher.

PAUL BLAIR   Finally, the chaplain came and told Jim why his family was in Massachusetts. Then Jim made a phone call.

ALYCE   I was glad he was alive and coming home, I told him. He sounded depressed.

"There was nothing for me when I got here," he said.

Other POWs got folders with pictures of the family. I didn't remember my family assistance officer asking for anything.

"We have to talk when I see you," I said.

"Well, talk now."

"No, there are things I have to say when I see you."

I hung up and called Harold to come home. I called Willa and Marty in Honesdale. They already had their bags packed and headed up from Pennsylvania. I called my mother. Then I waited for the kids to get home. Suddenly we had newspapers calling again and TV people knocking at the door.

PAUL BLAIR   After the phone call, Jim became very despondent. I could see he'd been crying. He didn't know which way to turn or what to do. A lot of POWs were getting bad news. Broken marriages. Deaths in the family. One guy found out his wife, who'd been receiving his checks for five years, now had nothing in the bank. All his wages down the tube. It wasn't an amazingly joyous atmosphere, not by any means.

DON MacPHAIL   When I called my wife I got my mother and father instead. So I knew something was wrong. Turned out she was on the verge of marrying somebody else. My folks didn't tell me anything, though. "Wait until you get home," Dad said. "You can talk to her." I couldn't even get my wife on the phone. We were taking turns making calls. Now I could feel the others watching me. And as much as we had shared with each other in 'Nam, we now became tight-lipped, feeling terrible, wanting to be left alone. I took my wedding ring, the only thing the Vietnamese let me keep, and threw it away.

FROM the *New York Times*, MARCH 17, 1973

LONGEST-TERM P.O.W. FREED WITH 31
by James P. Sterba

CLARK AIR BASE, the Philippines, March 16—Major Floyd J. Thompson of the Army's Special Forces, who spent nine years in captivity, longer than any

American military prisoner of war known, was released by the Vietcong in Hanoi today.

Presented with a green beret, the symbol of the Special Forces, while on his way to Clark, the 39-year-old major put it on and was reported to have said "They're going to have to fight like hell to get this off my head this time. . . ."

Major Thompson was the first American soldier known to have been captured in the Vietnam War,* though Pentagon officials said for years that the first was Lieut. Comdr. Everett Alvarez of the Navy, the first pilot shot down in North Vietnam. Major Thompson was captured more than four months before Commander Alvarez.

PAUL BLAIR   Jim and the other returnees stayed in the Philippines a couple of days to complete initial medical exams.

DON MacPHAIL   I only weighed one hundred four pounds when I got to Clark. The doctors there said I would need a few operations. I also saw a psychiatrist, some colonel. He didn't help much. He looked at my fingernails and toenails and burst out crying. The communists had pulled them out. They'd grown back but I had no feeling on the tops of my digits. The medical term is "clubbing." This psychiatrist cried the whole time he was with me. We needed more support than that.

TED GUY   It quickly became apparent we had come home too fast.

DON MacPHAIL   Too much thrown on us at one time. That's my biggest bitch. The Army had no idea what our emotional state would be. They shouldn't have allowed us to contact our families so quickly. Most of us had stayed alive to see them again, only to come back and find we didn't have a family. It was a tremendous shock.

I said, "What the heck did I come home for?" I blamed myself first. She had the kids to think about. But then I thought, She was running around while I was getting the shit beat out of me! Suddenly I lost trust in all women, and in everyone around me. It's hard to trust anyone when the person you trust most lets you down.

PAUL BLAIR   Touring Clark was an eye-opener for the men. Jim saw a girl with a big chest and said, "She doesn't have a bra on!"

TED GUY   It was a tremendous culture shock. When I left, men wore pinstripes and had their hair cut short. Women dressed conservatively. I returned to long hair on the men and women wearing see-through blouses and miniskirts.

---

* Thompson was not the first captured. Those few American servicemen captured earlier, however, either died, escaped, or were released years before.

PAUL BLAIR   Jim was surprised not just by the way women dressed but by what he saw as lax morality. When he left there was a lot of censorship. Now there was total nudity in *Playboy*. Some magazines they saw on the flights back from Hanoi. Others in the base exchange. Jim reacted strangely. He didn't understand how society could come to that so quickly. Like, "What is this country coming too?"

––––––––––

HERVEY PEEBLES   With each returning group of prisoners, *Pacific Stars and Stripes* published their names. My wife, Fran, looked at them out of curiosity. When she came upon Thompson's name she noticed his capture date was the same day that our son Bill was born.

FRAN PEEBLES CWYNAR   We explained this coincidence to my son and thought Billy should write this returnee a letter. So he did.

Dear Major Thompson
You are proble so glad that you are going to see your family. You'v might forgot what they look like. I was born on the day you were capcherd and that was on March 26, 1964. All my life you've been in prison and now I am so happy you are out. I hope you feel good and I want you to be happy for ever.

LOVE Billy

PAUL BLAIR   After talking more with the chaplain, Jim's spirits picked up. He'd already made up his mind what kind of person I was—a liar. It was as poor a relationship as I could have with a man I was sent to help. He did tell me he wanted his family back. So when he got the letter from Billy Peebles, he wanted to ask him what a boy his age might want as a gift, what he would play with. Jim was worried whether his own son would welcome him home.

FRAN PEEBLES CWYNAR   They had closed the hospital for everyone unless you were a returnee or emergency patient. But we were able to arrange to visit the next evening. We took an elevator down from the lobby and walked through this long corridor toward the returnees' recreation room. I'd never seen anything like it in my life. The hallway seemed a hundred feet long, yet from eye level to our feet, the walls were covered by telegrams, drawings, letters of love from schoolchildren. Hundreds of them taped to the wall.

On many letters the children had just drawn stick people and messages like "We're glad you're home" or "We're glad you're alive." The men, as they walked back and forth to the lounge, wrote the children back on the same letters. This circle of love, back and forth, was heartrending. And it was through this incredible scene that we walked to meet Jim Thompson.

HERVEY PEEBLES   Having heard of this man's captivity—nine years, five in solitary—I expected to see some slow-witted guy in pajamas. But there in the lounge, waiting for us, was this magnificent man, standing tall, decked out in his Green Beret uniform and jump boots. He spoke articulately and was so lucid.

FRAN PEEBLES CWYNAR   To me he looked tired, maybe a little nervous. His hair had turned gray. His face was craggy and I felt a tremor in his hand. But he was very cordial.

HERVEY PEEBLES   He took Billy's hand and they sat together on a couch. Fran and I took other seats, giving those two time to talk. Jim had no idea what a nine-year-old boy was like. Billy didn't totally comprehend what was going on. He was a quiet kid anyway. But Fran and I were numb. The guy before us was a hero! Just being there was . . . well . . . we were more shook up than Billy. After his brutal captivity, a time when I was piloting an Air Force desk, he looked fit, at ease in these surroundings. It all struck me as remarkable.

FRAN PEEBLES CWYNAR   Billy asked what Jim ate in captivity; he had heard they ate mice and rats. If that's what Jim had, he didn't want to tell this child. "Billy," he said, "we had pumpkin soup!" Billy asked about Jim's experience in a cage, another thing we had read about. Jim talked a little bit about it but not his rougher times. We stayed maybe thirty minutes. Then he hugged Billy and shook our hands. Billy had brought him a lei of flowers, so as we were leaving Jim squatted down, pointed to an insignia on his uniform. He had Billy take it off and Jim pinned it on Billy's shirt. We still have that.

PAUL BLAIR   I saw Jim change after that meeting with Billy Peebles. His mood started an upward swing.

———

PAUL BLAIR   Immediately after his return, it was Jim's choice that his status as longest-held POW was not more widely publicized. He didn't know what his family situation would be like, so he didn't want publicity. Something appeared in *Pacific Stars and Stripes* about Alvarez, but Jim said, "Leave it where it is. Let Alvarez have the notoriety. I don't want it."

DON MacPHAIL   I'm not taking anything away from the Navy and Air Force pilots, but a lot more of them survived than did those of us held in the South. I know about Stockdale and what he went through, but

Thompson went through a hell of a lot more. No medication, no attention. At least those in the Hanoi Hilton got to talk to each other. I was flat on my back in stocks twenty-three hours a day. My body fluid built up so that if I stuck a finger in my arm the indentation just stayed there. Some of us literally drowned in their own fluid. Yet when the Army guys got back, none of us got the attention that was paid to the pilots.

FRED KILEY   Jim Thompson was either unknown or this mystical figure only the Army guys knew about. Army guys, see, were never a "group" in prison, not like Air Force and Navy guys up north. Army POWs had been captured all over the place, held in jungles for the most part, in isolation. Some had been released in the middle of the war; many escaped; many died in captivity. And only a tiny percentage of them were officers. No one made a conscious decision not to celebrate them when they returned. They got their share of decorations. But Operation Homecoming brought back mostly Navy, Marine, and Air Force pilots, all well-spoken, all presenting a virile, reassuring figure. Compare them to Army kids with hyphenated Latin names captured at age eighteen while slogging through the delta someplace. It was a whole different group. They were heroes, all right. I've catalogued twenty-six successful escape attempts—none of them from the North. But much of the Vietnam POW story has been monopolized by the prisoners of the North. And though there was no organized torture of guys held in the South, I predict they will die younger than the pilots. Their bodies will just give out from all they went through.

———

PAUL BLAIR   Before leaving Clark, we took the returnees to the base exchange. Jim bought watches for the children and for his wife. They weren't cheap.

HERVEY PEEBLES   Fran heard they were laying on another trip to the base exchange for returnees and hoped to meet up with Jim there to give him a gift to take home to his son.

FRAN PEEBLES CWYNAR   The men had the whole store to themselves. People gathered outside to express their love and concern. So many people only wanted to catch a glimpse of them. One time a children's choir was there. As the men got back on the bus the children sang, "This land is your land, this land is my land." The men laughed, cried, waved.

That day we gave Jim a couple of wood carvings and on the front of a *Stars and Stripes* newspaper where his picture appeared, Jim wrote us a note, "To my family away from home."

The next day Jim was leaving. We got to the flight line early to be on the front row. They had a red carpet rolled out on the tarmac. The bus pulled up and the men disembarked in full uniform. Walking toward the aircraft they passed through a receiving line, an admiral and some other high-ranking people. We yelled as Jim walked up to the dignitaries. When he saw us he left the carpet and came across the tarmac, maybe a walk of a hundred yards. He took Billy by the hand, asked me if it was all right, then took him back to the receiving line. Reporters pounced all over me, wanting to know who the boy was and why he was going out there. After introducing Billy to the receiving line, Jim walked him back. We hugged and said goodbye. And he got on the aircraft.

HERVEY PEEBLES   I watched all this on closed-circuit television back at the personnel center. The whole experience was the most outstanding and memorable of my entire Air Force career. The emotions and the historical significance were overwhelming. I had been commissioned in late '62 when the buildup in Vietnam began. The war had continued through all my years of service. Now, that long dirty war was over. And they were back. It was such a thrill to be there.

FRAN PEEBLES CWYNAR   I saw these men when they first came off the planes there in the Philippines; I saw most of them when they got back on days later. Coming off, they waved, but almost in disbelief. They were overwhelmed by the reception. On many faces I could still see the pain. I wanted to run up, put my arms around them, and say, "It's okay. You'll be okay." But watching them getting back on the planes for their return to the States—after they had been in the hospital, had been around other Americans for a while, had returned somewhat to society—we saw how moods had changed, like black turning to white. They bounced off the bus with a kick in their step, a light in their eyes, and a smile on their faces. They were reborn.

Billy was bewildered by it all. He only knew something terrible had happened to these people and now something good was happening. But for me it was the most poignant thing I ever hope to see. We cried a lot during those days.

HERVEY PEEBLES   Right now, even recalling that time at Clark, the hairs are raised on the back of my neck. The whole thing was so bittersweet. Bitter that they went through that captivity and the torture, sweet that they came back.

FRAN PEEBLES CWYNAR   When some men finally met their families, they didn't get what they expected, and it hurt to read about that. But they were gone so long. Family members left behind didn't know what happened to them. We followed news of Jim Thompson as best we could after that. Our first Christmas back from the Philippines we were in Florida and got a Christmas card with a line or two and Jim's signature. That was all we would get.

35 ■ REUNION

Seven months before the release of U.S. prisoners of war in Southeast
Asia began, Julius Segal, a psychiatrist with the Center for Prisoner of
War Studies at the Navy's neuropsychiatric research unit in San
Diego, warned in a report that returnees would face far greater challenges
than POWs from previous wars in adapting to changes that had occurred in
their families and in society.*

"Few episodes of captivity endured by American military personnel have
resulted in so wide a psychological gap between the prisoner and the outside
world," Segal wrote. "For many men, the period of captivity now exceeds by
far that known by POWs of the past. More important than the actual time
factor alone, however, the long years of imprisonment during the decade
past have seen broad and dramatic social and technological changes that
now pervade virtually every element of American life. Consider any aspect
of society—from modes of dress to liberated role of women, from the youth
culture to space technology—and one realizes how much of America in
transition that today's captives have missed. The culture shock for the
returnee is likely to be enormous. . . ."

Segal recommended that the POWs be returned by ship, to allow them
and their families more time to prepare for the changes ahead. News of
deaths, divorces, or "the fate of children" could have a "devastating impact"

---

* "Therapeutic Considerations in Planning the Return of American POWs to Continental
United States," Report 72-37, Navy Medical Neuropsychiatric Research Unit, San Diego,
Calif., July 1972.

on POWs, warned Segal, as they tried to process such information "through impoverished emotional channels."

"It is well to remember," he wrote, "that the image of the world with which the POWs return is the last one they remember before capture. That image and today's reality will need to be bridged in an environment as free as possible of stress and the intrusion of external demands."

It's unclear how seriously the leaders of Operation Homecoming took Segal's recommendation. From the Philippines, however, POWs were flown home on military transport jets.

PAUL BLAIR   The plane made a stop in Hawaii so we could get a meal and refuel, followed by a brief stop in California to drop off some men there. Then it was on to Pennsylvania.

LARRY RYAN   I was assigned to a tenant activity of Valley Forge Hospital when the hospital commander asked my boss to provide an escort for a POW patient coming in. He wanted somebody special, he said, an officer who could handle a delicate situation. There might be problems in the man's family life. I reported to the hospital Saturday morning, March 17 [1973], along with other escorts. We got briefed on our duties.

———

ALYCE   Marty and Willa arrived in Massachusetts in time to watch the kids as I prepared to leave for Valley Forge. They would travel back down to Honesdale, Pennsylvania, and stay there until I called.

JIM JR.   My mom said this man, my real father, would be at a hospital and we might have to go there to be with him. I didn't care for that idea. What kid wants to pick up and leave nine years of his life like that? Just forget it and start anew? I didn't care nothin' for that.

TED JOHANSSON   As her family assistance officer, I arranged to drive Alyce down to Valley Forge.

ALYCE   I didn't want Ted coming to the house, so I said I would meet him at a highway exit on the excuse that he wouldn't have to travel fifteen miles out of his way and double back. Marty drove me to the interstate. When Ted pulled off, I put my suitcase in his car and off we went.

TED JOHANSSON   Alyce was smartly dressed. She looked well. Not long into the ride, however, she said, "Ted, I have something to tell you. I don't know what you will think of me after this but I have to tell you."

Then she told me the whole story. How her family had been taken in by this man, how he had looked after them. The melding of two families. That they lived as husband and wife. She talked about getting rid of her in-laws and away from Bragg. She described her life in full detail.

How her husband had been a heavy drinker because it was a macho thing to do.

Alyce was distraught in recounting everything. She felt she'd deceived me. But when I heard the whole story I said, "That's tremendous!" I really thought it was. And I still do. Here was a woman who had been abused emotionally by this macho officer before he went to Vietnam, and later she found someone willing to take her in. Why should one condemn the other? You need to be gods; these were only people. She described how she had explained the situation to the children. "The family," she said she told them, "was going to have to decide whether we're going to live with Daddy Jim or Daddy Harold."

ALYCE   We stopped for lunch at a Howard Johnson's. Jim loved chocolate-covered cherries. I knew I had a tale to tell, so as a peace offering I bought him a box. It was all going to come to a head within twenty-four hours. The closer we got, the more I knew what I had to do and what a terrible time it was going to be. I was a wreck. My stomach was . . . ah, you have no idea. Ted had to stop for me often, especially that last hour. But I knew the quicker I did this the better off everybody was going to be. We got to Valley Forge in the early afternoon.

———

LARRY RYAN   While we waited for Jim's arrival there at the hospital I saw Alyce's hands shaking. She used a lot of Kleenex throughout the afternoon, becoming more high-strung and nervous as the time approached.

ALYCE   About five o'clock they told me the helicopter was landing.

———

DON MacPHAIL   It was windy as hell at Valley Forge. Cold and windy. Jim was in the first helicopter. When he got off, he made a brief statement.

JIM THOMPSON: I don't know as I rate the title of "Dean of the PW corps." The fact that I had been there longer than anybody else is a somewhat dubious distinction at best. However, I would like to try to express to all you kind people the feelings we have at finally getting back to the good old U.S.A. To try to put these emotions into words would be a flat impossibility. I would like to offer a salute to the President of the United States to whom we pledge our undying loyalty and our readiness to do our part whenever we're called upon again to do so. Every one of us feels the same way. To conclude my brief talk this morning I would like to say, "God bless you, Mr. President, for having had the courage and the determination to bring us home in dignity and in honor, that it should all not have been in vain." Thank you all.

PAUL BLAIR   We were put in cars for the drive to the hospital. Now Jim got very reserved and clearly filled with apprehension about meeting his family. He had no idea what was coming.

———

ALYCE   They brought all family members into one large room to greet their POWs. That's when I saw Jim's parents. I gave Elizabeth a big hug and kiss and she hugged me back. I didn't tell her where I had been all those years.

———

PAUL BLAIR   The returnees walked in. Jim spotted Alyce and his parents among the waiting families. It was very tense. I gleaned from the expression on Alyce's face that she didn't want to go back to him.

ALYCE   I was shocked at Jim's appearance. He was emaciated. He had gotten so old. White hair. He looked at least sixty. He had always been good-looking, if not handsome. Now his face had deep lines and a scar. His nose had been broken. The sight turned my stomach. I hate to say that. But he looked so bad. I hugged him. He said, "Hi, babe." That's what he used to call me.

He greeted his mother and dad. I gave him the chocolate-covered cherries. He laughed. Then he asked where the kids were.

"They're up at Marty's."

He asked why.

"Because there's something I have to tell you."

"I knew something was wrong," he said.

The two of us went back into the suite where he would stay. He had a sitting room with a TV, a couch and a couple of chairs, a table and lamps, a separate bathroom, and a hospital bedroom. He sat in one chair and I sat across from him. I told him that after he heard me out, if he didn't want me around anymore, I would leave. My coat and pocketbook were right there. I'd leave and that would be the end of it. He'd get to see the kids, I said. It was their right and it was his right. Then I told him the whole story.

———

LARRY RYAN   The two of them were in there together for twenty minutes when Jim came out and asked for a bottle of scotch. Paul Blair turned to me and said, "Can you get it?" I sent somebody out to the club and had it brought back.

———

ALYCE   While I talked, Jim seldom interrupted. He asked at one point why I went away with Harold. I tried to explain, but, well, I didn't know if I got through. He let me finish. There was no anger. He just sat there. Then I said, "There it is. How do you feel? Do you want me stay or what?"

"I guess I want you to stay," he said. "I think we can overcome this and start over."

He asked again where the kids were. They would be down the next day, I said. "I didn't know how you'd react. I didn't want them going through something unnecessary."

———

TED JOHANSSON   They came out of Jim's room after about an hour, both wearing big smiles. I thought Jim looked snappy in his uniform.

LARRY RYAN   Alyce was smiling, as though things had gone well. At least she didn't look distraught.

TED JOHANSSON   "I know everything, now," Jim said, coming up to me. "I want to meet this man who took care of my family."

LARRY RYAN   I quickly told Jim who I was. I said we had a thorough physical exam scheduled and a debriefing requirement in the days ahead. They were to be done quickly but with Jim's feelings in mind. He understood.

That first evening was pretty hectic. The exuberance of the reunion, getting received into the hospital. Jim looked drawn, thin, tired. But he didn't seem like someone who'd been a prisoner for nine years. He was very sharp and vigorous compared to some we had. Jim, Alyce, and his parents accompanied the escorts to the mess hall for supper. During the meal Jim went on and on about the butter. He could never have any while in prison. Still he didn't have a great appetite. I attributed that to the excitement. I couldn't detect depression.

Jim and Alyce treated each other with affection and warmth, as you would expect of a couple who had been away from each other for nine years. Happy reminiscing. They discussed the kids. Jim was eager to see Jimmy and the three girls. About eight o'clock, Jim and Alyce phoned them together. I was relieved that the first day had gone so well. Finally, about eleven, Jim's parents left, and Alyce did so a half hour later.

ALYCE   He wanted me to stay that night, but I couldn't. I couldn't.

LARRY RYAN   I instantly liked Jim. In fact, I never thought we were strangers. After Alyce left he was still excited, all hopped up about everything. When I left him at one in the morning, sleep wasn't something he was ready to take on.

March 19, 1973

Dear Major Thompson,

No words can compensate you for the ordeal you have passed through for your country. The captivity you have undergone for nine years, the longest in American history, required a strength of faith, patience and patriotism which can never be fully comprehended by others. However, I do want to impress on you the heartfelt gratitude that I and millions of other Americans feel toward you on your return.

Some things about America may appear to have changed since your departure. That is inevitable. But I can assure you there has been no change in the pride and gratitude the American people feel for what our servicemen have done in Indochina and the thankfulness we share on your safe return.

Your resolute courage is a source of inspiration to us all. My sincerest wishes for your future success and happiness. Welcome home.

Richard Nixon

PAUL BLAIR   I was staying in the same hotel as Alyce, so a military chauffeur took both of us back to our rooms. On the way I asked Alyce how things had gone, how she felt. One thing led to another and I became a marriage counselor.

ALYCE   We went into the hotel bar, had a drink, and talked. Finally, I said, "I'm going to my room." Paul took me back but I was so upset we sat in my room and talked and talked. He was sympathetic. He went out and got a bottle of scotch.

PAUL BLAIR   Alyce was feeling mixed emotions. She discussed where her life had gone after Jim's capture. Her attachment to the other guy appeared strong. He had provided well for the kids. The kids liked him. They were doing well in school. She was not ashamed that she had been living with him. I had no reason to question her. We developed a close rapport. I encouraged her to give Jim a chance.

ALYCE   Before Paul left that night he asked what I was going to do.
"I have a lot of thinking to do tonight," I said. "I'll let you know in the morning."

PAUL BLAIR   Alyce said it all depended on what transpired the next day when the kids came down. No one knew how they would react.

ALYCE   I stayed up the rest of the night thinking this thing through. I drank four little bottles of scotch from the room's refrigerator as I debated whether to go back with Jim. I might just as well have been drinking tea. I'd never drunk so much and not gotten drunk. About four a.m. I made my decision. I would go back to Jim. Not because I loved him. I didn't. I was repulsed by his appearance and I was hurt by what he had caused to happen to our lives in the last nine years. I would go back to him because of the kids. I know that sounds like a cop-out, but that's the damn truth. I thought the kids would be happier back with their father and would live a better life than I could offer at Willa and Marty's. I called Harold near dawn. He'd been awake, he said.

"I have come to a decision," I said.

"What is it?"

"I'm going to go back with Jim."

"Why?" he asked.

"Because of the children."

"Well, you do whatever you think best," Harold said. He wasn't angry. He never showed anger. He choked up and cried. Then I called Marty and Willa, and told them to bring the kids down.

March 21, 1973

Dear Jim,

After all these years I doubt you will remember my name, so let me jog your memory a little bit. We were both in Ethan Allen Chapter[*] in Dumont. You had me by a few years but we went on quite a few visitations together. In March 1964 I was living in Lodi when word was published in the Bergen Evening Record you were lost in 'Nam. I didn't know how to reach your family or even know you had married. The usual church services were held but nothing else was ever heard.

I moved my family to California. In time an organization known as VIVA became active in this part of the country and started to put out POW/MIA bracelets with the names of people on them. Tried with all my might to get one with your name on it, but the organization said they had no permission from your next of kin to do so. Even wrote to the chief of information in Washington to try to find your family to get permission. No luck.

The unbelievable happened when they published those darned lists of POWs. You were on it. Since then my family and I have watched every telecast about returnees, collected all the information from the local and

---

[*] Of the Order of De Molay, a national young men's organization sponsored by the Masons.

Los Angeles papers and, heck, I've even ordered the Bergen Record hoping to find a little more information. Caught the TV shots of you getting off the C-141 in McGuire and got pictures of the TV with you in front of the microphones. You sure were a sight for a pair of hopeful eyes. Welcome home soldier, we've missed you.

Fraternally yours,
Arthur L. Gunzel

Psychiatrist Segal, with the Center for Prisoner of War Studies in San Diego, explained in his 1972 report on therapeutic considerations for returning POWs that a serviceman's self-image often is "severely altered," that is, damaged, by long periods of captivity.

"It is not simply that he has moved precipitously from freedom to enslavement, from a potent military role to degradation and impotence. He has also altered physically, aged and deteriorated by the passage of time and the privations and stresses of captivity. The devastating changes in self-concept are a long time being undone. . . . [T]he released POW's first experiences with important figures in his life will often help shape the quality of his adjustment over the long term, and it is of considerable importance, therefore, to allow for a period immediately upon repatriation which the POW can utilize to begin altering his self-image, the image he presents to the world. . . .

"We comb our hair and straighten our tie—even smile into the mirror—when we anticipate an important appointment," wrote Segal. "The POW must be allowed a moment in time to do likewise, as he struggles to erase the years of physical deterioration and psychological squalor imbedded in body and mind."

JIM JR.   Memories of my father start that March day in 1973. Before that, he didn't exist for me.

LAURA   It was a sunny day. A beautiful day. The air was so chilly we wore winter coats. I didn't understand a thing about the Vietnam War. I was just a twelve-year-old whose father was returning from it.

ALYCE The guards at the gate were alerted to expect my aunt and the children. Finally the call came, "They're on their way in."

PAUL BLAIR The hospital, a low red brick facility, had been built during World War II. Outside the back entrance was a concrete ramp with steel-pipe railings. It was there that we waited. Suddenly the kids came around the corner of the hospital. Three girls and the boy.

LARRY RYAN I watched from the hallway inside, through the glass doors. All around me were white-uniformed hospital staff.

ALYCE Jim and I had walked to the top of the ramp to wait.

JIM THOMPSON Jimmy was the first to look up and see me. He took off on a run.

JIM JR. My dad wasn't ready for it, or maybe he was too weak. But I ran, jumped, and knocked him dead on his ass.

JIM THOMPSON It was a tackle that would have done justice to a professional football player. The girls then piled on top like a football skirmish.

LAURA "I love you," my dad was saying. "I love you. I love you. It's so good to be home! I missed you!" I'll remember that till I die. When I looked up, nurses, orderlies, doctors were peeking from every window. Every one of them crying.

ALYCE It was the first time Jimmy had seen his father; the first time Jim had seen his son. He cried. The kids cried. All the people lining the windows. Only Ruthie laid back on seeing her father.

RUTH I felt the excitement of the moment, sure, but I didn't feel happy. Jimmy was giving him all kinds of hugs. Not me. I was scared. He was a stranger. And I wasn't used to being the center of attention. All these people staring out from doors, from windows.

LAURA My father looked sick. So thin and pale. He had no cheeks, only bones. We could tell he'd been through hell. Hugging him I remember thinking how skinny his neck was. His head looked so big on that neck. He could have worn my pants he was so thin.

PAM He looked a whole lot older than I expected. Of course, he was floored by the change in me.

JIM THOMPSON I didn't recognize my daughters. Pam was not yet six when I left. The three girls all had blond curly hair. Now I had three brunettes. All very pretty young ladies but I doubt I would have recognized them. But Jimmy . . . well, I could have picked him out of a thousand boys. He was the spitting image of me as a kid.

LAURA My brother was in awe, seeing the man said to be his father.

LARRY RYAN   Those kids looked great. Neat, clean. Smiles on their faces. Nice manners. And so happy to be with their father. I was impressed. Someone, I thought, had spent time with those children. You don't get kids like that by accident. We took the whole group inside.

LAURA   The hospital was old and creepy but the people were as good as gold.

ALYCE   We went into a dayroom reserved for us and it turned into a party. They had snuck in some booze, of course, and it flowed freely.

TED JOHANSSON   Jim wore a grin that wouldn't stop.

LAURA   He had bought us all gold watches with our names engraved on them. We began vying for his attention. Each of us had a million questions and wanted them answered at the same time. We asked what he had gone through. He didn't want to talk about it. He wanted to see our report cards and school pictures and how our looks had changed from year to year. We began to talk about what it was going to be like being a real family. We began making vacation plans, discussing what kind of house we wanted. He told us silly things we used to do when we were toddlers. Through all the fun there were plenty of tears.

I could see our reunion was hardest on Ruthie. As youngest daughter she had no idea what to expect. Pam and I at least had talked about him coming home.

RUTH   There were so many people, all wanting me, expecting me, to be so happy, so glad he was back. I didn't know what was going on. Suddenly I just missed all my friends. I wanted to get away.

LAURA   We needed time to get used to him. It was like, "Yes, you're my father. But who *are* you?"

PAM   After a while his attention pretty much focused on Jimmy, "the boy he hadn't seen." I slid into the background and out of everybody's way.

LAURA   We could sense he was mostly excited about seeing his son. Jimmy knew it too. The only boy. He had heard this in the press. It's what the kids back home talked about before we left. He was the spitting image of my dad. All the staff and the brass there at Valley Forge said, "Oh, his only son! Look at him!" We listened as Dad told Jimmy different stories of what he did when he was a child, how similar it was to Jimmy's experience. Jimmy hogged Dad's attention. Got such a swelled head. It bugged me. I smacked him a couple of times when we were alone. I said, "Knock it off!"

JIM JR.   Yeah, he sort of favored me over the rest of 'em. I was all wrapped up in trying to get to know him, and he was trying to get to know me. We laughed and carried on. He was all dressed up in his uniform. I took his beret and wore it around the hospital.

LARRY RYAN   That afternoon Jim's parents left. There was too much hustle and bustle going on for them. Before they left they talked with Jim and had their say. Jim obviously was close to his mother. He told me she looked older, more tired than he expected. She dressed like an older European woman. Jim and the kids went shopping at the exchange before returning for dinner. In the evening the adults went to the officers' club on post, where the drinking continued. In those first couple of days Jim was partying pretty good and it became a concern. He was partying far more than the other POWs. And we didn't know yet how sick he was.

ALYCE   Jim's feet were rotten. He also had worms and trouble digesting normal food. But booze didn't bother him at all. The amount of drinking began to disturb me too. But I thought, well, he didn't have a drink for nine years. Maybe the problems from before are past and this drinking will ease off.

LARRY RYAN   All of us escorts met daily with the homecoming team chief to tell him what was going on with our returnees. I said I thought Alyce and Jim were going to make it. Then another problem surfaced. We got word a story was about to break in a Massachusetts newspaper that Alyce was really married to somebody else. The POW project officer called me and Alyce's escort into his office and asked if the story was true. Captain Johansson said, no, Alyce had not remarried. He didn't volunteer anything else. That seemed to be the end of it.

FROM THE *Worcester Evening Gazette*, MARCH 20, 1973

NO RECORD OF THOMPSON IN HUDSON

Reports that Major Floyd J. Thompson, 39, longest held prisoner of the Vietnam War, is a resident of Hudson, Mass., have not been officially substantiated.

The *Hudson Sun* has checked the records of the Town Clerk to see if he has ever been a resident of the community, and there is no evidence he has been.

Persistent reports that his wife, Alice, is residing in Hudson with the major's nine-year-old son who he's never seen, and three other children, also haven't been substantiated. There is no record at the Town Clerk's office that an Alice Thompson and family are residing in Hudson.

A *Hudson Sun* reporter talked with the woman living in Hudson who was first believed to be Thompson's wife, but she said she was not Thompson's wife. The same Hudson woman, however, is at the Valley Forge Hospital outside

Philadelphia this morning conferring in private with Major Thompson, according to a report from United Press International. (See photo on Page 3.) As of
this writing, she still hasn't admitted to being the wife of the freed prisoner.

LARRY RYAN   The next morning, on March 21st, Jim went to the gym
and did his PT, then we started the rounds on his physical. Different specialists came by to see if he wasn't suffering from this or that—urology,
dermatology, ear, nose, and throat, and X-rays. My job was to keep him on
schedule yet let him do what he wanted to do. Trouble was, he didn't want
to do much else once those kids came.

LAURA   There was a champagne breakfast at the hospital one morning.
Dad started to get a little drunk. When I said something about Massachusetts, I saw his temper flare for the first time. That was it. Breakfast was
over. He and my mother stayed in the room alone.

LARRY RYAN   Later that day we had a birthday party on the ward for little Jimmy.

PAUL BLAIR   It was a few days early, but Jimmy wasn't going to be there
for his actual birthday. So the hospital baked a cake.

LARRY RYAN   Jim continued to drink, there and elsewhere, and his physicians started to worry. Too much drinking and staying up late. We didn't
get the drinking down to where it was manageable until Paul Blair left.
The two of them were in a party mood, like two airborne buddies boasting
about how much they drank.

PAUL BLAIR   I was trying hard to win Jim's confidence and improve our
rapport, to overcome the fact that I had lied to him when we first met.
Meanwhile, he was trying to overcome a nine-year deficit and get back in
the mainstream of life. Alyce told me Jim didn't seem like the same guy
who had left nine years earlier. In her mind, a lot had changed. This definitely was the best mood I had seen Jim in since we met in the Philippines.
But after a few days, I returned to Okinawa.

———

LAURA   As those first days passed, me, Ruthie, and Pam became more
withdrawn. Part of it was all the moving around. We had gone from Massachusetts to my aunt's house, and to the hotel at Valley Forge, then back
and forth to the hospital every day. My parents talked a lot behind closed
doors. We got sent to the cafeteria or to the rec room.

ALYCE   Finally the kids had to get back in school. Ruthie was scheduled to
have her tonsils out. So the kids went back with Aunt Willa. I lived out of
a suitcase there at the BOQ.

LARRY RYAN   He had spent so much time with the kids we had fallen four days behind his hospital schedule. Jim's biggest physical problem became lack of sleep. He looked very drawn. There were dark circles under his eyes. He said he was having nightmares.

ALYCE   The doctors said he was reliving bad times. What he had been through for nine years. He woke up screaming, soaked with sweat.

LARRY RYAN   An Army finance team came to Jim's room and gave him two checks, one in payment for all the leave he didn't use during captivity. The other was the difference between what Alyce had been paid and what Jim had earned. He gave both checks to me and asked me to take them home. I was uneasy about doing that. "I insist," he said. "I will decide what I want to do with them later on." It shocked me that he didn't want to do something else with the money.

ALYCE   Jim didn't talk about his captivity at first. Then they had people come to question him. I sat through some of it. I demanded to. After all, he wanted to know what went on in my life. I had a right to know what went on in his. He talked about eating rats and bugs.

LARRY RYAN   Debriefing by Army Intelligence was one of the last things on Jim's schedule. He didn't want to do it. He didn't indicate why. Even after a few weeks with Alyce and the kids it took him a while to get started. After the first session or two, Jim said it was slow going but he felt good he could remember so much. He talked to me about having built a special home in his mind. In retelling the stories, Jim had a mental sharpness. He answered all my questions lucidly, intelligently. He said he wanted to write a book to tell soldiers what to expect if captured. That had been a serious failure in his own training.

ALYCE   Jim had expected everything to be like it was. Clothing, hairstyles. When I met him at the hospital I was wearing a red minidress with white polka dots and white boots. Jim looked at me odd. But one young POW, paralyzed from the waist down, asked, "Is that what the ladies are wearing now? Boy, I sure like that." Not Jim. Within the first week at the hospital he said, "What's happened to you? You're not the Alyce I left."

"No," I said, "I'm not. I had to learn to fight my own battles and be my own woman."

"Well, I don't like it," he said. "I want what I left."

"Well, you ain't going to get it."

I was not about to give up my independence and go back to asking him for a dollar every time I needed a pair of stockings.

————

GAIL MEYER   There was a lot of suspicion that women had been unfaithful. At Balboa Naval Hospital, where Lew was taken, it was like the Spanish Inquisition. Everyone asked how the wives had behaved. I could hear beatings in some rooms. A lot of women had been swinging. I didn't. I didn't think it appropriate. I kept real close to our children, my boys.

I believe Lew suffered some brain damage in Vietnam. He had had an infection in his ear from the moment he was captured. Now his mind wandered and he had black moods of depression. There were times when he could not think a thought through. I had to remind him what he was talking about. For five years Lew probably had fantasized day and night about our marriage and how I and the boys would be there for him. I began to understand this after he had been back a few days. Our whole world had to revolve around Lew. I was at the hospital day and night, rushing back and forth to take care of Jeff, our youngest, then a high school senior. One day Jeff called me hysterical about one of our terriers being injured. I was under tension anyway. Lew heard only one side of the phone conversation. "Who?" he asked. "Who is hung up on a fence?" My side of the conversation was shaking him up. I put the phone down and told him one of the terriers.

"The goddamn dog?"

At that I was angry. I said I was going home. Then Lew's mother gets into it. "You don't dare leave this room and my son."

"And I don't think I will come back," I said. "You're all crazy."

The priest caught me in the lobby. I returned. But that episode put everything into perspective for me. I'd been very happy by myself. I was well on the way to a degree. My kids were good human beings. I was not about to change, to go back to where I was when Lew left. Yet I was doing all these things the doctors were telling me to do, saying all the things they were telling me to say. I thought, Someday Lew's going to come home and believe that's the way the world really is! I decided not to have all this game-playing.

Yet many POW wives hung on to this role, acting as if all they had to do was say, "You're the heroes and the world revolves around you." As a family we needed to know that not only was Lew important but I was important and Jeff was important and Bill, our oldest, was important. Lew was sympathetic. He was pleased with the changes in me but it was still hard for him to cope.

———

DON MacPHAIL   My wife wasn't doing any explaining in the hospital, but I could tell everything was different. Her hairstyle, the way she carried herself. She didn't look bad, just different. She had an air about her. Very independent. My kids were as cute as buttons, but they didn't even call me "Daddy." You shake it off, saying you can change it in time. I was willing to give the marriage a try.

Jim was even more upset than I was. "Mac," he said, "I love her. I blame myself for what happened, but I just don't know if I am adult enough to accept the situation." Jim was bullshit about his money situation. He threw up his hands. Didn't know what to do. I told him I would give it a shot.

But the anger comes out. You can destroy everything with anger. You begin thinking every time you were tortured, every time you buried a friend, she might have been making love to another guy. There were awful feelings of guilt, too. "If only I hadn't got captured. If I had done something different that day." We expected our wives to be angels—take care of the kids and adhere to our code of conduct. Then you get more angry at yourself because you can't accept it. You spent your time not letting these communist bastards get to you, looking forward to your family, and when you get home you find that goal tarnished. You don't know how to react. If you show emotion and yell and scream you say to yourself, Am I doing this because I am a prisoner of war?

No one gave us any time to sit back and put things in perspective. Psychiatrists, everyone, were telling us what to do. We were tired of being told what to do. But we did what they said because we didn't know what to do ourselves. The psychiatrist at Valley Forge used to get me so damn mad. He was trying to find my flash point. Was I living in reality or off on a trip someplace? They gave us every test in the world, even down to classes on having sex again. A lot of guys had problems having sex when they got home. At Valley Forge they told us it was something upstairs, something in our heads. Afraid to expose our emotions. Then you start feeling inferior and want to go rip someone's head off.

ALYCE Jim was interested in me staying overnight in the hospital, but I didn't want to. The idea of sleeping with him turned me off.

LARRY RYAN On the afternoon of the 24th of March, Jim finished his debriefings with military intelligence. Then my escort diary says, "To Guest Quarters." For the next two nights, Jim and Alyce got off the ward and shared a room.

ALYCE Jim had by no means been a lover before he went to Vietnam. It was always "Slam, bam, thank you ma'am." Nothing to it. He hadn't cared if he satisfied his partner. Back then you didn't talk about such things.

That night it was just like it had always been. Wham, bam. When he fell asleep I got up and wrote a long letter to Jean Ledbetter. I questioned whether I had made the right decision. I said I was glad for Jean, that she didn't have to go through something like this. I poured out my heart and soul to her. And when I got done, when I got it all out of my system, I took the letter and burned it.

37 ▪ PULLING UP ROOTS

LARRY RYAN   Jim was a pleasant guy to be around—cooperative and friendly. Doing his best to get through this adjustment period. I was eager to get down there each day. The Army wanted returnees brought back into the world at their own pace, so my whole family had to keep quiet about my being Jim's escort. My only confessor was my wife, Obe. I'd unwind each day by talking to her.

SAM DEACON   The Army was no help to me in trying to contact Jim. They said he was somewhere out of town. "Can you give me a phone number?" It was unlisted. There was too much press interest, too many well-wishers.

LARRY RYAN   Nothing Alyce said suggested to me that she and Jim were having problems. I thought they were adjusting fine. One Sunday afternoon I drove them out to my house in Pottstown for supper.

OBE RYAN   Jim looked very drawn, eyes still sunken, even after days of care. We drove them through neighborhoods and towns and the state park. It was marvelous to see Jim react to the outside world. He couldn't believe the cost of cars and houses. Everything was a faster pace than he remembered. It overwhelmed him. Back at our house a neighbor family joined us for a cookout.

LARRY RYAN   My son brought over his friend as if to say, "Look what my dad brought home." Jim was super with the kids. He answered all their questions, then had his picture taken with them.

OBE RYAN   We sat around the dining-room table with our mouths open, listening to Jim's stories. Completely captivated. He described an experience none of us could relate to. He didn't talk about the torture, not with the kids there. The neighbors' seven-month-old, who normally wiggled and twisted, sat on Jim's lap contented as could be. Jim was glad to hold him too.

Jim and Alyce seemed to be trying very hard to be close, to stick it out. But Alyce didn't hide anything when she and I talked alone. She told me about the house in Massachusetts and the pool. It was by way of saying "This is how I survived" rather than expressing any guilt. I could understand her too. I couldn't do what she did but I didn't condemn her either.

LARRY RYAN   Jim talked a great deal about his dreamhouse. How in captivity he tried to figure the cost of all his materials to build it. I thought he'd try to build it, too, he was so strong-willed. When we'd walk the hospital grounds he'd talk about this and about his family. He complained that the Army hadn't watched how Alyce spent his money.

Jim had more psychological testing done, at his initiative. He complained that he had lost some ability to remember. That was funny, because the doc came out and he said, "If he's lost any of his mental faculties, I would have liked to have seen him before Vietnam!" He was sharp as a razor. For instance, I had been asking him every day what he wanted me to do with two sizable paychecks he gave me. Finally he said that he remembered the name of a man at Fort Benning who had opened a checking account for him almost a decade earlier. We called down there and damn if that man wasn't still there, now vice president of the bank. They made the necessary arrangements over the telephone.

I got Jim a new uniform. He got a haircut and a new ID card. He made sure his ribbons were correct and his boots spit-shined. He did his own boots too, because he wanted an airborne finish. He was an absolute perfectionist. And on the afternoon of March 29 we held his first press conference.

DON MacPHAIL   Jim and I were the first Army POWs allowed to talk with the press.

THOMPSON: Ladies and gentlemen of the press, thank you for the opportunity to meet you and, through you, to speak to the American people. Each and every one of us ex-POWs has a story to tell and is more than anxious to tell it. I had planned to begin with a prepared statement. However, I

feel you know better than I what the American people want to hear. Therefore I shall defer to your questions.

REPORTER: Major, a Navy captain said today he estimated ninety-five percent of prisoners held in the North were either tortured mentally or physically. Were you tortured?

THOMPSON: Yes, definitely so.

REPORTER: In what way?

THOMPSON: Both physical and mental torture. Five years in solitary confinement, for example. Physical torture was applied on several occasions.
Beatings, my arms tied behind my back, strung over a rafter on the ceiling. I was strangled at one point, beaten with hands, fists, forced to bow
to Vietnamese cadre by being kicked in the belly, my head smashed on
the ground. . . . The list is rather lengthy.

REPORTER: When did this end?

THOMPSON: When I was moved into a prison in Hanoi in July '68.

REPORTER: Did the Vietnamese give you any reason for doing this?

THOMPSON: I believe they were interested in forcing propaganda statements out of prisoners.

REPORTER: Did they break very many people in the POW camps?

THOMPSON: I have no idea. I know what they did to me.

REPORTER: Did they break you, major?

THOMPSON: I was forced to sign a statement. But I don't consider this being
broken, because my spirit was never broken, my attitude never changed.

REPORTER: Could you elaborate on what type of punishment you received,
Sergeant MacPhail?

MacPHAIL: When I was first captured I was hanged over a tree limb and
beaten for about four hours with bamboo sticks. There were three graves
below me. I was told I would be the fourth one. I had been shot in the
upper part of my leg. During interrogation an iron rod was stuck through
my leg many times while they were asking me questions. For the next six
or eight days I was beaten unconscious. And every time I regained consciousness I was beaten until I was unconscious again. I weighed one hundred and ninety pounds when I was captured. In less than four months I
was down to one hundred thirteen pounds. I bled every time I urinated or
defecated for about nine months.

REPORTER: Why were they doing this to you? To what end?

MacPHAIL: I had escaped a couple of times, although I had been beaten
even before I escaped.

REPORTER: Major Thompson, did you try to escape?

THOMPSON: I made five escape attempts, yes.

REPORTER: What kind of punishment did you get for escaping? How far did you get?

THOMPSON: The first three escape attempts I received rather severe punishment. On the fourth one it was even worse. On the fifth escape attempt, which was in October of '71, I received no punishment whatsoever.

REPORTER: Did you get far?

THOMPSON: A day and a half was the longest I managed to stay from them.

REPORTER: Major, you mentioned signing a statement. What did that statement say?

THOMPSON: That I was receiving very kind and humane treatment and had never been beaten or tortured or maltreated in any way.

REPORTER: How did they get you to sign that statement?

THOMPSON: [Laughing] That question has already been answered.

REPORTER: Sergeant, did they force you to sign anything?

MacPHAIL: Yes, sir. One statement. . . .

REPORTER: There has been discussion of America providing financial aid to help rebuild North Vietnam. What is your reaction to a proposal like that?

MacPHAIL: I think we ought to spend more money building B-52s.

REPORTER: Major, there has been talk of possible dissension among POWs regarding signing of statements, et cetera.

THOMPSON: None of us signed those statements voluntarily. . . . It was a matter of death staring you in the face. It was either die or sign it. I felt these propaganda statements weren't worth dying over.

REPORTER: Did the presence of antiwar people like Jane Fonda and Joan Baez in Hanoi improve your conditions, major, or did they aggravate the treatment you received?

THOMPSON: Considerably aggravated it. These people contributed more to prolonging the war than anything else that's happened. These people created the atmosphere that there was dissension in the American population. Capitalizing on this attitude caused the Vietnamese to hold out longer in the negotiations.

REPORTER: Are you saying you don't believe there was dissension in the American population?

THOMPSON: Do you believe there was?

REPORTER: Yes sir.

THOMPSON: Apparently it's so. And this is one of the most disheartening aspects of this entire war. It's certainly the toughest thing we had to bear as prisoners. To know some people didn't believe in what we were doing.

REPORTER: Major Thompson, state legislators around the country are getting together, drafting bills for special consideration for all POWs, like tax breaks and things like this. Do you think because you were incarcerated in

Vietnam the country or your state or your family or your township owes you something more than any other Vietnam veteran?

THOMPSON: Certainly not. Being a prisoner of war was a hell of a way to spend the war. I'd much rather have been out and fighting for it. I don't believe we are entitled to any special consideration.

REPORTER: Major, in a very general way, could you describe what a day is like in a prison camp?

THOMPSON: That could range anywhere from absolute boredom to twelve-hour indoctrination sessions. The sessions took the form of material read to us, movies, lectures, tape recordings, some from Americans like Dr. Spock. We heard several other prominent people—senators, congressmen, American writers, Nobel Prize winners. Their quotes were read to us or we heard taped broadcasts.

REPORTER: Major, what would you say to somebody like Dr. Spock who was working in that movement, if you were facing him today?

THOMPSON: I'm afraid I wouldn't talk with my mouth.

REPORTER: Major, what contributed to your ability to survive for nine years in prison?

THOMPSON: Just making up your mind you're gonna make it. I can say with complete assurance there are three phases. One, faith in God. Two, faith in country. Three, faith in the love of a good woman. It was these three things that saw me through. . . .

REPORTER: Major, are you from Hudson, Massachusetts? Is that correct?

THOMPSON: No, I'm not. I'm from New Milford, New Jersey.

REPORTER: Have you ever been in Hudson?

THOMPSON: No. My wife and children are living there now.

REPORTER: With relatives or . . .

THOMPSON: She was obliged to move to Massachusetts because the press hounded her to death and she had to hide somewhere.

HOSPITAL COMMANDER: Thank you very much.

[The press conference ends abruptly.]

LARRY RYAN   Jim felt he had done a good job. Now CBS wanted to interview him in Washington. Jim agreed to go only if I could too. That evening we flew by helicopter to Bethesda Naval Hospital outside D.C.

ALYCE   I decided to have my tubes tied at Valley Forge. I wasn't about to get pregnant again. But the day I had my operation, goddamn if Jim didn't go off to Washington. I went down to surgery and come back from surgery all by myself.

LARRY RYAN   Everyone knew who they had on the chopper when it arrived at Bethesda. Jim was treated like a VIP. We landed on a medical center helipad and were met by a Navy captain who asked if Jim would be willing to meet his admiral, the hospital commander. Jim said, "By all means." A Navy car took us about a half block to the front door, where a rear admiral stood waiting. We were escorted up to a ward by a medical service corps officer.

There was a common bond among the returnees, and Jim quickly began sharing experiences with the Navy POWs. Then we had a driver assigned to take us wherever we wanted to go. We went to the club for supper, then left the grounds. I don't recall when we called it a night, but it was late.

The next morning a woman from Defense Department public affairs met us and we headed for the CBS studios. They did a little makeup work. I sat behind the glass, on the other side of the studio. Not a penetrating interview. After the show, we went to the Mayflower Hotel for breakfast, then walked around Washington. Jim looked in every window we passed. Bought a few jackets. A tuxedo and a cabana set. I can't recall where the money came from, but returnees got all kinds of free gifts and offers for goods at reduced prices. We flew back to Valley Forge later that afternoon. It had been a good day, Jim's first in public. He had handled himself extremely well.

FROM THE *Bergen Record*, APRIL 3, 1973

WINTER OF DESPAIR ENDS
by George James

It takes two and a half hours to travel by car from Bergen County to Valley Forge General Hospital. For Floyd J. Thompson, measure the trip in light years. It was not made without great pain. Major Thompson was a prisoner of war. He holds the unasked-for distinction of being the longest-held American POW. When he arrived at the hospital March 19, three days after his release from a North Vietnam prison, he had not seen his wife and three daughters in nine years. He had never met his son. The boy was born a day after a plane in which Thompson was riding as an observer on a recon mission disappeared over Quan Tri Province. Floyd Jr. is nine. . . .

The skeletal-like face with the dark hollows around the eyes softened in a grin as he recalled the homecoming incident that occurred only a week and a half before.

Thompson sat on a low platform facing reporters in the hospital conference room not far from where George Washington's troops survived the most difficult winter of the American Revolution. A Green Beret, Thompson was captured in 1964. He was thirty-one. When he came to Valley Forge two weeks ago, his face belonged to an old man. But now, with the military crew cut and the Class A uniform decked with ribbons, he looked young and vigorous. . . .

When he went into solitary confinement for five years, he took with him that attitude, fortified by eight years of Army service and the traditions of a country that was not questioning the war yet. There were no Harlem or Paterson riots for Thompson, no Watts or Detroit or Newark. There were no campus demonstrations. Robert Kennedy and Martin Luther King had not been assassinated. The Democratic National Convention in Chicago, in which the very process of selecting a leader seemed to be shaking apart, was in the future. There was no slow, steady assault on individual and national beliefs and assumptions.

Instead, there was the enemy, a hut in a South Vietnamese jungle and later the prisons in North Vietnam. There were beatings, political indoctrination and boredom. One could not believe the stories about division in America. There were statements against U.S. involvement attributed to prominent Americans. Thompson and the other prisoners eventually had to believe there was dissension. It was, he said, the most disheartening aspect of their situation: That some Americans doubted America's role in Vietnam. Thompson must have clung steadfastly to that world he left in 1964. He could not afford the luxury of questioning his country's actions. The things that saw him through, he told reporters, were "faith in God . . . faith in country . . . and faith in the love of a good woman."

He made it sound as simple as an act of the will to survive. Listening to him, you could imagine Thompson reliving the small and great things from the day he was born in Englewood Hospital. Growing up in Cresskill. Remembering things like setting up audiovisual equipment for teachers at Bergenfield Junior-Senior High School. Of his parents in Lodi. The classic lines of the red brick Old North Church in Dumont where he met his bride-to-be, Alyce, in the Sunday school when they were kids, how it looked when they were married there. . . .

What emerged at the press conference was a blend of human courage and a bitterness against his captors and the people of the antiwar movement. The movement prolonged the war, he said, a theme repeated over and over

again by other POWs. At best, the peace people were sincere but misguided, Thompson said. You got the impression that just as the POWs had
been a kind of reason for staying in Vietnam, now they had become a symbol to prove the enemy's inhumanity. The message that seemed to evolve
wrongly implied that any action against the enemy had been acceptable
because he was not human.

The reporters as well as hospital and military people applauded Thompson when the press conference ended. He was making preparations to get to
know his family again, to leave Valley Forge where the Continental Army in
1777–78 made it through what since had been termed a winter of despair. It
had been a symbolic setting for a press conference, both for a prisoner of
war who had risen above despair, and a country that has come through a
long, hard winter and has yet to resolve its differences about a war in
Indochina that still may not be over.

OBE RYAN   Ford was giving returnees a car to use for a year. Somebody
else gave them baseball tickets for a lifetime. Clothes stores said, "Just
come on down and we will fit you." They could telephone anyone in the
world for free.

LARRY RYAN   So many organizations tried to do right by the POWs. A
year's ticket to Disney World in Florida. Education opportunities for the
kids. As the offers came in I put them into a book. I didn't want Jim to lose
any of it.

OBE RYAN   It was an exciting time, and Alyce was drawn into it. When
she visited our home a second time she seemed more upbeat.

ALYCE   Jim was only back a couple of weeks when the Army promoted him
to lieutenant colonel. A lot of pressure comes with the silver oak leafs.

LARRY RYAN   Jim worried about his career, that he lacked experience for
such a senior rank. But it was a handicap he thought he could handle.

———

LAURA   As we kids settled in with my aunt and uncle in Pennsylvania, we
began to realize how much we missed Harold. I missed the house too. I
missed our routine. Finishing school that year in Honesdale was rough.
We didn't get along with the other kids. My grades were terrible. And I
didn't know what to expect when I came home anymore. Sometimes my
mother would be in tears. Sometimes her and my uncle would be fighting
over little things like grocery shopping or laundry. My aunt and uncle had
lived alone for years, and suddenly they had four children and a grown
woman. We were always underfoot. Mom still was unsettled about the

decision to return to my father. She had let one man go and she was setting her sights on another but the relationship was shaky.

_____

DON MacPHAIL   Three POWs got our noses fixed there at Valley Forge. Jim and me and Richard Perricone. We had bad noses from beatings which made it hard to breathe.

LARRY RYAN   Jim also wanted his ears pinned back.

ALYCE   He was trying to look handsomer. He even had Jimmy's ears done there at Valley Forge because they were big too. Jim also had extensive dental surgery, and later a vasectomy. Every time I turned around he had another operation. That's why he stayed in Valley Forge so long. I wanted him out so we could begin life as a family.

LARRY RYAN   As the weeks passed I began to look upon Jim almost as a brother. Escort duty was about over. They didn't want me to be a crutch he leaned on forever. The night before Jim was due to leave, he told me he didn't think the marriage to Alyce was going to work. He couldn't get it out of his mind that she had been with another guy all those years, and that his money had been squandered. It was a festering sore. "It keeps gnawing away at me," he said. "I can't forget."

_____

ALYCE   Jim insisted on going with me to Harold's house in Hudson. I wanted to go to my aunt's place in Pennsylvania, and then me and Willa could go up to get my furniture. I tried to talk Jim out of a Massachusetts trip. "What do you want to put yourself through that for?" He said he had to do it. Maybe he had visions of it being a shack. If so he was in for a surprise.

We both drank on the plane. In Boston we rented a car and Jim insisted on driving. I said, "That's foolish. I've lived around here and I know where I'm goin'." Oh God, he got all ugly after that. We finally pulled into the driveway. Harold was home. It was very tense. I introduced them and they shook hands. There were no harsh words. Jim was too much of a gentleman to hit Harold. A lot of anger was building up inside him, though. He eventually would let it loose on me.

TED JOHANSSON   Jim wanted me there that day in Hudson to "meet the man who had looked after his family." He introduced Harold that way too. The whole thing was so very strange. I accepted it because these people accepted it. I only spent the evening there, but they were going to stay together, at the house. Harold was like a brother-in-law in the background.

Given the emotional pain Jim Thompson must have endured during that trip to Hudson, the anger he had to control upon meeting Harold and seeing the house that his paychecks, while a POW, helped to finance, the obvious question for Jim was why he made the trip.

So I asked him that during one of our interviews in 1985.

I went to Massachusetts to meet the sergeant. That's all. No-good bastard. [*Laughing*] But I met him.

That must have been terribly painful.
Yes. Painful. But I want to look. That's all. Look.

Nice house?
Gorgeous house.

You emptied the house of furniture?
I determined, "Take it all!" All of it.

ALYCE   As we packed, Jim wanted to know where his parachute was. The damn thing was silk and it had started to rot while he was gone. So we had made big tents out of it in the backyard. The wind caught it and tore it to shreds. He got all over me about that. He also got mad that I couldn't find his camera, and that clothes in his footlocker smelled damp and musty. Shit, they came back damp and musty from Vietnam.

I went to bed that night exhausted. Downstairs something happened between Jim and Harold. Words were said, but I never learned what. My neighbor Sheila came by the next morning and gave me the prettiest charm bracelet with little memories of our years of friendship. "I'm losing one of my best friends and I hate it," she said, crying.

Saying goodbye to Harold was emotional too. I knew it was breaking up a home. But I had to give living with Jim a chance. I didn't want my four kids coming back to me later and saying, "Why didn't you?" Or even myself saying, "Maybe I should have."

Harold and I hugged. I got in the car. He might have cried. I didn't see it. We headed down to Pennsylvania.

38 ■ POWER OF FAITH

DON MacPHAIL   Living by the Code of Conduct during the war was easy compared to the code we had to live by when we got home. And the longer we were home, the worse it got. I found out more and more things my wife didn't tell me. When I finally did leave her I had worked up so much hatred it was like fighting the enemy again. And the anger didn't leave. I shut myself off from the whole world. Months later I was back in the hospital. I never did regain the lost trust.

TED GUY   I estimate that seventy-five percent or more of us got divorced. And it wasn't that we didn't love our wives anymore. But the changes were so dramatic. I had three boys, my youngest in first grade, when I left. When I got home all of them had long hair. The wives were liberal with the children compared to how we would be. We wanted to know where our kids were going with the cars. We wanted them to live by our rules.

One day I even sat them down and asked my boys, "What do you think about the Vietnam War?" They said they were against it. They were sorry I got shot down but all three said they would have gone to jail instead of going there. And here I thought it was a good war, fighting for humans who wanted to be free.

LEW MEYER   It wasn't until October of 1973 that Gail said I was clear-eyed. "You're finally back," she said one day. Before that I was apathetic. I wouldn't even turn on the television. I'd just sit there. "What do you want for dinner, Lew?" she'd ask. I couldn't say.

———

JEAN LEDBETTER   I was stunned to learn Alyce had gone back with Jim. Perhaps after all he'd been through she wanted to give it a chance. Or maybe she did it to save face. Back then people tried more often than they do now to make their marriage work for the kids' sake. In her letters Alyce said Jim was a different person. I wrote back that she probably should have stayed with Harold. Jim found it and was furious. And it was during their first year together again that the kids began having all their problems. My, how it affected their lives.

———

ALYCE   Finally out of the hospital, Jim spent his first period of rest in my aunt's house in Honesdale before he had to report to Fort Benning. The house was crowded. The girls slept in her attic. Jimmy in the den and Jim and I slept on a pullout couch in the living room.

LAURA   Seeing him in the hospital and leaving was one thing. Learning to live with somebody . . . well, it was hard.

JIM JR.   By then we were more like friends than father and son. You can't start a real father-son relationship nine years late.

RUTH   Here I was, an eleven-year-old kid, and suddenly a stranger comes in, takes me away from my school, my friends, and screws up all that was familiar to me. And everyone is telling me how much I must have missed him, how much I should love him.

PAM   I thought at first we would go back to the good times I remembered as a little girl. Maybe they weren't as good as I remembered. But my image of him changed very fast after he joined us. He didn't like to show his emotions or to see someone else show emotions. I felt this coolness. Maybe because I had changed so much too. I wasn't doting on him like a six-year-old. I was strongly attached to Mama.

LAURA   We started getting into a routine. Each morning, for example, he had a soft-boiled egg and coffee.

RUTH   I noticed when he picked up his cup, the coffee would go round and round and round. I said, "How come you shake like that?" You know, kids ask dumb questions like that. He looked at me like I said something awful.

———

ALYCE   A guy from *Reader's Digest* came by and did an extensive interview with Jim. My aunt had a big bedroom with a sitting area. They went in there, shut the door. I wasn't allowed in. I couldn't even make any noise. Willa and Marty had gone off for a couple of weeks. The kids were at school. But Jim made me feel like, "I don't want you hearing this. It's none of your business."

———

LAURA My dad was impressed by so many things we took for granted. Stay-pressed shirts. Teflon cookware. Automatic steering. Color TV. Modern architecture. Soil-resistant carpet. Air conditioning. Men using beauty salons. The first time he drove he couldn't keep the car on the road. It was like learning to drive all over again.

RUTH When we went shopping he laughed at the clothes. He does have a great laugh. Right from the gut.

LAURA He wanted to look cool, to look modern. So we helped him. He started accepting the latest fashions, looking on people who wore them not as creeps anymore.

RUTH He wouldn't wear a straight tie for nothing. He had bow ties, and not just those bitty ones. I'm talking about bow ties! We kidded him but he wouldn't take them off.

LAURA We talked him into bright shirts and plaid pants, chains. He loved to dress cool when out of his Army duds.

RUTH I thought he began dressing kind of feminine. Wild-colored clothes. Wild-looking silk shirts. His socks didn't match his pants but usually matched his shirt. I thought that was crazy.

LAURA More than anything it was the younger generation that surprised him. Kids were so open about different things. Sex, for one. He couldn't wait to see an X-rated movie. He and my mother went to one called *Meatballs.**

ALYCE Oh, God, that was the first X-rated movie I had ever seen. I sat there like this [*hands covering her face*]. Jim watched the whole damn thing.

FROM THE *Bergen Record*, APRIL 26, 1973

POW TO SPEAK AT OLD NORTH

Floyd "Jimmy" Thompson, America's longest held prisoner of war, will speak to the congregation of Old North Reformed Church, Dumont, Sunday at 4 p.m.

The special welcome home service of thanksgiving was organized as a tribute to its former member, says the Rev. Albert Van Dyke, pastor. Thompson and his wife, Alyce, met in Sunday school at Old North, and their three oldest children were baptized there.

---

* This film is not the PG-rated comedy with the same title that was released in 1979.

The youngest child, Jimmy, 9, will be baptized at the regular 11 a.m. service Sunday. Jimmy was born March 27, 1964, the day after his father was shot down over South Vietnam. . . .

Dr. Van Dyke said young Jimmy was never baptized because his mother waited for his father to return. "She's been waiting in faith all this time," Dr. Van Dyke says.

LAURA   With Dad home we began going to church. Before that we hadn't stepped foot in one. We didn't know what going to church was about. That bothered him. Suddenly we were going every Sunday.

ALYCE   I had talked to my mother about getting Jimmy baptized after he was born. She said, "Why don't you wait until Jim gets back?" So I did. And it went on and on and on. After a while I wasn't going to be a hypocrite and go to church with my son when I wasn't going to church myself. I got soured on the church. I went faithfully until this Vietnam mess happened. Then I couldn't understand—why me?

———

RUTH   Dad didn't want anyone to think his marriage was less than perfect. Everything had to be perfect for appearances. We never were to argue or disagree in public. He and my mom had to be happy. The kids had to be happy. We were supposed to be one big happy family. What went on behind closed doors was a different thing. But as far as the newspapers and our friends and everyone else, we were the perfect family. That's the way he wanted it.

———

FROM THE *Bergen Record*, APRIL 29, 1973

A POW ADJUSTS TO FREEDOM
by George James

Just getting used to being free after nine years in prison is the hardest adjustment he has to make, says the longest-held POW of the Vietnam War.

"Freedom is something the average person just doesn't really appreciate until he has it taken away from him," says Lt. Col. Floyd J. Thompson of Bergenfield.

"Just getting used to the very simplest—little things, like walking through a door without having a guard opening it first. Or being able to go for a walk when you feel like it, or driving a car. Or deciding what you're going to have for dinner. . . . just that you have this privilege of thinking and making a decision for yourself to decide what you want to do and when you want to do it. . . ."

Today, Thompson and his family will attend services at the Old North Reformed Church in Dumont where he and his wife, Alyce, met and were married. . . . Thompson will speak to the congregation at four p.m.

There have been problems in readjusting to family life and society again, but these are not insurmountable, he said. Thompson, who spent five of his nine years of captivity in solitary confinement, spoke most strongly about the adjustment of being free again.

"The privilege of going to church. Of getting up when you feel like it or going to bed when you feel like it or reaching over and switching on a light. Picking up a newspaper or turning on a television and finding out what's going on in the world. . . . I'm talking about small things, but just all of these small things put together make a completely different way of life. The precious thing we call freedom is something I'm afraid you really can't appreciate until you have it taken away."

On the lighter side of his readjustment, he said he has had difficulty getting used to new clothing styles, especially men's styles, and long hair and beards. Looking down at his own light blue knit shirt, blue checkered knit trousers, white belt and tan loafers he laughed and said "Anybody that would wear clothes like this ten years ago, why you'd think he was queer. . . ."

On May 24, the Thompsons will attend a presidential reception in Washington with the other POWs and their families.

LAURA   This newspaper wanted a photograph of the whole family walking together up the dirt road in front of my aunt's house.

PAM   I thought it was a dumb idea. And in the rain. But that's what the guy wanted and that's what he got.

LAURA   I was soooooo pissed off! To dress up and go out in the rain for this stupid picture. I had a bad attitude. My Dad sat me down and said, "You know, this really means a lot to me. I would like you to do it and do it with a smile."

"Okay," I said, "let's go.

FROM THE *Bergen Record*, APRIL 29, 1973

POW'S WIFE HAD PATIENCE TESTED
by George James

For almost nine years, Alyce Thompson had to fight her own war.

For almost nine years, Alyce Thompson was not sure her husband, Floyd, was alive. She had doubts she would ever see him again.

To make her trials worse, she was hounded by crackpots and reporters. And right wing groups tried to use her. And through the ordeal, she had to try to raise her four children with faith their father would come home. Perhaps the worst time came when it should have been the best of times.

"When the report came out that he was on the [returning POW] list in January, I got a nice little report from somebody that, yes, he was alive, but he was a mental and physical vegetable," Alyce Thompson says, not wanting to go into details who told her that. . . . As she talks the clock on the wall behind her ticks loudly in the Pennsylvania mountain silence.

"So until I spoke to him on March 16 from the Philippines and I knew he was not at least a mental vegetable, then I told the children he was alive and coming home."

After her husband was captured in 1964, the John Birch Society offered her a lifetime membership. Maj. Gen. Edwin A. Walker, a conservative activist, called saying he had news of her husband. When she returned his call, she discovered he knew nothing about Thompson but wanted her help in his drive to impeach President Lyndon Johnson.

"Newspaper reporters and crackpots were calling me in the middle of the night," she remembers. "The crackpot calls were that they had been praying for us, and some that Jim got just what he deserved because we shouldn't be in that country in the first place."

Then it started with Pam, her oldest daughter. "Pam was coming home in tears every day because the children were teasing her. 'Ha-ha, your daddy's not coming home tonight. Mine is.' Cruelest people in the world, children."

"As for the press, they wanted constant stories," she says. "Is there any news, any news, any news . . ." Her voice trails off. These incidents forced her to take the children away from Ft. Bragg, N.C., and seek seclusion in Massachusetts.

"Now everything's fine," she says in a flat voice. "I think I've got four beautiful healthy children, especially in today's day and age. I'm glad he's home with us again. I'm glad he's as well as he is. I've seen some of them."

Behind her the clock ticks loudly; only now, her husband sits in a rocking chair across from her, smiling.

BERNIE WEISSE   I had just come to know the Lord, and started going to church up the street, when Jim Thompson came back to Old North. It was a spring day. The service was Sunday afternoon. Everybody who was anybody in Dumont was there. Many in the church that day remembered Jim as a young member of the congregation.

LAURA   Old North Church was beautiful. The pews had the old-fashioned trim. It was packed when we got there.

BERNIE WEISSE   To see my old classmate, looking so lean and trim in his white uniform, I couldn't believe it was the same Jimmy Thompson I went through school with. I knew him but I didn't really know him. He looked so fine. Maybe a little haggard in the face but happy.

THE REV. ALBERT VAN DYKE: We welcome each one of you to this special service this afternoon, a homecoming and service of thanksgiving. . . . We cannot mention Jim this afternoon without thinking equally of his devoted wife, Alyce, and their children, and their persistence in faithfully waiting, seeking to keep alive hope and humor in the constant struggle to be brave and true. We remember also the constant concern in this parish of his parents, his brother and family.

CONGREGATION: Amen.

VAN DYKE: Through the open windows we hear childish voices. Jimmy and Alyce were children in the Old North Church, grew up together here. . . . Old North Church has always kept all of our servicemen in our prayers. Just nine years ago the word came that young Captain Floyd Thompson was missing in action. From that day to this we have prayed for him and his family and now our prayers are answered. . . . American prisoners of war have survived an ordeal that defies the imagination, and emerged with a strength and a spirit that surpassed even the wildest expectations of their families, the military and the nation. Throughout the land their homecoming has touched off a surge of national pride and a burst of uninhibited emotion. The prisoners' courageous bearing seemed to give America a new sense of hope, hope that these impressive men who have become the symbols of America's sacrifice in Indochina might help the country heal the lingering wounds of war. Their happiness seemed matched by a rare exhilaration in the spirit of the land they had come back to. Whether or not their return somehow helps heal the wounds laid upon us by Vietnam, the fact is the homecoming was one of the few events in the war's long history in which Americans joined together in unity and joy.

   You this afternoon with me are puffed with the unity and joy with which we welcome the return of all the prisoners of war, all of whom have suffered for their country. I now present to you Lieutenant Colonel Floyd James Thompson.

JIM THOMPSON: Thank you, Pastor Van Dyke. Dear friends of Old North, I never expected, nor do I deserve, such a tremendous welcome home. The warmth of the welcome has touched us deeply. I accept it on behalf of all of us.

A professional soldier and his family must forgo putting down roots in the civilian community. Nevertheless, our taproot is firmly entwined in the foundations of Old North. Home is often defined as where the heart lies. Old North is more than that to us. Alyce and I were born and brought up here at Old North. It is where our parents dedicated us to God's service almost forty years ago. It is here we received our Christian education, were confirmed into the church and were married. As I look around the congregation I see many familiar faces. Mother was active here at Old North for many years. At one time she was president of the Ladies' Aid, the Missionary Society, taught Sunday school, and was in the choir, all at the same time. When my wife, Alyce, was a little girl she was a student in my mother's Sunday school class. I have fourteen years of perfect attendance pins from Old North sunday school, and later I too sang in the choir.

I have many pleasant memories of the various activities during those years—the annual fair, the rummage sales, the potluck dinners, and much more. I must confess I was one of those boys forever getting into mischief. I remember one Sunday morning when the temptation to climb the ladder up into the steeple here proved too much to resist. Many times as youngsters we would go up to where the clock is and ring the bell and just kind of explore. So we had frequently been cautioned that it was unsafe. However, this one Sunday we succumbed to the urge and began to climb the rickety old ladder into the steeple. The ladder began to creak and groan, and just as we were about to chicken out and come down, the sexton began ringing the bell for the eleven-o'clock service. The whole thing started to shake, and, terrified, we hung on for dear life, too scared to stay and too scared to go back down and get caught. When we could stand it no longer we scrambled down the ladder and bolted for the door, two very scared and very dirty little boys. I think perhaps the most startled was the poor sexton. He nearly collapsed as we ran by.

So you see Old North holds many memories for both of us. Two of our three daughters were christened here and this morning we were blessed with the privilege of dedicating our son, an event I've looked forward to for a long, long time. During these past years I relived my memories of Old North and drew considerable strength from them. And I determined that one day I would come back and share these experiences with you. Today, by the grace of God, we are together again. I shall try to tell you how faith brought me back. . . .

It is only fitting and proper that this altar be flanked by both the Christian and American flags. This great nation of ours was founded on religious freedom. These flags are part of our nation and Christian heritage. They are the symbols of what we believe in, of our way of life, of what we have fought and died for. Although separation of church and state is a fundamental principle of our democracy, they are inseparably linked together. As American Christians we cannot serve one without serving the other. It is all the more important today in the struggle against these godless communist devils that we reaffirm our faith in both of these flags and instill in our youth an awareness of their heritage. . . .

My friends I have been asked many times how I managed to survive nine years as a prisoner or war, five of them in solitary confinement. Years of incredibly poor food, inadequate medical care, subhuman living conditions, torture, interrogation, communist indoctrination, and all the rest. My answer is simple: it was the power of faith.

Christ tells us, "If ye have faith even as a grain of mustard seed ye shall move mountains." I say, a man without faith, faith in Almighty God, could never come through such an ordeal alive and sane. I should like to share with you the most moving experience of my life, an experience that occurred about a month after the plane crash. It would be impossible to recreate my state of mind. Contributing factors were, first, concern for my family. Our baby was due about the same time as I crashed. I never knew such agony or torment wondering which came first, the baby or news of the crash. Was Alyce all right? And the baby? Was it a boy or a girl? What a terrible time to receive such news. How did it effect her? Would she find the strength to hold up?

And what about my mission in Vietnam? I was the commander of a Special Forces detachment charged with the responsibility of preventing Viet Cong infiltration into Vietnam from Laos. Extensive operations were underway and even more in the long-range planning stage. Much of the plans was still in my head and not yet reduced to paper. Could they carry on effectively? Would all the work we had accomplished so far be lost? I don't mean I was indispensable, but when a new commander comes in, it takes a while to get started again, to get his feet on the ground. And of course I was concerned with my own personal safety. In the plane crash I received a concussion, a broken back, a bullet wound, severe burns, and internal hemorrhaging. Would I live? Would they torture me? Would I ever see my family again? Would I ever know if I had a son or a daughter?

All these, and a thousand more things, raced through my mind. The days were an agony of torment, the nights pain-filled, all but sleepless. Then one morning I awoke to a very strong, unusual sensation. It took me a while to figure out what it was. It was peace of mind. Overnight, the worry, the anxiety, the tensions had completely vanished. For the first time since the crash I felt calm. I was absolutely certain Alyce and the children were all right, that the baby had been born and it was a fine healthy boy. And I knew I would make it back home. This feeling never left me all the time I was a prisoner. From that moment I never once lost faith, never once doubted.

Was this Christ's message? Was it God's word? Under these circumstances how else could a man know peace? It was the "peace that passeth understanding," a peace that never left me all the time I was a prisoner. Until it is denied, we never fully appreciate our freedom. It is a great, wonderful privilege to be able to attend church every Sunday and yet how many times do we fail to take advantage of it. We often let personal considerations take priority. The Bible tells us to put first things first . . . and many a Sunday morning Alyce and I had things to do besides attend church.

After this experience I just described I felt a terrible longing to attend church services. Obviously physical attendance was impossible under those conditions. So I decided I would build my own church. The result was a small but a very beautiful chapel in the sky. It was made out of pine and oak. I had a simple cross on the altar, very much as it is up here on the altar at Old North. A very fine church perched on a cloud somewhere. Each Sunday and each holy day thereafter I simply closed my eyes, met my wife and children, and went to church. I felt closer to my family at this time than at any other. This Sunday-morning worship service began the high spot of each week for me. . . . Faith in God is one thing no man can take away from you. On the contrary, the more they try to destroy it, the tougher the test, the stronger becomes a man's faith.

Undoubtedly the most discouraging and disheartening aspect of the communist propaganda were reports of the antiwar effort back home. Of course, this is a free country and as such we enjoy our freedom of speech. In truth it is one of the privileges we are fighting for. However, these privileges, these freedoms, carry with them a grave responsibility. I frankly don't understand the thinking of people who took an antiwar stance. I don't understand how anyone who understands the international communist movement and their stated goal to communize the world could take issue with our position in Vietnam. Furthermore, knowing that antiwar activities provide moral support for our communist enemies and grist for their propaganda mill, people should think twice before they speak or act in such a way. . . .

My friends, the most important aspect of the Vietnam War is that we have shown the communist bloc we will not stand idly by and watch them swallow up one country after another. We had to take a stand in Vietnam today, or tomorrow we would be defending our own shores.

These then are the things from which I drew strength to survive the nine years: faith in God; the conviction that we were doing a job that had to be done and a wonderful family to come home to. . . . I decided one day I would go back to Old North Church to bear witness, to tell you my impressions based on experience. I'm not much of a public speaker but I meant this straight from the heart. I hope and pray we will never have to go to war again. But if we do, I hope the next time we are all together.

VAN DYKE: There are perhaps six hundred of you here. . . . Had Colonel Thompson been speaking under a different circumstance, perhaps you would have been moved to rise to your feet at the conclusion of his message and clap like mad. I was torn on whether to do that or just let out one great "Amen." While we didn't do that, although I know many of you were moved in that direction, we are going to express it through the hymn, number 510, "Oh Beautiful for Spacious Skies."

LAURA   I cried. The reverend cried. The choir cried. He had everybody in tears. I've never seen anything like it in my life.

JIM JR.   I don't remember what he said. I do remember he got sentimental. [*Jimmy pauses to choke back his own tears.*] He's got a good deep voice and he knew how to talk. He sure did.

RUTH   He could move you with his stories.

PAM   It was just a little bit too much for me. I thought, I don't know where he came up with this. It was something maybe he believed in but I wouldn't tell it out loud. The part where he knew Jim was a boy and was doing fine. That was too much. I thought, Oh, God!

BERNIE WEISSE   It was a blessing to listen to him, to hear him tell how he used his faith to get him through. While he didn't describe the real bad things, deep down I knew he went through hell.

ALYCE   They had a big open reception before we went to the pastor's house for dinner. A lot of old high school classmates showed up. Some asked where I had gone while Jim was in Vietnam. I told 'em I wanted to get away. That's all.

RUTH   Little Jim stood near the doors. People walked by, kissed him, and stuffed money in his pockets. Those pockets were full! I decided I wanted to get christened again.

BERNIE WEISSE   My wife, my children, and I waited in the reception line an hour and a half to see Jim. Finally we got up to him. He looked in my eyes and said, "Bernie Weisse." I was so proud he knew who I was. So proud. It was such an honor to see him and say hello. I have spoken to many people about that day, even described his talk to my own Catholic church. With pride I've said, "Jim Thompson was my friend."

––––––––

LAURA   Have you seen the drawing? An artist drew his impression of Dad's "Chapel in the Sky" speech. It depicts a man wearing the prison uniform my dad wore, sitting on a bench hanging his head. The chapel is above him. It's in black and white and, well, it's worth a million words. Dad had it framed. He might have thrown it away now since he no longer believes in God.

39 ▪ THE WHITE HOUSE

LAURA   Dad loved making speeches. Always started out with a joke. "The way to get the crowd's attention," he said, "is to get them laughing." He practiced in front of the mirror and in front of us kids.

ALYCE   Can you imagine the kids sitting down and listening to that? Sure, it was good. But he gave the same speech over and over.

LAURA   After hearing a couple of them we pretty much knew what he was going to say. I'd be shifting my weight, getting impatient, thinking about going home or eating a tuna fish sandwich.

After a while it was, "Come on, Dad. We heard it."

PAM   I refused to read anything about him or his speeches. I wanted things back to normal.

ALYCE   Despite everything else, it was a high time for us through the summer of '73 when all that attention was focused on the POWs. Good Lord, yes, it was fun. There were lots of gifts. A year's lease on any Ford we wanted. We got to go places and didn't have to pay nothin'.

It would be fun for anybody, wouldn't it?

JIM JR.   At first I didn't understand my dad was a celebrity. But as time wore on I did. I knew for sure after he was invited to the White House.

———

GAIL MEYER   In late May 1973, the former POWs and wives were invited to Washington as Nixon's guests. I didn't have the nerve to say no. But unlike so many others who were going, I didn't feel it was just mar-

velous that our men had served or that they were real heroes or that the
cause was worthwhile. I thought it was a wasted period of life.

But with Lewie back only a short time, we were on a plane to Washington.

ALYCE   We visited the Vietnamese embassy. I got to meet Gerald Ford
while he was vice president. We got to meet a lot of big people. It was
there in Washington that I first met Lew Meyer and his wife.

GAIL MEYER   Lewie had described Jim Thompson as his very best friend
in the whole world, someone who showed courage, intelligence, and
strength of character in confinement. Jim and Alyce stayed at the same
hotel with us, so we spent most of our time in Washington with them,
starting with cocktails that first evening in our room. But that wasn't a
nice chitchat. In fact, I thought Alyce was one of the worst bitches I had
ever met. Everything Jim said she contradicted or put him down some
way. He was tolerant, but any little thing he said about the kids, or reminiscing about where they had been, what they had done, Alyce corrected
him or turned critical. And this was before we even left for dinner!

Jim himself struck me as very militaristic and authoritarian but with less
compassion than Lewie had. And while Lew was quiet, Jim was a great
talker. He bragged about being the longest-held. Both of them talked
about their escape attempt. There was camaraderie between them. That
was obvious. They had been leaders in their camp. They had been in their
element over there in Vietnam. They were stars. That came across with
everyone I talked to. But while Lew didn't talk about his POW experience, Jim loved to tell stories. In fact, he wasn't interested in anyone else's
conversation. Alyce kept him in his place, though. She made sure he didn't
monopolize conversation. Soon he was criticizing her in public too, with
put-downs about her weight. They were not a happy couple.

During all this bickering, Lewie was a pussycat. Anything I wanted to
do was okay with him. Anything I said was fine. He was on heavy doses of
Valium, totally concerned about his health and getting through this period
in his life.

Friday afternoon Alyce still hadn't bought a dress for the White House
ceremony the next night. So we went shopping.

ALYCE   Jim gave me money to buy a dress. He didn't approve of any
dresses I had.

GAIL MEYER   Jim got behind the wheel. We rode to the waterfront,
where the guys stopped off at the package store. Then we headed downtown. Jim was going out of his way to kill all four of us. Passing in front of
people, driving through red lights. Totally nuts. When Jim finally stopped
at a red light, Alyce just pushed Lewie forward in the front seat, pressed

him against the dash, opened the door, pushed me out, and she followed. "We'll meet you back at the hotel," she said. I was flabbergasted. Here we were alone in the middle of Washington, D.C., at noon. But suddenly I trusted her. She had made sure we escaped the car with our lives. We went into the first teashop we came to and sat down. Then we both began to cry, pouring out our feelings to one another.

Alyce said she knew she was misbehaving terribly this trip but she was so unhappy. She loved Jim, she said, and wished to change the situation, but she felt the marriage would never work out. The kids, she said, had seemed happy with that other man. He had been good to her and to them, and it was a much more satisfying relationship than she had had with Jim even before he left. We shared a lot that afternoon. Alyce, I discovered, was not a bitch at all.

ALYCE   Gail couldn't stand her situation either. Like Jim, Lew came back expecting everything to be the same. He wanted her under his thumb, and she said, "I can't do it. I've been on my own for too long."

They wanted to take away our independence. Everybody had problems. Don Rander's wife said he came back expecting her to be living in the same place with the same furniture and have the same car. They all came back expecting everything to be like it was. It couldn't be. The world had changed.

GAIL MEYER   The wives compared notes at these shindigs and the real stories came out. Very few marriages got back on track without difficulty. That afternoon in the teashop I learned that Alyce had been getting the same psychological baloney at Valley Forge that I was getting in San Diego.

"If you would only change and be like you were," the psychologists told her, "everything would be all right. Return to the little women of the fifties and sixties and these guys would be okay."

We ended up finding her a dress about four-thirty that afternoon. By then we had had fun together. She was a different person than the one I first met. I liked her. That afternoon we had evolved into something we liked very much. From then on, that weekend, the boys could do anything they liked.

DON RANDER   The night before the president had us all over, we accepted an offer for an evening out on a boat on the Potomac. Dinner and dancing. About half of the ship were POWs. Alyce and my wife, Andrea, got along great.

GAIL MEYER   It was a pretty night. Everyone was in good spirits. We had a delightful dinner. Jim asked me to dance. That was the first time I had been alone with him. He was a different man away from his buddies and Alyce. Very charming. No longer the guy determined to entertain the group. By the end of the evening everyone was back in sync, although I still didn't want to be there.

Saturday evening [May 26, 1973] we went to the White House on buses. It had rained that day and we stood ankle-deep in water on the lawn. Alyce and I both thought it ridiculous. Later we went into the library with the Nixons and then on a tour.

ALYCE   I met a lot of people that night. The Nixons and Sammy Davis, Jr., Edgar Bergen, and Bob Hope.

PAM   We were excited when they came back. They brought gifts. Jimmy got a pair of White House cufflinks. We girls got earrings. Then it was off to Disney World for the whole family.

———

SAM DEACON   By the summer of '73 I was a policeman for the Dade County Sheriff's Department living near Miami. One night I got a phone call and this very familiar voice says, "Damn, Sam!" It took me a few seconds to recognize it. Jim Thompson. Without me asking he said he and Alyce were back together with the kids and coming to Disney World.

"By God," I said, "you'd better come see me or I'll never speak to you again!"

———

RUTH   We drove down, first to Disney World, then Cyprus Gardens. We had good times!

JIM JR.   Some of the trip was good; some wasn't. I got my first whuppin' from him down there. I was just bein' a regular kid. I guess he did the natural thing and took me out and whipped my ass. But he put more force behind it than Harold ever did. It hurt more. It scared me. With Harold, I'd bare my bottom and he paddled me. Whap. Whap. Whap. But my dad picked me up and . . . boom! Right there in public. I knew the fun was about over.

———

SAM DEACON   The Thompsons spent several days with us. I had to work nights, so Jim came over to the sheriff's station with me. That wasn't such a good idea. He kept trying to get the keys and let the prisoners out. My partner would say, "Hey, he's got those damn keys again." Jim was back in the holding cells talking with the drunks and the criminals.

"Jim," I said, "you're not allowed back here."

He'd say, "But I know how these guys feel."

"But these guys are criminals, not POWs!" He couldn't understand why we had them locked up. I mean, he was sincere! He said, "Can't you do something? Nobody should be behind bars."

Jim had changed since our early days in Vietnam. He wasn't the same flamboyant person. He was more serious. Before he'd give some arm-waving explanation of what he was thinking. Now he looked directly at me and talked sincerely. Like about those prisoners. "Can't you do something?" There was no arguing with him. He wanted to let those prisoners out. His mind was made up.

———

LAURA   We began to realize what we had left—our friends, the town and state we loved, the father we had—to have this stranger boss us around. I wore low-cut bell-bottom jeans and small shirts. That was the fashion in 1973. But Dad kept telling me to put clothes on. He was living behind the times. Perhaps if I had more understanding, what followed wouldn't have been so traumatic.

ALYCE   Laura one day walked into the kitchen at my aunt's place wearing jeans with a peace patch on the pocket. Lots of kids wore that patch.

"What are you doing," Jim said, "wearing a communist symbol?"

LAURA   He was enraged. I didn't understand. He claimed it had something to do with communism.

"It does not!" I said. "It's a peace sign. I've had these jeans a long time!"

ALYCE   I tried to tell him too. I said it was only the peace symbol the hippies were wearing. He wouldn't have any of it. He cornered Laura there in the kitchen.

RUTH   He had her backed up, trying to rip it off her jeans.

I was thinking, God, Laura, just let him have it! But while he was determined he was gettin' it, she was just as stubborn he wasn't.

JIM JR.   That was the first time I seen him in a violent rage.

LAURA   He was so sure it was a sign of communism he flipped out. He ripped the thing right off my pants.

ALYCE   Harold had never once laid a hand on Laura. Never once. Now Jim was like an insane person, beating the hell out of her. It happened like that [*snapping her fingers*]. It took my uncle and myself to get him off of her. Then he walked out. I got Laura quieted down and went looking for him. I found him four miles away, in a bar, and well on his way to getting drunk.

Laura had always been such a sweet girl. After that beating, she was never the same. Soon she was getting mixed up in drugs and going downhill.

————

EVERETT ALVAREZ   I met Jim Thompson for the first time at that show in Oklahoma City in July of '73.

ALYCE   We all got invited. The kids too. Bob Hope was featured, along with Tennessee Ernie Ford.

EVERETT ALVAREZ   The night before the main event they had a dinner for us at the Quail Creek Lodge. Lou Rawls was sitting at our table. He got up, sang some songs. Jim was at a separate table but I sat with him for a while. I was impressed. I turned to the lady I was escorting, a local they had fixed me up with, and I said, "This is Jim Thompson. He was longest-held. He was there nine years."

She looked at him and said, "Am I supposed to be impressed or something?"

Right there I wrote her off. I mean, I was awed to be in Jim's presence.

Earlier that day we had some rehearsing to do in the morning for the Bob Hope TV show. It was to be one of those extravaganzas with Tennessee Ernie Ford and Anita Bryant, the Kilgore Rangerettes. The TV people brought by captions that would be superimposed on the screen. They wanted to make sure they spelled our names right.

Below mine it said, "Longest-held POW."

"Wait a minute," I said. "I'm not the longest-held. He is."

"Who is he?"

"Colonel Thompson."

"Oh."

To me, Jim was a hero. Yet people still referred to me as the longest-held. I wondered why. Well, that night I asked him.

"Jim," I said, "how come they don't call you the first?"

He didn't answer me.

40 ■ HURTING TIME

LARRY RYAN   By the time Jim returned that summer to Valley Forge he had gained weight and looked better. He wore flashy clothes, was driving a free Ford station wagon, and showed me his lifetime pass to baseball games.

But other things were changing too. The POWs were slipping from the limelight, which was exactly what Army officials had hoped for. They wanted them back into mainstream America.

———

DAN RICKARD   I was senior administrator at the Infantry School at Fort Benning when we got briefed that three former POWs—Jim Thompson, Marc Smith, and Ben Purcell—were coming down. Thompson was the one we had to figure out what to do with. He had gone from captain to lieutenant colonel without any training. The plan was to bring him up to speed on everything. Department of Army people warned us there might be some problems.

As Infantry School secretary I made some recommendations on handling these men. I said we should give Colonel Purcell the Blue Plate Special, our orientation program for top-ranking visitors. He could visit whatever department he wanted, the same as if he'd been a general given a special command someplace. Whatever briefings Purcell wanted he got. And no problem at all. He had his head screwed on right. Smith was only a captain, so he fit in.

The challenge in handling Thompson was to get him into the advanced course without treating him like a student. My plan was to make him a monitor, to have him attend classes, absorb the material, but not be a student. He was to provide input to me on the attitude of the students toward the instruction and toward the school. It wasn't essential but it might be helpful.

NATHAN VAIL   I directed the school's leadership department, so let me sketch out what Jim missed while held captive for nine years.

In Vietnam he was a team leader. Team leaders don't even equate to a company commander. A company commander is responsible for a battery of troops, probably two hundred men. Whether in combat or peacetime, company-level command is the single most important command job in the Army. It is the most demanding. It's where people try to challenge you.

While a captain is in that billet, his wife for the first time becomes an integral part of the process of command. She is the first lady of the company. All the wives gravitate to her. Their families gravitate to her. She becomes counselor or mother hen. She begins to grow too.

Next, the officer goes to the advanced course where captains are taught battalion and brigade operations and tactics. The maps are up and you're armed to the teeth. You fight the war from various positions, from the role of commanding general of a division down through the staff positions. Officers are taught the intricacies of command, of managing resources, the budget process. They learn a full range of staff functions and every discipline—operations, logistics, and so on. It's their first formal in-depth instruction in those areas.

Then officers are assigned to units where they serve as staff officers. They develop position papers and briefs. They function as the primary personnel or intelligence officer, or as an action officer. There they evolve into field-grade officers. After three years they head for Leavenworth as a major or lieutenant colonel. There they are taken beyond the range of larger unit operations to logistics or support of corps and field armies. They learn about installation management and tactics. The whole spectrum of professional functions is studied in depth. They leave there and go to a joint staff, Army staff, major command staff, or some higher level. As a colonel or lieutenant colonel they become assistant to a star rank, and professional development continues. Many go off to get their advanced degrees during this time.

What I just described are nine of the most important years in the development of a senior officer in the profession of arms. Jim Thompson missed all of that.

More troubling, as it turned out, he didn't realize it.

ALYCE   I drove the new station wagon down. Jim drove the Tempest. We were in high spirits. I still thought this might work out.

LAURA   Two kids rode in each car. After a hundred miles we switched. The cars were packed. We couldn't move.

ALYCE   When we reached Benning, Jim went about getting us a house on post. We had to wait for quarters, so we stayed in one of the apartments we used to live in on Madison Avenue. That's where we were July 18, our twentieth wedding anniversary. To celebrate I figured I'd do something special. The communists had taken Jim's rings, so I gathered up money for the kids to buy him a birthstone ring and I bought him a new wedding band. I would give my gift to him that night. Even bought a bottle of wine. After dinner, though, Jim went out with the kids to check on the house on post. "I'll be back," he said. When they got over there, neighbors came out and the first thing you know Jim was inside drinking and the kids played. I stayed in the apartment by myself all evening. When I went to bed I put the wedding ring under his pillow. Jim and the kids didn't get home until two in the morning. That's when he found the ring.

"What in the hell is this?" he said.

"I got you a new wedding band."

"Only one ring meant anything to me. And the VC took it."

That hurt. Later he decided to wear it, but he'd already let me know it didn't mean anything.

———

NATHAN VAIL   The Thompsons moved in across the street from us on Miller Loop. After our first contact I thought Jim to be very rational, very pleasant. We had begun our Army careers the same way. We both entered as privates, both went to officer candidate school, and we were close in age. I felt we must share many of the same basic values. I quickly concluded I was wrong. We didn't have very similar notions at all. We were not compatible, either professionally or socially.

———

LAURA   Georgia at first was an adventure. Getting there, moving in, meeting new friends. But when we started settling down, the glamour and glory faded. Reality set in. The year ahead turned into hell.

JIM JR.   The house on post was big. Upstairs had a master bedroom and two smaller bedrooms. A bedroom downstairs had its own bathroom with shower. My sisters were all fightin' over who was goin' to get the downstairs bedroom. My dad said, "He'll get it."

PAM Harold had treated us all the same. It soon became clear Jimmy would be treated differently.

LAURA Even before Dad came home, Jimmy was babied. He never had to work for anything. Now it just got worse.

PAM Where in Massachusetts we had fun and games in the house, the colonel set up what might be called a "perfect operation."

ALYCE Jim insisted that the kids call him "sir" and me "madam." If we asked them a question they couldn't answer "Yes, Mom" or "Yes, Dad." It had to be "Yes, sir" or "Yes, madam."

———

STERLING WETHERELL The Thompsons lived six houses away, so my first visit was both as neighbor and as post chaplain, to welcome them and invite them to come to church. My first impression was of a household in turmoil. I detected it mostly in the behavior of the children, from their actions and reactions toward their mother and father and each other. It was clear their father was in charge, a man whom they had grown up without. It caused them great wonderment and much anxiety. They ran in and out of the house. I heard a lot of shouting and antagonism, more between them and their mother than with their dad. Jim was the stranger in charge.

I sensed from the language, from the attitude they showed toward each other, that these were not happy children. No matter what any one of them said, it was not accepted by the others. The two older girls were the most stressful and obviously the most unruly—mouthing off, running around, giving Dad a fit. Sometimes the language was a bit colorful. Not at all ladylike. I sensed insecurity. The youngest little girl, Ruth, and the little boy seemed the least tension-filled, but still they had that sense of wonderment.

Alyce kept a clean house. If anything, I thought she worked out a lot of her problems scrubbing and cleaning. She was struggling. It was a hurting time for all concerned.

———

LAURA We were rotten kids, yeah. But we had been uprooted and then given only scraps of information to understand why. We couldn't learn the truth from each other. None of us knew more than the rest.

RUTH We fought for our parents' attention, but they were too wrapped up in their problems to notice. So it got to the point where we couldn't stand to be around each other. Laura once pushed me down the stairs because I wouldn't do what she wanted. Another time she conked me on the head with a pressure cooker lid because I wouldn't dry the dishes for her. Only months earlier, in Massachusetts, we had been close. Now I hated Laura's guts and she hated mine.

LAURA   It might have been different if our parents had fallen in love all over again. We could have fallen into step as one happy family. But we all sensed something was wrong. They argued from the first. He harbored so much resentment, and Alyce fought back. They fought continuously over the life she had lived with Harold. He didn't approve of how she had raised us, the way we dressed, the way we talked, our table manners. And they made no attempt to argue in privacy. These were full-blown fights where Ruthie and I would hold on to each other—as much as we didn't like one other—thinking, My God, someone's going to die tonight. I didn't want to come home after school. Every muscle tensed when I walked into our yard.

RUTH   The only time we were noticed was to be punished, and the only way to be punished was to raise a little hell. That's why Laura did the things she did. Today she hates to remember the way she treated me. But I treated her just as bad.

ALYCE   Pam got hurt the most. He had once called her "princess." Now he didn't want nothing to do with her.

PAM   It took a while to figure it out, but I wasn't his little princess anymore. I had my own way of doing things, my own way of thinking.

LAURA   Pam withdrew. She dove into her reading and studies. She became very quiet. A bookworm.

ALYCE   Jim wanted a social butterfly.

PAM   The colonel thought there was something wrong with me. He pushed me to go out more. I wouldn't do it.

RUTH   In the early sixties, women stayed at home and raised the kids. Husbands paid the bills and bought the cars. That had all changed while my dad was gone. Women's rights became a big thing, and Mama had changed along with everybody else. She learned not to follow behind a man like a puppy dog. So the two of them argued about things like who would start a fire in the fireplace. None of us knew what Dad expected of us. I always felt there must be something I could do that I wasn't doing. But he never said what it was. It was as though there was something wrong about me as a person. I used to think that if I were a boy he would love me more.

———

NATHAN VAIL   For a month or two at Benning, Jim was seen as a champion. And with good reason. So he was on a high. After a time, however, that exhilaration began to yield to reality. Jim began to think about the way Alyce had lived during his own absolute privation. He tried to reconcile that and couldn't.

STERLING WETHERELL   The family was on an emotional roller coaster—euphoria at one point, absolute depression at the next. Jim would come to my home so happy one day and so depressed another. Underlying it all was this great sense of tragedy and suffering in the family. The two older girls knew what was going on and suffered right along with Mother and Dad. Jim said he wanted to be close to those children but he couldn't. He was totally out of touch. He wasn't able to control events in his own family, so he became more and more disillusioned. The freedoms and liberties he saw the children exhibit were not part of his own youth. He couldn't bridge that gap. And of course his relationship with Alyce interfered with understanding the children. He wanted the family together, but he saw things in blacks and whites, no grays. He could never again trust Alyce or, I think, really love her. That was a big part of the problem.

Finally, Jim had difficulty understanding the changes in society. He wanted Mom, apple pie, and the flag. But that wasn't America in 1973. Kids had bad feelings about the war. Sons were telling fathers they would go to Canada rather than fight. Jim couldn't understand this. His dreams of what it would be like back in the United States were very different from what he saw around him. And his answer to it all was a very easy one—discipline. Shine those shoes! Cut that hair!

———

ALYCE   I dreaded suppertime. Every night Jim had us eat dinner in our formal dining room. The kids had to be on their absolute best behavior and sit there picture-perfect.

PAM   Suppers in Massachusetts had been relaxed. It was the only time we could gab with each other. Mama never worried too much about table manners.

LAURA   It was grab what you can and eat. Now, in Georgia, we had lace tablecloths and chandeliers every night.

PAM   If we wore jeans and a T-shirt, he made us change for dinner. Then we sat down and ate. That was it. No fooling around. No laughing. No jokes. We sat in silence.

ALYCE   Jim told them to keep quiet unless they could contribute something worthwhile to the conversation. He wanted the kids to read the newspaper to learn about current events he discussed at the table.

JIM JR.   I had to sit right next to him. If I set my left arm on the table, he'd take a knife, grab the blade end, and swat me on the elbow with the handle. It didn't take long to learn to keep my left arm off the table.

ALYCE   Little Jim's elbows didn't hurt nothing! It's a wonder he didn't bust 'em, hittin' 'em like that.

PAM   We complained to Mama about all the changes, but she didn't want to rock the boat.

RUTH   One evening Laura invited a boyfriend over for dinner. Mama had fixed pork chops, but they were tough!

LAURA   I was sawing away at my chop when it flipped off my plate.

RUTH   It come flying across the table. We about died laughing. Mama too. I mean, here's Laura trying to impress her boyfriend and jumped her chop off the plate. Dad jumped up and said he wasn't eating with a bunch of pigs. Then he looked at Mama and said, "You're worse than all of them because you ought to know better!" And he stomped off to his office. Of course, after he made that big speech we laughed even harder.

STERLING WETHERELL   Jim was a man of compassion, he really was. But all those years he had spent thinking about what it would be like to be with his family—and it was nothing like he had imagined.

DAN RICKARD   Jim became a very popular guest speaker—Rotary Club, Kiwanis, the Lions. He gave a tremendous pitch. Listeners wound up with tears in their eyes and giving Jim a standing ovation. I used to get calls of congratulations from every club in town and anywhere he appeared.

STERLING WETHERELL   The Army was flying Jim all over the country. His POW experience gave him something he knew that others in the Army didn't have. The speeches became important to Jim because, professionally, he really was feeling out of step.

DAN RICKARD   He liked having the freedom to come and go as he pleased. And the Army always was interested in how he was being treated. It was a foregone conclusion he would graduate from the advanced school without taking a single exam. He didn't even attend all the classes, unfortunately. If he had something else to do, he did it.

NATHAN VAIL   Jim had a whole range of expectations. Common among them was that he was going to be champion. As a former POW he expected the limelight and actively sought opportunities to maintain it.

LAURA   At speeches and outings, people would tell Mom, "Step up and take a bow!" Dad, though, was concerned about how she looked. Mother had been beautiful in her youth. Now he thought she was overweight. He also felt she couldn't carry on a conversation at his level.

ALYCE   After a while he didn't invite me to the speeches anymore.

———

LAURA   Dad had terrible nightmares. We all heard them.

ALYCE   He'd start thrashing about, then screaming. I'd wake up and find him drenched in sweat. I couldn't make out what was going on. He'd let out these blood-curdling screams! Oh God! I'd hear it coming and jump out of bed.

PAM   In the morning they didn't talk about it and I didn't ask.

———

STERLING WETHERELL   Jim was getting some psychiatric care down in San Antonio. They were checking on all the POWs to see if they were doing okay. I was not the only one talking to him about his problems. My pastoring to the Thompson family, apart from observation and prayer, was nurturing, trying to give them inner support. I felt both Jim and his family lacked a strong church background. It's true Jim was grateful to God for his deliverance and for the support he had gained from his faith while in prison. He was able to express that rather clearly in his speeches. Not theologically, but emotionally. However, he was unable to translate that into action.

The "Chapel in the Sky" image epitomized Jim's relationship with his faith. It was otherworldly, up in the sky, rather than something on earth he could relate to. The reality of faith escaped his everyday life. With the POWs' return, there was a venting of emotions, a tremendous experience that caused a lot of grief on the one hand and some rejoicing on the other. Jim's expression of faith came about in the reality of that celebration—the freedom of being back in the world. I never was able to tell whether the "Chapel in the Sky" really existed for him or if it was just a figment of his imagination.

41 ▪ WILD STREAK

NATHAN VAIL   When I'd get home from work, the Thompsons would be sitting out in the yard.

"Going out tonight?" Jim would yell over. "No? Well, come over and have one."

So Mary and I would walk across the street to chat for a bit.

MARY VAIL   Or Jim would visit, drink in hand, and stay for hours. Other neighbors began avoiding Jim.

NATHAN VAIL   Don Whitlock was one. He was a solid guy who didn't put up with a lot of nonsense. His family didn't socialize with the Thompsons, in part, because Jim came across as rather egotistical. He'd pontificate. Almost search for an argument.

MARY VAIL   Most people wouldn't challenge Jim's view, given all he had been through. Nat, however, felt since Jim was back in the real world he should have some of his thinking challenged. So Nat challenged Jim, and Alyce went after Nat. In public she was extremely protective.

About this time Jim got a letter from the Army saying he would not be given a regular promotion to lieutenant colonel. Both Jim and Alyce were furious. The Air Force, Jim said, automatically gave their POWs regular appointments. He was incensed.

LARRY RYAN   Jim called me about that. He sounded upbeat, saying they didn't have half his records. But the board must have said, "How much promotion potential does this guy really have?" They probably thought his chances of making colonel or general were so slim there was no sense bringing him into the regular Army. Still, the decision offended me, given Jim's sacrifices.

NATHAN VAIL   Most often Jim and I talked about the program of instruction at the Infantry School and changes going on in the Army. We were evolving into an all-volunteer force then. I tried to provide Jim some rationale for the direction the Army had taken. It had gone through the most intense introspection any profession had ever gone through. Ever. Coming out of Vietnam, the atrocities like My Lai, the failures in combat, the breakdowns of leadership. This coupled with changes in society and public attitudes about that war challenged the very fiber of the Army. I tried to explain the evolution to Jim.

STERLING WETHERELL   Jim couldn't understand. "How come soldiers have longer hair, and act and behave the way they do?" he asked. They no longer kept their uniform properly and didn't act with military bearing. Discipline was not as brisk. Jim couldn't accept that. He saw the changes as a personal attack.

NATHAN VAIL   Jim is opinionated. I am too. But I like to think I'm informed. I had been to Vietnam twice, both times in combat. I was an absolute student of the profession. I was well read. I had been to college. I finished my master's degree in political science. Jim had been a Special Forces captain when captured and was made a field-grade officer upon his return. A lot was lost during the interim—in professional development, in training, and in values instilled by the process. Despite this, an awful lot of credence was being assigned to what Jim said. The expectations were so high and that aura of celebrity captured him. He became a self-styled PR artist. His ego got in the way of his judgment. He was a zealot and took advantage of his special status. He made suggestions to Brigadier General Bill Richardson, assistant commandant, that I thought inappropriate. Dogmatic things having to do with the school's curriculum, the code of ethics, training for junior officers. All required a more rigorous treatment than a comment from Thompson. Jim became a disruptive force.

Bill Richardson was part of the problem. He was a very fine gentleman but he literally indulged Jim. Jim didn't know tactics, yet he was trying to tell others how to teach tactics! The man couldn't function in the school, yet he was offering all this advice, and in a very critical way. We couldn't abide it. I, for one, wanted him out. I sent a memo to Richardson telling him so. Bill did not like controversy, though, and he wasn't going to chair that scene.

Jim spoke a few times at the school. He had a very condescending way about him, as though he had all the answers. People were very courteous, though. They put their arms on Jim's shoulder as if to say, "Hey, Jim, you've been out of the perimeter for a while. You may have jumped the track on that one."

He wouldn't pick up on it, though. In his mind he was there to teach, not to learn.

STERLING WETHERELL   Jim got rave notices as a hero and speech-maker, but no one was listening to him professionally. He was out of touch and in disagreement with so many things.

DAN RICKARD   No, Jim was not a guy you immediately fell in love with. He and I talked about his marital problems two or three times a week. He seemed overwhelmed by it all. Extremely nervous and out of place, like he couldn't adjust. He looked old beyond his years and would get the shakes. Yet standing in front of a crowd he was absolutely marvelous.

––––––––

ALYCE   Nobody at Benning knew about my life in Massachusetts. Occasionally someone asked, "Why'd you move there?"

"I just had to get away from Army life," I'd say. I wouldn't go any farther. The ones who brought it up most were psychologists who'd talk to Jim and then would come to me. Much of what he told them wasn't true or was only partially true. It was such a messy time.

MARY VAIL   The neighbors on our circle were close. We cooked out together on weekends. Wives gathered in the afternoon to drink iced tea. Alyce socialized with the rest of us, but we never talked about her life while Jim was gone. She did speak often about how many POW friends were divorcing.

NATHAN VAIL   Jim one day cited the names of POWs whose families had failed them when they returned. It seemed the men were keeping track of broken marriages. Mary and I said, "My gosh!"

MARY VAIL   "You know," Alyce would say, "Jim and I are a statistic."

––––––––

STERLING WETHERELL   Sometimes I saw Jim daily. Sometimes weekly. He'd come by, sit down and talk. Feelings and responsibilities were overwhelming the guy. He was nervous, distressed, distraught, angry. He felt great stress as a father. He felt additional stress as an Army officer. Sometimes he discussed the issue of military professionalism to the total exclusion of anything in his personal life. The next time we talked it would be all family and total neglect of anything military. He seemed to work in compartments as though the problems were so overwhelming he could deal with only one group at a time.

––––––––

NATHAN VAIL   My children knew his children very well. And, gosh, we empathized.

MARY VAIL   Our son Tom was the same age as Pam. Kent as old as Laura. Nan and Ruth were very close. Jimmy and Susie too were the same age, both still in elementary school. Jimmy was the star—first boy, the child born after Jim left for Vietnam.

NATHAN VAIL   He was a good little fella. A typical towhead nine-year-old racing around the neighborhood on his bicycle and everyone trying to control his life.

MARY VAIL   Ruth, the youngest daughter, was an absolute, vivacious character. Very truthful. A marvelous sense of humor. Laughed and enjoyed life. If Ruth was affected by the family's situation, it was difficult to tell. Pamela was a very studious young gal, and perhaps that was her saving grace. She got excellent grades. As far as extracurricular activities, though, she had none. She came home and that was it. Maybe she hid in her books. She had to carry a lot of burdens. Quite often she was the one to tell the other children what they could and couldn't do. And, of course, they resented that.

Laura, now. Well, Laura had a wild streak. She soon got a terrible, terrible reputation. She wore her jeans a little too tight, her sweaters a little too tight. She appeared to be, as my son would say, "on the make."

––––––––

LAURA   I still hadn't slept with anyone. I was a big tease, I will say that. I pushed it to the very limit and then said "no." I used to stop by the NCO club because I knew that would royally piss off my dad. Noncommissioned officers were like an absolute "No!" An officer's child didn't associate with them.

––––––––

ALYCE   After Jim got back I had had surgery, so we couldn't have sex. Then he had his vasectomy and we couldn't. It suited me just fine. After we got down to Benning, though, he started requesting me to do things I didn't want to do. It was against my nature. Then he began going to sex stores. It was terrible for a while. One time we pulled up to this sex store in Columbus. He said, "I'll be out in a few minutes." I sat there an hour and a half. He would spend forty dollars, fifty dollars on magazines and crap and bring them home. It didn't bother me so much his bringing novels and magazines with women and men like *Penthouse* and *Playboy*. But he started bringing in male-only sex books. I was petrified the kids would find this crap.

MARY VAIL   There was one thing the other wives in the neighborhood could not get over. We assumed Jim had received a very large amount of money when he got out. Alyce made us feel like they had close to a hundred thousand dollars to spend. But they bought furniture that was . . . well . . . less than tasteful.

STERLING WETHERELL   After Jim and Alyce fixed up their bedroom, they invited me up. Of course, I was surprised at the invitation. It was a very warm, garish sort of room. Drapes matched the headboard. All was red or pink, and so lavish. They called it the Sex Room. They invited me to see it, I thought, as a way of saying, "Look, we're going to make it."

As the months went by, though, and the money was spent, the challenge of living on a lieutenant colonel's budget became very real. Money troubles added to the stress. They had spent so much to buy things that supposedly spoke of a new life together. Yet those expenditures . . . well . . . they didn't pay off.

PAM   The high school on Benning was being integrated with an all-black vocational school, and I was scared to death. They couldn't discipline the students. I told my parents to get me out or I'd quit. So, a couple of weeks into the school year, they put me in a private school, Brookstone Prep. Five other kids from the post went there. We had to keep a certain grade average. They didn't take just anyone. I loved that school. Teachers cared about what we were doing. We could ask a question and not feel dumb. We could work with the class or work at our own pace, which I loved. I was a sophomore and that was to be my best year of high school.

RUTH   Laura began to get involved with drugs. Here's a photograph taken in our basement in October 1973. Sitting with her there is her boyfriend. Look at her eyes and tell me she wasn't on drugs.

LAURA   A distant relative had come to visit that summer. He was older than I was. The first time I ever smoked pot was with him. He said, "Come on. It's great. Give it a try!" So we went down into the woods with a few friends. Before we knew it, there were two MPs behind us saying, "Come on. Let's go."

ALYCE   We were having a party at the house when the MPs came knocking on the door. They said they had Laura and some other kids down in the hoosegow.

LAURA   My dad picked me up at the MP barracks. He was very calm. He wouldn't make a scene at the station. He asked me how the pot was. He said, "Now that you have tried it, do you think you'll do it again?" Turns out it wasn't my pot-smoking that pissed him off. It was that I got caught and embarrassed him. When we got me home he said, "If you had to do that, why on post?"

ALYCE   I don't believe Jim ever engaged in homosexuality before he went to Vietnam. But the tendency was there. He was very feminine about some things. His walk, for one. He had a wiggle. He always put clear polish on his fingernails. I learned to accept this as part of his life. But my thinking changed during the Thanksgiving holiday of '73. Mom and Jack came down. Another young man, a relative on my side, came too, as a surprise to my mother. When Mom and Jack went back, this relative spent a couple more days with us. His last day there, it was getting close to his time to leave. Jim was going to take him to the airport. I went upstairs to get them but the study door was shut.

I knocked but didn't wait for them to say "Come in." I opened the door to find them embracing on the couch. And it was more than a friendly type of thing. They separated as soon as the door opened. All I said was, "We have to leave to the plane."

I turned around and left.

Another night Jim was going out and I asked if I could go. He said no. About three-thirty in the morning the telephone rang. It was one of his friends, a guy with the sweetest voice you'd ever want to hear. He said I was not to worry but Jim was at the Fort Benning hospital. He had had his nose broken at this bar. Got the crap knocked out of him. I learned later it was a gay bar.

I told mother what I suspected, what I had seen. Jim was the apple of her eye, so she didn't want to hear nothin' about it. But you have no idea what it was like to sleep in the same bed with a man you know is . . . well . . .

Because Alyce alleged that homosexuality put additional strain on their marriage, I asked Jim about her claim.

Alyce said the first Thanksgiving after you got back, one of her relatives came down.
Oh, yeah. All right. I got it.

Alyce said she opened a door and found you two embracing.
Oh, yeah. I remember that. He is, ah, a woman or a man.

Bisexual?
And I encourage him to say [to Laura] marijuana is no good.

Well, how do you feel about your own sexuality?
I don't know, frankly.

Any homosexual activity in prison?
Not a bit.

42 ▪ DREAMHOUSE

DAN RICKARD Jim's speechmaking was looked on very favorably at first. He gave a tremendous presentation. Put the Army in a good light. But it started to interfere with his training. The speech dates went on and on, involving more and more trips away from the school.

J. J. WALSH As deputy assistant commandant I met with Jim when problems developed. He wasn't doing what he was supposed to. He had irreconcilable differences with his academic counselors. I was the last buffer before the general got involved. I never thought assigning Thompson to the school was a good idea. He took advantage, acted as though the course were beneath him. So when I talked to Thompson it was not to congratulate him.

———

LAURA By March '74 my dad had found his dreamhouse off post in a neighborhood called Novena Woods.

ALYCE The house was gorgeous. A split-level with six bedrooms. So big I would just get done cleaning it when I had to start over again.

LAURA Dad was happier about the house than my mother was. He picked it out, then went to Ethan Allen and furnished it, even picking the upholstery.

ALYCE New carpeting. New drapes. With all the furniture stores in North Carolina, he had a dining-room set shipped down from Pennsylvania. It cost a fortune.

LAURA   He had never had luxury as a kid and certainly not in prison. But that's how he wanted to live. And that's how he wanted us to live.

PAM   I had a room to myself way in the back. I could work on my oil paintings—I paint by numbers—and had enough room for all of them. I closed the door and the problems stayed outside.

ALYCE   Our bedroom was pink. More Jim's idea than mine. He saw a hot pink carpet he wanted. He had hot pink valances made, pink satin drapes, and a white satin brocade bedspread. It was swank. Not masculine by any means, but that was his taste. I didn't need such luxury. This dreamhouse was something he fantasized on.

———

LAURA   My dad's heaviest drinking began after we moved to the new house. Things really began to deteriorate.

ALYCE   He bought himself a nine-hundred-dollar chair, one of them lounging chairs with heat and a vibrator. He began coming home in the afternoon, saying he had a headache, and upstairs he went. He'd swallow tranquilizers, then drink booze to make the headache go away. And then he'd sit there. In the dark. Glass in hand. Ice bucket full. Night after night after night.

LAURA   The more he drank the more often the violent nightmares came. Some words he screamed in Vietnamese. Sometimes he talked in such a low voice we couldn't understand at all. He never talked about them in the morning.

ALYCE   He went through better than a fifth of gin a day. Sometimes he'd fall asleep in his chair. Other nights he'd come out roaring, falling-down drunk. Oh, it was a hell of a life.

———

STERLING WETHERELL   Jim and Alyce didn't speak often to each other about their problems. When they did, it was after they drank, which of course was the wrong time. They talked openly about it as a problem, each complaining about the other's drinking.

RUTH   At one point Mama was drinkin' just as heavy as my dad.

LAURA   We stood around wondering what the heck to do. It was like my father stood alone, outside the family.

JIM JR.   Once in a while he'd try to jump into that father-son thing. I didn't want to be around him.

LAURA   After a while he gave up on trying to know us. The family was falling apart right before his eyes.

JIM JR.   Then the fightin' got worse. It seemed like about every day. I never asked what it was about. I just found something else to do, some other place to be.

RUTH   I'd go in the closet and put my hands over my ears.

PAM   Even if they argued in their bedroom I could hear it. My room was right below. He said he couldn't believe Mama stayed with Harold that long and still claimed there wasn't anything to it.

LAURA   Everything he felt about her, about what she did, came out. "You don't understand!" Mom cried. "What was I supposed to do?"

RUTH   It was such an incredibly emotional time, yet they ignored their children. Our needs didn't matter. The only attention we got was during drunken rages if we happened to be in their paths. So we sought affection where we could find it. Laura in particular needed somebody to tell her she was wanted.

PAM   Laura turned wild.

LAURA   I couldn't stand the insecurity, the fear. I started failing in school, fighting teachers, rebelling against everything and everyone.

ALYCE   In Massachusetts Laura had been this sweet, peaches-and-cream little girl who'd come up, put her arms around me, and say, "I love you Mama."

That Laura disappeared.

———

STERLING WETHERELL   It was no use talking to the girls about their behavior. The family began taking a lot of my emotional strength. They were so disoriented there wasn't much anyone could do.

———

RUTH   My parents one day were going to a meeting about Laura. I wanted them to drop me off at the library because a report was due. But that morning I had broken my wire-frame glasses. Mama said, "Put your old ones on until we get the others fixed." My old pair were these ugly plastic things. I wasn't going out in public with them.

"But you need that report," Mama said. "Get them on and let's go!"

My dad was in the living room where I couldn't see him.

"Mama," I said, "I'm not going nowhere!"

He came downstairs, grabbed me, and said, "What did you say?"

I didn't say nothin' now 'cause I was scared to death. I remember how his eyes looked, 'cause I had nightmares about them for a while. Like a crazy man's eyes. He took me to my bedroom and began hitting me with a belt. There wasn't nothin' Mama could do. She just stood there.

ALYCE   It was almost unbelievable.

RUTH   I tried to get up. He pushed me down again and kept on hitting me.

LAURA   I don't know whether he was thinking about Vietnam or what, but I told him to stop.

"Harold never would do that!" I said.

I regretted that right after I said it. He stopped, walked away, and locked himself in his study. He wouldn't accept phone calls. He sat there in the dark, hours upon hours, and got so smashed. He never laid a hand on Ruthie again. Ruthie wouldn't have anything to do with him either.

———

PAM   The colonel complained I was always in my room reading. I wasn't getting enough friends. I wasn't as outspoken as he was.

ALYCE   He expected only the best from Pam after we put her in a private school. Tuition was twelve hundred dollars. Pam completed her first year and loved it, taking chemistry and calculus. Real whizbang things.

PAM   One night he told me to come up to his office after dinner. The school, he said, wasn't helping me. "You're as introverted as you were in public school. You're not going back."

"You can't mean that, Daddy," I said. "I realize I don't go out that much, but my grades have improved. I do have quite a few friends over there. I like it over there. I enjoy it!"

Well, he said, he wasn't going to throw money away. Good grades weren't what he was after. He wanted me to be popular.

RUTH   Pam begged. I mean she begged him.

PAM   He said he couldn't talk to me about anything. "It isn't necessary," he said, "to show that kind of emotion."

RUTH   After that Pam wouldn't have much to do with him either.

———

ALYCE   Jim's mother, Elizabeth, had been sick for years. A bad bowel problem. I'd say, "Mom, why don't you go to the doctor?"

"No," she said, "Ben won't take me."

She finally collapsed in the spring of '74. After surgery the doctor called and said, "It's so bad I just closed her up." We drove to New Jersey. As I was walking in the door of the hospital, the staff was paging me. Elizabeth died up on the table. The only store-bought dress Elizabeth Thompson ever had was the one she was buried in. I bought it for her.

Before Elizabeth Thompson's death, a year after her son's return, she privately told Jim something that made it more difficult for him to forgive Alyce's decision to leave with Harold. Alyce admitted she had obtained a reel-to-reel recording of a taped broadcast of his propaganda statement. A New York radio station station had sent her the tape while she still lived at Fort Bragg with Jim's parents. But Alyce said she couldn't get anyone to play it for her. Having no real evidence that Jim was alive, she made the difficult decision to move on with her life.

In May 1990, Jim told me his mother had shared with him a different version of events before she died.

"My mother saw story on tape in captivity," Jim said. "Someone sent to United States. And my mother, and Alyce, saw the tape. And Alyce and my mother said, 'He's alive!' Alyce and my mother rejoiced!"

" 'Saw the tape?' You mean your mother listened to the tape?"

"Hell yes," Jim said. "My mother . . . She told me she had heard the tape."

Was it true? I asked Alyce in September 2000. Had she and Elizabeth listened to the tape recording, together, in 1964?

"I really don't remember," she said.

43 ▪ BROKEN-HEARTED

STERLING WETHERELL Jim Thompson was feeling torn by professional responsibilities, family responsibilities, and the marital relationship. And finally, one night in June of 1974, it all exploded.

PAM Mama got tired of taking it from the colonel every time they argued. She started fighting back.

ALYCE The one night that Jim beat me up I accused him of being a homosexual. It started with a friend of his going to California on leave. This fella had a swanky sports car and didn't want to leave it on post unattended. We lived not too far from the airport, so he asked Jim if he could keep the car in our garage.

"As long as you're doing that," I said, "why don't you have dinner here and we'll take you on to the airport."

I made lasagna. It got to be time to go. While Jim put the suitcase in the car, this kid said, "Aren't you going to ride with us?"

I didn't have anything else to do. But when I started out of the house, Jim said, "Where are you going?"

"To the airport."

"There's no need," he said.

"Well, I just want to take a ride."

"There's no need."

This guy interfered. "Why, she can take a ride."

I knew Jim was mad. I could see it. On the way back home he said, "Can't even stop for a goddamn drink 'cause you've got flip-flops on."

"I can go in a bar with flip-flops on."

"No, you can't!"

When we got home, one thing led to another. The next thing I knew we are in his study in a battle royal. He called me a whore and a slut. I picked up a martini set, pitcher and glasses, and smashed them.

PAM   Ruth and Jimmy were in Pennsylvania with my aunt and uncle for two weeks. Only Laura and I were there. From my room downstairs I could hear it getting loud and nasty. After the glass hit the wall I couldn't ignore it anymore.

LAURA   I was asleep when it sounded like the whole house exploded around me. I heard glass smashing and my sister running upstairs. I went up after her.

Dad was screaming, "I don't know you anymore! Get out of my life! You're driving me to my death! The kids are rotten!"

ALYCE   He picked something up and threw it at me. I picked up a bust of Abraham Lincoln the kids had given him and smashed it. He started punching my head with his fist. I put my hand up to protect myself. The Good Lord must have been on my shoulder that night, I'll tell ya.

Pam come in and started screaming, "Don't hit my mama!"

I swear to God if she had had a knife she would have killed him.

PAM   Mama was scared and wanted to get out. She looked awful. Her face was red and her arm and hand swollen.

LAURA   When I got there, I saw my dad reaching for a drawer where he kept a gun. He stopped when he saw us kids.

PAM   In the hallway Mama said, "Go pack. We're leaving!"

ALYCE   I went into the bedroom, opened up the suitcase, and threw in what I could. I was scared for my life and my kids' lives.

PAM   I grabbed some clothes. After a while we couldn't hear the colonel anymore. He might have passed out.

ALYCE   The kids had been saving their allowance for a trampoline. Pam thought enough to grab their jar of money.

PAM   It was filled with dimes and a couple of dollars. Mama had five ones. That was all we had.

LAURA   My mother tried to push both us girls out of the house and into the station wagon. I didn't want to go. I didn't want to leave my dad alone. I don't know why. I just ran. I hid underneath a highway bridge, on a cement ledge. I could see my mother but she couldn't see me. She drove around the block a couple of times, calling my name.

PAM   We went to some of her friends' houses and asked if they had seen Laura. We drove back to the house once. After a couple of hours we took off. Mama just wanted to get away. She was scared.

ALYCE   I took valuable time looking for Laura, all the while looking over my shoulder that he wasn't coming after us. We stopped at a gas station before I got on the main road and called the minister, Wetherell. I told him what had happened and that I couldn't find Laura. I was afraid Jim was after me with a gun so I had to go.

"You go," he said. 'Don't worry about it."

STERLING WETHERELL   That they had fought didn't surprise me. I'd been concerned about their physical safety. Jim had the potential to be violent. He was drinking heavily and had this intensity about him. And he was a man of many moods. There was nothing anyone could do to move these people from feelings to thought processes. So Alyce drove out of town.

Jim at that point was broken by the experiences of his life—the torture he had undergone, the tragedy of his marriage, the loss he felt in his own sense of pride and professionalism. He had good qualities but he just couldn't cope. And the end result was tragic for him and his family.

———

ALYCE   Pam counted the money. We had thirty-eight dollars. We drove from Columbus to Atlanta when I stopped. My head was hurting so bad I couldn't see anymore.

PAM   We got a motel room with a credit card.

ALYCE   I called my mother and told her what had happened and that we were on the way up.

PAM   We got four or five hours' sleep, had some breakfast and coffee, and drove on.

ALYCE   The whole way to New Jersey I was thinkin' about gettin' an aspirin. Then we had a blowout on the New Jersey Turnpike. When we finally got to Mama's my head was so swollen my glasses dug into it. Mama put me to bed. Next day the doctor said I had a severe concussion. My hand was badly bruised but not broken.

PAM   My grandmother kept saying, "Why would you leave him? He's a great man."

I never heard Mama talk about homosexuality before, not until she explained why he hit her. My grandmother didn't believe her.

———

LAURA   I stayed under the bridge that night, popping No Doz so I wouldn't fall asleep. But I did. I woke up early the next morning. Walked around. Smoked a pack of cigarettes. Finally knocked on the door of one of my male friends' house. He encouraged me to go to my dad and to talk to him, let him know somebody still loved him. I was afraid. But that afternoon I did go back home. I didn't know what to expect, so I knocked rather than walked in. I'll never feel again the way I did at that moment. It could have gone either way. Dad opened the door, obviously surprised to see me. "Can I please come home?" I asked.

He started to cry. I never saw such a broken-hearted man.

————

PAM   We stayed a few days at grandmother's. Mama called Ruth and Jimmy from there and said they would have to stay at Uncle Marty's longer than expected. She didn't explain further.

RUTH   Me and Jimmy were swimming in my aunt's pool when I looked up and seen the station wagon coming down the road. We both said, "What is going on?" Mama's hand looked awful, all bruised and swollen. The side of her face was blue-black. She told us they had a fight and were gettin' a divorce.

PAM   Jimmy had just gotten to know his father and he liked all the attention. So now he was hurt and upset.

JIM JR.   I didn't want to accept it. It was so soon after he come back. Now she was tellin' me he was gone again.

RUTH   I got mad. Real mad. It had seemed everything finally was going to be all right. We were getting some normalcy in our lives. Even though I was scared of him, he was spending more time in his study. I had nice friends. We were in the new house. Had nice things. Yet here she comes and tells us it all blowed up again. He flew into our lives and when things got steady again he was gone. That pissed me off. I crawled up a tree near the swimming pool and just sat there.

I didn't understand a lot of the decisions my mom and dad made and probably never will. But the way they decided to divorce was the worst thing of all. Her just pulling up in the driveway like that and saying this is the end. To me it meant my dad had rejected me. I wasn't what he expected. It was an even longer fall for Jimmy. He was hurt bad. He went from believing he was one of the greatest persons who ever walked the earth to being someone his new dad didn't want to live with anymore. After that day Jimmy never let anyone know how he was feeling. He turned into a cold, closed-off person so he wouldn't be hurt again

LAURA   My father apologized to me about the fight. The drinking didn't stop, though. It was bad. At one point while we were together he said he wanted to try pot, to see what the big craze was about. So I shared some with him. We got a kick out of it. Started laughing together. He pretended like it was nothing, though, maybe to try to discourage me from using it.

Within a few days I went back to live with my mother. I knew I wouldn't get to know my father well until he got his head on straight.

44 ▪ DIVORCED

J im Thompson was referred to a staff psychiatrist at Martin Army Hospital on Fort Benning in July 1974, complaining of depression, headaches, insomnia, loss of appetite, and a reduced ability to concentrate. He was sleeping only four to five hours a night. He had nightmares, or he would wake to "bursts of energy" but then had difficulty even reading a book. He described to his physician "a great deal of bitterness" toward his wife and anger that his children called another man "father" and had been raised "in a manner not to his satisfaction," according to the psychiatrist's notes. He was beginning to feel emotionally out of control, which was "unlike me."

"The patient is basically reliant on obsessive compulsive mechanisms and denial of dependency needs," one doctor noted. Thompson also was using alcohol, the doctor said, "as a medication." The psychiatrist prescribed Valium for Thompson's depression and a sedative, Dalmane, for sleep. A change of jobs, into a less stressful environment, also was recommended.

DAN RICKARD   After his stint monitoring the Infantry School, Jim was made deputy director of Army-wide training support at Benning in August of 1974.

BILL GUTHRIE   My deputy had just retired when I got a call from the school secretary. "Colonel," he said, "we have a guy who was a POW a long time. He may have some problems, but would you consider taking him as your deputy?"

Without talking to this former POW, Jim Thompson, or anybody else, I said, "Sure."

I sat him in the same office as Doris, my secretary.

DORIS SONGER   There was a little wildness about Jim, although he was always very charming to me. In fact, he went out of his way to do gentlemanly things. But his job wasn't much really. A twelve-year-old could have done it. Colonel Guthrie made all the decisions. But the Army was doing what any big, lumbering organization might think was right. It was trying to give Jim Thompson something to make him feel worthwhile.

BILL GUTHRIE   He helped handle personnel problems, budgeting, operations. He visited other elements of the support program, speaking to sub-employees to get ideas and learn what was going on. I encouraged him to get out and talk to people. I knew going in I would have to fill a lot of gaps in Jim's experience. And I did. Jim made snap judgments the way a young officer would. Every time he screwed up I told him so, and I explained, "Jim, don't jump to conclusions." He was willing to take the criticism.

DORIS SONGER   Other officers didn't have the same compassion for Jim. They made derogatory remarks behind his back, like "Damn fool!" After a while, Jim became so erratic, making snap decisions and getting impatient. A secretary who filled in for me while on vacation said Colonel Thompson had thrown his telephone across the room.

————

ALYCE   My mother supported me and the kids for a while. She even called Jim and asked for money to help with food and expenses. He sent a hundred dollars. Soon we moved down to Pennsylvania again. But Aunt Willa and Uncle Marty couldn't afford to feed me and my kids for long.

PAM   We only planned to stay until Mama got on her feet, found a job and a place to live. She went to work for Moore Business Forms in Honesdale, taking orders in the office.

ALYCE   Jim filed for divorce in Columbus. When he tried to give me the shaft I got my own lawyer. He wrote Jim's lawyer, telling him I needed a place for the children to live and transportation, that I was going to make it hell for him if he didn't supply them. When I couldn't find a house to rent, I insisted Jim buy me a house trailer. I picked out a cheap two-bedroom. Only ninety-five hundred dollars with a bare minimum of furniture. I insisted he buy a washer and dryer too.

RUTH   Mama didn't want alimony, just money for our support. One hundred dollars per month per child, until we turned eighteen. She also got the Cutlass station wagon. Mama got a bookkeeping job paying eighty-five dollars a week.

PAM   Between Mom's pay and the support payments, we were just able to pay the bills.

ALYCE   Since Jim had returned in March of '73, we had moved as a family from Massachusetts to Pennsylvania to a house at Fort Benning, Georgia, to a big house in Columbus, then back to Pennsylvania to my aunt's, and then to a trailer. Five moves in eighteen months.

RUTH   By that time I didn't want nothin' to do with my father. I associated him with a lot of damn problems. Hurt and pain and trouble.

PAM   I was happier cramped in a trailer than I had been in that big house. Getting away made me realize how uncomfortable we'd all felt living with him, where being ourselves wasn't acceptable. Now we could relax. We could get loud every now and then. We could talk at the dinner table again. If we showed up looking scruffy it didn't matter.

ALYCE   The trailer was long but only twelve foot wide. I gave the two oldest girls the biggest bedroom. With a sliding partition we made two bedrooms out of the second. Jimmy had one part and Ruth the other. I slept on a sofa bed.

RUTH   As for money, we were never worse off. We didn't have a TV. She cooked with an electric skillet. We wanted to buy clothes like everyone else but Mama bought the cheapest she could.

––––––––

BILL GUTHRIE   After I fussed with Jim, he became an effective deputy, and we became awfully good friends.

My role was to say, "Let's get back to the real world, Jim."

That was very difficult for him. He came to me on Valium. Returning to Columbus from one of his trips, he had a martini on the plane on top of Valium. Walking out of the airport he flat passed out. In uniform. A visiting brigadier general witnessed the episode. I got a call from the assistant commandant, who asked what was going on. No formal report was filed, but it shook Jim up.

BARBARA GUTHRIE   Jim lost time to headaches and digestive pain. Many thought he was an alcoholic. But it was those drugs in his system. Some people didn't give him the benefit of the doubt. He was not as respected as he should have been there at Benning.

In October 1974, eighteen months after regaining his freedom, Jim Thompson began to receive medals and awards recognizing his gallantry and sacrifice in Vietnam. The first nation to honor him was South Vietnam, which, ironically, stood on the brink of extinction. Thompson still wasn't well known among other former POWs, including prominent returnees like Commander John McCain, a Navy pilot and the son and grandson of admirals, and George "Bud" Day, an Air Force officer whose leadership through torture and deprivation in Hanoi would earn him the Medal of Honor.

But all the returnees seemed to share a deepening sense of dread that America was abandoning both the cause and the country for which these men had sacrificed so much.

JOHN McCAIN   The South Vietnamese had invited several former POWs to return to see the country. South Vietnam was struggling. Their government hoped the trip would produce a little favorable publicity. They were desperate. They saw the North Vietnamese buildup occurring inside their own country and knew it was only a matter of time before a major attack.

It wasn't until we took that trip together in the fall of 1974 that Jim Thompson and I had a substantive conversation. I noticed how his hands shook and sometimes he was not articulate. I chalked it up to physical problems he had in captivity.

Yet he was very courteous. In fact, Jim was almost nonmilitary he was so friendly. But he lacked self-confidence and needed to be told what to do. He seemed a bit like Rip Van Winkle, uncomfortable about his rank and not well informed.

GEORGE "BUD" DAY   I sat with Jim on the airplane. He struck me as very odd. He seemed depressed, extremely quiet. Only if I pressed him would he talk. In the slammer we called it the "Solo Syndrome." He drank heavily, even on a daylight flight.

Still, I liked Jim, and by the time we reached Saigon, he had opened up. He said his wife's conduct hadn't been that great, so he got rid of her.

At the old Vietnamese Palace in Saigon we received that country's highest decoration, the South Vietnamese equivalent of the Medal of Honor. It was a touching, very dignified ceremony attended by many Vietnamese. President Thieu extended special recognition to Jim, making laudatory remarks about him as a prisoner. An eloquent commentary. Jim lightened up after that.

JOHN McCAIN   For me, coming home from the war had been wonderful. I never had a flashback. I never had a nightmare. I don't think about it anymore. A lot of POWs, however, couldn't come back. The same is true among combat veterans. Some never think about it. For others it's the most searing experience of their lives. I can better understand Thompson having problems than most anybody else. The conditions under which he lived were far more severe than in North Vietnam. Experienced over nine years it had to have some effect.

At Fort Benning that November, Army officials held a special awards ceremony for two former POWs, Thompson and Staff Sergeant Stanley A. Newell. Both men had managed to escape their captors in Vietnam, at least for a time.

In recognition of his October 1971 escape from Rockpile with Lew Meyer, Thompson received the Silver Star, the nation's third-highest award for heroism. The citation said Thompson had escaped "knowing that the odds for success were slight and that if recaptured he would receive torture and long periods in solitary confinement."

For his years in captivity, Thompson also received the Bronze Star and the Legion of Merit. The Bronze Star recognized his "continuous resistance to an enemy" from January 2, 1971, to March 16, 1973, "in extremely adverse conditions of Communist prisons of Southeast Asia." At Rockpile and Hoa Lo he "demonstrated his professional competence, unwavering devotion and loyalty to his country."

The Legion of Merit recognized his suffering from March 24, 1964, to January 1, 1971. "For the first four years he was kept either in bamboo huts or small cages and never had sight of another American," the citation reads. "He escaped from the enemy several times but was recaptured each time."

Thompson had no family at the ceremony.

A few weeks later, worried that he might have suffered brain damage from his 1964 plane crash or from the torture that followed, Thompson had himself admitted to the psychiatric ward of Martin Army Hospital for a complete psychiatric and neurological evaluation. He complained of "blackouts" and difficulty with equilibrium. His handwriting had become illegible. He reported passing out at his desk at home while writing letters, after only a single martini, on top of three or four Valiums taken throughout the day. He would pay all his bills correctly, he said, and then forget that he had paid them. He recalled other episodes of clumsiness and indecision.

During his two-week hospital stay, Thompson assumed a "protective role" toward other patients and had "frequent skirmishes with the power base," according to physicians' notes. "He appeared quite satisfied when he successfully challenged authority figures without retribution."

Test scores confirmed Thompson's intelligence to be in a "very superior range." No neurological disease was found, however, to explain his amnesia, headaches, or unsteadiness. He showed no withdrawal symptoms from an absence of alcohol or drugs during his stay.

Doctors concluded Thompson's symptoms likely had been brought on by stress from "severe personal difficulties."

One psychiatrist suggested that Thompson was, in effect, a fish out of water.

"His self-enforced personality traits are highly adaptive to a prisoner role," he wrote, "yet maladaptive to this society"

45 ■ NEW PARTNERS

LAURA   We finally had a little peace and quiet at home. Had it, that is, until John stepped in.

RUTH   Mama met John at a bar on my thirteenth birthday.

ALYCE   I lucked out when I found John that December. Not too damn many men would have a woman ten years older with four kids. He knew my whole story, all about what I'd been through.

LAURA   I couldn't stand him. Not from the first.

RUTH   I would go in my room and close my door until he left.

PAM   Ruth kept hoping our parents would get back together, and Laura resented John because he started helping Mama with the discipline. John can't stand anybody being disrespectful to parents. And Laura was forever smart-mouthin' Mama.

RUTH   Mama saw John as her last chance for happiness. She was willing to sacrifice anything for him. Bent over backward to keep him happy. I thought she had sacrificed us.

PAM   John moved into our trailer a few months after they met. The two of them slept on the love seat. John even started fixin' things around the house. I thought it was great. Every now and then John got wild, roaring drunk. Then he slept it off and would be fine. He never got nasty.

LAURA   John wasn't interested in my mother's past. He got upset when we talked about Dad and he left the trailer whenever Dad called. That really pissed me off. My dad was upset about John living there in a trailer he had bought and paid for. But my mom had left two men already. She wasn't about to lose a third.

ALYCE   Jim came up one day to see the kids.

JOHN   Alyce insisted I meet him. I'll tell you, I didn't want to meet him as much as go to hell. I figured some Green Beret dude was going to come out of a jeep with a bandolier over his shoulder and bang me up.

ALYCE   We looked out the window as Jim pulled up. I thought John was gonna burst his britches laughing.

JOHN   He come out of the car wearing a strawberry-colored sports jacket, patent-leather shoes, and walking through the mud like this [*tiptoeing*]. I thought, My God!

ALYCE   It tickled the fire out of John. Cowboy boots is all John wears, and here comes Jim in patent leather, tiptoeing through snow and mud like a woman afraid of gettin' her little toesie wet.

LAURA   My mother started an ugly rumor that Dad was under a gay influence. It didn't make any difference to me. He'd been through a hell of a lot, and if it's true I can surely understand it. People need love. But she tried to turn us against Dad.

DON RANDER   In April 1975, Saigon fell. I was the staff duty officer at the Pentagon that night. We had the Associated Press and UPI wires and a telefax. I sat there reading the reports, watching television. And when I saw us leaving I cried my fucking heart out.

FROM THE *New York Times*, APRIL 30, 1975

MINH SURRENDERS, VIET CONG IN SAIGON
1,000 AMERICANS AND 5,500 VIETNAMESE
EVACUATED BY COPTER TO U.S. CARRIERS
by the Associated Press

SAIGON, South Vietnam—President Duong Van Minh announced today the unconditional surrender of the Saigon government and its military forces to the Vietcong.

Columns of South Vietnamese troops pulled out of their defensive positions in the capital and marched to central points to turn in their weapons.

Within two hours, communist forces began moving into Saigon. A jeep flying the Vietcong flag and carrying eight cheering men in civilian clothes, armed with an assortment of weapons, drove along the street a block from the United States embassy compound.

This action followed by hours the ending of the American involvement in Vietnam through the evacuation of most of the approximately 1000 Americans still here.

[In Washington, the White House said that President Ford had "no comment" on the surrender of Saigon but a White House spokesman said the surrender was considered "inevitable."]

The surrender announcement, made in a broadcast to the nation, signaled the end of three decades of fighting. It came 21 years after the 1954 Geneva accords divided Vietnam into North and South and a little more than two years after the Vietnamese cease-fire agreement was signed in Paris on Jan. 27, 1973. The last American troops left the country in March of that year. . . .

ALYCE   It was a damn shame the way the war ended. All that heartache and they turn around and hand it to them. My stepbrother died for nothing. But the main thing that made me mad was the draft-dodgers getting amnesty. I don't think that was right. I sure don't.

PAM   John and Mama got married in June 1975. The wedding was in the Honesdale mayor's house. He was also justice of the peace.

ALYCE   Some friends gave us a little reception at the bar where I worked. Me and John never did have a honeymoon.

BILL GUTHRIE   Lois was an Air Force lieutenant colonel assigned to the protocol office at Patrick Air Force Base, Florida. She had made arrangements for Jim to speak there. That's how they met.

DORIS SONGER   Lois was a little taller than Jim, a large-framed woman. Very pleasant face. Charming. Soft-spoken and gentle. Jim seemed crazy about her.

BARBARA GUTHRIE   Lois offered the support and compassion Jim needed. They were well suited for one another.

PAM   The colonel came to Honesdale once with Lois. Took us kids out to dinner. I went because Mama made me. Lois wasn't beautiful. "Handsome" is a better word. Nice face and real good figure. About five foot eight. Red hair, cut short.

BARBARA GUTHRIE   She carried herself well, made a very good appearance. Lois was easy to know and to converse with.

DORIS SONGER   Jim went to great lengths to try to get his first marriage annulled so Lois, a Catholic, could be married in the church. I worked for weeks typing up papers to send to the diocese in Savannah.

PAM   Mama wouldn't sign the annulment papers. It would mean her first marriage never existed, she said, making us kids illegitimate. We learned Lois was retiring from the Air Force early to marry the colonel. We tried to warn her she needed more time to know him better.

ALYCE   On the phone one night I said, "Lois, you're going to regret this. You're giving up a career and Jim is homosexual."

Boy, she went at me. She called me a slut and a whore and everything else.

"You just mark my words," I said.

PASCAL BATSON   As Jim described it years later, it seemed to be a marriage of appearance as much as of convenience. They made a nice couple. But they didn't know one another well. Jim was attempting to reestablish himself, to build a relationship with another person. On the surface Lois may well have represented to Jim the ideal wife, given his realistic limitations.

————

DAN RICKARD   Jim's fiancée called me one day. She wanted me to sit in on a counseling session. The subject would be Jim's drinking and depression. She was concerned. Deeply concerned. The shrink there at Benning did the talking. I was the father figure, the old guy in the room. Jim admitted having a drinking problem. Lois was grateful for the session.

————

DORIS SONGER   They were married in Florida in a civil ceremony. Colonel Guthrie was the best man.

BILL GUTHRIE   My wife and I thought highly of Lois and thought her the right person for Jim. She was an outgoing career woman who seemed to understand her new husband and was tolerant of his failings. She accepted that he had problems, and tried to help him with them.

BARBARA GUTHRIE   It took a lot of courage to move into that situation. Lois tried hard to have Jim put things from the past behind him. I was impressed too with Jim's attitude and spirit, considering all he had been through. Together they did a beautiful job charting a new life together. They even talked of adopting a child.

STERLING WETHERELL   The newlyweds moved into Jim's home in Columbus. He thought the marriage would be his salvation.

PASCAL BATSON   From the start they did not communicate well. For example, Lois didn't understand the importance of the house to Jim, what it represented for him. She began changing it in ways he considered heavy-handed.

LAURA   He had taken a lot of care decorating that house. He'd bought everything he ever dreamed about. Now here came this woman who hated his lamps, who hated his paintings. His tastes were rich. Hers were practical. Crystal chandeliers weren't necessary, she said. Little by little, without consulting him, she changed his dreamhouse.

———

BARBARA GUTHRIE   Lois expressed concern about Jim's drinking. She said alcohol changed his personality. He didn't eat a balanced diet. With his digestive problems even a little bit of alcohol had a powerful effect. At parties we started keeping a watchful eye on Jim so he didn't have a problem.

———

PAM   In Honesdale Laura had serious problems almost immediately.

RUTH   She hit a teacher and broke her glasses.

LAURA   I tried to put one over on her by reading a book inside a book. She nailed me. It was as though somebody put a match under a thermometer. I absolutely lost it.

RUTH   The vice principal termed her incorrigible and didn't want her back. They told Mama they might take court action to commit her.

ALYCE   We got hold of her father. Him and Lois drove right up. "Oh, poor baby," they said. They decided to take her back down to Columbus. It was that or she was going to reform school. Laura figured she would get away with murder down in Georgia.

———

LAURA   I hated the Benning area as soon as I got there again. Lois was a very strict Catholic who had had an extremely strict upbringing. She had her own ideas about how a teenage daughter should grow up. By then my father had learned to accept some of my ways. I caused fights between them.

He'd say, "Goddammit, leave my daughter alone. She's not yours."

Sex was a no-no to Lois. Good girls didn't do those kinds of things. That wasn't my Dad's view.

BARBARA GUTHRIE   Lois warmed toward Laura, tried to reach her, to have the teen confide in her. But it was difficult. This was a very troubled child. Laura got into trouble as a form of rebellion from the unnatural environment in which she was raised. In Georgia she enjoyed the special attention, enjoyed being away from her brother and sisters. But Lois and Jim were too consumed with their problems to have their lives revolve around this young girl. After Laura ran away a couple of times, Jim decided he couldn't handle the responsibility anymore.

———

PAM   Laura returned to Honesdale but couldn't go back to school. Instead she got deeply involved in drugs and guys. She picked the worst friends and turned hostile to everyone in her own family.

RUTH   She was attractive and just loved the boys' attention. Mama and John couldn't do nothin' with her. She did what she wanted and piss on everybody else. She started hanging around with a motorcycle gang. One night she came home with a tattoo on her chest, a cross with three bars, something to do with Hell's Angels. She said she couldn't remember how she got it, she was so out of it. Another time she went out to a party, came home screaming, locked herself in the bathroom, and said she was going to kill herself. We got a neighbor to kick the door down. They pumped her stomach at the hospital. Laura never did tell me what drugs she was taking but it was more than pot.

LAURA   I was into 'em hot and heavy. Cocaine and angel dust. We laced our dope with the angel dust too. All the stuff that made me forget.

ALYCE   She even stole my engagement ring to pay for her drug habit. The ring her father gave me.

RUTH   I was walking down our hallway and saw she was into Mama's jewelry box. She got the ring, then threatened to beat the shit out of me if I ever told. I knew she'd do it too.

LAURA   I got twenty-five bucks for it because it was in really poor condition. I know it was a spiteful thing to do. I still have no remorse. I wanted to hurt her. She started it all by turning our lives upside down. Now I was going to make her life a living hell.

———

ALYCE   Six months after a soldier becomes a POW, Social Security considers the soldier disabled due to lack of proper food, medication, and proper housing. And his family begins accruing benefits. After Jim's release, I received a check for almost forty-five hundred dollars, and another worth four times that amount, almost eighteen thousand. The last was on behalf of the four children. Both checks were made out to me. I put them into a joint savings account to be used for the children's education.

When we moved to Columbus, Jim said I could earn more interest if we put the money into a trust fund for the children. So, stupid Alyce signed the withdrawal card. By March 1976, almost three years later, Pam had picked out a college in Pennsylvania. She called her father.

PAM   "I'll send you the tuition bill," I said, "and you can pay for it out of the trust fund."

"I don't know what you are talking about," he said.

"The trust fund for college."

"There's no such thing."

But we had talked about it. It was being held for our college.

"I was with you when you set it up," I said.

"I can send thirty or forty dollars a month," he said.

"That's not going to pay my tuition!"

He said he didn't want to spend all that money for me to go to college only to get married and drop out. He didn't approve of educating women.

"This isn't something I'm doing to pass the time. It's something I want to do," I said.

"You should have applied for a scholarship," he said.

"I didn't think I needed to."

"You did."

"You son of a bitch," I said. I hung up.

ALYCE   I listened to her end of the conversation. I thought, Good girl.

Asked about the incident years later, Jim Thompson said he considered the Social Security money paid to his family for his years of hardship in Vietnam to be assets he should control. He had offered to pay half of Pam's college expenses, he explained, if Alyce would pay the other half. But Pam, he said, "wanted it all. And cried and cried like hell."

As to Alyce's contention that they had agreed the money would be used as a college trust fund, Jim suggested the issue was more complex than that, more complex than he could explain now, given his difficulty communicating since his stroke. But he also noted how the Army for nine years had sent his every paycheck to Alyce and her "sergeant," and they were used in part to remodel a home and buy a fancy out-of-ground swimming pool.

"All my money, shot to hell," he said. "All my money!"

For Jim, it boiled down to a question of equity. But his phone conversation with Pam that day severed all ties with the daughter he once had called his "princess."

ALYCE   Jim had treated Pam so damn rotten. This was the final blow.

PAM   I wanted more than anything to go to college. And he knew my plans.

ALYCE   Pam stopped calling her father "Dad." After that it was "the colonel."

Ben and Elizabeth Thompson with sons Danny and new-
born Floyd "Jim" Thompson on the day of his christening,
July 1933.

Danny, left, and Jim with the family dog outside their home in Bergenfield, New Jersey, 1947.

In a school portrait, Jim wears medals earned for perfect Sunday school attendance at the Old North Reformed Church, Dumont, New Jersey, ca. 1947.

Jim and his father, Ben, in his bus driver's uniform, ca. 1947.

The groom's wedding party toasts Jim's future on his wedding day, July 1953.

Alyce, the eighteen-year-old bride-to-be, before the ceremony.

The couple drives to the wedding reception.

Jim Thompson, reluctant draftee, at Fort Dix, New Jersey, July 1956.

Alyce beside the couple's convertible, August 1956.

The Thompsons' first Christmas as an Army couple, 1956.

Thompson and daughters Pam, Ruth, and Laura (left to right) before Sunday service at Fort Bragg, North Carolina, spring 1962.

Laura, Ruth, and Pam (left to right) outside family quarters at Fort Bragg, June 1964.

Special Forces A-team at Khe Sanh shortly before Thompson's capture, 1964.
Front row (left to right): Gerald Blais, Jim Oller, Thompson, Dan Hannah,
Frank Rose. Back row (left to right): Herb Hoff, Don Donkin, Robert Rooney,
Ed Trent, Max Jones, Nelson Smith, Lindsay Carr. Donkin and Rooney were
Australian warrant officers.

The Special Forces compound at Camp Khe Sanh, Laos in the
background, 1964.

Viet Cong cage of the type used to hold Thompson during his early years of captivity in the jungles of South Vietnam and Laos.

Aerial view of the North Vietnamese prison nicknamed Camp K-77, or Skid Row, where Thompson was held from July 1968 until June 1971.

Aerial view of Rockpile, nickname of the prison from which Thompson, Lew Meyer, and Speed Adkins escaped on October 1, 1971.

The Hanoi Hilton, where Thompson and other prisoners who were being held in outlying camps were brought after the peace accord of January 1973.

At Gia Lam airfield in Hanoi on March 16, 1973, Thompson is escorted to a waiting C-141 transport that will fly him to freedom.

Inside one of the C-141s that brought POWs out of Vietnam during Operation Homecoming, 1973.

On Thompson's flight out of Vietnam, Special Forces Sergeant First Class Lonnie Johnson presents him with a new beret.

At Clark Air Base in the Philippines, Thompson is welcomed by Admiral Noel Gayler.

Thompson is knocked off his feet when Jimmy, the son he has never seen, leaps into his arms at Valley Forge Army Hospital. Surrounding them are Alyce, Laura, Pam, and Ruth (left to right).

Thompson reads a letter he received from President Richard Nixon, with Pam, Laura, Ruth, Jimmy, and Alyce (left to right).

Thompson and Army Sergeant Don MacPhail answer questions from reporters at Valley Forge Army Hospital, March 29, 1973.

In late April 1973, Thompson and Jimmy hug for a photographer from his hometown newspaper, the *Bergen Record*.

In another posed newspaper shot, taken in the rain outside the home of Alyce's uncle in Honesdale, Pennsylvania, in April 1973, the family hides its troubles behind smiles.

Thompson honored during a Memorial Day parade in Bergenfield, May 1973.

Alongside then–Navy
Commander John McCain,
Thompson receives South
Vietnam's Medal of Honor in
a formal ceremony in Saigon
in the fall of 1974. The city
would fall to communist
forces within six months.

Thompson accepts congratulations at his Pentagon retirement
ceremony on January 29, 1982, at
which Army Secretary John
Marsh presented him with the
Distinguished Service Medal, the
nation's third-highest
military honor.

President Reagan presents the Prisoner of War Medal to Thompson, June 24, 1988, with Mrs. Reagan and General Robert T. Herres, then vice chairman of the Joint Chiefs of Staff.

Thompson's daughter Ruth accompanies him to the White House ceremony. She walked away from a television news reporter who asked about her family's past.

46 ■ TENNESSEE

LAURA   The guy I was seeing was no good and his family was no good. They were very rough people. But bad boys appealed to me.

John knew the family. He didn't want me having anything to do with them. But life at home was constant tears. It became my escape. I told my mother, "You don't want me here. Sign these [marriage] papers. I'll get married and be out of your life."

RUTH   Mama couldn't control Laura anymore. The choice, she figured, was sending her away or signing the papers. Dad told her it was her decision. So Mama signed. Laura was fifteen.

ALYCE   I didn't want her in my house. She was into drugs. I didn't like the people she brought home. I didn't want the other kids subjected to it.

LAURA   We married in February of 1976. We had no money, so we lived with his parents. You don't learn about somebody until you live together.

ALYCE   He started beating the hell out of Laura.

LAURA   He stayed out all night and then took it out on me. One night, when I was three and a half months pregnant, he hit me so hard I had to go to the hospital. I was in danger of losing the baby.

———

RUTH   John built houses for a living. But during hard winters in Pennsylvania no houses were going up. Times got tough. Spring of '76 he went to work in New Jersey for Jersey Zinc.

ALYCE   John learned the company was opening a new mine in Tennessee and needed experienced people. The pay was good, he said, and there were supervisory opportunities. He went down, called back, and said that's where we were going.

RUTH   Laura was still awfully sick and in the hospital.

ALYCE   Mother said, "Alyce, don't cancel your plans to move. Bring Laura to my place." So we did. A doctor there did an ultrasound and found trouble. The baby would be badly deformed, mentally retarded or born dead. The doctor suggested a therapeutic abortion. Mother made all the arrangements.

While Laura recuperated we got ready to leave Honesdale. With two days to go, John was sitting there stewing.

"Goddamn," he finally said, "I'm not gonna leave town without giving that boy a lesson."

We drove around until we saw him on a street corner. We stopped the truck and he got in. We took him up the road and got talking to him about how he had beat the hell out of Laura.

"She's a defenseless little girl, and pregnant and your wife at that," John said. "You want to know what it's like to be beat up?"

John gave him a couple in the jaw. He went down. I went over and kicked the hell out of him. We got in the truck and left. We felt better.

———

LAURA   Mom and John bought a very old farmhouse with eleven acres. They got animals, planted a garden, and farmed the land.

RUTH   Mama loved living in the country, having to drive forty miles to the nearest Kmart. The little town nearby had a general store, post office, and five or six churches. That's about it.

———

LAURA   In New Jersey, Grandma nursed me back to health. I never felt so good as when I stayed with her. No tension, no hassle. I wanted to stay. But if I did, Grandma wanted me back in school.

ALYCE   By August, with school about to start, Laura decided to come to Tennessee.

LAURA   My mother said things were going to change. They had lots of land. It all sounded so nice. She even put John on the phone. He apologized for our arguments. Said he had gone through a tough time too and I should understand.

"I really want to start a family with you guys," he said. "We can do it."

———

PAM   That year I worked at a shirt factory in Tennessee. I saved enough to buy a car while I established residence. The next year I borrowed to rent a room at Middle Tennessee State. I got part-time work in the cafeteria.

LAURA   In Tennessee I wanted to be good. Everyone pretty much tiptoed around me because of what I had been through.

RUTH   We had tired of people asking questions about our lives, so we decided, while starting a new life, to take John's last name.

JIM JR.   I began calling John "Dad." For a while there he acted like a dad. We'd go hunting. Fishing. We'd talk. Every boy needs a father. All my sisters, except Laura, called him Daddy too.

RUTH   Jim Thompson will always be my father, but John became my daddy. There's a big difference. John was there when I needed him. And I seen how happy he made Mama.

JIM JR.   But soon after we got to Tennessee, John was getting drunk a lot. If he wasn't working he had a beer in his hand. On weekends, he'd stay up late, get drunk, pass out, then wake back up and put another one in his hand. I didn't like that scene. I done been through it with my real father.

LAURA   John and my mother went through a case of beer a night. Sitting on the front porch, drinking themselves into a stupor.

I thought, Here we go again.

RUTH   John held his temper with Laura as long as he could. Every time she screwed up, he gave her another chance. Then she'd turn around and screw up again.

LAURA   My girlfriend had a car. We liked to ride around, go to the fair, the Dairy Barn, the general store. John put the almighty thumb in there and said absolutely not. He wouldn't let me go. Suddenly all those rebel feelings came pouring forth.

———

LEW MEYER   After we'd been back from Vietnam a couple years, I heard about Jim's drinking. There was something said about him not being fully dressed in public on one occasion. There were stories about homosexuality and stories linking him with marijuana. When I heard such reports I turned them off. But I knew Jim was having problems. I went to see him in Columbus. Jim was out of shape. That night he had some drinks and fell asleep. Lois and I talked all evening. I liked her. She was more domineering than I had expected. She was retired military and outranked Jim. He resented that, she said. Jim was becoming a problem, she said. He was inconsiderate. Drinking too much. The Army had pulled him off the speaking circuit. Something about drinking in travel status. All in all my visit was a big letdown. I realized as I left I wouldn't be back to see Jim again.

———

PASCAL BATSON   Jim said Lois put on a very good appearance. She dressed well. She knew how to handle herself. But when they got down to the business of day-to-day living together, both were too accustomed to making decisions for themselves.

DORIS SONGER   Lois tried to plant the seed in my mind that Jim was homosexual. She mentioned it two or three times. He made trips to Atlanta with somebody, she said. I just thought when any marriage begins to break up both parties feel rejected and grab at straws to explain what happened.

———

ALYCE   Laura hung around the general store and hooked up with any guy who would have her.

LAURA   I was reaching out, for any kind of love. I would find affection somewhere. I wasn't sleeping around. I slept with two people. That's bad enough in a hick town. While seeing a guy named Michael, I got pregnant again.

RUTH   I only knew she was pregnant because we shared a bathroom. I never talked to Laura about it, though. She didn't eat right, trying to hide the pregnancy. She gained no weight in her face and arms.

ALYCE   One morning Laura said, "Mama, I don't feel good. I'm not going to work." She'd get pains in her stomach and would go running into the bathroom. About eleven o'clock she was laying there on the couch, moaning.

"Laura, you sure you're okay?"

"I'm fine," she said. "Just leave me alone. I've got a kidney infection."

About one-thirty she was doubled up. "Laura, if I didn't know better I'd swear you were in labor."

She looked me in the eye and said, "No I'm not."

By two, she was still doubled up. I told Pam we were taking her to the doctor. "I think she's got appendicitis." There was a waiting room full of people, but Laura was screaming so loud the doctor took her right in. He called me in a few minutes later.

"Alyce, you'd better get Laura up to the hospital."

"Her appendix, huh?"

"No," he said, "she's about to give birth."

LAURA   My mother's face hit the floor. "Why didn't you tell me?" she said. "Now what am I going to tell John? Holy shit!"

The baby was born within an hour. She was real tiny.

PAM   Mama was in total shock. We had to go home to tell Daddy. I didn't want to do that myself.

ALYCE   We hurried back. I didn't want John coming home to an empty house. When he got home I said, "John, I've got something to tell ya. I don't know how to tell ya."

"The best way is just to come out and say it."

"Laura had a baby an hour ago."

He was dumbfounded.

RUTH   The school bus dropped me and Jim off at the general store and we were surprised to see Pam waiting for us. For a long time walking home she wasn't saying anything. Then she said, "Laura had a baby this afternoon." "Oh man!"

ALYCE   We got Laura home within a few days. Catherine had to stay another three weeks, she was so tiny. When the baby did come home she wouldn't have wanted a better mother than Laura.

LAURA   I didn't need anybody else. This baby was my sanity. I stopped seeing guys. I finally had somebody I could love and who would love me back. I'd have long talks with her and she always listened. John was so upset we stopped talking completely.

PAM   When Catie was six weeks, Laura was working, Ruth was off on a date, I was in college, and Mama was outside feeding the animals. The baby started screaming. John told her to be quiet. He called for Mama but she couldn't hear him. John couldn't stand the crying. Finally he picked Catie up. She won him over right there.

PAM   Somebody called county welfare and they tried to take Catie from us. We got a good lawyer and fought it. Mama and John got awarded temporary custody. Mama warned Laura that if she didn't get a job they'd take the baby. So Laura began work at a shoe factory in town.

RUTH   There ain't much to the first couple of months of motherhood. You feed 'em and burp 'em and change 'em. And Catherine was so tiny and sweet everybody doted on her constantly. But when the newness of motherhood wore off, it turned into more of a chore for Laura. She didn't like having to care for a baby.

LAURA   It put a giant squeeze on me. Here, before the baby, I thought I couldn't go out. Now it was worse. Motherhood wasn't the loving picture so many books described.

RUTH   Catherine woke up several times a night, and Laura began screaming at her. "Why don't you shut up! I have to go to work in the morning!" So more and more, me, Mama, or Pam got up to feed her. After a while Laura wouldn't get out of the bed.

ALYCE   One evening Laura said she was going to a movie. Okay. I had had the baby all day but I would take care of her that evening too. The following week it was two evenings Laura was gone. The next week she wanted to go out every night. Finally I said no.

"Well then the hell with it," she said. "The hell with it."

The next day, Saturday, Ruth and I went to the Laundromat in town. We came back a couple hours later.

RUTH   Laura's bedroom was on the other side of the house, but from the driveway we could hear her screaming at Catherine. "Shut up! Shut up! I want to go to sleep!"

ALYCE   She was calling Catherine a bastard. She never heard us come in.

RUTH   Catherine was in the playpen and Laura was in her face, screaming at her to shut up.

ALYCE   I don't know what would have happened if we hadn't come.

RUTH   That's when Mama decided Laura couldn't handle the responsibility. I picked up the baby. Mama and Laura had a long talk.

ALYCE   "I've had it," she told me. "I don't like doing it. I don't want no more part of it. I'm going to put the baby up for adoption."

"The hell you are," I said.

We filed papers and John and I got legal custody of Catherine. She became the child John and I couldn't have. And in the years that followed, Catherine brought us a lot of happiness.

47 ■ SIMPLE NEGLIGENCE

RICHARD McKEE In the summer of 1976, Jim Thompson began attending Columbus College full-time. Technically he was still an Army asset but his real status was student. After a few months it was clear Jim was not doing well. He was drinking and had stopped attending classes. By early 1977 he was out there on his own, getting no direction.

I was director of personnel and community activities at Benning. On my previous Pentagon tour I had served on a prisoner of war group where I got to know Jim's background. When I heard about his troubles I wanted to salvage him. With support from his second wife and officials at the military personnel center, we decided to jerk Jim in, pull his student status, get him under control. He wasn't happy about it.

My office dealt with recreational facilities on post. I defined a position and made Jim my deputy. We bent over backward to give him a position of dignity. On the job he was very pleasant, very anxious to please. But he was never very good. While on duty he never showed like a typical alcoholic, but after hours . . . well . . . we became concerned.

SID LEVINE I had two roles in Benning's alcohol treatment program—acting director of Benning House, our residential treatment facility, and program psychologist. One day, after I had finished group therapy and was walking toward my car, Colonel McKee came tagging along behind. "Sid," he said, "I have a project for you. A VIP with a major alcohol problem."

McKee gave me some history: longest-held of the POWs; the Army had an investment in him; it wanted him well. The bottom line was they dropped him on me, saying, "Fix it." I put Jim in our four-week residential treatment program. Rank there was immaterial. Residents worked their usual job during the day and returned to the dormitory in the evening. Everyone was responsible for maintenance and upkeep. That meant Jim occasionally got down on his hands and knees with a private first class to clean the bathroom. He did pretty well. In a very short time he assumed the position of house president.

In our sessions, Jim described how, when he came back from Vietnam, his wife had dumped on his life. Then with the second marriage he thought everything would be great. It wasn't. He indicated some sexual difficulties. His wife also had a hard time with his mood swings and drinking. After four weeks of counseling, the report back from McKee was that Jim was doing better. Job performance had picked up. His thinking was clearer. He was less depressed. He seemed to enjoy his work. For a short time it seemed we might be out of the woods.

But gradually I began to feel Jim was manipulating me. For years he had behaved similarly to survive. He had become an expert at giving those in authority the wrong information. He'd claim he hadn't had a drink in five weeks. I suspected it was five days. He said he was taking Antabuse to reduce his craving for alcohol; I felt he wasn't. When alcoholics say everything is going all right, your antenna goes up.

RICHARD McKEE   I kept in contact with the infantry branch at the Army personnel center. We discussed protecting Jim, getting him back on the street without bad publicity. After a while, however, it became clear Jim was drinking again. Levine and his people pulled him out of a couple of bars. Once he disappeared for a couple of days.

SID LEVINE   McKee wanted Jim fired.

RICHARD McKEE   He was AWOL, goddammit. We took his car keys away, over his strenuous objections, and confined him to quarters. We leaned on him. We reached the point where we needed to box him in. Benning House was only bailing him out. He wouldn't stay with the program. He found it too demeaning. Finally I forced the issue. I gave Jim a letter that said either he attended the tougher drug and alcohol program run by the Navy in Jacksonville, Florida, or he resigned. He chose Jacksonville. The program was rigorous, one of only three centers like it in the United States. But shortly after returning from that program Jim would leave us altogether.

———

SID LEVINE   One afternoon I got a call. The man sounded a little drunk. "You wouldn't believe it," he said.

"Jim, is that you?"

"You have to see it."

"What's wrong?" I said. "Hang on, Jim, I'll be right there."

I jumped in the car and drove over to his house. It was the most bizarre scene I'd ever walked into. Jim was sitting on the living-room floor. He reminded me of a helpless baby, just whipped and beaten. He had a drink in his hand.

"Don't finish it," I said. "It won't help."

He hung on to it, though, while I inspected the house. Other than a few mementos from Vietnam on a lone desk in the study, the house was bare. Lois must have had a trailer back up to it while Jim was away for the weekend. She'd taken everything, including drapes. The one pair of curtains still hanging looked as though they had been slashed with a knife. She had even taken some wall-to-wall carpeting. Cabinets in the kitchen were bare except for a couple of cans. Everything else downstairs was gone. Jim's shock was phenomenal. He was pale as a ghost. It was the first time I'd seen him cry. When you know the enemy, you can protect yourself. It's the emotional blindside that catches people. At that moment, watching Jim on that floor, I thought, This woman has gotten to him in a way no Viet Cong could.

RICHARD McKEE   My sergeant major and I went over . We saw where the rugs had been torn out. I don't remember anything being left in that house. Jim always looked half sick. This day it was worse. He looked bad. Big-time hungover. He was in tears.

SID LEVINE   That house was everything to Jim, perhaps the only thing that helped him hang on. Somehow it gave him the strength to keep going. From that point on he began to deteriorate fast.

———

ALYCE   I tried to warn Lois that Jim was homosexual. After they split she called me.

"Alyce," she said, "this is Lois."

"What?" I snapped. I was immediately on the defensive.

"You've got a right to be mad at me," she said. "I owe you an apology. God, how I wish I had listened to you. I have thrown my life away for a queer."

She said Jim had been going to a camp on weekends where a bunch of gays got together. Before leaving she had gone through Jim's papers and found the documents on the Social Security accounts. She sent them to me. Twenty-two thousand, three hundred and sixty-nine dollars. Until then I had no way to prove what happened to that money. Jim had denied that it existed.

———

SID LEVINE   The day after the incident at his home, I had Jim come in to begin working through that crisis. But it was a terrible setback. He made arrangements to sell the house. He started describing his nightmares from Vietnam. In one he was a skeleton limping down a trail and no matter what he ate it fell through his bones. In another, he was chased by a headless person.

In the days that followed Jim claimed he wasn't drinking, but others saw him in the club. Besides therapy, it was clear he just needed a friend. He was wallowing in emotional poverty. His hooks with humanity had been ripped out. He needed a haven. For starters my wife and I decided to have him out to the house for dinner.

SANDRA LEVINE   It seemed he had an awful lot on his mind that he wouldn't talk about. Just knowing what he had been through made me standoffish. I didn't want to say anything that would remind him of past incidents. I noticed how very observant he was about everyday things. Like that first dinner at the house, I fixed a garden salad, steak, and baked potatoes. I set the table very colorfully. But I hadn't put out salad forks. Jim commented on it. I thought, Those things really mean a lot to him.

SID LEVINE   Within a few weeks, Jim closed the deal on his house and moved into bachelor officers' quarters. There were more slip-ups, more drinking episodes. McKee wanted him declared a rehabilitation failure. It became increasingly clear to me that alcoholism was a major problem, but I didn't think it was Jim's primary problem. The guy's whole world had been turned upside down. The enemy was everywhere. At least with a nightmare you can wake up. Jim couldn't wake up from this. He was slipping into a psychotic depression.

Late one afternoon, I met another officer, a major, who was staying in the same BOQ as Jim. I said I hadn't seen Jim that day. The major said that afternoon he had seen Jim sacked out, nude, on his bed. His door was open. Psychologists are supposed to pick up warning signals. I didn't. When I got home, my wife, Sandra, happened to ask if I had seen Jim. I told her what the major had said. My wife is a nurse.

"Sid," she said, "doesn't that seem strange to you?"

"Damn. . . . Yeah."

I remembered that at our last therapy session Jim had been neither way up nor way down. Typically, persons contemplating suicide find peace with themselves. I sped off to the bachelor officers' quarters. Jim's door was open. Most of his clothes were scattered over the room, although his uniform was hung neatly on the chair. I saw an empty gin bottle and whiskey bottle on the desk. The closet was open and in disarray. And Jim was sprawled across the bed. I tried to rouse him. He was nearly comatose. Besides the empty booze bottles Jim had more pill bottles there than a pharmacy. Valium, Sinequan, Dalmane, phenobarbital, an assortment of other barbiturates. Mix any of those with alcohol and you're going out the door. All the vials were empty.

There was no doubt what happened. Jim hadn't given up all those years as a prisoner. But he had now.

He was ashen gray. A half breath away from death. There was little motor response. Pupils were dilated. The body was cold. His whole system was shutting down. I grabbed a pair of underpants and trousers and slipped them on so as not to embarrass him. Then I picked him up, slung him over my shoulder, and carried him to the car. I drove eighty miles an hour to the emergency room of Martin Army Hospital, three miles away. They started lavage treatment immediately, putting a plastic separator in his mouth to keep it open and running a plastic tube down to his stomach. Then they sucked out everything they could. At the same time, they started giving Jim an antagonist for narcotics.

After three hours Jim started to come out of his coma. The doctor ran some charcoal into him to help absorb the drugs still moving through his system. Then they gave him something to induce vomiting.

Jim was transferred to intensive care, where, for the next two or three days, the medical staff kept a close watch. I was amazed at how he began to respond. Fears about brain damage disappeared.

STATEMENT OF MEDICAL EXAMINATION AND DUTY STATUS

Investigation revealed that Lieutenant Colonel Thompson drank some alcohol in the course of taking his prescribed medication of valium and sinequan at his home, resulting in his hospitalization on 17 November 1977 at Martin Army hospital, Fort Benning, Ga. There is no indication officer attempted suicide or self destruction in this action. No known witnesses to incident. No MP report on file. Records reveal that officer was a Prisoner of War for approximately 9 years and suffered great mental and physical anguish and discomfort as a result of incarceration. . . . It is my firm belief and conclusion that this incident can be classified as a case of simple negligence as opposed to willful misconduct on the part of LTC Thompson.

First Lieutenant Michael Wallace
Investigating officer
Company A, Headquarters Command

SID LEVINE   McKee said Jim was not fit to be in the Army, regardless of his background. He wanted him out, either medically retired or as a rehab failure. All those years as a POW and now they wanted to cancel him out. He was becoming an embarrassment. But when McKee started pushing, I started pushing. As soon as Jim was stabilized, I had him transferred up to psychiatry, where I knew I could keep McKee away from him. With the suicide attempt, psychiatry agreed to review his case. I wrote a discharge summary on the problems, what occurred at our treatment center, what the diagnoses might be. I said the primary problem was combat neurosis; a secondary problem was alcoholism. Everyone was looking at it the other way around. The chief of psychiatry agreed the best thing would be a transfer, to get Jim the hell away from Benning.

RUTH   In Tennessee, Laura couldn't stay out of trouble. The police picked her up a time or two for being out past curfew, for drinking underage. The judge, who had granted Mama custody of Catherine, told her, "If you can't keep Laura at home and out of trouble, I'll take them all away from you." So Mama and John forbid Laura from going out. One night Laura said she would come and go as she pleased. She was goin' to the car and leavin'.

John, who drank every night back then, told Laura, no, she wasn't leaving.

"You watch and see."

"You watch and see me, by God," he said.

John got his shotgun and went outside. We heard him scream, "You ain't a-leavin' in this car." Next thing we heard was Bam! Bam! Bam!

He blew her car all to shit. Shot the radiator, shot the windshield, shot the windows, shot the tires. "Now let's see you leave. You're not goin' to get into more trouble with the law. That's all there is to it."

LAURA   I don't know if I was more petrified or angry. There was a point, when he was done with the car, that I was curious what he was going to do with me. He didn't put the gun down.

RUTH   Laura screamed, "I want to get the hell out of here!" John said he'd give her money for a bus ticket. So the next day, a few days before Christmas 1977, Laura left. Mama gave her her Christmas presents. She was seventeen with a ninth-grade education.

PAM   Laura's car stayed a couple of months down on the back lot, in the brush. Then somebody hauled it away.

PASCAL BATSON   At Walter Reed's Forest Glen Annex, patients had to earn a change in status. "A" patients, like Thompson, were restricted to the ward. "B"s had to be accompanied by a staff member if they left the ward. "C" status meant the patient could be accompanied off the ward by "D" patients, who, in turn, come and go without supervision. One thing we needed to consider regarding Jim was privacy. He had been in prison for so long, where he was constantly intruded upon, that it was a delicate balance for us. To be intrusive enough to get the information we needed to understand Jim, but not so intrusive we recapitulated his POW experience.

RONALD ERSAY   He came to us depressed, but the medicines they had him on were depressants. If drinking wasn't causing his depression, the pills were. As a psychiatrist I knew Valium was just a very dry martini.

PASCAL BATSON   Benning psychiatrists had entertained several diagnoses. The only clear one for me was alcoholism.

RONALD ERSAY   We agreed that needed to be the focus of treatment.

PASCAL BATSON   Also, Jim had been displaced from a house that had become a major focus for him. Indeed, this was a dreamhouse, literally, which had occupied his waking hours in captivity. He built it in his mind over and over again. He had renovated and remodeled a home in Georgia to match it, planning the rooms down to the wall coverings.

RONALD ERSAY   I heard about his house. But his response to both his captivity and to what his second wife had done were red herrings, in my opinion. What he was responding to with the suicide attempt was the deterioration of his life through alcoholism. His moods and his judgment were affected by drink. Things fall apart from that alone. He denied any problem with alcohol prior to being shot down, and he even claimed no problem now. One would think, after a suicide attempt, the patient would be willing to discuss it. Instead Jim still tried to hide it.

PASCAL BATSON   There are many philosophies about alcoholism. That it's a repetition compulsion, or an organic dependency with a genetic loading, or that some people are just more susceptible because of a combination of enzymes. A medical model is used as the basis for most treatment programs. Jim had obsessive-compulsive traits. There are people who are very meticulous, very orderly. They make lists and get things done. It's only when faced with some monumental decision that they become less than methodical and make a rash decision. So there was some question whether Jim had a major affective disorder, or if he was manic-depressive. But we knew for sure he was alcoholic.

———

DON RANDER   I got word in early January 1978 that Jim was at Forest Glen, where the Army had its Ward Eight. I went up there to visit. It was a snake pit. He was on a ward with these young soldiers who played loud rock and roll. The noise alone could drive him up a wall. Some walked around like zombies, with eyes lowered or wearing blank stares. It was very discouraging. I wanted to talk to Jim alone, so I flashed my security badge at the head nurse; I may have even said something about national security. She gave us a private room to talk. Jim was lucid but depressed. Very depressed. When I got back to my office I made some frantic phone calls to POW friends of mine to try to get Jim's conditions improved.

———

RONALD ERSAY   Even into the late 1970s, alcoholism was not considered a bona fide illness. Jim and a lot of other people said his problems involved far more than alcoholism. He had served his country so well, they reasoned, it had to be something else. He couldn't be just a drunk. But, in fact, booze was killing Jim. Since his return the Army had allowed Jim to avoid responsibility for his alcoholism. Like an alcoholic with lung cancer. He'll say, "I'm not going to deal with alcoholism because the cancer will kill me." In Jim's case, everyone excused his drinking, saying, "He went through so much. It only made sense that he drank." But a person in Jim's situation who is not alcoholic finds another way to cope with his prison experience, his family problems, his professional setbacks.

In Jim's case the alcohol only impaired his judgment. He knew his mind was not as sharp as it had been. Once, he said, he could have looked at a seven-digit number and dialed it. He couldn't do that anymore. But instead of alcohol he wanted to blame it on wartime malnutrition.

The military solution to alcoholics typically is to discharge them. Jim knew we wouldn't do that. That's why he could fall down drunk in front of a general and not be put in jail. That's why he got shipped up here to Walter Reed. My recommendation—and I let Jim and everyone else know it—was if he didn't take care of his alcoholism he should be discharged. Anything short of that allowed him to continue to be sick. Kicking him out, I said, might be the only way to save him.

48 ▪ PLACE IN THE SUN

PASCAL BATSON   One evening I had the duty and received word Jim Thompson had left the ward. After a search I found him outside. We talked out there for an hour or so. And in that time our relationship changed. We gained mutual respect, I believe. He agreed to return to the ward and be more cooperative in a genuine way. He became more active in therapy, working with young troops. He became sort of a senior adviser even though his POW status was not widely known among the other patients.

————

ALYCE   Things got quieter at home after Laura left. John enjoyed his work in the mine. I spent my time caring for the baby and the house, getting dinner for the family, gardening. John and I still drank. I didn't need it but I wanted it. You get a high from alcohol and begin to think that's all there is. I used to buy six cases of beer a week for the two of us. If we had company I bought more. On weekends we'd start around nine o'clock in the morning and drink all day. During the week we began when John got home. I suppose a parent misses a lot when drinking that heavy.

Ruth and young Jim were still at home. Ruth and John developed a very strong bond. But there was tension between him and Jim Jr. Jim was so much like his father. He had that superior attitude.

JIM JR.   In Tennessee school was easy. When I entered seventh grade it was like I was back in fifth. I never took a book home. Didn't study much in eighth grade either. By ninth it caught up to me. I hung out with the guys at a gas station. Probably missed a hundred days of school that year. Sure enough, I flunked ninth grade. Flunked it bad.

———

PASCAL BATSON   After several weeks Jim was promoted out of the "pit" to an open ward, so he could come and go as he pleased. On at least two occasions he returned from a weekend having clearly been drinking. He made no attempt to conceal it. I found no cause-effect relationship between his prison experience and his drinking as much as he would have liked one. In fact, part of my treatment was to move Jim away from that identity as a POW. We focused on what was going on in his life currently, and what factors before his POW years affected how he felt about himself. I wanted Jim to understand things that had been conflicts for him, to deal with them rather than retreat as he would often do, denying they were important or painful. Denial had been a very effective method of coping as a POW. Rather than think about how he might be killed or die of malnutrition, he developed a survival skill: deny the seriousness of his situation. It kept him alive. Now it would take a long time for him to stop denying his problems with alcohol.

During our sessions, Jim revealed the great and stormy course of his life, to the point where he now found himself questioning the very values he had pegged his life's efforts on—the middle-class dream of children, a big home in the suburbs, life at the country club. He recalled how he and his father had very different value systems. The Army had been a way to break free, to get out of what was sort of prison, with his father as the jailer, a man who chained up Jim's dreams of bettering himself. Jim spoke of his early Army career in very glowing terms. It didn't matter who his father was—John Astor or a bus driver—superiors judged him on what he could do.

He talked too of an ideal family life before Vietnam. A devoted wife, three doting daughters, and another child on the way. But our memory is kind. We remember good things, particularly if we seek comfort in those memories. We don't dwell on the thorn. So what Jim remembered while a captive was an idyllic life, like situation comedies of the 1950s. *Donna Reed. Father Knows Best.* Everything clean and neat and loving and no problem that couldn't be solved before sundown. He didn't talk about the times the Army separated him from his family. That would have made it less than idyllic, and that ideal life was a memory he still wanted very much to hold.

So when Jim came back he felt betrayed. Not only betrayed but abused, as if he had been written off, as though Alyce had buried him in her own mind. Still, Jim had built this dream and wanted to try to fulfill it by living with Alyce and the children. If he could survive nine years of what he went through, he could somehow make this right. But within a few years of his return he was questioning everything he once thought so important.

RONALD ERSAY   The Army found a job for Jim in Washington, so he left the hospital in the spring of 1978. Our recommendation was that he continue therapy as an outpatient.

PASCAL BATSON   Certain patterns of behavior emerged. Clearly the main deterrent to his recovery and a successful career was drink. People who drink are never all there. All they think about is the next drink. All else is on automatic pilot. Somebody like Jim, who is orderly and method- ical, can still get things done but can't make changes. Jim would come to a session, be very animated, and say he was going to do this or going to do that. It was wishful thinking. The drinking bound him to previous behav- ior. I'd see improvement and then regression. Improvement and regres- sion.

RONALD ERSAY   The Army didn't know what to do. Here was a man who went through more than any other prisoner of war. But how could they promote him?

PASCAL BATSON   Jim resumed his speechmaking, regained his place in the sun. But as the seventies droned on, Americans wanted to forget that war. There were fewer and fewer calls for him as a speaker. Annual cele- brations of POWs became less frequent, less grandiose. Jim bitterly com- pared the reception POWs had received from Nixon, who welcomed them back as heroes, with the Carter administration's attitude. Carter, he said, treated the war as if it had been a national disgrace and that somehow it was no longer fitting to honor them.

HILDA SIGDA   In July 1978 I moved into the Fountains, a condominium complex in Alexandria, Virginia. There I met Jim Thompson in the hall- way. He welcomed me to the building and asked if I was interested in get- ting a certain type of drapery, a very fragile material called Tregal, that would cover the huge condo window in my apartment and had no seams. I said I was. It turned out beautifully and our friendship began. Though our first discussion involved curtains, my initial impression of Jim Thompson was macho. There was something in his attitude toward women. He assumed the air of a swinging single, not some sad and lonely person. I saw him frequently at social gatherings. He always looked nice, wore fine clothes. But I very quickly became aware of his overindulgence in alcohol. Sometimes when we passed in the hall he'd slur his speech or show a different personality than I'd see when he was sober. Sometimes when drinking he'd take out pictures of his family. He still held on to one showing him with his three daughters taken before he went to Vietnam. He'd recall how his marriage and world fell apart. Then he'd cry. He said his children didn't know or understand him. In fact, resented him. They had had a stable family life with another man. When Jim came home, a skeleton with a bad disposition, he disrupted their lives.

I'd tell Jim his children were victims of the war as much as he was. He knew that was right, but he had a terrible amount of pride. He could feel rejected very easily. After a while I saw through the macho image and found a man with very low self-esteem.

PASCAL BATSON   Jim was trying to reconcile with his family, particularly his son, whom he had never really known. There was one daughter he felt closer to, also, and took pride in her accomplishments. The others, he said, had been turned against him.

RUTH   Laura came to spend more time with my dad than the rest of us after she moved north. She liked him. She cared about him. And she couldn't afford to be wild any longer. She didn't have much money.

LAURA   After leaving Tennessee, I returned to Honesdale, the only place I knew. I got a job my first week there and a cute apartment. I stayed for two and a half years, putting money away. I got myself a car. Little by little, things began to work out. My dad and I got real close. I called him when the chips were down. He gave me the old lines, "Keep your chin up" and "If I can ever help you out, let me know." He was my backbone. If it weren't for him, I might have folded. When I got my high school diploma he was so proud.

He would describe in our talks how he and my mother had had a storybook romance. Married right after high school and lived together quite a few years before Pam was born. So they had time to develop a close relationship. He described how, before the war, he'd take us girls to lunch. Obviously the memories were precious to him.

He became fun. We'd sing together. We'd breakfast on his balcony. We went for motorcycle rides. We got high together. We talked one on one. I could tell him anything. Absolutely anything. We used to tease each other about being black sheep of the family. Barry Manilow had a song out at the time, "I Made It Through the Rain." That was our song. The two of us had been through hell and back again, we said, and came out shining.

RUTH   In the summer of 1978 I got a job. As soon as I had enough money for a bus ticket I quit and went to visit Nan Vail, my friend from our days at Fort Benning. Her father by then was a full colonel and stationed in Washington. Sometime during my visit Colonel Vail asked me where my dad was. I told him Alexandria.

"Well, aren't you going to go see him?"

"I don't reckon I will," I said.

But he set me down and talked me into calling him. When I did I found out Laura was visiting too. So I spent the last couple of days of my visit with them. We had a ball! We went out, we partied, we went down into Washington. My dad had a convertible and we drove with the top down. Saturday night when we got back to Dad's condominium, me and Laura saw the big fountain out front, and we jumped in with fancy dresses on. "Get the hell out of there," Dad said. "You're going to get me in trouble!"

LAURA   Instead we pulled him in. Oh, it was great fun.

RUTH   I called Mama to tell her where I was, and that I wanted to stay a few more days. She got upset.

"I know he's going to talk you into staying! You won't come back home."

She cried and cried. So I packed that weekend. On the way home I realized me and Dad hadn't had any time to sit down and talk. We were too busy having fun. I wouldn't see him again for six years. I went back to pretending he didn't exist.

JIM JR.   Dad began inviting me up during the summertime. One visit up there he was havin' a bad dream. I went in to wake him up, to shake him out of it. Bad mistake. He was runnin' from something. When I shook his shoulder he about ripped my arm off.

After he saw it was me he started cryin'.

EVERETT ALVAREZ   We had quarterly lunches of former 'Nam POWs in the Washington, D.C., area. Jim came to a few. He brought his son to one. He told me how his son was going to grow up to be a paratrooper. The next time I saw Jim at one of these—this one at the Fort Myers officers' club—he frightened me. He sat beside me and out of the clear blue Jim said, "I've been having some difficulty. Actually I want to go out and kill myself."

He told me he had already tried it once. I'm sitting there shocked.

"Jim," I said, "are you seeing anybody, a counselor?"

"Oh, yeah."

I didn't know what to say. What do you tell a guy when he says something like that?

"Jim," I said, "look on the positive side. You still have much of your health and you still have your life. If you want help, don't be afraid to ask for it. I'm sure we all need it."

He wasn't listening. He was having a one-way conversation. I felt sorry for him.

――――――

MARY VAIL   When our daughter Nan wanted to visit Ruth in Tennessee, we drove her down to a highway exit where Ruth met her. After a week, on our way back from Kentucky, we picked Nan up. This was our first visit to Alyce's farm.

NATHAN VAIL   I said to Mary, "We should have looked at this before we brought Nan up here." When I went inside to use the bathroom the condition of that house made me sick.

MARY VAIL   Nan was totally oblivious. She had had so much fun and had done so many things. Alyce taught her to can tomatoes. They had all those animals. Nan couldn't stop talking about it.

NATHAN VAIL   Alyce wasn't at all displeased with her life. She saw it as a kind of refuge.

MARY VAIL   She was back in her comfort zone, happier than I'd ever seen her. As we were leaving, a bull got loose. They had to coax it off the road. Alyce turned to me and said, "This is a lot different, isn't it, Mary?"

"Yes," I said, "but are you happy?"

"Oh, extremely."

And she was. She was as happy as can be.

――――――

PASCAL BATSON   While Jim was an outpatient, he wrote a note to Lois, outlining why he found the situation with her intolerable. It was very intimate and revealing, perhaps the first intimate communication he had with this woman. By then Lois too was living in Alexandria.

Nov 78

Dear Lois,

It is with heavy heart that I write this letter because it is the coward's way out and because of the many memories of the good times we shared. I

thought I could get over the bitterness and the cynicism but I cannot. It is
said that to forgive and not to forget is not to forgive at all. As much as I
have tried, I have not been able to forget. Now, as then, you show
absolutely no regard for me as a person nor for my feelings. I know this is
not deliberate but you are insensitive to my feelings and to my emotional
needs and therefore ride roughshod over them.

It all started when you insisted on redecorating my home. I loved that
home; it was me; it represented the realization of a cherished dream. Every
change you made was a personal affront and made over my protest. It
wasn't easy to be overruled at every turn. I voiced only mild objection
because I loved you and placed your happiness above my own. I waited in
vain for reciprocal empathy. The way I walked, the way I talked, the way I
danced, the way I dressed, the way I drove a car, my preferences in enter-
taining, my friends, etc., etc., ad nauseum, all fell short of your definition
of right and wrong. You even tried to force your value system on my children, exacerbating an already difficult situation. It had to be your way or
the wrong way. Hasn't it ever occurred to you that what is right for one
may not be right for another? And that there is room in this world for
more than one right? Then, as now, I could take no more. Continuing
such a relationship under the guise of a happy marriage would have been
the epitome of hypocrisy. Many things I am, a hypocrite I am not. Therefore my decision to get a divorce.

I hold you responsible for having me pulled out of school and sent to
Jacksonville. Yes, I was drinking heavily, but I did not deserve that. It was
overkill, an overkill that probably ruined my career. And once the decision
to divorce, your actions bore out—no, exceeded—my worst expectations.
You stole, yes stole, $5,000. $1,000 from my checking account and $4,000
from my savings account to which you contributed absolutely nothing and
to which you had absolutely no right. I wonder if your conscience bothers
you that you took money from an insurance policy on Alyce that I can-
celed. And then you literally decimated my home. I can still hear you
brushing away my protests to redecorate that house with phrases like
"Don't worry. I won't break you," and "When we leave it will all go with
the house." I could never put into words how devastated I was when I saw
my once beautiful home literally decimated. I could not believe that anyone in her right mind could do such a horrendous thing to what was once
so beautiful. Is it any wonder that I find it so difficult, even impossible, to
trust anyone, especially a woman again?

You did things I would never have believed you capable of. You tore up
everything, left my kitchen looking like a pig sty with a dirty oven, my
china soiled, encrusted with dried food, windows open, doors unlocked, air

conditioning going full blast. All of this and not even the decency to tell me you had left. My reaction of total devastation is the understatement of the year. This desecration of that which I held near and dear contributed in large measure to my attempting suicide.

Further, I'll never believe my lounging pajamas and my autographed copy of Dr. Carr's book just vanished, nor will I ever believe my shirt and shell necklaces just disappeared; they were souvenirs from our honeymoon and just the thing a mean, jealous, spiteful, vindictive woman would destroy. And all this I am supposed to forgive and forget? I can't and I truly regret that I can't. It's a hell of a thing to live with. You still attempt to impose your value system on me. You still feel free to express your opinion about anything and everything that crosses your mind including what my children should and should not do. This chair isn't right. The planter should be there, the secretary should be open, the terrarium is lost in the kitchen. Never mind how sensitive you know I am (or do you know) and how much of me is in these things. Would it ever cross your mind to be just a little considerate of my feelings and have the good graces to say something nice or not say anything at all? Even knowing how difficult it is for me to assert myself, you continue to do your thing with my things and I resent it just as I resented what you did to my home in Georgia. I wouldn't dream of commenting on your home in a critical way much less rearrange it to suit my taste. Why must you do it to me? Why must you sit in judgment on everything I say or do? I'm getting to feel crowded just as I felt crowded before we separated. I've had enough of the nightly phone calls; enough of the true confessions, because you consistently take advantage of my reluctance to unpleasantness. You are unwilling or unable to sense my feelings now as before. You think nothing of prying into my personal life, asking personal questions I would never dream of asking another person and I refuse to be subjected to this any longer. The last prying question you asked was about my wedding ring. You will find it enclosed. I hope you have the good graces to return your wedding and engagement rings to me. I feel in all fairness you should return the diamond pendant and earrings. I would also like to have whatever portion of the $100 I loaned you that you feel you owe me.

Goodbye, Lois, and good luck.

Sincerely yours,
Jim

PASCAL BATSON   It was easier for Jim to write than to talk to Lois. He could accomplish such frankness only at a distance, and perhaps he never mailed it. The letter speaks to the power of his desire for intimacy but also to his frustration when he couldn't achieve it. In this case, intimacy is accomplished as he is telling her, basically, he doesn't want to ever see her again. He is telling her why now, instead of having dealt with it when something could have been done. He couldn't tell Lois then that her redecorating meant a lot more than putting color schemes together. He couldn't express anger. The idea being that you can't be angry and still love someone. This may go back to Jim's childhood when anger was not something he could express. Anger in Jim's childhood home could be really very dangerous.

————

LAURA   Grandpa Thompson died in '78 in a run-down apartment in Lodi, New Jersey. He had been dead several days when they found him.

RUTH   He didn't have any friends who would wonder why they hadn't seen him. Nobody liked him. It took three days before somebody smelled something.

LAURA   I went with Dad to the funeral and then to help clean out the apartment. It was pathetic. Extreme poverty. Dad had had a monthly allotment set up to help his parents. Grandpa, a very proud and stubborn man, only stuck the money in a bank account. Every allotment was still there in the bank when he died.

RUTH   Grandpa was tighter than bark on a tree. And all that money became part of Grandpa's estate. It turned out only Jimmy was in Grandpa's will. Not my dad. Not me, Laura and Pam. Grandpa didn't like girls. So Jimmy was to get seventy-five hundred dollars when he turned eighteen.

49 ■ BRIDGE PLAYERS

CHARLOTTE FAIRCHILD I found it very difficult to be a single person. I think Jim did too. I met him in 1979 through a bridge group.

LOIS VERMILLION At first he was just Jim Thompson, a regular guy who plays bridge. He didn't come to us as any major story.

CHARLOTTE FAIRCHILD He came across as cultured, well-educated, a classy guy. I understood he was in the military but didn't know until later about his war experience.

HOWARD FISHER His politics surprised me. I thought, given his background, he'd be a superhawk. But his opinions were moderate.

LOIS VERMILLION He was a hell of a bridge player. But rating wasn't important to him. Bridge was an easy way to meet people.

CHARLOTTE FAIRCHILD Jim was a very good declare player. For that you need concentration, you need to listen to the opposition and figure out what you've got. You need to know every card played and to communicate with your partner.

LOIS VERMILLION In some way his experiences colored for each of us our own perception of life. Yet he seemed to take the whole POW experience in stride. I mean, it didn't make him weird in any way. But he said it was almost like he had died, like people didn't know he was alive.

CHARLOTTE FAIRCHILD He said he thought the experience would shorten his life. He felt cheated to have been out of circulation so long, to have missed his son's first nine years. My reply was, "You're here, you're safe and you're healthy. What more could you ask for?"

LOIS VERMILLION   As Jim became more comfortable with the group he socialized more. We all loved him.

CHARLOTTEE FAIRCHILD   It became sort of an extended family. Bridge, beach, parties, theater, movies, board games. A very caring group. None of us was married. I had just moved to Alexandria from Dallas and was going through a very painful divorce. I had had a perfect marriage for twenty years. By the time I got to Washington I was mentally and physically devastated. Jim became a wonderful friend.

We dated a few times. He was absolutely a gentleman. Very bright. Obviously self-made. A delightful person to be with. I could talk about anything with him. And any social grace you wanted in a human being this man had. He oozed class. Most guys in the bridge group, when it was their turn to host, brought out the cheese and crackers. Jim always put on a special spread. Spinach dip, sometimes caviar or deviled eggs, expensive nuts. Jim enjoyed cooking. A maid came in twice a week, so his apartment was spotless. He had her clean the crystal and prided himself on his Wedgwood china. Perhaps because of his horrible experiences in captivity, he appreciated beauty more than anyone I had ever met. The apartment was so tastefully decorated, right down to the draperies that were custommade and expensive. He had the best of everything. Furniture was incredibly gorgeous. He had a king-size bed and very pretty black dressers. Fine crystal, fine china, nice art objects. He had quite a nice library with a big desk, a leather chair, books, and some very nice pictures on the wall. Some military memorabilia but not overwhelming.

Everything about his personal appearance and environment was immaculate. His car, a big Pontiac convertible, was in beautiful shape. When we went out he dressed beautifully. Anyone would be very proud to be with such an escort. The night he took me to the theater he was dressed in a tuxedo with a bow tie he had tied himself. He looked gorgeous. Status, you see, was very important to Jim. He prided himself on his rank in life. He's a snob. I can say that because I'm a snob too. There are certain things in life I want—or want to do—regardless. Every time I set my table it's perfect. I never put a wineglass to the left. Ever. So I could relate to Jim wanting top of the line in clothing, furniture, everything.

And he treated me like a queen. One Sunday, when I was so very depressed and hurt over the divorce, and my daughter and ex-husband were having problems, I spoke with Jim on the phone about it. "You stay right there," he said. "I'll be there in a few minutes."

Half an hour later, he was on my doorstep.

"Come on," he said, "we're going for a drive."

He had the top down. We drove around the Beltway into Maryland, just beyond the D.C. line, where he showed me around a group of old buildings on grounds that were charming. Old architecture. Yes, Forest Glen, that's right. He said it used to be some sort of old college or retreat. It was lovely. Then we drove up Rock Creek Parkway, stopped at a picnic area, and out of his car came a bag with wine and bread. We sat there and talked. I'm telling you it cheered me so.

Lois Vermillion had a family beach home in Bethany. She would invite several people down for the weekend. Jim was there three or four times. We sat on the porch and sang songs, then went for a walk on the beach. There was a lifeguard stand where we sat and sang and had a wonderful time acting silly for a couple of hours. Gosh, Jim was a happy drinker. He really was. He had such a good time.

———————

PASCAL BATSON By Jim's description the amount of drinking very much depended on his work. He felt he had a do-nothing personnel job there in Alexandria. He was treated as a special person but they had no expectation his work would be used. They'd start him on a project he found very important and it turned out to be just busy work. No work he ever did came to fruition.

ARMY OFFICER PERFORMANCE EVALUATION

Lieutenant Colonel Floyd J. Thompson
Position: Military Job Analyst,
                MOS Structure Branch
                USA Military Personnel Center
Performance: Lieutenant Colonel Thompson has performed all of his assigned duties in an outstanding manner. He rapidly became conversant with and able to apply policies, precedents and procedures pertaining to both officer and warrant officer actions to provide continuity and depth within the branch. He utilized his expertise by acting as MILPERCEN's representative on a DCSPER team that reviewed all LTC and COL positions in TAADS in preparation for promotion by specialty. He directed an extensive study that developed the first objective system of grading officer positions in TDA.

Potential: Capable and ready to perform as a colonel in his specialties. He could best serve the Army in positions requiring public relations work.

CHARLOTTE FAIRCHILD Jim was spending quite a bit of time with his shrink. He told me when he had been to see him but never what was discussed. I didn't want to open wounds.

THERAPEUTIC GOALS
prepared by Floyd J. Thompson for Dr. Batson
June 1979

Acting on your suggestion that we renegotiate the contract, and after a great deal of thought, I elected to put my ideas on paper, not with a view toward engaging in written negotiations but to assist me in organizing my thoughts. Each time I wrote this paper, I put it away to reread it in the morning (as is my habit) and each morning I was obliged to rewrite it. This represents the fifth iteration. The thought occurred to me that this is a good time to renegotiate our contract because, a year ago, I doubt if I would have been able to clearly identify the problem much less to articulate it. I discovered that this is a dynamic process that could, and in fact should, go on indefinitely. I feel differently today than I felt yesterday and I know tomorrow I will feel differently than I do today. This paper then represents how I feel today.

My ultimate goal is to eliminate or at least diminish chronic depression and thereby be able to lead a normal life without medication. In the course of this therapy I expect to learn how to deal with potentially depressing situations and be able to preclude a recurrence of depression. To accomplish this goal I see two objectives to be addressed in therapy: one, make my life more meaningful and therefore worth living and, two, develop the capacity for close interpersonal relationships.

A third objective is to deal effectively with my drinking problem. Fourth is to capitalize on the heightened sense of well being that derives from being in good physical condition. I fully understand that to pursue this goal will require a great deal of hard work, some serious soul-searching and will involve painful self-examination and evaluation. I also realize no progress will be made if I continue to use alcohol to ease the pain. I accept as my part of the contract to refrain from alcohol and should I elect to discontinue treatment I will so state and return for six additional visits.

In order to make my life more meaningful and therefore worth living I must:
1. Establish realistic, attainable goals.
2. Accept failure realistically.
3. Accept life as it is and not try to make it the way I want it to be—become more realistic, less idealistic.

4. Find job satisfaction—be able to work, concentrate, produce.

5. Regain the zest for living—awake each morning eager to savor what this day will bring instead of dreading a new day.

6. Replace too much time and not enough to do, with not enough time to do everything I want to do.

7. Raise sense of self-worth.

8. Increase self-discipline.

9. Eliminate self-pity.

10. Acknowledge weaknesses and be willing to accept help.

To develop a capacity for establishing close relationships I must:

1. Resume a normal sex life—not feel threatened with loss of freedom, not be intimidated with anxiety over not being able to produce.

2. Reduce inappropriately high defensive and repressive mechanisms.

3. Respond spontaneously to stimuli—allow love, hate, anger, grief, joy, etc. a normal, healthy expression.

4. Develop self-confidence to the point that I am able and willing to risk being hurt again.

5. Accept loss of the family I knew and loved and develop a realistic relationship with my children as they are today.

6. Be able and willing to make a personal commitment to another person.

7. Expand circle of friends and social activities.

I must accept the fact I may never be able to drink alcohol again. I see the campaign against alcoholism as a three-pronged attack: attempt to remove or at least reduce the motivation to drink through therapy; directly address alcoholism with Dr. Ersay and . . . construct support system devoid of alcohol.

I see the possibility of three levels of success: one, stay sober with the use of antabuse; two, stay sober without the use of antabuse and, three, return to social drinking. I am at the first level now. I realize I could progress, regress or remain at level one. However, if I never progress I must learn to accept it and be happy with it. I don't want to die a drunk.

I know too well how great it feels to be in top notch physical condition. I have no excuse for being out of shape. The sense of well being that derives from being in good shape and, conversely, the down feeling that comes with poor condition, defies description. And more important than the physical sense is the emotional sense. Good physical condition breeds quiet confidence. It raises one's sense of self-worth. I am firmly convinced a sound body means a keener mind. Physical strength breeds emotional strength. Getting back in good physical shape may be half of the battle to get back in good emotional shape.

This has been a difficult paper to write. It was particularly difficult to evade the enticement of speaking in philosophical terms and vague abstractions. Subdivisions of the principal goal did not fall into place nor did any logical order emerge. Prioritizing was impossible. There appears to be no first step, second step, etc. but rather it is a multi-faceted enigma that requires a multi-lateral approach. The subdivisions chosen do not even represent major categories. They represent different avenues of approach: objectives one and two we work on together; objective three includes Dr. Ersay's help and objective four I see as my responsibility.

—Jim Thompson

CHARLOTTE FAIRCHILD   I had a romantic interest in Jim. I thought he did in me too. But after I knew him awhile, he made no moves on me whatsoever. We did sleep together once but nothing happened. Really. Nothing. That evening was very strange. I ended up sleeping in one of his T-shirts, and very close together on his silk sheets. We kissed a lot. But that was it. Perhaps he was afraid of getting too close to people. He had been burned by his first wife. His second marriage didn't work out. God only knows what happened to him while he was in prison.

He never spoke about that night. I didn't either. And I didn't care. He was a good human being.

———

PASCAL BATSON   Physically, Jim was able to have sexual relations, but he was dysfunctional by his own accounts. How much of that was alcohol, which can cause impotence, and how much was psychological would be hard to know. This was a man depressed, alcoholic, anxious, and at the end of his rope. There is not much room for the relaxation and spontaneity necessary for a satisfying relationship. Impotence had been a concern in his relationship with Lois too. He anticipated the problem if he were dating someone and felt additional pressure. His prison experience certainly could have been contributory. He was without a sexual partner for so many years. More importantly, he had problems with intimacy in general. That's certainly understandable given his solitary state in prison and need to survive by closing himself off to people. Jim's experience with intimacy was that it was very dangerous. You could get hurt, if not killed.

———

CHARLOTTE FAIRCHILD   When angry, Jim's reaction was silence. And he really got angry at me once. He had invited me and my friend Petra over to his apartment for a drink. He had a ficus tree in his living room with a dead leaf. I said something like "Let's pick that leaf off."

"Don't touch it," Jim said.

But it was dead. I had the leaf in my hand already. One dead leaf. The end, right? Well, Jim was furious, in that very cool way.

"I asked you not to touch that plant and you touched it," he said. Then he got quiet. He talked to Petra the rest of the evening but not to me. I felt iced. I wasn't sure what was happening.

Days went by with no word from Jim. I told Petra I had not heard from him.

"I bet it's over that tree," she said.

Two months passed with no word. He was a good friend—a really good friend—so I called him. I had to pull teeth to get him to tell me what the silence was all about. Finally he said it was the leaf. I had violated his kingdom. I had violated his trust.

"All right," I said. "I didn't respect your wishes. I'm really sorry. Had I known taking a dead leaf off of your tree would cost this silence and maybe cost our friendship I wouldn't have pulled it."

He wasn't embarrassed by the incident. Not at all. And he didn't think it was silly. I hadn't taken him seriously enough. That's the way he felt. That's the way it was.

———

HILDA SIGDA   In the fall of 1979 we had a fire in the Fountains. I went to Jim's door and knocked, trying to get him to come out. He wouldn't. He was drinking again. Later that evening he left the building very late and had an accident with his car. Ran it off the road. The Army got involved. Later he came to my apartment in a very deep depression. He was despondent and disgusted.

CHARLOTTE FAIRCHILD   A few weeks later Petra had some of us over to play games in her apartment in McLean. Jim got so drunk he became violently ill. Petra had two bedrooms, so Jim asked if he could stay over. The next weekend, for the Cowboys–Redskins game, Petra had another party. Jim had such a good time, singing and laughing. But again, he drank too much. This time he decided he needed to go home. He left and we didn't hear from him for a couple of days. He told us later that he had pulled off the road to sleep when the police came along and took him to jail. He was there for a day or two. You can imagine how that experience scared him.

RONALD ERSAY   Jim continued to get worse, sliding into the late stages of alcoholism, to the point where he was killing himself with drink. Finally, after an interminably long time, Jim joined Alcoholics Anonymous. It seemed, at last, he might turn his life around.

50 ∎ TURNAROUND

PASCAL BATSON Jim had an obsessive-compulsive way of organizing even emotional experiences, to try to understand them intellectually. We see that in this letter.

5 Dec 79

To Dr. Batson:

The Big Bingo!

Starting Sun 2 Dec I began to experience an "up" mood, a feeling of general well being. After reveling in it for a couple of days I began to feel this "up" mood was here to stay. I hadn't felt so good so long in years. I was enjoying all the signs of the "up" feeling: clear, sharp mind; energetic; enthusiastic; decision-making functioned well; willing and able to plan ahead (work, evening activities, vacation); memory functioned well; used sound logic; remembered phone numbers and appointments etc.; played excellent bridge; could grasp concept that had been eluding me; awoke each morning feeling refreshed even after minimal sleep; feel alert, eager to go to work instead of drudgery; played improved racquetball as opposed to sluggish, slow reflexes, poor eye-hand coordination, poor control over shots, poor judgment of ricochet. Bottom line—ALL SYSTEMS GO!

Why? Realized depressions were fewer, not as deep and further between. Brain less foggy, feelings of futility almost gone. "Up" periods last longer; almost happy. Willing to engage in and enjoy casual banter with others instead of "smile for the audience" and then conscientiously return to down. More sociable. Firm realization that good or bad times, enjoy or be irritated, productive or non-productive AA meeting—it all depends on my attitude over which I can now exercise a measure of control.

Now comes the bingo—the revelation. What in the past I've described as the pits is in fact depression; what I've described as an "up" feeling (akin to euphoria) is in fact NORM. It was only because I had been in a depressed state so long and so low that, by contrast, normal seemed euphoric and was described by me as euphoric.

I see now why Dr. Dirksi at Fort Benning and the psychiatrist at Brooke Army Medical Center favored a diagnosis of manic depression and Lithium. I marvel you did not fall into the same trap. I feel now that I have only one major obstacle to overcome: interpersonal relationships.

Jim

MOOD CHART

+2 Manic state
0 Normal range
−2 Depressive state

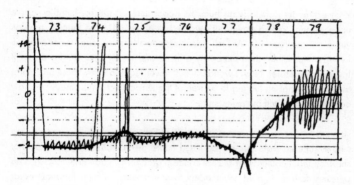

	Positive	Negative
1973	Repatriation	Reality
1974	Separation & divorce	Personal/professional problems
1975	Marriage	Back to reality
1976	College	Sustained depression
1977		Alcohol rehab, divorce
		Despondency → suicide
1978	(1st half) New diagnosis and treatment	Slow progress, many setbacks
	(2nd half) Better progress	Increasing painful, desire to quit

1979	(1st half) Upward trend	Violent mood swings
	(2nd half) Rapid progress	Diminished mood swings
	Tendency to stabilize	

1980	Reality - stable - normal

HILDA SIGDA   Joining AA was a turning point in Jim's life. He found some inner strength and self-worth. He seemed at peace, and over a lot of his bitterness about the war and his family.

Alcoholics Anonymous encourages its members to be brutality honest with themselves during a self-evaluation process that helps them face their addictions. The process is part of Step Four of AA's twelve-step guide to recovery. Excerpts of documents in Jim Thompson's psychiatric files hint at the depth of his own self-analysis as he struggled to cope both with alcoholism and demons familiar to most of us.

THOMPSON ON HUMILITY

I never thought I could learn humility. I considered it OK for humble people upon whom I looked down but I wanted to be proud. I see humility now as virtue not as weakness. At first, admitting powerlessness and unmanageability was impossible, then extremely difficult and repugnant. With practice it has become easier. Now I wonder why I never learned this without becoming alcoholic. What a blessing to be free of the zero-defect syndrome. I can now accept criticism without resentment.

ON FALSE PRIDE

I have suffered from this all my life. I could never admit a mistake or any shortcoming. I could never accept criticism graciously. I equated criticism with personal failure. I could never admit to any feelings of fear, inadequacy or lack of knowledge. My entire sense of self-worth was predicated upon what other people thought of me. I spent my life looking for positive strokes.

ON PERFECTIONISM

I have always been willing to accept mistakes, shortcomings and less than perfection in others. Never in myself. I could always be kind and tolerant of less-than-perfect performance in others but my motive was not genuine kindness or tolerance; it made me feel superior. I had to be the best. Never gave myself the right to be less. Fear of not being the best prevented me from doing many things. I couldn't enjoy golf unless I could shoot par so I never tried. I don't play a musical instrument for the same reason even though I always wanted to. No instant pay-off, no play. Breaking free of the zero-defect syndrome has enabled me to try to enjoy many new things without having to excel.

ON ACCEPTANCE

This is perhaps the greatest lesson learned in AA. Fears and defensiveness have diminished and I can accept less than perfection in myself. Only in AA did I come to realize that as a human I have the right to err, to fail.

HILDA SIGDA   At parties Jim drank only Perrier water. He was very determined to straighten out his life. Suddenly he seemed very pleased with himself. He even felt his career was going somewhere. He began to trim down—he had gained forty pounds since we met—and bought a lot of nice clothes. He became more active in Big Brother, working with a black youth of about fourteen. Jim took him to football games and other events. He was becoming a different person.

ON SELFISHNESS

I am very selfish, particularly in materialistic ways. I have never done anything without asking myself, "What's in it for me?" But I'm clever enough not to let it show. No matter what I say or do there is always a calculated payoff even if only the ego-feeding superior feeling I get from donating to charity. I need work here.

ON SHARING

I'm pretty good at this. I do love people, particularly kids and people less fortunate than me. I am more than willing to share my time, talent and, to a certain extent, money. I do feel my motives are not completely genuine. I'm still looking for the payoff: respect, admiration, a good feeling, a certain smugness, even self-aggrandizement. I find it most difficult to share my feelings without being phony and holding back.

ON BEING PHONY

I have never been happy with what I am. No matter what I was or had or did, I wanted to appear better. I used every deception in the book: misleading statements, omissions, half-truths, deliberately creating false impressions. Although I have made some improvement here, it has not been much. I wear more expensive clothes and jewelry than I can afford. I make every effort to create the impression I lead an exciting, glamorous, carefree life. I pretend to be happy when I want to cry.

WANDA MERCER   One evening Hilda, her boyfriend, and I were returning from a party. Jim Thompson was having a few friends over so he
invited us in. He wasn't drinking but offered us drinks. Hilda had had a
few already and we took her home. Jim asked if I would like to come back,
so I did. He sat on a chaise longue and I was on a barstool.

"Why don't you sit here with me," he asked.

"No, I don't think so."

"Wanda, I won't bother you," he said. "I'm impotent right now."

He said it was because of his drinking or his stormy relationship with
two past wives. We spent the rest of the night on his balcony talking. We
became good friends.

ON BEING YOURSELF

It does feel good but the temptation to revert to old ways is strong. It's great
not to have to live a lie but at times I still like the fantasy better than reality.

WANDA MERCER   Jim was polite, considerate, well-spoken. Knowledgeable about so many things. He had a good sense of humor too. But I
noticed too that he always was careful in all he said or did. Still we kept an
easy relationship. He liked music, cards. I went to AA meetings with him if
he wanted me to. We went to plays, movies, and dancing. We didn't live
together, however. He kept his apartment and I kept mine. But people in
the building assumed we were having a love affair. I did love Jim. I think
Jim loved me. But it was not sexual. Jim felt safe with me. I didn't demand
anything.

ON TAKING THINGS FOR GRANTED

I have enough adversity in my life to keep from becoming complacent. Boredom is a self-inflicted wound. Anyone suffering from it deserves it. Depression
is my stumbling block.

ON SELF-PITY

I wallowed in self-pity for years. When I saw the things I valued most—health,
happiness and career—shot to hell, not only did I feel sorry for myself, I
wanted everyone else to feel sorry for me (even though I vehemently denied
it). I'm coming out of it now but still slip back occasionally.

ON RESPECT FOR OTHERS

My friends in AA are the best example. Alcoholism is the great leveler. Differences in age, sex, race, nationality, religion, political orientation, socio-
economic background, education pale into insignificance. We all stand

naked together. And we love each other. I had a hell of a time getting into this but it sure feels good now.

ON FEAR

At one time fears dominated my mind. I knew no peace. I cannot say these fears have been eliminated, but they have been reduced to a tolerable level. My greatest fear now is recurrence of depression, despondency leading to drinking and possibly suicide.

WANDA MERCER   Jim commented to me once that he wasn't a very nice person to live with before Vietnam. "I guess I never had a good father figure myself," he said. He began to see there were two sides to a story, that there were problems before Vietnam and some were his fault.

ON GUILT FEELINGS

The greatest guilt feelings I've ever felt were because I didn't feel guilty. Regardless of my expressions of love and concern for my children and guilt feelings over the harm to them that the divorce might have caused, I really don't feel that way. For a long time I felt guilty because I felt no parental love.

ON HONEST THINKING

The biggest problem I have here is recognizing what I really think and why. A good example came up today, 14 March, 1980, when I tried to answer this question posed by Dr. Batson: "What would make you happy?" I replied in terms of wife, kids, home, car, stars on my collar and money in the bank. Is this a conditioned response? I think so. I like my lifestyle now but the answer I gave was "acceptable." What do I really want? I don't know.

ON BEING GRATEFUL

I feel better about myself now than I have in a long time, better than ever, really. And I am grateful: grateful to several professional people who helped me, grateful to AA and to my AA friends. And above all grateful to God. Without these I would be dead. Because of these I have a new lease on life. The only way I know to express this gratitude is to share my experience with others and hopefully help others find what I have found—life itself.

WANDA MERCER   AA became such a major factor in Jim's life. He was even counseling others through the local chapter and would get calls to go help somebody else. He was going to church too, really trying to put his life back together. And succeeding pretty well.

If Jim was still bitter about anything it was not having a relationship with the children, especially his son. Young Jim came up to visit his father in the summer of 1980. He brought a girlfriend. He said it was a really bad scene at home. Jim Jr. seemed immature and insecure.

CHARLOTTE FAIRCHILD   I was struck that his son, to be very blunt, was a redneck. His grammar was horrible. He seemed to have no ambition.

WANDA MERCER   Jim and his boy were very careful around each other. Overly polite. Overly caring. For a few days everything was fine. Then Jim Jr. started needing money, wanting Jim to do more and more favors. Jim went along until it became excessive and he felt used. Then Jimmy went back to Tennessee.

———

PASCAL BATSON   Not having much of a job, Jim put his energies into seeking promotion to colonel. He had been passed over twice and each time asked that the promotion board's decision be reviewed. Finally he got a special board. While awaiting the results, Jim pressed for a more significant assignment.

WANDA MERCER   He won a transfer to the commander in chief's office, to work as a public information officer. He felt so much better about himself and his job.

PASCAL BATSON   In the fall of 1980, Jim was selected for promotion to colonel. A major personal achievement.

WANDA MERCER   He felt like he finally had put his life back together. And all things considered, he had. He decided to have his own promotion party and asked if I could host it. We set up a buffet in his apartment. The party lasted three or four hours, a come-and-go type of thing, with sixty to seventy people there at any one time and a lot more than that through the evening.

CHARLOTTE FAIRCHILD   Jim talked about how he had gotten his act totally together—mentally, emotionally, everything. He even bought a fancy motorcycle. Jim had missed a lot during his childhood. "I'm in a position now," he'd say, "that when I see something I'm going to buy it or get it or do it. I'm going to be a kid again."

———

RUTH   I didn't tell Mama until the Monday before the wedding that me and Kenny was gettin' married. Then it took me a long time to convince her I was serious. Mama goes on first impressions. Kenny done me dirty once. I got over it but Mama didn't. She begged me not to marry him. But we got married in her living room.

KENNY   I drive a truck for a living. They gave me an easy day that Friday so I had time to get home and get ready.

RUTH   Mama made me call Dad and tell him. She said he had the right to know. I just wanted to say, "Hi, I'm your daughter, I'm gettin' married." But before he even said "Congratulations" or "What's the man like?" or "Are you sure you're going to be happy?" he said, "Let me fly you to the Bahamas." He had rented a condominium down there for two weeks in January.

"Damm it," I told him, "I don't want your money! That wasn't why I called!"

Then I hung up.

———

WANDA MERCER   In the Fountains' party room New Year's Eve we had forty or fifty people. Jim was my escort. About eleven-thirty, he disappeared.

LAURA   He called me near midnight that night.

"Hi, Love, how you doing," he said.

"Gee, Dad, great. But you sound like you're doing better."

No, he said, he was cold sober. "But guess what I'm wearing."

"I give up."

"A diaper."

"What are you supposed to be?"

"Baby New Year!"

WANDA MERCER   A diaper and a hat. Somebody else was Father Time. Everyone thought it was wonderful.

CHARLOTTE FAIRCHILD   Finally Jim began to enjoy life.

WANDA MERCER   But, you know, Jim Thompson is the classic example of how bad things keep happening to some people.

Part V

NO REPRIEVE

1981–1992

51 ■ CAPTIVE ONCE MORE

MICHAEL CHAMOWITZ   A former law school classmate had referred Jim Thompson to me for a traffic charge. We resolved it and that was my only contact with him until 1981.

WANDA MERCER   That January Jim took a vacation in the Bahamas.

HILDA SIGDA   He had had a good week in Nassau until his last day.

While lying on the beach this 47-year-old patient experienced severe subternal crushing chest pain which at first he thought to be gastrointestinal in nature. He forced himself to belch several times without any relief. When he climbed three flights of stairs to his room, his discomfort grew to frank pain and he became profusely diaphoretic. Feeling warm and very weak he lay on a cool tile floor where he was found. He was taken to Princess Margaret Hospital for evaluation. EKG findings were consistent with inferior MI.

—from Thompson's military medical file

FRED KILEY   The heart attack hit only days before Jim was to return to Washington to attend President Reagan's inaugural. He was to be on the platform with other invited guests.

The patient remained quite anxious but otherwise asymptomatic. On 13 February he underwent cardiac catheterization. . . . Patient was scheduled for coronary artery bypass graft surgery on 1 April 1981. Because of resting

tachycardia and severe coronary artery disease he was started on Nadolol
80 mg. per day.

—from Thompson's military medical file

WANDA MERCER Jim was very worried about his condition but doctors
at Walter Reed said surgery would take care of it.

HILDA SIGDA They scheduled him for a triple bypass.

WANDA MERCER While awaiting the operation, those people he had
met in the Bahamas invited him to come back, stay a few more weeks. But
in late February, a day before he was to leave again, Jim had a stroke. It
was massive and severe.

———

LAURA When I got the call I was living in Holly, Pennsylvania, and
engaged to a guy named Paul. I got on an airplane that night. When I
reached the hospital in Alexandria my dad opened his eyes and said, "Hi,
baby. How you doing?" But there was swelling on the brain, and little by
little, in the days that followed, he became a different person. It got to the
point where he didn't know me.

CHARLOTTE FAIRCHILD Laura was frantic. She asked the doctor over
and over, "Why can't we get something done here?"

RUTH Laura called to say Dad was critically ill. She got angry when I
wouldn't drop everything and fly up there. I had no job at the time and
Kenny wasn't making good money. I told Laura there was nothing I could
do.

KENNY I was surprised Ruth didn't react to news of the stroke. It was like
her feelings were all knotted up inside. I could tell it had done something
to her emotionally but it was days before she showed anything. She kept
going over how bad it had been for the family after he got back from the
war. I said, "Sure." But I figured the guy must have gone through a lot too.

———

WANDA MERCER Jim was unconscious and looked terrible. His mouth
was drawn and pulled up. His whole right side was black. He was hooked
up to all kinds of tubes. We weren't sure how much damage there was or
whether he would survive. If Jim lived, they said, one whole side of his
body would be impaired. I thought it would probably be better if he didn't
make it. In recent years he had kept himself in such good condition. He
liked to do for himself. It would be very hard for him to overcome a severe
disability. He remained in a coma, so they transferred him to Walter Reed
in early March.

An EEG showed a slow focus over the left frontal region. An examination by an ophthalmologist discovered a right homonymous hemianopsia. An echocardiogram revealed left ventricular dysfunction without evidence of a source of embolization. Initial evaluation by a speech pathologist documented profound impairments in listening, talking, reading and writing. His prognosis for independence in communication is guarded.

—from Thompson military medical file

LAURA   I called Jimmy. "Why don't you come up and see him. You might be the key that will jar his memory."

RUTH   Jimmy was going through a wild period. He didn't give a care about school anymore.

JIM JR.   For a couple of years I'd been trying to get my mom to let me quit. She knew I done lost all interest in school and I'd found other things to occupy my mind. She knew I was having problems gettin' along with my teachers and my principal. Most of the time I was expelled or something like that. I was always doin' what shouldn't have been done. Smoking outside or throwing a firecracker. I was gone more than anybody else. My grades weren't no good. So finally Mom lost hope. About halfway through my junior year—right after my dad had his stroke—I quit. I wanted to develop my own lifestyle. My mother didn't approve. We argued night and day. Going up to be with Dad was just my escape.

RUTH   Jimmy left to take advantage of the situation. With my dad too sick to know what was going on, he went wild.

MICHAEL CHAMOWITZ   I got a call from Jim Thompson's commanding officer. He said Jim had suffered a stroke but had no close family. Jim didn't have a close relationship with the children, this officer said. It was a fractured family. He was afraid trouble was descending and asked if I would agree to act as guardian for Jim's estate. I had never talked in depth to Jim about the family. But I was persuaded it might be appropriate for somebody to watch over his assets.

JIM JR.   I enjoyed that trip to Washington. Not because my father was in the hospital. He didn't even know I was there. He couldn't walk, talk, speak. He couldn't do nothin'. He didn't know nothin'. But my sister Laura was there, and I hadn't seen her in years. I liked Laura too, maybe because she had the same conflict with my mom and John I was having. We never had gotten to talk none before.

LAURA People were very generous, always stopping by to see how Jimmy and I were doing, bringing meals. Many were buddies from AA.

ALYCE My mother called from New Jersey and said, "You know, Jim had a stroke."

"Yes, they called me," I said. "And young Jim is up there."

"Well, Jim is my favorite and I'm going."

"Do what you want," I said. "I don't want to get involved."

MICHAEL CHAMOWITZ The court appointed a temporary guardian, another lawyer in town. He went to Walter Reed and found Jim catatonic. Eyes were open but fixed to the ceiling. Vital signs were good but there was no movement. This lawyer concluded it was in Jim's best interest to get a full-time guardian. About this time I got a phone call from Jim's daughter Laura, who said she and her brother were in their father's apartment. They needed to do something about his money. She had found my name among his papers. We arranged to meet before a judge from the circuit court in Alexandria. Laura was a very attractive girl but a young kid. The judge convinced her I should be guardian of the estate.

LAURA Chamowitz began to take care of the bills. He gave me an allowance for groceries or other household expenses. But I wasn't included in any decisions. That upset me. Then Jimmy and Chamowitz began to fight like hell.

JIM JR. Chamowitz said, "You're going back to school." He said he done enrolled me in such-and-such high school. I had to be there at this time, on this day. I said, "No."

"You're living under your father's roof," he said. And blah, blah, blah. He knew I didn't like him. He also knew I loved wearing my father's motorcycle jacket. It was custom-made for him and I loved it. And I loved riding his motorcycle, a year-old Honda. So Chamowitz sold the motorcycle.

LAURA When Jimmy wouldn't go back to school, Chamowitz found him some really gross jobs and expected him to take them and bring money into the house.

MICHAEL CHAMOWITZ Laura asked for some of her father's money to pay for her wedding. I said no. It was not an expense that, as guardian, I could approve. It didn't contribute to Jim's welfare.

LAURA Dad and I had talked about my wedding. I was on my own, so he wasn't going to pick up the entire expense, but he had been more than willing to help pay for a lot of it. Chamowitz put the ax on every bit of it. He felt I was only there to collect. But all I wanted was to give my dad support. By now Dad was on so much medication the hospital only let me stay a few minutes at a time. After a few weeks he came out of the coma. But he had lost all word association. If I picked up a spoon he'd call it a cup. One day he looked at me and said, "Who are you?" It killed me. After a while I didn't feel I was doing my dad any good. I had to get on with my life.

"Okay," I told Chamowitz, "just keep me informed. I will call every day."

Jimmy stayed at the apartment and took Dad for a ride.

———

MICHAEL CHAMOWITZ   I was a young lawyer called upon to take care of this guy's affairs. After Jim got out of the hospital he still had trouble controlling Jimmy.

JIM JR.   I got a reckless driving ticket in Virginia. The police got me doing eighty-five at three o'clock in the morning.

MICHAEL CHAMOWITZ   He also had an accident with Jim's car.

JIM JR.   There wasn't enough room to fit two cars where I had to park at the condo. It was the person who parked next to my dad who hit the car. Chamowitz said I did it. I didn't like him at all.

While I was there my dad got better and better. I stayed on to do things for him. But the stroke had affected his mind quite severely. He was not the same person. Still, my visit there had been kind of nice until Dad tried to calm me down. I liked to go out nights and sleep days. That didn't jive well with him. Then I got another ticket.

LAURA   Dad was more furious Jimmy had dropped out of high school. It was one thing for a girl to do that, but not his only son.

MICHAEL CHAMOWITZ   Jim couldn't get Jimmy off his butt. He wouldn't do what Jim wanted. He couldn't be motivated. Jim said his son never had a proper upbringing. When Jim tried to impose some discipline, it was a complete failure.

JIM JR.   Things was goin' bad. Instead of making more trouble I decided to leave. In my life, when there's a problem, I leave.

———

WANDA MERCER   I visited Jim frequently at his apartment, never for very long. He didn't seem to want company. He had a terrible time communicating. All that came out was gutter language. Profanities. And it bothered him.

I'd say, "How are you, Jim?"

He'd say, "Fuck, goddamn, all right."

It was terribly frustrating for him.

HILDA SIGDA   Jim became very uncomfortable around sympathetic people. He never, ever wanted sympathy. Just the reverse. He wanted to be admired. When that wasn't possible he withdrew.

CHARLOTTE FAIRCHILD   We'd often discuss Jim in our group. Someone would ask how he was doing and we all said how sad it was.

LOIS VERMILLION   We felt a certain amount of grief when we lost Jim to the stroke. Because we did lose him. He never came around again.

52 ■ REHABILITATION

VIRGINIA BACHE I was working in the home care unit of Alexandria's health department when Walter Reed called. They had a forty-seven-year-old white male who had had a stroke. The patient couldn't speak, they said, had almost no use of his right arm, and limped on his right leg. They said he was going to need twenty-four-hour care.

I had been a military nurse, so my boss thought I'd have more background on this one. The next day I visited the condo and was surprised when the man answered the door himself. He had dressed himself, too, in trousers and plaid shirt. Yet he could barely walk. He couldn't use one arm. And he was all alone.

Jim Thompson was glad I had come but about the only thing he could say was "goddammit" and "hell." I did a physical, emotional, and neurological assessment, then an assessment to determine if Jim was able to live in his home. Physically, he had more strength than I expected. Mentally he had no reading comprehension. He did not know a single letter of the alphabet. He couldn't identify parts of his body. I told him to pick up his hand and touch his nose. He couldn't. I showed him how. Still he couldn't. Emotionally, Jim seemed like a time bomb ready to go off. When I asked questions he couldn't answer he pounded on tables or chairs. He said "goddammit" and "hell." He was so upset. It was as though he were saying to himself, "How can I get out of this one?"

I'd been in nursing twenty-one years and had handled a lot of stroke victims. They either have the will to get themselves back into the mainstream of life or they don't. Some want to give up. I don't criticize them for it. Rehabilitation is the hardest job they've ever had. Every day is an uphill battle. This day Jim told me with his eyes that if I gave him the right tools it was going to work. I had come expecting to find another young man unable to do anything for the rest of his life. I left believing I could get this guy back on his feet.

I scheduled Jim for speech therapy, physical therapy, and occupational therapy. The loss of speech was the most frustrating aspect of the stroke for Jim. He knew what he wanted to say but his brain couldn't communicate the words. The therapist had to go back to using flash cards of things like houses, spoons, and cats. She sat at a table, turning card after card over, forming the word and having Jim form the word. My nine-year-old son flipped cards for Jim during some of my visits. Everybody wanted to help this man.

The physical therapist began Jim on stretching exercises, moving his arm and leg in directions he couldn't. Pushing and squeezing and turning. The occupational therapist taught him to do what he needed at home—the coffeepot, the alarm clock, the stove—using his weak hand in concert with his good one. During rehabilitation, Jim's mood went up and down. There were wide swings, which I thought was positive. Frustration meant he wasn't giving up. He would sit down and think about his difficulties for a while and bounce back.

I liked Jim. Part of it had to do with me being an Air Force nurse. I had a lot of military friends and knew people who had been lost in Vietnam. So I could identify with Jim's experience. His greatest strength was his determination. He was an extremely particular man. Even though he had had this massive stroke we never saw him when he wasn't neatly dressed, his hair combed and his face shaven even if he had nicked himself a few times. One day he had the flu and was very embarrassed that he hadn't felt up to getting dressed. He was an extreme gentleman. He continued to use "goddammits" and "hells" but after a while we didn't hear them because we knew they were expressions he couldn't help using. We never figured out why. People who knew Jim before the stroke said he seldom swore.

Three or four months after we began therapy I came into his apartment one day and Jim was very excited about something. After I settled in he took his finger, pointed to his eye, and said, "Eye." It was such a great achievement for him. By the end of the day he could point at his nose, his eye, his mouth. He messed up a few times, but it got to the point where he could laugh about it. He was coming back.

MICHAEL CHAMOWITZ   Even though Jim had had a stroke, and was battling a serious speech disability, he demanded that other people "do it right, or not at all." The phrase is emblazoned in my memory. "Do it right or not at all." He said it over and over and over again. Jim did his own firing too. Cleaning people. Speech therapists. He'd complain; I'd tell him how much he needed somebody to do these things for him; he'd say he'd already fired them.

———

RUTH   I started medical technician school that September [1981]. As intense as that was, I still worked the night shift at Burger King to make ends meet. Kenny and me didn't see each other hardly at all. About this time my brother returned and wanted to stay with us. This cult he joined was after him to move off somewhere. Instead he came back here. He tried to preach to me and Kenny how we was living our lives poorly and we ought to quit drinking. Me and Kenny was smoking a joint once and Jimmy said, "You shouldn't do that. It puts impurities in your body." He scared me. Then, just as suddenly, he dropped the whole mess.

———

VIRGINIA BACHE   About six months into therapy I asked Jim what he did that weekend. He said something about going out. I asked him where. He cocked his hand back like he had had a drink. "You're not drinking, are you?" I yelled. "That will not help!"

For a while after that confrontation he didn't drink. But then I suspected he was. It got so he didn't want to say anything about how he spent his time because I would scold him. His real fear was that we would stop the therapy.

———

RUTH   Me and Kenny wasn't making ends meet but I couldn't turn Jimmy away. Mama was going crazy with worry over him. She thought he'd end up in real trouble.

KENNY   We helped him out all we could but we were struggling ourselves. And he didn't make any attempt to get a job.

RUTH   He was the laziest kid I ever met. He wanted everything handed to him. Wasn't willing to work for nothing.

KENNY   Young Jim's as likable as they come but he's not going to turn his finger for ya. He'd stay up all night watching HBO. Then he'd sleep all day and get up grouchy 'cause he was hungry and wantin' supper. Then he'd proceed to watch TV again.

RUTH   This went on and on. And Jim was a pig. I mean gross. I'd have to force him to strip his bed. He'd need a crowbar to peel them socks off. I forced him to use deodorant, forced him to bathe, forced him to brush his teeth. He was terrible.

———————

VIRGINIA BACHE   Every once in a while I asked Jim how many children he had. Sometimes he got all their names right and sometimes he wouldn't. His opinion of them varied. Sometimes he couldn't wait to talk about his children. He wanted me to know more.

At other times he referred to them by saying "Go to hell." And it seemed he meant it.

———————

KENNY   That first Christmas back from Virginia [in 1981], young Jim tried calling his dad. The colonel hung up on him. That hurt Jimmy real bad. He just wanted to wish him a happy Christmas.

RUTH   Still, Jimmy did take advantage of Dad. As always, he wanted everything handed to him. We kept thinking he'd grow out of it. He would have given anything if all he had to do the rest of his life was sit on the couch, watch TV, and have somebody wait on him.

———————

VIRGINIA BACHE   After some progress Jim thought for a time he might get back to full duty. But as the months passed he became more resigned to retirement. He started talking about a boat and Florida, but clearly he was very unhappy about leaving the Army.

HILDA SIGDA   He tried to make people think he was on top of everything, but those of us who knew him well knew he hated the thought of retiring. It made him terribly sad.

VIRGINIA BACHE   The ceremony took place in an executive conference room in the Pentagon [on January 29, 1982]. I had sent a letter to the White House asking that someone representing the president be there. I got a polite letter back saying it was inconvenient. Jim looked so great in his uniform that day that the whole world should have been there looking on. The secretary of the Army was there along with representatives from several service branches and a lot of Jim's friends. The ceremony was very touching. Jim's face showed total disappointment that he couldn't continue his career. He was very much an Army man.

Chamowitz read Jim's speech. Everyone I looked at was crying.

I am honored to receive this award (the Distinguished Service Medal) today but at the same time I am saddened to be leaving active military service. The

Army has been my life and I am proud of each of my twenty-five years of service.

Of those 25 years, I spent nine as a prisoner of war. Those days were grim, and survival was a struggle. I was able to withstand that long agony because I never lost my determination to live—no matter how painful that became—because I love my country and never lost faith in her, and because I had dreams of what my life would be like upon my return to America. Those dreams were always, unquestionably, of a life that was Army. I found that the dream of continued service gave me a goal that helped me survive my years as a POW.

After my return from Vietnam, the opportunity to serve became the motivating force in my life. Military service has given me my greatest challenges and my greatest rewards. I have worked hard for sound leadership development in the Army and for realistic training. The greatest problem faced by POWs was fear of the unknown. This fear can be reduced, not only for the potential POW but across the awesome environment of the battlefield, by training which is honest enough to address the real issue of combat and which is tough enough to approximate battlefield conditions.

No, I do not now retire freely—there was much I still wanted to do—but circumstances present me no alternative. I leave active military service because I must. But for the rest of my life, the Army will be no less a part of me, and of what I am, than what it has always been.

ENTRY IN THE *Congressional Record*, FEBRUARY 1, 1982

COL. FLOYD J. THOMPSON, U.S. ARMY
by Honorable G. William Whitehurst of Virginia

MR. WHITEHURST: Mr. Speaker, on Friday, January 29, 1982, in a quiet ceremony in the Pentagon, the Secretary of the Army awarded the Distinguished Service Medal to Col. Floyd J. Thompson in appreciation for his 25 years of service to this country as an Army officer. Colonel Thompson has the distinction of being this country's longest held POW returnee.

After his return from Vietnam, Colonel Thompson devoted his efforts to improving the Army's survival training and leadership programs. He was instrumental in developing modifications to the Code of Conduct in the hope that others would gain from his experience. Unfortunately, a debilitating stroke has brought an end to what he had hoped would be a full 30-year Army career, and he was medically retired effective December 31, 1981.

The Army and the country have lost the services of a true American hero, and I extend my deepest appreciation to Colonel Thompson for his service, devotion and sacrifices in the name of this country's defense.

I would like to share with my colleagues the citation that accompanied the Distinguished Service Medal. . . .

"[H]e made a truly incalculable and remarkable impression on the entire Nation through his nine-year internment as a prisoner of war. As the longest held prisoner during the Vietnam era, Colonel Thompson demonstrated truly magnificent powers of faith, physical endurance and trust in the Nation during years of almost unfathomable deprivation and hardship.

"That he emerged from this experience with a determination to continue to serve and to share his experience with his fellow Americans, no matter how uncomfortable to him personally, is a true testament to his indomitable spirit and belief in his country. The value and dimension of Colonel Thompson's many accomplishments, singular dedication to duty, and overall extraordinary and distinguished performance represent meritorious achievement and distinction in the most honored and cherished traditions of the United States Army."

53 ▪ DISAPPEARED

RUTH My brother's stay with me and Kenny grew from weeks to months. He kept sayin', "I really appreciate y'all lettin' me stay," and "As soon as I get some money I'll give y'all some."

KENNY It was gettin' close to the time young Jim would get that inheritance from his granddad's estate.

RUTH He could have the money when he turned eighteen. Mama tried to get it changed to twenty-one but the lawyers wouldn't do it.

Jimmy kept telling us, "As soon as I get that money, I'll help you all out." But enough was enough.

KENNY John realized the strain young Jim put on our finances. "You run him off," he said. "He can come stay here for a period." That's what we did.

RUTH In March 1982 my brother got that money, that seventy-five hundred dollars. He bought an old junk car. He let everybody smoke all his dope. He partied and partied and partied.

I said, "Jim, if I were single and eighteen and got that much money I'd like to party too. But put some of it away!"

"It's my money," he said, "and I'll do what I want, so you leave me alone." So he blew it in six months.

KENNY He lived his life's ambitions. He must have fulfilled them, too, because if it were me and I'd blown that much money, I'd still find days I'd want to kick my own butt. Evidently he don't regret it. As for us, well, young Jim took us out for supper one time. He thought that was payment in full for four months with us.

387

JIM JR.   I did my own thing. I partied. I'm not going to hide it. I stayed out late hours raising hell. Savin' money never meant nothin' to me. When I spent what I had, I started to work on farms. Haulin' hay, cuttin' tobacco. I made enough each day to where I could party at night. And if I didn't work, I laid around, slept, took it easy. I never thought nothin' about the future. The future was tomorrow or later on tonight. It seemed anytime I made a future plan it didn't work out so I didn't make 'em. I just took 'em as they come.

Meanwhile, I did a lot of drinkin'. Alcohol had become a friend to me. Never told me things I didn't want to hear. Otherwise, life wasn't meaningful. I only looked forward to seeing how drunk I could get. And stayed drunk quite often. In the back of my mind, I'd think about my father. I'd think about my mama. I'd think about Harold. I'd think about all of it. I'd get drunk and slip into my own world where I tended to think about it all. But I'd never been one to put my emotions out in the open. I believe I've talked to you more than I've talked to anybody in my life.

———

ALYCE   Pam earned a bachelor of science degree in 1982 and became a medical technologist. She paid for her education by working after school and on weekends and got student loans for the rest. And she did it without owing her father a damn thing.

PAM   When I graduated I felt like sending the colonel a note to let him know.

———

HILDA SIGDA   It hurt Jim so much to think he had overcome the alcoholism, had put his life back together, and now had been slapped down this way. He grew very bitter. Even about religion. Any kind of religion. He wouldn't go to a church service with me anymore.

LAURA   My dad told me he'd become an atheist. I cried my eyes out. We had gone to church every Sunday after he got back. If I had said "goddamn" he smacked me across the mouth. Now he had stopped believing. After everything he'd been through it was finally too much.

———

WANDA MERCER   Jim stayed in the Fountains a little more than a year after his stroke. By then he had become estranged from all of us. He just didn't feel comfortable with people.

MICHAEL CHAMOWITZ   I never understood why, or how, he developed this affinity for Key West. Apparently he had stopped there on a vacation once, fallen in love with it, and always wanted to go back. Now he wanted to get away to someplace warm.

HILDA SIGDA   Jim didn't let anyone else know he was leaving, so there was no party. He gave me an unlisted telephone number where I could reach him, but there was no way anyone else could. His kids couldn't find him if they wanted to. Then he left. I thought it was a mistake moving to an area where he had no friends, no support group. At least at the Fountains he was highly regarded. Still is.

I still have people say to me, "What do you hear of Jim Thompson?"

––––––

LAURA   He just disappeared. Chamowitz wouldn't tell me where he was or how he was doing.

"Your dad," he said, "does not want to see you."

Chamowitz had nothing more to say, under my dad's instructions. After that my phone calls went unanswered.

––––––

DORIS SONGER   On the 17th of September, 1982, Jim Thompson came to Fort Benning to be inducted into the OCS Hall of Fame. He had appeared in my office the day before. We hugged and in his broken way he asked me to have dinner with him that evening. We had a good conversation, although I must say he was better making his points than I was at understanding. I asked for his mailing address. He couldn't provide it. But after I drove Jim back to guest quarters he told me to stick around a minute. He went to his room, picked an envelope out of his trash that had his address, and gave it to me. He was very clever.

Over the years I've accumulated a number of things about Jim Thompson—newspaper clippings, photographs, a program from his induction. You might say I'm almost haunted by the man.

54 ■ SEPARATE MOVES

MICHAEL CHAMOWITZ It's not accurate to say Jim cut himself off from his children. He cut himself off from the world. He didn't want to be bothered by anybody. He was embarrassed by his physical condition. He asked me not to give out his address, even to his children.

A week before the Vietnam War Memorial was dedicated, in November of 1982, I went to the office of Jan Scruggs, who had led the effort to get the memorial built. I asked for a place of honor for Jim Thompson. That effort failed. They'd already selected those who would be seated near the podium. They gave me VIP tickets, but Jim would not get any special recognition.

The morning of the dedication there was a parade down Constitution Avenue, the longest seen in Washington since President Kennedy. As Jim and I sat in the stands, Everett Alvarez, the grand marshal, rode by. The announcer identified him as the longest-held prisoner in Vietnam. I'm not the shy, retiring type. I wanted to make a scene. Jim restrained me.

"No bother. No matter." That's all he could say. But his tears said much more.

EVERETT ALVAREZ Scruggs might have introduced me as the longest-held. Once in a while people checked the wording of introductions with me, but . . . well . . . what am I going to do?

MICHAEL CHAMOWITZ There followed an article in the *Washington Post* that again described Alvarez as the longest-held prisoner of war. I attacked with a letter to the editor. While I ranted and raved, all Jim could say was, "Goddammit, can't speak."

EVERETT ALVAREZ I'm still often introduced as longest-held. But I always say, "Look, I was the first one shot down in North Vietnam but there was a fellow captured in the South who was the longest-held. If there's notoriety for that, let him have it."

———

JIM JR. I could live in the country forever. I like to hunt and fish. Always liked the woods. But by early 1983 I moved to Nashville to find work. I didn't care nothin' for the city but was forced to get used to living there. I continued to drink heavy.

RACHEL PERRY I was manager of the Nautilus Submarine Sandwich Shop when the owner hired young Jim Thompson to work for me. My first impression was of a little country hick in a big city where he didn't belong. He had just turned nineteen. Had long hair. A beard. He wore a floral shirt missing two buttons, blue jeans, and off-the-wall tennis shoes. He took to sleeping in people's backyards. Sometimes in their cars. All he had to his name were two pair of blue jeans, a shirt, two pair of socks, two pair of underwear, and one pair of shoes.

And he hated me. I was nineteen myself but had grown up in the restaurant business. Any new employee had to empty the trash, wash the dishes, slice the meat, and bus the tables, none of which Jim wanted to do. He wanted to make sandwiches and run the cash register but I didn't have time to teach him. So he told everyone who worked there I was a bitch. Mostly, though, he kept to himself.

I grew up in a bar and could spot alcoholics. Jim was a drinker. During breaks he'd go next door to a bar called Boggies and drink as many White Russians as he could in fifteen minutes. One night after closing Jim asked me for a ride home. I didn't think anything would come of it. But the morning after our first date Jim called.

"Rachel," he said, "I made a decision. I'm not going to drink anymore."

"Don't stop on account of me."

"No," he said, "I don't want to be like my mother or father."

So he quit.

JIM JR. I got away from drugs too. I'd found something to live for and didn't want to go through life drugged out and drunk.

RACHEL PERRY We were total opposites, Jim and me. It took him for-ever to make friends. He wouldn't open up to people, wouldn't show his feelings. He said his world got messed up when he was nine years old. But he was the first guy I dated who didn't have his hands all over me. For three months the most we did was sit together on the couch and hold hands. He bought me everything I wanted too. I fell in love.

At the shop Jim picked up on things so quickly. But whenever I sat down to do payroll, Jim figured it was a signal for him to take a break. Eventually he got fired. We were living together when Jim asked me to marry him. I thought he was crazy but he kept asking. Finally I said okay. Thanksgiving of '83 we set the date.

———

ALYCE   Young Jim and Rachel came down the Wednesday before Thanksgiving. I got out of bed to greet them. Next morning when John woke, I said, "I just want to tell you, Jim and Rachel are in the living room sleeping. And John, she's big. Don't say nothing."

He walked to the bathroom past the two of them. He come back and said, "You told me she was big but you didn't tell me she was that big!"

"Well," I said, "you ain't seen it until she stands up."

———

HILDA SIGDA   Jim wanted to go to Nassau for vacation but he wouldn't go alone. So in January of 1984 I went down to Key West with him. When we came back from Nassau I stayed next door with his neighbors for several days. I urged Jim to get back in contact with his children. He hadn't talked to any of them for years. They didn't even know where he was.

RUTH   One night, out of the blue, the telephone rang. I picked it up and my dad started talking. He couldn't speak well but that he called at all blew my mind. By then my daughter was several months old. When I told him about Elizabeth—his mother's name—he cried. I told him we had tried to get in touch.

HILDA SIGDA   Jim was tearful, happy. "I missed you," he told Ruth. Afterwards he recalled for me the little things they had said to each other. He made several more calls over the next several days. Reached all four of his children. There was so much joy in those conversations. Jimmy told him he was getting married in February and wanted his dad to come. Jim asked me to go. I didn't want to. I thought it was his time to heal wounds. And my going might lead Jim into even stronger feelings that, for me, weren't there. I tried to explain, straining my words through his limited vocabulary, but clearly I let him down. That's the way life is sometimes. You get angry sometimes with your children too but you never stop loving them or caring about them. Jim, though, was unforgiving if you disappointed him. I'd never met anyone with such feelings of betrayal.

ALYCE   In February 1984, John almost died. He was vomiting blood. Doctor said it was pancreatitis brought on by drink. Next time, he said, he might not be able to save him.

John and I talked about it.

"That don't mean you got to quit," he said.

"No reason I gotta drink either."

We haven't had a drink since. We could stop cold because we did it together. We supported one another. And after we quit we realized there's a lot more in this life than drinking. Everything got better.

———

JIM JR.   My dad couldn't make my wedding, unfortunately, but he sent his best wishes. I felt good about that.

RACHEL PERRY   We moved into a little bitty apartment. The first thing we bought was a twenty-five-inch console color television, and for three months that was all the furniture we had, except a mattress on the floor my mother bought us. Every other wedding gift was for the kitchen. People knew I could cook.

Jim got work at the Number 1 Tire Store. My best friend ran the place. I took Jim up and filled out the application. Jim bought me roses every day and said he didn't want me to work. That fantasy lasted about six months until he realized I had to work for us to make it. From the beginning I waited on Jim hand and foot. I got up with him every morning, laid out his clothes, put his belt through his loops, put his power gauges in his pockets, turned the water on in the shower. I had his wash rag and towel right there and I fixed his lunch. He didn't have to do nothin'. And he didn't fight it. Jim turned out to be the laziest guy I ever met. Had an attitude about work. If I'd go out and get him a job, Jim was fantastic. Everyone he ever worked for said he was great. But he wouldn't look for a job himself. Every job he ever got I found for him. And at home he wouldn't do a thing, not empty an ashtray, not take out the garbage. And he hated to get out of bed.

———

ALYCE   That summer young Jim bought John's old Ford truck for five hundred dollars. He picked it up on a Sunday; told John he'd have the money to him Wednesday. When I called Jim to ask about it, he shouted at me like I wasn't his mother. Then he hung up. I didn't hear from him again. Not at Thanksgiving. Not at Christmas.

———

RACHEL PERRY   By the second year of marriage, I realized my Jim didn't care about bettering himself. He didn't want to work, period. And for months at a time he didn't. He laid on the couch and did nothing. I mean nothing. One night in '86 we were watching TV when an ad came on for a trucking school.

"That has always been my dream," Jim said. "To be a truck driver."

"Do it," I said.

Jim was a loner anyway. I thought driving a truck might suit him. We took out a government student loan to get him through three months of driver school. Companies who backed the school hired graduates under various deals. Jim figured the best one was to buy his own truck, be an owner-operator. It cost fifty-five thousand dollars.

So before Jim received his check each week, North American Van Lines deducted the truck payment and whatever other expenses Jim charged against his company credit card, like fuel and tolls. They sent what remained home to me. At first I got a couple of good checks. But then I started getting checks with big Xs through them, which meant Jim spent more money than he made that week. The dispatcher began sending Jim places where he wouldn't have a load coming back. He'd wait for days, racking up expenses to eat and shower. When he did get loads they were short runs. Tires started to blow. Insurance and taxes came due. North American even talked him into having a personal accountant. Jim kept calling me to ask for more money. Finally I'd had it. "You park that truck and come home," I said.

Another trucking company finally hired him. The job paid twenty cents a mile. But like everything else involving Jim, it didn't last long. He called me one day from the road, sounding like a lost puppy.

"Honey, I'm in North Carolina," he said. "They put me off the truck. Send me money to come home."

Turned out young Jim had tested positive for marijuana.

"I'm not sendin' you shit," I said. "You're a truck driver. Go to a truck stop, get in a truck."

————

MICHAEL CHAMOWITZ   In Key West, Jim established relationships with people but he had no friends. I never knew him to have a drinking buddy, or someone to go out to a movie with or to a ball game or dinner. From time to time he developed a friendship with a woman. Ultimately he ended up getting drunk and the woman ended up leaving.

————

RUTH   The first few times my dad called me he didn't say nothin' about lovin' me. The subject didn't come up. He just wanted to know how I was. I'd still go months without thinkin' about him. One night he called on the spur of the moment. Me and Kenny was already asleep. This time Dad said it . . . and I couldn't say it back.

KENNY   Ruth came back to bed that night and laid there quiet for a while. "He actually told me he loved me," she said. It was like she couldn't believe her own dad could say such a thing. It blew my mind. Showing love and affection is part of life in my family. Yet that was the first time Ruth had heard it since her dad first got back.

RUTH   He called a few months later and again said he loved me. This time I said I loved him too. I got off the phone and thought, Do I really mean that or do I just want to make him feel good? I knew that's what he wanted me to say. It got me so upset I couldn't sleep. I didn't know if I loved him. I didn't know.

LAURA   From the time my dad first called to let me know where he was living to the time I decided to fly down to see him, his condition changed. I heard progress in the way he spoke, in what he felt was important to talk about. He said he was exercising three times a week. Yet I didn't know what to expect from the trip. I hadn't seen him in three years.

The first thing that amazed me was his energy. Each day he got up early, made breakfast for us. When we went swimming he kept at it as long as I could. Then we were off to the Bahamas, where we communicated more in those few days than we did all the years he was able to speak well. We talked little about the war and his captivity. He told me how he had felt about Mom.

"You still love her, don't you?" I said.

"Love what she was," he said.

Our last night in the Bahamas we went to this very ritzy restaurant. He insisted on cutting the meat himself even with his bad hand. It went all down his front. The mood turned somber. Then the waiter started moving things around and knocked over our bottle of wine.

"See," I said, "it can happen to anybody!"

I could have kissed that waiter.

PAM   Laura rarely called to ask about her daughter, Catie. That upset Mama. Holidays passed, Catie's birthdays passed, and Laura didn't send anything. When Catie turned six she started asking about her mother. We didn't keep it from her. She knew her real mother was Laura who lived somewhere else because she couldn't take care of her.

ALYCE   It was awfully hard on Catie. She came home one day in tears. I said, "What's the matter?"

"Oh, I got kidded on the bus," she said. "I'm the only kid in class who doesn't know who her father is."

"Honey," I said, "you're looking at the wrong person, 'cause I don't know either. You'll have to take that up with your mama."

LAURA   I didn't visit because I didn't want Catie's life disrupted the way mine was when my father returned. She was happy. My mother gave her more than I ever could. Mom and John treated her like their daughter. Someday when she was old enough I knew I owed her an explanation. But I had to be sure that no matter what my mother said, I wouldn't go crazy. I wasn't sure whether to talk to her first and then see a therapist, or the reverse. There's so much in my childhood I don't remember. There's got to be a reason.

———

MICHAEL CHAMOWITZ   Jim worked hard enough on his rehabilitation that after a year in Key West he earned his driver's license. Not long after that he drove off for Central America. I didn't hear from him for two weeks. I called the U.S. embassy in Belize and had a tracer put out on him. He finally called.

"What are you worried about?"

"You proved your point," I said. " You can drive to Belize. Now put the damn car on a ship, fly back to Miami."

He did. A week later the U.S. Customs Office called and told Jim his car arrived and was ready for pickup. In Miami he finds the friggin' car's been stripped. Torn apart. Customs agents thought the longest-held prisoner of war in American history was smuggling drugs! I went through the roof! I finally got them to pay for the repairs. But it stunned both of us.

———

RUTH   My son, Michael, was born in September of 1984. Kenny called my dad and he was ecstatic. "A boy, a boy, a boy!" He's hung up on boys. He don't hardly ever talk about our daughter, Elizabeth. I love both my kids with all my heart. But my dad, well, even if he never speaks again to Jimmy, it wouldn't surprise me a bit to learn he's left everything he owns to his son.

That December my dad invited me down. Laura told me to go. She said I had to find out myself whether we could ever have a relationship. After Dad asked me, not a day went by I didn't think of him. I'd get up at four, work all day, come home, cook, straighten up the house, take care of Kenny and the kids, and crash in bed . . . only to lay there with my eyes wide open thinking about him. I was afraid if I didn't go to see him it would make me crazy.

I didn't know nothin' about my father's experiences in the war. I didn't even know his birthday, or his favorite color. I thought it was time I found out. Part of me wanted to be with him; another part was scared to death. I can't even describe my fear at the thought of him getting angry. Then you called, asking about him, and all the memories came swirling back. That night I sat down and wrote him a letter. I said a writer called me this evening to talk about him, that it was now two o'clock in the morning and I couldn't sleep. I told him I didn't know when I could come to Florida unless he paid for it.

I put the letter out in the mailbox the next morning, and went out three times to get it back. I was so relieved when the mailman picked it up. The next Saturday I came home with food for Kenny and the kids. I hadn't eaten all day.

We was setting here pigging out when Kenny said, "Oh, by the way, your dad called and said something about a travel agency and some tickets."

I could hardly swallow the food in my mouth. I got so nervous knowing he was down there in Florida and I could go to see him anytime.

Until the plane took off that Thursday, I was afraid the weather would turn bad and I'd chicken out. During a long layover in Atlanta I had three drinks and two more on the plane. My dad met me at the airport. We didn't say much, just hugged. I remembered the way he smelled. His cologne. He seemed a lot thinner and weaker but I was too scared to look closely. Back at his apartment I recalled other things about him, like how he kept everything so clean and what a good cook he was. I asked what he did with all his time.

"Get up," he said, "make coffee, drink coffee. What to do today? What to do today?" He was too busy for me when he got back from Vietnam. Now all he had was time.

We talked quite a bit that first night. Until then I had only heard Mama's side of the story, how Dad had fantasized about a perfect marriage, about a perfect wife. Now he was telling me everything had been perfect. He talked about Mama before Vietnam, described her as gentle and soft-spoken.

I said to myself, That is not my mother! I can't imagine her being submissive. Today it's "Agree with me or go to hell."

Dad said he couldn't believe it himself how much she had changed. I could see it hurt him to talk about it. By eleven that night he wanted me to call Mama to verify what he was saying. No, I said, I didn't want to start any shit.

We talked about the others. It killed him that Jim quit school. It didn't bother him that I quit but Dad would have paid to send Jim to any college he wanted. I told him I was going back to school. He pressed me about it for a little while, then said, "Be devoted mother."

The whole time there he waited on me. Poured my coffee. Cooked the meals. We were both nervous and smoked like crazy. Saturday we went shopping. That was a disaster. He got mad when I wouldn't let him buy me nothin'. When we got back to the apartment neither one of us spoke. Finally he asked why I wouldn't accept a gift. I said I knew he had money and it didn't matter. That didn't cut it. He went into his room and slammed the door. I heard him crying. I went next door to his neighbors, the Blubaughs.

Mrs. Blubaugh said, "Your dad thinks gifts are the only thing he has to give now."

Later that afternoon my dad came out and hugged me. He said he respected my independence. But he wanted to give me a wedding present. I knew better than to turn him down again. He gave me a check.

That night a movie came on television called *Gulag* about a reporter in Russia who gets put in prison on a trumped-up charge and eventually escapes. My dad said, "Good movie. Let's watch. I watch it to the end," as though for another movie that might be a chore. Well, we watched, but it upset him. The whole time this guy is in prison thinking about his wife. Dad cried like a baby.

Sunday he cooked dinner. Steak, broccoli with a cheese sauce, baked potato smothered in sour cream, strawberries, and fresh Colombian coffee, the best I'd ever had. He stuck a bottle of champagne in my suitcase. All week he'd treated me like a princess. After dinner he took me to the airport. I got on the plane but it didn't take off for fifteen more minutes. All that time I watched him standing there. He looked so alone.

————

ALYCE   In the spring of 1988, Ruthie called to tell me her father was getting some goddamn medal from President Reagan. I got angry.

"When is he and the government going to let this shit die!" I said. "It's been fifteen years! Let it alone!"

I mean, there were POWs in Korea, in the Second World War. You don't hear all this shit for them. And they went through hell too. But Jim loves publicity, loves the pat on the back.

———

MICHAEL CHAMOWITZ   Jim was elated to learn he would be honored by President Reagan. But then we found out Alvarez was going to be honored too. We were angry. Alvarez knew the Reagans personally. In fact, I found out later, it was Alvarez who recommended that Jim alone receive the first newly struck POW Medal. The Reagans, however, insisted that their friend Alvarez be honored too. Not knowing this, I contacted White House officials to say Jim alone ought to receive the medal on behalf of Vietnam War veterans. I said honoring Alvarez too would be an affront. The White House, however, had already decided to pick two representatives each from World War II, Korea, and Vietnam.

I wanted Alvarez off that podium. There was not a medal, not an award, Jim Thompson ever got that Alvarez wasn't somehow associated with. And that's unfair. Alvarez can be a guest speaker, he can tell jokes, he can tell stories, he can stand on his own. Jim can't. I thought it was time he got some special recognition. When I could put Jim in the spotlight I wanted to keep him there, and by himself.

The ceremony was held June 24, 1988. Before it began, this guy I'd been dealing with came up to me on the South Lawn and said, "I hope you're not going to make a scene."

WHITE HOUSE OFFICIAL: Good afternoon. . . . The Prisoner of War Medal which will be awarded today is a new medal recently authorized by Congress. Every prisoner of war is eligible but today six men will receive the medal as symbolic representatives of all prisoners of war.

Now, ladies and gentlemen, the President of the United States.
[Warm Applause]

RONALD REAGAN: In my lifetime, America has fought four wars. The First World War, World War II, Korea and Vietnam. You, the men here today, are the Americans who fought those wars. . . .

You symbolize the sacrifice our nation has made and you can be proud of what you helped achieve: a Western Europe strong and free; a democratic and prosperous Japan that is our critical ally in the Pacific; a South Korea with its remarkable economic and political achievements has become a model for developing freedom in a developing world, and in Vietnam you fought a noble battle for freedom. On the battlefield you knew only victory, only to have your victory lost by a failure of political will.

Nonetheless you did honor to America. Your resistance to the evil of communism foreshadowed a growing movement toward democracy we see today around the world. Through blood and valor you won time for the rest of Southeast Asia, and for the rest of humanity you sustained the dream and leave as your legacy the free and vibrant nations of that region and the recognition that only free nations can prosper for their people. You, all of our former POWs, embody America's indomitable will to be free. Through your heroism you have woven your lives into the fabric of American history and bound your flesh and spirit into our two-hundred-year unbroken chain of freedom. Through your courage you have demonstrated to the world that the American people shall always do that which is necessary to remain free. . . .

When the Vietnam POWs returned I was governor of California and Nancy and I were fortunate to have several hundred of them, in a number of groups, in our home. And we heard such stories, and saw such courage. One night afterward, when they had gone, I said to Nancy, "Where do we find such men?" The answer came almost as quickly as I asked it. We found them where we've always found them—on the farms, in the shops, in the offices and stores, on the streets in the cities. They're just the product of the greatest, freest system man has ever known.

55 ■ MURDER SUSPECT

RACHEL PERRY My Jim got hired by another trucking company, and things went on as before. We had a routine. When he'd come home from weeks on the road the first thing we'd do was make love. Then we'd shower, go to his truck, get his belongings, wash his clothes, and put 'em back in the truck. We did this together. We did everything together.

But in November of 1989, when he returned after forty-seven days, I knew something was wrong. I went to kiss him. He said he was too dirty and went straight to the shower. He didn't want to be with me right off. Then we made love—and I knew for sure something was wrong. For seven years it had been the exact same thing. I could set my watch by it. This time it was different.

"Jim," I said, "have you been with somebody else?"

He started to cry.

"I know I didn't do right," he said. "Please give me another chance. Please let me try to make it right."

"It's too late."

I wanted a divorce. I knew Jim would go back to drinking, to being a nobody. But I'd been miserable too long so he could be happy.

———

KENNY We planned a special Christmas [1989]. The colonel was coming.

MICHAEL CHAMOWITZ Jim was so excited. For the first time in more than a decade he, Ruth, and Jimmy would be together as a family. And with grandchildren too. We sent Jim a ham to take along.

KENNY   Jimmy called about a week before Christmas to say the dinner couldn't be at his apartment. Rachel had moved out while he was on the road. The place was empty.

RUTH   Rachel had every reason in the world to leave my brother. I didn't blame her. But the way she did it was wrong.

JIM JR.   My dad still came up. I hadn't seen him since I left Washington, eight years earlier. While personal problems clouded the reunion we still talked about things fathers and sons are supposed to.

RUTH   For the first time I was comfortable enough to ask Dad to stay in our house. Every other visit I couldn't breathe until he went back to a motel. But we'd worked hard to get to this point.

KENNY   The colonel lit up like a Christmas tree that holiday. He showed us how he could read a little from one of those Time-Life books. We even had him wearing a Tennessee sweatshirt.

MICHAEL CHAMOWITZ   Jim called and used expressions like "best Christmas ever." After years of failing to reconnect with his kids this trip had been a great victory. He was elated.

KENNY   Jimmy had his problems, though. He hadn't had a drink in years, but Christmas Eve he grabbed a beer as we set up the kids' toys. He also said he was cutting short his vacation to go on the road. He'd start sending his checks to our house.

RUTH   Jimmy had told Rachel she could have a divorce. She could have everything from the marriage except his clothes and one of his cars. It was just out of meanness then that Rachel sold that car to Joe Luna.

———

RUTH   Saturday morning in mid-January, Kenny picked Jimmy up at a truck stop out on the interstate, three miles from our home. He was with a friend, Justine. She was short with long straight black hair. Jeans, boots, and a leather jacket.

I had to take Elizabeth to a birthday party that day and asked Justine to come along. Coming back, I said, "Justine, I have to ask you something. Jim's a really nice guy. But what in the world would make a girl as young as you get in a truck in Texas with a total stranger and drive all the way here? Are you nuts?"

"I don't worry about it," she said. "I've got this baby right here."

She pulled a gun out of her purse. I about ran off the road.

"Put that away!" I yelled. "Justine, I have two small children. You either lock that in my car or keep it in your purse, but put the bullets somewhere else. Whatever you do, keep it away from my kids."

That afternoon we listened to music and danced and talked. Even got out pictures of me and Jimmy as kids. It turned into a wonderful weekend. The best time I'd spent with my brother in a long time. I was glad he wasn't boo-hooing over Rachel anymore. He seemed in better spirits than I'd seen him in years. It was all an act, of course. Inside, Jim knew we wouldn't be together again for a long, long time. Sunday when Jimmy woke he wanted to see a newspaper. When I got back with the *Nashville Banner* and the *Tennessean* he sat in the living room and read 'em both. Suddenly he decided to leave that afternoon. So I fixed a really nice dinner. Even made desert. Then we drove them to his truck and said our goodbyes.

————

KENNY   Wednesday night, Jimmy called.

"Hey," I said, "did you drop off your load already?"

"No. I guess I'm going to be in New Jersey for a while. I'm in jail. They got me for murder one."

First thing I thought was he hit a pedestrian.

"No," he said. "I killed a man in Nashville Friday night."

"Friday night!" That wasn't possible. He'd spent all day Saturday and Sunday with us.

"Come on, man, you're pulling my leg. Cut the shit."

But he wasn't kidding. I asked if it was self-defense.

"Yeah," he said. "The guy had something in his hand. I pulled the trigger. . . . Don't tell Ruth."

"Jimmy, don't give me that shit!"

That boy don't show his feelings for nothin'. It was like he didn't understand what trouble he was in. Besides shooting a man, he ran! He and Justine were parked at a truck stop in New Jersey when state police yanked the door open and found them naked. Charged them with carrying a concealed weapon, illegal ammunition—.38-caliber hollow-point—and marijuana.

To add to Jim's troubles, Justine was a minor.

RUTH   Soon as I got home I could tell something was bad wrong. Pulling me into the bathroom where the kids couldn't hear, Kenny said, "I've got something to tell you. It's bad, Ruth, it's bad." I went numb.

————

MICHAEL CHAMOWITZ   Jim called me from Key West, sobbing. "That's the end of Jimmy," he said.

What could I say? It was devastating. Particularly after Jim's wonderful Christmas with Jimmy, Ruth, and the grandchildren. I told Jim I'd look into the matter.

FROM THE *Nashville Banner*, JANUARY 24, 1990

TRUCK DRIVER HELD IN MAN'S SLAYING

A truck driver who apparently thought his wife was having an affair with a West Nashville man is being held for the man's slaying.

[James] Thompson of Waverly was arrested Tuesday in New Jersey with a female companion, [Justine], who may also be connected to the case. Thompson is being held without bond pending extradition to Nashville. Thompson is accused of gunning down Joe Luna, 27, of 5508 Tennessee Ave. late Friday night outside a West Nashville bar.

Witnesses identified Thompson as the man they saw shoot Luna in the parking lot of the Silver Dollar Saloon, 5511 Charlotte Ave. "A confidential informant told us where he was going," said murder squad detective Larry Flair. "The informant knew because he (the suspect) drove an 18-wheeler out of state. We contacted New Jersey State Police who pulled surveillance on Interstate 81 and located the suspect."

Thompson, [27] and [Justine] were charged in New Jersey with possession of an illegal firearm, possession of ammunition and possession of a narcotic. "We will be checking to see if the weapon found was the same one involved in the murder," Flair said. The detective refused to say what kind of weapon was used. Flair said the possible motive was jealousy.

"Thompson and his estranged wife were getting divorced. He probably thought there was a romantic situation between Luna and his wife. Our investigation showed there was no relationship between the two of them whatsoever."

MICHAEL CHAMOWITZ   Jim's life had been a roller coaster since his return from Vietnam, but this was the abyss. I worried about suicide. None of us would have been surprised.

I contacted authorities in Tennessee, then the New Jersey police. I talked to Ruth. By the time Jim came up from Key West, I had a better sense of what had happened. He walked into my office and cried. I mean cried. I tried to be his friend. I tried to comfort. But I knew Jimmy was going to serve some time.

I drove Jim over to the Marriott Suites, where I had reserved a room, and returned to the office. That evening I called to see if he wanted to go out to dinner together. He didn't answer. I called throughout the evening. I didn't sleep well. I showed up at the Marriott at seven-thirty the next morning. The desk clerk said Jim had just left. I ran outside in time to see his car exit the underground garage. He pulled over and got out. I hugged him. "I'm so sorry," I said.

"It's okay," he said. "It's okay."

"What happened to you last night?" I asked.

"AA," he said. "One day at a time."

I sent him on his way.

"I'm not worried anymore," I told my wife. "He knows it'll be tough but he's going to survive—again."

KENNY   After extradition, Jimmy had a preliminary hearing in Nashville February 12th. The colonel came up from Florida. We drove together to the criminal center. He said the pain of his POW days was flooding back.

RUTH   Dad at first believed the trial would be over in the blink of an eye. The district attorney would see inconsistencies in the witnesses' testimony, the police would unlock the door, and his son would be free. He couldn't stand the thought of Jimmy in prison.

KENNY   This woman comes into the courtroom with Jimmy at her side. Said she was the court-appointed defense attorney, Sue Evans.

RUTH   Jimmy wore his hair down to his shoulders. He had a full beard and mustache. I told him later to make himself more clean-cut.

KENNY   We heard nothing good at the hearing. The state had a star witness, the drummer of the band who'd been playing at the Silver Dollar. He testified that while standing outside on his break he saw Jimmy and Joe Luna arguing in the parking lot. Jimmy drove his car ten feet away, stopped, leaned out, and shot. If true, it means Jimmy could have kept on driving. Worse, they didn't find no knife at the scene like Jim said. They found a switchblade in Luna's jacket, but that was hanging behind the bar door. Investigating detectives described the wound and the blood and the morgue scene. The DA showed he had enough to take the charge to the grand jury. Luna's family protested the fifty-thousand-dollar bond. There was a whole row of them, a tough-looking bunch. Tattoos, biker jackets, and chains. I worried they might be revengeful. But I also felt bad for 'em. It's unfair to think they weren't hurtin' too. Jimmy, the little shit, didn't seem to understand yet how he hurt people. He was so nonchalant when we visited. Like, "Hey, it happened."

RUTH   He saw it as self-defense. Period. "Ruth," he said, "I didn't go there to start no trouble. I just wanted my car." He thought everybody was going to believe him.

KENNY   Chamowitz didn't want the colonel to put up the bond because Jimmy had no place to go. And with fifteen relatives protesting the bond, even Jimmy's lawyer said it might be good to stay in there.

RUTH   Jimmy wrote Mama a letter. He sent it to me, saying, "I don't want to cause any trouble. You read it first." He poured his heart out in six or seven pages. Told her he cared about her and he knows he hurt her by leaving home. He'd only realized in the past year how important family is. He wanted to build those bridges again. I read the letter to Mama over the phone except for one paragraph she wouldn't have liked. Jim said he thought she deliberately deprived him of material things while he was growing up.

———

RUTH   My dad came to Nashville again in September and wanted to see Jimmy. Trouble was, a new sheriff had just fired the whole department. I spent four hours on the phone trying to arrange a visit, but with the sheriff's office in turmoil, none was allowed. "It wouldn't matter if your father was president of the United States," one officer said. When I explained this to Dad he jumped off the couch, said he was going home. I exploded. Here I done everything within my power to get him a visit. "If you didn't come to see me, then get the hell out."

He left. He drove back two hours later, saying he couldn't leave like that. It was time to talk.

"I hope we have a strong enough relationship I can be honest with you," I said. "I'm fed up. Ever since I can remember, you put Jimmy before me. He's all you ever talk about."

Jimmy could treat him like dirt and it was all right, I said. But if Laura or Pam or me make one mistake he's ready to write us off. After I said my piece he was standoffish. He said he was afraid he'll never see Jimmy again outside of prison. Then he left.

I didn't know what would happen. I'd been ready to move forward with our relationship. Now, I thought, I made a mistake.

Dad called a few weeks later. He said he'd thought about what I said. I was right. He had put Jimmy first.

"But Ruth," he said, "you . . . taught me . . . how to love again."

It marked a turning point in our relationship. Finally I could say, "Hey, I don't like what you're doing." I could piss him off . . . and he wasn't going to leave me. I felt wonderful.

56 ■ A TENNESSEE TRIAL

For a year following his arrest, Jim Thompson Jr. occupies one of twenty-four cells in the Davidson County jail in downtown Nashville. Each cell has two bunks. From eight in the morning until eleven at night, prisoners congregate in the jail's dayroom to watch television or play chess, checkers, or card games. They are allowed forty-five minutes on the roof each day, for fresh air and exercise. Jim Jr. prefers to sleep. He sleeps as often as possible, including three or four hours during the day. It makes the time go faster.

An argument with a guard lands Jim Jr. some time in a maximum-security cell over the Christmas holidays of 1990. Otherwise, he stays out of trouble. He thinks often of his Dad's long ordeal. Though Jim Jr., knows his own confinement doesn't approach the physical and mental hardships his dad endured, he still hates prions life and craves freedom.

Jim Thompson visits his son several times in the months after his arrest. Each visit is painful for the former POW. He gives Jim Jr., money for cigarettes and phone calls. Communicating through the thick glass of the visiting area, however, is frustrating for a stroke victim. Special contact visits are difficult to arrange. Thompson promises his son he will be there for the trial.

It begins January 28, 1991. On the fifth floor of the Davidson County Courthouse that morning, Alyce sits alone in the marble hallway, smoking. Jimmy's trial will begin in half an hour. Alyce is surprised to see me. She seems even more surprised to be here herself.

"I'm a wreck," she says.

Jimmy and his lawyers, public defender Sue Evans and court-appointed attorney Beau Taylor, are seated at the defendant's table as Alyce and I walk into the courtroom. Jimmy nods to his mother. They have not seen each other in five years. His narrow shoulders slope sharply from his neck, reminding me of his father. The beard is gone. His long, light brown hair is parted in the middle and swept back along the sides. He has his father's oval face, too, I see. His skin is prison pale.

"All rise," the bailiff commands. Circuit Judge Walter C. Kurtz enters from behind a curtain.

RUTH   Me, Kenny, and my dad were late getting to the courthouse, so I missed witness roll call. As I stepped off the elevator somebody was calling my name. When I raised my hand, this guy grabbed me and rushed me in. I was glad to see Mama.

Then I thought, Oh my God, they're here together!

After jury selection, Judge Kurtz orders the jurors removed while lawyers argue prosecution and defense motions. Assistant Attorney General Tom Thurmond asks that the defense be barred from introducing testimony that the victim, Joe Luna, carried a switchblade in the pocket of his jacket, which was hanging inside the bar when he was shot. Thurmond's argument is interrupted.

JIM THOMPSON: Judge! Judge! I can't . . . I can't . . . Stroke victim. Un . . . in . . . tell . . . igble! Un . . . intelligible! Can't concentrate!

ALYCE: Jim, sit down.

BAILIFF: Sit down sir.

JUDGE KURTZ: Who is he?

JIM THOMPSON: I am Jimmy Thompson.

TOM THURMOND: I think it's the defendant's father, Your Honor.

JUDGE KURTZ: Well, what's the problem?

SUE EVANS: Your Honor, I think what he's saying is he's had a stroke and he can't hear, he can't understand.

JUDGE KURTZ: Okay. Mr. Thurmond, Ms. Evans, will you approach the bench.

Kurtz and the lawyers confer for a moment, then the judge looks up.

JUDGE KURTZ: The court will recess for five minutes.

JIM THOMPSON: [*Turning to son-in-law, Kenny*] I am sorry too but . . . my son.

JUDGE KURTZ   I don't have many people jump up in court and say they can't hear. I didn't even know Thompson's father had been a POW. In chambers the prosecutor said the jury shouldn't know about the colonel, that his status didn't have anything to do with guilt or innocence. He was correct.

RUTH   The judge had me come back there too. Made me feel I was responsible for whatever my father did. "I'm only his daughter," I said. "He's an Army colonel and I can't do nothing about it."

> In the courtroom, Jim Thompson, now under the watchful eye of the bailiff, is agitated. As he paces, he seems suddenly desperate to keep Jimmy out of prison. Alyce tries to calm him, inviting Jim to sit beside her. Jim rudely declines. She tries again to talk with him but Jim walks away. When he paces back her way, Alyce asks Jim if he wants a cigarette. He declines, saying he doesn't smoke anymore. Alyce grabs his hand awkwardly and shakes it, congratulating him for kicking the habit. "I quit myself once for five weeks." It's a small attempt at reconciliation.
>
> Jim isn't interested.

RUTH   I called my father out of the courtroom.

"Listen," I said, "you're not head honcho here! Don't think for one second the judge won't throw you out. You're going to have to control yourself or wait in the hallway."

> When the trial resumes, Jim and Alyce sit side by side in the first row, where presumably Jim is better able to hear. In a strange way, he still seems to have a hold over Alyce. She treats him with a level of respect I had not detected in any of our interviews, but which Jim refuses to return.

RUTH   When I saw them sitting together I about fell off my bench. God, I thought, what's going to happen? It used to be if I said Alyce's name in front of my dad, his face turned purple. And if I mentioned him to Mama, smoke came out her ears.

> By the end of the first day, the seriousness of the case is painfully clear. Jimmy's confidence seems to fade. The whole family feels it, too. The defense team is clearly outgunned by a savvy prosecutor.
>
> "Jim, honey, I'll see you in the morning," Alyce calls to her son as the courtroom clears.
>
> His face brightens as he waves good night.

For day two of the trial, Alyce again is the first family member at the courthouse.

"I haven't heard from Jim in five years and I just want to hug him," she says. "I just want to hug his neck for a minute."

That morning Jimmy takes the stand in his own defense.

JIM JR: Friday afternoon I parked my trailer behind McDonald's and went over to my apartment. No one was there and my 1971 Cutlass was gone. I called Chris Waxman, Rachel's brother, and asked him to come over and get us. . . .

I saw my Cutlass parked in front of this duplex. A man there told me the car belonged to Joe Luna. We went back to Chris's house to unpack. Then I asked him if I could borrow his car so me and [Justine] could go back to my apartment and I could shower. While we were driving back there I thought I'd stop at the Silver Dollar again and ask Joe why my car was in his parking lot.

I knew from my first visit that a man at the door was collecting cover charges. So I asked someone going inside if he would tell Joe Luna I wanted to talk to him. Joe came out and asked me what I wanted. His attitude was that I was taking him away from what he was doing. I asked him why my car was parked in his driveway. He told me he bought it from Rachel. I told him it wasn't hers to sell. He said it didn't make no difference, that he had paid Rachel one hundred dollars and was going to fix her car as part of the deal. He said he wanted the car he got.

All the while I made my points, Joe was getting madder and madder and madder. He started cursing. I couldn't believe he was getting so mad. He beat on the car and kicked the door. Then he started to walk away. He said the car was his and I should forget about it.

"Man," I said, "this ain't over with. That's my car and I'm not going to sell it." As I was saying that he came running at the car. The only thing I could think of was I'm not going to let him cut me like he cut Bubba Rohmein.

I had [Justine]'s gun in my pocket. I pulled it out. Joe was three or four feet from me when I fired.

In less than a second he would have cut me.

I have gone over this again and again in my mind. I really believed he had something in his hand. It was as if pulling the gun to shoot was a reflex action. I couldn't believe it happened. I was dumbfounded. [Justine] was saying, "We've got to go!" So about the time Joe was falling, I was leaving. I drove back to my truck. My truck to me was home. I lived in that truck. It felt secure to me. I carried on with business. That's all I could think to do. It shocked me to think I had shot somebody. [Justine] and I spent the night together at a truck stop and then I phoned my sister.

JUDGE KURTZ   Colonel Thompson insisted on speaking to me when court recessed. He expressed frustration at being unable to follow what was going on in court. He could hear the defense lawyers all right, but he couldn't hear the prosecutor. I told him the acoustics in court were bad, that I'd be surprised if he could hear anything. I said I was a Vietnam veteran myself, a graduate of the Citadel, and had been a lieutenant in Vietnam. That seemed to register on him. I had been with the 1st Infantry Division north of Saigon, along Highway 13, up into the Cambodian border area around An Loc. I wasn't a career officer, but thirty-eight months on active duty, twelve in Vietnam, is a fairly intense circumstance. So he knew I felt empathy toward him.

I'll tell you, the Vietnam War—I can never get away from it. Several of the biggest cases ever tried here—one a death-penalty case—involved delayed-stress syndrome. And for some reason every case that has a Vietnam overtone gets sent to me. It's solely by chance, but the only judge who's a Vietnam veteran seems to get these cases.

That afternoon, on cross-examination, prosecutor Tom Thurmond asks Jimmy to reenact the shooting, by sitting in a high-backed green leather chair and pulling a handgun from the side pocket of his suitcoat. At the prosecutor's insistence, Jimmy is to stick his head out an imaginary car window, look toward the rear, and show how, after seeing Luna charging, he pulled the gun from his jacket and fired.

Jimmy complains that the jacket he wore that night was a short-pocket windbreaker, not a suit jacket. Even with Jimmy's life at stake, his lawyers don't insist that the actual jacket be brought in for the demonstration. Jimmy, alone, is no match for Thurmond. Jimmy's attorneys raise no objections as Thurmond presses the attack. For the first time, Jimmy seems confused and, to the jurors, on the defensive. Thurmond decides to press his advantage. He asks Jimmy, now flustered, to explain the path of the bullet through Luna's body. If Luna was only a few feet away from the car and coming toward Jim in a threatening manner, why did the bullet enter high on Luna's chest and, moving on a downward path, lodge in his lower back?

One obvious explanation is that Luna was crouching, preparing to lunge as he approached the car. But Jimmy says he can't explain the bullet's path. Neither, it seems, can his own attorneys, who watch in silence as Thurmond tears into their client's credibility. If they have an alternative theory for the bullet's path, they don't raise it.

God controls the universe, says Beau Taylor. It's later that afternoon and Taylor, seated in his car, is assessing his client's testimony that day, and speculating on what the future might hold for a young man with such a troubled past.

Jimmy fared pretty well under a tough cross examination, says Taylor. He was personable, credible. Taylor also thinks whatever lies ahead for his client he's been moving toward all his life. He was born, for example, the day after his father was captured in Vietnam. The trial brings Jimmy to a new crossroads in his life. At one point, Taylor thought about arguing the case as a simple moment in time, when the paths of two fools crossed. A fateful, unfortunate moment in history—the first time Jimmy ever had a handgun in his pocket, the first time he ever got involved in any violence.

Taylor says he was surprised to see that Jimmy's father is a retired colonel. Sons of senior officers usually have more promising starts in life than high-school dropout and truck driver. But that background as an officer's son likely explains the ability to communicate so well on the stand, Taylor says. Children exposed to the world at an early age usually grow up faster, and gain more savvy, than others.

Taylor declines to speculate on Jimmy's guilt or innocense. As a defense attorney he accepts Jimmy's account of events that night and certainly doesn't believe the state's version. Defendants who are guilty often lack the courage to go to trial to prove their innocence. Whatever the verdict, Taylor expects Jimmy to take it well. After his father's return from Vietnam, Jimmy once told him, he didn't know which parent to turn to. Today he talks about both of them in a detached manner.

After the trial, Taylor says, Jimmy's life will start over and perhaps on a more positive path. Jimmy already understands that he loves his mother, he adds. Resentment and anger are easing. He knows he loves his father, too, although they haven't had time to develop that love. Jimmy looks forward to strengthening both relationships, Taylor says.

The morning of the trial's final day, Jim Thompson paces the cold hallway outside the courtroom. He is alone. Although retired from the Army now nine years, he wears his service dress uniform again today, with its chestful of ribbons. Jim Thompson hopes it will somehow help his son.

JUDGE KURTZ   I've had people in my courtroom who've had to leave because they can't stand it when the prosecutor says something about their loved ones. So I decided to talk again to the colonel's daughter. She listened and went out. When she returned she indicated her father didn't like getting all these instructions from a guy who had only been a lieutenant in Vietnam. I had to laugh.

His being here really had no effect on the trial. His status as a former prisoner of war is not relevant. The Supreme Court has ruled twice in the last several years that the prosecution can't put extraneous information about victims into evidence. If it's not relevant to guilt or innocence, it's an attempt to pander to the sympathies of the jury. We can't have cases tried differently because the defendant's dad is a POW.

But his presence did have an effect on me, as a Vietnam veteran. I really felt for him.

None of the Thompsons has slept well for days. Any hope they harbored when the trial began has been replaced by resignation. The evidence, says Jim Thompson, "is damning."

More disappointing, say Ruth and Kenny, is the conduct of the trial. Judge Kurtz, on several occasions, has had to rephrase Evan's questions to make them understandable.

As the courtroom fills this day, co–defense attorney Taylor is glued to his notepad like a college student cramming for a final exam. When the trial resumes, he recalls Jimmy to the stand to smooth over some of yesterday's rough spots.

JIM JR.:   It's difficult to reestablish what was going through my mind. The essence of the whole situation would be impossible to do in the courtroom. There's no way I can reproduce the feelings I had. There's no way I can re-create in my mind, or for General Thurmond to re-create for me, the way things were that night. I was afraid. I was afraid of what Joe Luna would do next. I'd known he cut up another man and I was afraid I was going to be next. Around the time he was beating on the car, I became afraid I might be a victim of his violence.

BEAU TAYLOR: Did you aim when you shot?

JIM JR.:   No sir, I did not. The only way I can see why there would be a discrepancy would be [if the] witnesses were not watching what was going on. If they were attracted by the sound . . .

TOM THURMOND: Objection, your honor. . . .

BEAU TAYLOR: How did you feel?

JIM JR.:   I was in a daze. I really couldn't tell you what was going through my mind except that I had to leave. [Justine] was saying, "We've got to get out of here."

BEAU TAYLOR: Did you feel you killed someone?

JIM JR.:   No sir.

Closing statements are scheduled for the afternoon. During the luncheon recess, Alyce and Jim walk separately to the basement cafeteria in the courthouse. Jim gets coffee and slides into a booth. Alyce, with her cup of tea, asks if she can join him. Jim waves her into the seat opposite, not in welcome but to indicate Alyce can sit wherever she likes.

"Are you all right?" she asks.

"Forget it," Jim snaps. End of conversation.

Alyce, angry, returns to the fifth floor to drink her tea alone outside the courtroom. As the trial resumes, Jim Thompson is sitting by himself on the far side of the courtroom, legs crossed, mouth twitching occasionally, eyes staring ahead at nothing at all.

Thurmond describes Jimmy to the jury as a man humiliated in his marriage, who found in young Justine someone who made him feel important again. When confronting Luna he wasn't about to back down and harm this new relationship. Not this time. Not with a gun in his pocket.

Taylor, closing for the defense, virtually ignores Jimmy's original plea of self-defense. He concentrates on explaining the lesser crime of manslaughter. His summation seems to seal his client's fate.

RUTH   The final argument by Jim's attorney sucked. You could pull Joe Schmo off the street and he'd have done the same thing. He showed no passion whatsoever. No conviction that his client wasn't guilty. Hell, I didn't believe him and I knew what he was saying was true.

ALYCE   I believed things would have turned out different if Jimmy had had proper counsel, if his father had come across with the money. I couldn't stick around for the verdict. I had to get home to feed John.

JUDGE KURTZ: Has the jury reached a verdict? Will you state the verdict?

FOREMAN: We the jury find the defendant guilty of second-degree murder.

RUTH   I felt my guts jump to my throat. I wanted to stand up and yell, "That's not right! You don't know what really happened! That's my baby brother! He's not like that!"

The courtroom clears quickly and quietly. In the elevator, Taylor explains that second-degree murder carries a minimum sentence of fifteen years, which means Jimmy might serve only three or four. Jim, Kenny, and Ruth greet the information with stony silence. In the lobby, Kenny helps Ruth into her coat. Outside he hustles her across four lanes of rush-hour traffic. Behind them limps Jim Thompson, a small figure bent against the cold. As the trio disappear into a maze of headlights, I think of Jim Thompson's son returning to his prison cell. Now, it seems, it's Jimmy's turn to dream.

As I promised to do, I call Alyce with news of the verdict.

"Second degree, huh?" she says. "Well, that's better than first. What was young Jim's reaction?"

"None."

"That's good. Cool throughout."

57 ■ THE SENTENCE

JUDGE KURTZ   Sentencing is the most difficult thing judges do. To do it well we need all the information we can get about a person. Family background and dynamics. Why a person might be more likely, psychologically, to commit a crime. The sum total of a person's life. A judge looks at all these factors. In the Thompson case, I had only bits and pieces of his story from conversations with his lawyers. I didn't get much more at the sentencing hearing.

EVANS: Your honor, I would like to start with the defendant's mother.
JUDGE KURTZ: All right.
EVANS: Can you tell me a little bit about your son, his background, as far as growing up.
ALYCE: Well, he was born the twenty-seventh of March, 1964. In July 1965 I moved my family up to Massachusetts where we stayed until March of '73. In March of '73 I moved to Pennsylvania. We went to Fort Benning Georgia after that. His father and I separated in June of '74 and divorced in October. I remarried in June of '75.

Evans seeks details that will show the turmoil of Jimmy's childhood and encourage the judge to support a lighter sentence. But Evans treads too near the tender regions of Alyce's life for her answers to be very helpful.

EVANS: Where was Mr. Thompson's father when he was born?

ALYCE: He was missing in action. I found out at five o'clock on the morning of March 27, 1964. I was ten days overdue. Jimmy was born that night.

EVANS: Describe the home situation when Jim Thompson Senior was away.

ALYCE: It was pretty rough those first fifteen months. Vietnam was kind of secret and I was made to feel like a black sheep. I moved to Massachusetts. Went up there and raised my girls in a home with a man and his two children until I found out Jim was not missing in action but a POW. I did not know that until January of '73.

EVANS: Growing up, did Mr. Thompson believe this other man to be his father?

ALYCE: I never told him so but I imagine he believed it.

EVANS: When his father returned from Vietnam you said you all got back together.

ALYCE: Yes, I went back for the sake of the children.

EVANS: How long did that last?

ALYCE: Fifteen months.

EVANS: Did you ever know your son to have a problem with alcohol or drug abuse.

ALYCE: No madam, not while he was living with me, he didn't.

————

EVANS: What is your relationship to the defendant?

JIM: Father.

EVANS: For the first nine years of his life where were you?

JIM: In prison.

EVANS: Not here in the United States?

JIM: No. [*Laughs*] POW in prison.

EVANS: During his adult life has he ever caused you any problems?

JIM: No, never.

EVANS: Have you had a very close relationship with him?

JIM: Oh, yeah.

EVANS: Mr. Thompson you were here for the trial.

JUDGE KURTZ: You'll have to excuse me, Ms. Evans, because of my background. But please refer to him by his military rank. Colonel.

EVANS: Colonel Thompson, you were here for the trial?

JIM: Oh, yes.

EVANS: You heard the evidence against your son. Knowing him as you do, do you think the charges against him are something he could have done intentionally?

JIM: Say again.

EVANS: Knowing him as you do, do you think he could have done that particular crime?

JIM: I don't know.

EVANS: You don't know. . . .

JIM: I'm sorry, a stroke victim. Simple, simple words I can understand. Complex words I do not get it.

———

JUDGE KURTZ: To the extent I am able, I recognize the tragedy suffered by this family as a result of the Vietnam War, and the imprisonment of Colonel Thompson for approximately nine years. That is taken into consideration by me in determining the sentence.

Mr. Thompson, would you stand.

The judgment of this court is you have been found guilty of second-degree murder. You are sentenced to serve sixteen years in the Tennessee State Penitentiary.

ALYCE   Sixteen years. It about killed me. Sue Evans comes up and says how great this is, he only got one more year than the minimum.

They let us visit with Jim before leaving the courthouse. Ruth and Kenny. Cate was with me. Pam came with her husband.

RUTH   As I came out, my dad was sitting there smoking one of my cigarettes.

"Dad," I said, "you don't smoke anymore."

He asked me to leave the pack. I had to work twelve-hour shifts the next two days, so my dad was staying at a hotel. He said if he didn't get to my place Friday night he would be there Saturday. I gave him a kiss and a hug and said, "Okay, I'll see ya there."

But he didn't come Friday night. Saturday morning comes and goes, Saturday afternoon and evening, and still no word. Not Sunday either. I didn't know the name of his hotel so I sat there, thinking a million different things that could have gone wrong.

MICHAEL CHAMOWITZ   Jim had been sure the judge would be lenient, that he recognized in Jim's experience a reason to keep Jimmy out of jail. So the sentence came as a blow and brought home the hopelessness of his son's situation. Jimmy would never get a government job. Never go into the military. Never be anything more than a truck driver. It represented a real embarrassment to Jim and a real failure for Jimmy.

Jim called me the night of the sentencing, totally drunk. "My son," he

cried. Over and over. "My son. Jimmy. In jail. Ruined forever." Then he
hung up.

RUTH   By Sunday night I was beside myself with worry. I called
Chamowitz.

"Have you heard from my dad?"

He didn't say anything for a few minutes. Then he said Dad had been
in touch. From the background sound of music and glasses, he said, the
call came from a bar. Nobody had heard from him since. I went all to hell.

MICHAEL CHAMOWITZ   I called Key West once, twice a day. Left
phone messages. For all I knew, Jim was at the bottom of a mountain
someplace. When I finally caught Jim at home he said he had gone to visit
friends. He didn't recognize how much he had hurt Ruth or what fear he
had put into me and my wife. Probably he didn't realize how much we
cared.

RUTH   I felt the way you do when you find a lost child. The first moment I
heard his voice I was elated. Then I wanted to ring his friggin' neck. I said
he had no right to treat me this way. He said he was sorry.

"Sorry don't cut it," I said. "I've been a wreck thinking you were dead.
When someone cares about somebody else they don't do that!"

"I was ashamed of myself," he said, referring to his drinking. I didn't
buy that and he hung up. I didn't care. I wasn't going to let him do this
anymore. I had gotten to where I cared about him and I wasn't going to let
him spit on that. If he couldn't deal with it, that was his problem.

Weeks later he called again. This time he explained why he really was
so upset after the sentencing. He said I had hurt him. He'd overheard me
tell Pam if we had had the money to hire a decent lawyer, Jimmy wouldn't
be in for murder. Dad took it personally.

I didn't do anything wrong, I told him. "So when you get over it let me
know." The next day I sent him flowers with a note saying I was sorry I
was so hateful.

He called me back that night and we cried together.

————

ALYCE   If anything good has come of this whole mess, it's Jimmy's changed
attitude. He doesn't have that superior attitude anymore.

RUTH   My mom's become Jimmy's number one supporter. She's on the
phone constantly to the parole board and to the guy in charge of deciding
where Jimmy serves the rest of his time. She's written a thousand letters
pleading his case, and she's been on my butt to write too. When she got a
date for Jimmy's first parole hearing, she asked me to call Dad. The more

support a family shows, the better. I wasn't going to be able to be there, so I said, "Mama, just tell me you'll be nice to him."

None of my family knows my dad now like I do. He tries to act like he's over his medical problems, but he's not. I know when he doesn't understand things he's heard but doesn't want other people to know. Mama was real cool about it. She said she understood and would take care of him, show him where to go, make sure he knows what's going on. It surprised me so. That deep hatred and bitterness was fadin'. The two of them had come to realize that whatever else came between them they did have four children together.

Then months after the trial, while Dad was here visiting, he said, "You'll never guess what happened."

I could tell he was excited, like he was about to tell me something incredible.

He said he was driving down a road when all of a sudden he realized he forgave Mama.

"For everything!" he said. "All that hate . . . all that bitterness. Gone! Like weight of the world off my shoulders."

"Okay," I said.

I mean, what do you say when someone says that?

MICHAEL CHAMOWITZ   Jim began to forgive Alyce years before this but it was an evolving process. Something, he told me later, he'd been thinking about for a long time. The trial and the sentencing were the end of that process.

RUTH   He even wrote Mama a letter telling her he forgave her. She said it was preposterous. He said he had lived for so many years with so much hatred but he had reached the point "where I can forgive you."

"I can't believe he would even say something like that," she said. For one thing, Mama said, she didn't give a shit whether he forgave her or not. For another, she couldn't understand what she'd done wrong that called for forgiveness.

58 ■ SURVIVOR

JIM JR. Obviously my life has not been normal. My dad's return threw a wrench into all of our lives. But if he hadn't come back I never would have known about him. I'd have thought some off-the-wall person was my father. I'm proud of him and always will be. But there was so much I didn't understand. Hell, as they was breaking up I was just getting used to the idea he was home. As I grew older, I had a lot of questions but it was too late to worry about answers. If I was nine again, the first question I'd ask my mother would be "Why didn't you ever tell me about my father?" That was a mind-boggler. Then to be told, "This man isn't your father, this man is. . . ." That was tough. My second question might be "Why didn't you wait for him?"

LAURA To this day, if I try to talk to my mother about our past, she changes the subject. Not long ago she wrote me a letter with her version of everything that happened. I don't know why she bothered. It was a lot of excuses. I just need to forget if I'm going to have any kind of relationship with her. As cheap and superficial as it is, it's better than nothing. If Alyce drops dead tomorrow, I don't want to feel guilty she died with a hole in her heart because I didn't stay in touch. It's a selfish reason, I know, but there it is.

RUTH One thing you must understand now about all of us Thompsons is we have very low self-esteem. We grab at affection anywhere we can. All of us suffer from this. In high school if a boy left the impression he liked me, that's all that mattered. As soon as Kenny was nice to me I thought he was the best person in the world. But I was lucky, 'cause he was. He's incredibly understanding. He knows a part of me has always been petrified that when we argue he's going to leave.

"Now Ruth," he'll say, "we're disagreeing about this one subject. We're not talking about our marriage." He knows I need that.

LAURA   Abandonment is a big worry in my own life. I feel sometimes if my husband, Dion, and I don't constantly agree he'll leave. I have a hard time even with my girlfriends. I wonder, "What are they thinking of me?" or "That last conversation, did I sound stupid?"

I blame Alyce more than my father. I felt abandoned during her desperate attempt to make a relationship with him. I blame her for not stepping in when we got beat, not taking us away when she realized how abusive he was. I don't care if she didn't have a dime. If someone beats your children you get the hell out.

RUTH   We were all so traumatized during those two years. Emotionally abused, really. Being a mother now, I can't imagine allowing my kids to go through something so traumatic. But my parents never once thought of what it was doing to us. They had so much to deal with themselves. It was like we were pawns. My dad admits that now. I tell him I was scared, I just wanted to stay out of his way. He wants me to understand why he was that way. He didn't think we were raised right. He thought we were unfit to be his children. He wants me to understand, and then to forgive and forget. But I can't forget. It affected the way I think about myself today. Nothing can change that.

LAURA   The war didn't give him the right to do what he did to us. But then how do you blame him after the stresses of Vietnam? Maybe the Army should have insisted on intensive counseling before fitting us into a family again.

RUTH   When I ask Dad why he had nothing to do with us after the divorce, he says they both decided it was best he stayed away.

Mom says, "I begged him to stay in touch!"

They both cry different stories.

LAURA   It used to be a day didn't go by I didn't think about that time. I have a happy life now, but I have to work at it. Dion and I just celebrated our fourth anniversary. Dusty is going to be two. We're hoping to have another child sometime. We live in a small town in New York State. Dion manages a little software company. I work part-time at an emergency care clinic. I can't say the past hasn't come haunting back. Like when I argue with Dion. I need to learn to love him enough to compromise, instead of screaming louder to get my way.

Other ghosts creep back. Even with Dusty. Some toddler things he does I have to stop and count to ten. I would never raise a hand to him, but I don't want to be a screaming, bitchy mother. I don't want what we had. If I don't work at it every day I'm going to lose it.

Earlier this year [1992] I considered suicide. We ran into financial problems in New Mexico and had to move back here, to live with Dion's parents. I began feeling we had nothing, that our marriage was falling apart in somebody else's house. I was so unhappy suicide seemed an easy out. I told Dion. That's when we started talking a lot.

I can't shake this feeling of being cheated, though. I would love to look into a crystal ball, to see where my life would be right now if it hadn't been for those years. I wanted a lot more than this. At least Dion and I are back living on our own. Who knows what will happen five years down the road, but I have a grip on things now. I'm in a happy marriage. I've got the most beautiful son in the world. As to the future, I see us back in New Mexico. . . . Trying to think happy thoughts. Maybe all of us will have our happy-ever-afters.

———

RUTH   Mama loves her life in the country. She's got friends. Goes to women's club meetings. She happier than I've ever seen her. Her blood pressure used to be awful. Now it's down. And she loves John.

———

ALYCE   John told them at the zinc mine a few years back he wanted to get away from underground work. A year went by and we decided it wasn't going to happen. So he opened this gunshop here on the farm. It's going good now. Our house is paid off. Our bills get paid every month. When you work hard for something you appreciate it more. And it's so darn pretty here. This weekend John and I got in the flowerbed together and got all the weeds out. When I came home tonight he had the truck in the street 'cause he was levelin' all the rocks in the driveway. The tulips were bloomin' and it looked so darn beautiful. I love the peace and quiet. The fresh, clean air. The tranquillity. Feeding the fish in the pond. Cutting the grass in the evening. Watching everything grow. Planting tomato plants. Going down a few months later and picking 'em and knowing they're mine.

I found out too what true love and marriage mean. John's so damn good. I haven't cleaned this house in a week. Haven't taken a dust rag to it. And he wouldn't give a damn if I didn't do it for the next month. Happiness is what I have now. Money can't buy that. Money can't buy love.

———

MICHAEL CHAMOWITZ A man goes off to Vietnam to fight for God and country. He comes back to find an unfaithful wife, a government that's taken all of his money, and a country still at war with itself over whether he should have been there at all. To half the population he's as much criminal for having fought the war as hero to the other half for having survived. His marriage is a disaster, his kids will have nothing to do with him, he's broke, and he's still, in effect, by himself. He turns to alcohol, he turns to therapy, he hits bottom. As he begins to come out of that nightmare over fifteen years he has high points and absolute lows. Disastrous, tragic low points. And all the while he's wondering: Why? Why did Alyce leave? Why did she do what she did?

It took Jim two decades to decide Alyce must have had good reasons. He can live now with the fact she had legitimate concerns. That's what he wanted to tell her in that letter.

———

PAM I tend to avoid the subject of the Vietnam War. It gets me too upset. I remember what it did to my family, how angry I was at the colonel.

LAURA Vietnam destroyed us. And what a senseless war it was.

RUTH My parents probably wouldn't have stayed together anyway. But the war made it so hairy for us. Jimmy's trouble had us all thinking again about how the war, Dad's coming home, affected us.

LAURA I wish Dad and I had talked about some things when he was well. Today he wouldn't understand if I explained the guilt I felt over the way we lived when he was gone. I understood how much he hurt. But there was nothing I could do, nothing I could say.

PAM I'm glad the colonel came back. I wish he would have been different though. I love him. I know I do. I guess I have all along. But I still have to get over the hurt and the bitterness and the anger.

JIM JR. He's a good man. I love him and I respect him. He's gone through one hell of a hard time. But as far as knowing him, I can't say I do. I don't know how he thinks. I don't know how to anticipate what he'd say in a certain situation. I am proud of him. I would like to believe one day I could deserve all the respect that man does. I hope one day we can get a better, more solid father-son relationship going. I don't look for it, but I hope. I don't ever see it coming but I do hope.

Between 1984, when I first met Jim Thompson, and 1992, when his son was convicted of murder, world politics had changed dramatically. I sought Jim's reaction.

Communism is disintegrating, Jim. . . .
Yes!

You spent nine years fighting it.
That's right. Success! USSR is done for. Everywhere—Germany, Latvia, Lithuania. All up in arms. But the ultimate goal, the ultimate goal, still yet determined.

And that is?
Peace. Peace and prosperity.

Did there need to be a Vietnam War? Would communism have collapsed anyway, under the weight of its own deficiencies?
Well, I'm in the Army. I'm a soldier. The president said, "Go to war." I'm going to war. Period.

In those quiet moments when you consider the whole of your life, what do you think about?
My first love is Army. I love the Army. And that's it.

You were held nine years, and now your son is in captivity. Do you see some parallel?
Yeah. Drinking.

But drinking didn't get you captured in Vietnam.
My son was drinking. Vietnam I drank. Same thing.

How do you feel about his imprisonment?
One day at a time.

———

LEW MEYER   There was a common theory among returnees that if Jim Thompson had died in captivity, he would have gotten the Medal of Honor. Some even say he would have received it had he gotten his life back together. But that didn't happen.

LARRY STARK   The Medal of Honor rewards heroic acts. That's interpreted to mean a specific act, or maybe two or three acts. But sometimes we get hidebound to regulations and lose sight of the spirit of the medal. I maintain it's deserved by someone like Thompson who persevered in captivity, who tried to the best of his ability to comply with the Code of Conduct, who never deviated from that while the rest of us sometimes did. Jim always tried to get the best out of himself and out of the other guys. That escape in '71, for example. He was complying as best he could with the Code of Conduct, even knowing the odds were against him. Maybe the dimensions of any one of his acts were not significant enough. But consider his performance over an extended period under extraordinary circumstances. Clearly he's deserving of the highest medal this country can give.

———

ALYCE   I was wrong in a lot of things I did. But I'm not wishing I could change 'em. If I could, if the Good Lord came down and said, "Okay, Alyce, you can go back to 1965. You can change everything from that year on," I would not have met John. I would not have Cate. Ruthie wouldn't have Kenny. I wouldn't have my two grandbabies and I wouldn't have the love of my family. I don't know where I'd be. Probably an alcoholic. A rich alcoholic.

Jim, well, he'll die rich. Until then he loves the praise and glory. His goal in life is being longest-held POW. And he ain't about to let it go.

———

RUTH   I thought after my dad got that POW medal from Reagan that that would be the end of it. Recognition was what he had strived for and with it he'd be able to rebuild his life. But that didn't happen, did it? His life is devoted to being some kind of hero, which to me and a lot of other people he was. He fought for what he believed in and sacrificed a hell of a lot for this country. But his whole life still revolves around the Vietnam War. Those nine years in Vietnam dominate his whole being. Every problem he has to solve he goes back to those years. Every time I tell him what I'm cooking for dinner he says, "Nine years POW eat anything."

My heart bleeds for him, because he'll never be any different.

LAURA   He has every right to feel cheated. But there comes a point if you're going to have normalcy in your life, you have to let it go.

LEW MEYER   I came out of the war with some handicaps and misfortunes, but for me, Vietnam is over. For Jim, it will never be over.

Can you ever stop being Jim Thompson, ex-POW?
No, never.

Why?
Experience, that's all. In prison nine years. Pure hell! I understand. You, a civilian, don't understand! You don't! You hear it but you don't think it!

MICHAEL CHAMOWITZ   Yes, Jim's obsessed with his POW experience. It has become a mark of character and of courage for him. He's the grandmaster in the parade in Key West every year. A couple of times a year there's an interview with a reporter. People continue to remind him about his past. He appreciates the attention. He's proud that he survived. And he has nothing else to identify with. He wanted his career as Army officer to continue, but he was involuntarily retired. He can't say he's a family man. He has no hobbies because he can't do anything. Is he obsessed with Vietnam? Does he have anything else to be obsessed with? I don't think he does.

Not everyone has the opportunity to be a footnote in history. Jim Thompson does. He never asked for it. But because of his courage and fortitude, that indomitable spirit, that determination, he survived. That obsession with survival created a place in history that nobody can take away. And with those same strengths he's been able to battle every tragic event in his life and move on. Unbelievable endurance, astonishing perseverance.

Clearly Jim is not the perfect hero. Not the perfect person. He freely admits that. But for the fact he survived longer than any prisoner of war in American history, he's like you or me. But being the longest-held POW makes him very special. And Vietnam, the war he survived, defines his character. You have to go back to that war to find the basis for Jim surviving all these postwar tragedies. He would never have survived that stroke if it weren't for Vietnam. He would never have survived Jimmy's fate but for Vietnam. Vietnam taught him a lesson. The same lesson he gets every day at AA: one day at a time. Tomorrow has got to be better than today. And if I live through today, there will be a tomorrow.

When our interviews began, Jim, you thought you only had a few more years to live. Remember?
Doctors at Walter Reed said "vegetable." Then, two years, I'm dead.

How do you feel now?
Confident.

Why the turnaround?
I'm a . . . survivor! [*Laughing*]

EPILOGUE

I f war begins in the mind of men, it must end there too. For Jim Thompson it does not end. Even as the years since the war turn into decades, Thompson's deep sense of loss and betrayal remains. By 2000, he had isolated himself once again from his children, including Jim Jr., who won an early release from prison, remarried, and moved on, promisingly, with his new life.

Alyce and John celebrated their twenty-fifth wedding anniversary that year on their Tennessee farm. All of the children were there, along with grandchildren and even two great grandchildren. Laura, who as a troubled teen almost ruined her mother's second marriage, brought the anniversary cake. Her bitterness is gone, she said. She and the other Thompson children hope their father finds peace too, one day, but they see no sign of it.

On occasion, it seems, a changing world mocks a soldier's sacrifice. In 1995, President Clinton, who avoided military service during the Vietnam War, restored full diplomatic relations with the communist government there. In 2000, Clinton announced a landmark trade deal with Vietnam, and that fall he became the first American president to visit the country since Lyndon Johnson, in 1967, as the war neared its peak.

Everett Alvarez, a successful businessman and prominent Republican, spoke briefly at the party's national convention in Philadelphia in July 2000. Journalists, broadcasters, and masters of ceremony still refer to him on occasion as America's longest-held POW. It's a mistake Alvarez has tried countless times to correct. Still he receives complaints periodically from misguided army veterans who can't understand why their hero, Colonel Thompson, isn't given his due.

On August 23, 2000, more than fifty-one million Americans watched the concluding episode of *Survivor*, one of the most popular television shows in history. Sixteen adults engaged in a staged contest of wills on a deserted Pacific island. The celebrated TV survivor left the island with worldwide fame and a check for one million dollars—after thirty-nine days. For trivia buffs, that was 3,236 days short of Jim Thompson's real-life, yet little-known ordeal. But as the new century dawned, Americans, perhaps thankfully, associated "survival" with entertainment, not war.

The remains of almost six hundred American service members have been recovered since 1988, when U.S. military search teams first were allowed into Vietnam. Two thousand still are missing, including Richard L. Whitesides, Thompson's pilot on March 26, 1964. Their crash site was found in July 1999, near the village of A Vao, beside the Da Krong River, several miles southeast of where Thompson believed the plane went down. Old-timers in the village confirmed that one passenger from the aircraft had been captured and turned over to the Viet Cong. The burned body of the pilot disappeared over the years. Only an aircraft seat frame, pieces of metal and Plexiglas, and a buckle from a lap belt were found. U.S. authorities added the crash site to their list for future excavations and vowed to find Whitesides's remains and bring them home.

Jim Thompson might one day like to visit the crash site where his saga began, said his friend Michael Chamowitz. Thompson turned sixty-seven in July 2000. The stroke of 1980, as well as recent major heart surgery and chronic back pain, have made him frail. But he still can travel and still insists on carrying his own bag, no matter how labored his steps, no matter how long the journey.

Alone, it seems, he survives.

POSTSCRIPT
TEN YEARS ON

Laura remembers a kind of pact she made with her mother after family members of Jim Thompson got their own copies of *Glory Denied* weeks before the book's original release date of Memorial Day 2001: They would read it and discuss while the sisters vacationed with Alyce on the Gulf coast in late May.

The heart-to-heart talk never happened, however. The book had stirred such deep emotions that "we read it but never talked about it," Laura recalled. Pam, Laura, and Ruth separately expressed to me sadness at what their family had endured because of the war, particularly their father, but also satisfaction at the truth of it all. "It's marvelous," Alyce said in the briefest of phone calls. We never spoke again of her life as an Army wife.

Jim Thompson had mixed feelings about the book, complaining to his friend Charles Ingraham, then director of veterans' affairs services in Key West, and later to a writer for the *New York Times* that too much attention had been given to Alyce and her experiences and perspective. At the same time, Jim was thrilled that, at long last, his captivity and heroics were chronicled and his status as America's longest-held prisoner of war affirmed.

Twice he appeared at local book signings. His condo association manager, Michelle Montgomery, who every Monday for eight years had sorted Jim's pills and helped him pay bills, invited Jim for dinner one special evening. After the meal they had cocktails while watching the details of Jim's life unfold on C-SPAN's *Booknotes* program with Brian Lamb. "He sat there in awe, I mean mouth hanging open, while I'm crying," Michelle remembered.

Jim soon was taking other steps to raise his public profile. Working with Michelle, he paid to have three flagpoles installed in front of Key West by the Sea, their condominium complex, to fly the American flag, the state flag and, most importantly, the distinctive black-and-white flag honoring U.S. prisoners of war and veterans missing in action. Beneath the POW flag, Jim had a bronze plaque mounted on a keystone pedestal to announce that Colonel Floyd "Jim" Thompson lived on the property. He bought a new black Cadillac and had bolted to its front fenders silver-plated mounts for a pair of American flags, which fluttered as he drove through town in a motorcade of one, his license plate proclaiming "POW."

Jim also contacted the director of Arlington National Cemetery to ask if he might be granted a place of honor there upon his death. By then Jim was nearer to death than his very few acquaintances might have suspected. In the fall of 2001, at the height of Jim's newfound celebrity, Michelle found him unconscious on the floor of his condo lying in vomit and blood. Rushed to a civilian medical center, Jim received emergency care for a bleeding ulcer and alcohol poisoning. Michelle visited the next day, posing as Jim's niece so as to get to see him. She found "the colonel" unconscious and in wrist and ankle restraints, his bed linens badly soiled.

"I went to the nurses' station and screamed and yelled. They said, 'Honey, you just wait a minute. You don't know what we've put up with this guy.' So they kept him strapped in. The doctor came. He looked right at me and said, 'If he has another alcoholic beverage he's going to die. Do you understand that?' I said, 'Yes, sir.' I understood. Of course, the person lying there was a different story."

Ruth Chamowitz, wife of Jim's lawyer and longtime advocate Michael Chamowitz, flew to Key West to be at his bedside. He still was unconscious and in restraints to control delirium tremens, the seizures associated with alcohol withdrawal in severely afflicted patients. Ruth visited daily through Jim's recovery and then arranged to take him home, wheelchair at the ready. On his release from the hospital, however, Jim had Ruth drive him straight to his favorite steak house on the waterfront. Too weak to walk inside on his own, too proud to use the wheelchair, Jim leaned on Ruth. Finally seated, Jim gave the waiter cash to find some cigarettes and ordered a double Scotch whisky. Ruth began to cry, asking Jim how he could do that after all he had just been through. Risking his wrath, Ruth even raised the touchy issue of Jim seeking long-term treatment again for his alcoholism.

The next day, Jim had Ruth drive him to the naval medical facility. Although he had no appointment, Jim insisted on meeting with his doctor.

When finally allowed to see the physician, Jim had Ruth repeat her suggestion that he seek treatment for alcoholism. The doctor listened. He then explained to Ruth that he and Jim had discussed his addiction on several occasions, and it was Jim's choice to continue drinking. Ruth wept. She soon returned home to Alexandria, Virginia. She and Jim never spoke to each other again.

To Ingraham, Jim acknowledged on occasion that cigarettes and alcohol might be killing him. "He just didn't care," Ingraham told me. "He'd say, 'Got to die from something.' "

Jim's final tenuous connection to family was his daughter Ruth. They talked by phone once in while. Ruth's son Michael had made a few visits to his grandfather's condo over the years. Knowing that her dad liked to entertain during the holidays, Ruth began sending a flower arrangement for his table every Christmas. In December 2001, the flowers arrived on schedule. But, due to clerical error, the card was signed only from Ruth's husband Kenny and the children. Jim called for an explanation. When Ruth delayed calling back for a few days, Jim was livid, saying she had made him worry needlessly. He refused to accept her apology. Kenny found his wife sobbing. Though unfailingly respectful of "the colonel" through the years, this time Kenny snapped. He phoned his father-in-law and blamed Jim for once again making Ruth miserable, turning a gesture of kindness into an excuse to cause more pain. With that, Jim severed his last tie to his own family.

By spring 2002 he also ended his personal and professional relationship with Michael Chamowitz, flying into Washington, D.C., unannounced to deliver the news in person. Michael's staff was shocked, Michael less so.

"You had to know him," Michael told me. "If you ever got on his wrong side, you were toast."

Jim had a long relationship too with Key West attorney Tom Sireci, but instead through Ingraham he arranged to visit the legal affairs office on the nearby naval base. There, a navy reserve lawyer serving her two weeks' annual active duty prepared for Jim a new last will and testament. Ingraham drove Jim to the pair of appointments with Lieutenant Commander Elena L. Escamilla, and on May 23, 2002, Jim signed the document that disinherited each of his children by name and made Ingraham his sole heir.

That spring, Ingraham later told me, Jim was both encouraged by and upset at news that President George W. Bush would be presenting the Medal of Honor posthumously to Army Captain Humbert Roque "Rocky" Versace, an infantry officer who had been wounded, captured, and, after two years of brutal captivity, executed by the Viet Cong in 1965. So with Jim's encouragement, Ingraham and some other Vietnam War veterans petitioned the Army anew to reconsider Thompson for the Medal of Honor.

Members of the Special Forces unit at Naval Air Station Key West had befriended Jim over the years, expressing open admiration and, whenever possible, celebrating the colonel's special status. On July 8, 2002, the unit held a birthday luncheon in Jim's honor. In what would be Jim's final public remarks, he echoed General Douglas MacArthur's famous quote that old soldiers never die but simply fade away. That morning at the White House, President Bush presented the Medal of Honor to Versace's family.

The following Friday Jim asked Michelle Montgomery to accompany him to a local restaurant for dinner. Afterward Jim was in no condition to drive, but he refused to let Michelle take the wheel. Instead he guided his Cadillac back to the condo at a crawl, never exceeding fifteen miles an hour. Michelle was livid at the colonel and let him know it. She therefore wasn't surprised when they had no further contact over the weekend and when he failed to call her on Monday to organize his pills and pay his bills.

On Tuesday morning, July 16, Michelle found three newspapers piled outside Jim's condominium door. Inside, at the dining room table, she found an evening meal untouched. Jim's body, clothed only in gym shorts, was on his king-size bed, legs drawn up in a fetal position. At age sixty-nine, the old soldier's heart could endure no more, ending one of the most remarkable lives from the Vietnam War era.

Jim left conditional instructions that his remains be cremated and his ashes spread on the ocean off Key West. "If, however, I am awarded the Medal of Honor, then my burial shall be in Arlington National Cemetery," he wrote. A final resting place was thus undetermined for several months until Ingraham received word that the Army would not be recommending Colonel Thompson for the nation's highest military honor.

On a cloudless morning in October, Major David K. Hsu, commander of the Special Forces Underwater Operations School, organized a pair of small boats to carry Colonel Thompson's ashes out to sea from Fleming Key. On the first boat were Hsu, Michelle Montgomery, and Charles Ingraham; the second held only three invited guests: the former prisoners of war Lew Meyer, Larry Stark, and Marc Smith. As Jim had instructed, the boats traveled south and cut engines within sight of his condo, where the turquoise waters above the reef gave way to the deep blue sea. A female chaplain gave a short prayer. Then, as Barry Sadler's "The Ballad of the Green Berets" played on a portable stereo, Michelle dropped a red, white, and blue wreath on the water. Together with Ingraham, and careful to wait for the right breeze, she spilled Jim's ashes on the calm water. The party listened to a recorded version of "Amazing Grace," then headed back to the island.

"The best part was coming back. We were the lead boat, and dolphins came along both sides of our wake and followed us in," Michelle recalled.

No family members had been invited to the ceremony. Jim's daughter Ruth had pleaded with Ingraham that she and her son Michael, then seventeen, be allowed to honor his grandfather. If they showed up, Ruth was told, they would not be allowed on the boats. "Michael cried his eyes out," Ruth said.

The John F. Kennedy Special Warfare Center and School at Fort Bragg, North Carolina, hosted a dedication ceremony in the fall of 2004 to rename a street in Jim's honor. Officials were surprised that Alyce would be with her children at the dedication; but, along with her daughters, Alyce was presented with roses during the ceremony. The remarks were delivered by the commanding general, by Jim Jr., and by former POW and Medal of Honor recipient Air Force Colonel George "Bud" Day. "In his heart," Day told attendees, "he loved his country as no one else could love it. He was truly a warrior."

Alyce's oldest grandchild Catie, whom Alyce and John had raised from infancy, sent a note in May 2011 thanking me for writing this book. Catie had read the story in nine hours, from Saturday afternoon through Sunday morning, feeling nauseous much of the time.

"There is nothing in this world so eerie," she wrote, "as to watch your own life unravel on the pages of a book. I am overcome with sadness at all that my family has lost, and amazed at what they managed to pull together for my sake and their own."

Alyce was diagnosed with lung cancer in January 2009. A few weeks later she lost the use of her legs and became bedridden with Guillain-Barre syndrome. She died from complications of that disease in her Tennessee home on April 18 at the age of seventy-four.

The day of her mom's death, Ruth suffered a heart attack, the first of three over the year ahead, cutting short her career as a medical technician. Already a breast cancer survivor, Ruth had her second heart attack soon after she and Kenny lost their son Michael, a troubled twenty-five-year-old, to suicide. Ruth and Kenny lived next door to Michael and heard the gunshot.

"The only reason I've survived this long," Ruth told me in December 2011, "is the strength I inherited from both my mom and my dad."

In 2003 Michael Chamowitz established the Floyd James Thompson Memorial Scholarship for children of POWs or students desiring a military career at a high school in Alexandria, Virginia. He said the scholarship pays tribute "to the good" in his old friend.

Jim Thompson was dead two years when the New York City Opera performed the first excerpts of *Glory Denied*, an opera from composer Tom Cipullo.

"Music is perhaps the most glorious tool for giving insight into the feelings and soul of another," Cipullo wrote in asking for the rights to base his first opera on the Thompson saga. "Somewhat magically, I believe, it allows us to empathize with others, even those whose motivations may seem selfish or base. To that extent, music heals."

Cipullo selected his libretto verbatim from the most meaningful passages of this book, allowing the characters of Jim and Alyce as both young and older adults to sing of their tortured lives. Full productions followed in New York City and Arlington, Virginia, and Cipullo's masterpiece won critical acclaim from *Opera Today*, the *Washington Post* and the *New York Times*.

Laura attended the Arlington premiere by the opera company Urban Arias. The performance left her overwhelmed emotionally, she told me, as the soaring music and her parents' own words evoked all of the anger and sorrow that had engulfed her family following her father's return from war.

New York Times reviewer Allan Kozinn wrote of the Chelsea Opera performance in New York: "It is Monteverdi's *Ritorno d'Ulisse in Patria* in reverse, the story of the returning warrior, but in this thoroughly modern version, everything has gone wrong, and redemption is out of reach."

—*Tom Philpott, January 2012*

ACKNOWLEDGMENTS

For a book that took sixteen years from conception to publication, there are a lot of people to thank for their guidance, encouragement and perspective. *Glory Denied* could not have been written without the sometimes painful, often courageous cooperation of the Thompson family—Jim, Alyce, Pam, Laura, Ruth, and Jim Jr. Special thanks to Kenny, Ruth's husband, to John, Alyce's husband the last twenty-five years, and to Catie, Alyce's granddaughter, whose impatience for the truth gave the author a final, well-timed push.

The book wouldn't exist in its current form without Kenneth Y. Tomlinson, former editor in chief of *Reader's Digest*, deciding to share transcripts of interviews he conducted with Jim Thompson during the summer of 1973. The transcripts originally were used by Tomlinson to help write *P.O.W.: A Definitive History of the American Prisoner-of-War Experience in Vietnam, 1964–1973*, by John G. Hubbell in association with Andrew Jones and Tomlinson.

I want to thank the following individuals for sharing their slice of the story with me, whether large or small: Everett Alvarez, Virginia Bache, Paul Blair, Tina and Lindsay Carr, Michael Chamowitz, Gail (Meyer) Clark, Fran (Peebles) Cwynar, George "Bud" Day, Sam Deacon, James DiBernardo, Ronald Ersay, William Evans-Smith, Charlotte Fairchild, Howard Fisher, Don Goulet, Barbara and Bill Guthrie, Herbert and Lea Hoff, Brenda Hunter, Ted Johansson, Franklin Jones, Bob Keyes, Fred Kiley, Samuel Kinchloe, Walter Kurtz, Jean Ledbetter, Edward Leonard, Sandra and Sid Levine, Don MacPhail, George Maloney, John McCain, Richard McKee, Wanda Mercer,

Lew Meyer, Mike O'Connor, Hervey Peebles, Rachel Perry, Ben Purcell, Don Rander, Frank Rose, Larry and Obe Ryan, Hilda Sigda, Robert Sironen, Roy Sironen, Nelson Smith, Doris Songer, Larry Stark, Beau Taylor, Francis Toomey, Eddie Trent, Mary and Nathan Vail, Lois Vermillion, J. J. Walsh, Joseph Weaver, Sterling Wetherell, Bernie Weisse, and Dick Ziegler.

Sadly, not all of those I interviewed lived to see their words in print here. Gone are three former prisonmates of Jim Thompson's: Claude "Speed" Adkins, Chuck Willis, and Colonel Ted Guy. Psychiatrist Pascal Batson, Sergeant Major Lonnie Johnson, Reverend Albert Van Dyke, and Colonel Dan Rickard also have died. I am indebted to them for having shared so willingly their time and remembrances.

Research on *Glory Denied* began in 1984 while I worked at Army Times Publishing Company, of Springfield, Virginia. In return for a magazine-length story, which I wrote in 1986, the company provided a telephone, for use as a research tool after hours, and some travel money to track down sources and conduct many of my interviews. My deep appreciation to my bosses at the time, James Doyle and Bob Schweitz, for their unflagging support.

For hard-to-find contacts, Richard Bielen, a retired Army officer and founder of the personal search firm, U.S. Locator Service of St. Louis, Missouri, was enormously helpful, particularly in finding Army colleagues of Thompson. Bielen, while a young Army captain, also served as family assistance officer to Thompson's parents, Ben and Elizabeth. Indeed, he brought the squalid condition of their apartment in Lodi, New Jersey, to the attention of local relief agencies and saw that improvements were made.

Not everyone interviewed for the book appears in its pages. Still, their insights, referrals, letters, recordings, or photographs were helpful. I especially want to thank Gerald Blais, Walter and Erina Buazzoni, Jean Dollman, Harry L. Ettmueller, Ray Foley, Pat Keyes, Dot McClellan, Evelyn Pemberton, and Richard L. Swick.

Over the years, several literary agents and prospective publishers advised me to abandon the oral history and write the Thompson story as a single narrator. I resisted, not wanting to lose the poignancy of the voices or to filter the facts through a single set of biases. I am indebted to friends who understood and offered timely encouragement, even as my file of rejection notices thickened. They include Phil Budahn, Lee Ewing, John Grady, and Randy Shoemaker. Thanks too to Tom Allen and Norman Polmar, for their publishing insights.

While others offered encouragement, Jean Ebbert, columnist and author, volunteered her time and considerable editing skills. Over several weeks, Jean turned an imposing tome into a publisher-friendly manuscript. I am forever in her debt.

I also owe special thanks to Robert DeStatte and Paul Mather of the Defense Department's POW-MIA Office in Arlington, Virginia. Bob volunteered his expertise on the POW experience in Vietnam to create maps showing camp sites where Thompson was held and his route north. Paul assisted on map research and explained how the crash site was located. Retired Air Force colonel Fred Kiley, coauthor of *Honor Bound: The History of American Prisoners of War in Southeast Asia, 1961–1973*, was always gracious in providing leads and perspective. The following news organizations granted permission to reprint select articles: the Associated Press, *Bergen* (N.J.) *Record*, *Fayetteville* (N.C.) *Observer*, the *New York Times*, the *Washington Post*, and *Worchester* (Mass.) *Telegram & Gazette*.

My profound thanks to Ethan Ellenberg, my agent, for his understanding and support, to Renee Schwartz for her legal advice, and to Robert Weil, a visionary editor at W. W. Norton whose infectious enthusiasm made my first experience with book publishing delightful.

Finally, I want to recognize the love and patience of my family, especially Barbara, my wife of twenty-seven years. I have worked evenings and weekends on *Glory Denied* through more than half of our marriage. She never complained nor expressed a doubt that the countless hours would produce a book, and that the book would be worthwhile. I am grateful for her sustaining love.

BIOGRAPHICAL SKETCHES

The Thompson Family

JIM THOMPSON Floyd "Jim" Thompson, the longest-held prisoner of war in American history.

ALYCE Thompson's first wife and mother of his four children—Pam, Laura, Ruth, and Jim Jr.

PAM The oldest of Thompson's three daughters. Pam was in first grade when her father was lost in Vietnam. She kept a photo of him hidden in her dresser drawer.

LAURA The Thompson's second child. She was only four when her father was reported missing in action. Laura had a troubled youth and was angry for years at her mother for pretending her father had died in the war.

RUTH The youngest of the three Thompson daughters. She had no memory of her father when he returned from Vietnam but proved to be his anchor years later.

JIM JR. Thompson's only son, born the day after he was captured in Vietnam. Jimmy spent half his youth believing another man was his father.

JOHN Alyce's second husband. They married in June 1975.

KENNY Husband of Ruth, Thompson's youngest daughter.

CATIE Laura's first child, she was adopted by Alyce and John.

BEN THOMPSON Jim Thompson's father.

ELIZABETH THOMPSON Jim Thompson's mother.

Others
(In alphabetical order)

SPEED ADKINS Supply manager for a U.S. defense contractor, captured in Hue during the communist Tet Offensive of January 1968. Adkins, a retired Army reserve major, became a cellmate of Thompson's in a North Vietnamese prison nicknamed Rockpile.

EVERETT ALVAREZ Naval officer captured after his plane was shot down during the Gulf of Tonkin Incident in August 1964. He became known as America's longest-held POW long before his release in January 1973.

VIRGINIA BACHE A home-care nurse in charge of Thompson's rehabilitation from a 1982 stroke.

PASCAL BATSON Thompson's psychiatrist during a three-month stay at Walter Reed Army Medical Center in the late 1970s.

PAUL BLAIR The first Army escort assigned to Thompson upon his repatriation.

TINA CARR Wife of Lindsay Carr, a member of Thompson's Special Forces A-team. Wives of enlisted team members looked to Alyce for comfort and information while husbands were in Vietnam.

LINDSAY CARR Junior member of Thompson's Special Forces A-team, trained in demolitions.

MICHAEL CHAMOWITZ Thompson's attorney and friend since 1982.

GEORGE "BUD" DAY An Air Force officer awarded the Medal of Honor for his service as a POW in Vietnam. Day first met Thompson on their return trip to Vietnam as honorees in the fall of 1974.

SAM DEACON Thompson's executive officer, or deputy, on the Special Forces A-team that trained at Fort Bragg, N.C., in 1963 and was sent to South Vietnam the day after Christmas that same year.

JAMES DiBERNARDO A Marine officer who ran the Armed Forces Television and Radio station in Hue when captured during the Tet Offensive in February 1968. He met Thompson briefly in a prison compound known as Bao Cao.

RONALD ERSAY A psychiatric consultant at Walter Reed Army Medical Center in the mid-1970s for patients with alcohol and drug dependency problems. He assisted in caring for Jim Thompson.

SUE EVANS One of two defense attorneys assigned by Tennessee to defend Jim Jr. on the charge of murder.

WILLIAM EVANS-SMITH Commanding officer of the 7th Special Forces Group at Fort Bragg while Thompson was in training there in 1963.

CHARLOTTE FAIRCHILD A friend who dated Thompson while he lived in Alexandria, Va., in the late 1970s and early 1980s. Fairchild met Thompson through a bridge group.

HOWARD FISHER A friend and fellow bridge player Thompson met in his condominium complex in Alexandria, Va., in the late 1970s.

DONALD GOULET A junior Army officer assigned with Thompson to the adjutant general's staff at Fort Bragg, N.C., in 1961.

BARBARA GUTHRIE Wife of Colonel Bill Guthrie, Thompson's first boss in an office setting after his repatriation.

BILL GUTHRIE Director of Army-wide training support at Fort Benning, Ga., in 1974 when Thompson was made his deputy. It was Thompson's first duty assignment after his repatriation.

TED GUY Air Force lieutenant colonel POW who earned a loyal following of fellow prisoners before their move to the Hanoi Hilton weeks before their repatriation. Guy resisted relinquishing his leadership role to Thompson.

HANOI HANNAH Americans' derisive name for the female broadcaster who delivered the communist propaganda to listeners in South Vietnam via radio stations in Hanoi.

HAROLD Pseudonym for the retired Army enlisted man that Alyce and the Thompson children lived with for most of Thompson's nine years in captivity.

HERBERT HOFF Assigned to Thompson's Special Forces A-team as the top noncommissioned officer.

LEA HOFF Wife of Herbert Hoff, the highest-ranking enlisted member of Thompson's Special Forces A-team. Lea became close to Alyce while their husbands trained together and deployed to Vietnam.

BRENDA HUNTER Alyce's cousin on her father's side. Brenda's father was Alyce's Uncle Lester.

TED JOHANSSON Alyce's family assistance officer in the early 1970s while deputy adjutant general at Fort Devens, the post nearest Alyce's home in Massachusetts.

LONNIE JOHNSON A Special Forces command sergeant major assigned to several flights into North Vietnam for Operation Homecoming. Thompson was aboard Smith's last flight in March 1973.

FRANKLIN JONES Director of psychiatry at Walter Reed Army Medical Center in 1977 when Jim was admitted following a suicide attempt.

JUSTINE Pseudonym for the girl who gave Jim Jr. the gun that killed Joe Luna.

BOB KEYES An older friend Jim met as a teenager working part-time at a local horse farm and stable. Keyes became a drinking buddy in the years before Thompson was drafted.

FRED KILEY A military historian who interviewed Thompson before Jim's stroke in 1982. Kiley is co-author of the Defense Department's official history of prisoners of war in Southeast Asia.

SAMUEL KINCHLOE Infantry officer who trained at Fort Bragg with Thompson in the early 1960s. He met Thompson again in March 1964 delivering payroll to Thompson's A-team at Khe Sanh.

WALTER C. KURTZ The Tennessee circuit judge for Jim Jr.'s murder trial.

J. C. LAMBERT The Army's adjutant general during the early years of the Vietnam War. He signed correspondence updating families of missing soldiers on progress in determining their fate.

JEAN LEDBETTER Wife of Tom Ledbetter, another Green Beret officer from Fort Bragg reported missing in Vietnam in the summer of 1964. She and Alyce leaned on each other for support for a year until Tom Ledbetter's status was changed in 1965 from missing to killed in action.

EDWARD LEONARD An Air Force captain captured during the Tet Offensive in 1968. He saw Thompson briefly at Bao Cao prison and thought he was an old man.

SANDRA LEVINE A nurse and the wife of Dr. Sidney Levine, Thompson's psychologist at Fort Benning in 1977.

SID LEVINE A psychologist in charge of Fort Benning's alcohol treatment program when he was called on to help Thompson in 1977.

LOIS Pseudonym for the career Air Force officer who Jim Thompson married in 1975.

JOE LUNA The man Jim Jr. shot and killed outside the Silver Dollar Saloon in Nashville.

DON MacPHAIL Army Special Forces sergeant who met Thompson in the final weeks of their captivity in Hanoi.

GEORGE MALONEY A seasoned combat officer and B-team commander for Army Special Forces A-teams assigned to I Corps in South Vietnam in 1963–64. Thompson's A-team was one of many Maloney had responsibility to oversee and train.

JOHN McCAIN A celebrated former POW who became a senator and presidential candidate.

RICHARD McKEE An Army colonel and director of personnel and community activities at Fort Benning in 1977 when he volunteered to accept Thompson, a practicing alcoholic, as his deputy.

WANDA MERCER A friend Thompson met in the early 1980s through Hilda Sigda, his neighbor at the Fountains complex in Alexandria, Va.

GAIL MEYER Wife of Lew Meyer, Thompson's best friend during the last half of his confinement. Gail confirmed for Alyce that her husband wasn't the only returnee unable to put the experience behind him.

LEW MEYER A Navy civilian fireman captured in Hue during the Tet Offensive. Meyer became Thompson's closest friend and supporter while a POW.

MIKE O'CONNOR An Army warrant officer and copilot shot down and captured north of Hue in February 1968. O'Connor was a prisoner in a cell near Thompson's at a prison called Bao Cao.

HERVEY PEEBLES An Air Force captain in the personnel office at Clark Air Base, the Philippines. Peebles volunteered to support returning prisoners of war as part of Operation Homecoming.

FRAN PEEBLES CWYNAR Hervey Peebles's wife. She joined the crowds at Clark to welcome home every planeload of POWs.

BILLY PEEBLES The Peebleses' nine-year-old son. He was the same age as Jim Jr., the son Thompson had not seen since birth. Billy visited Thompson in the hospital at Clark to provide insight into a nine-year-old's mind.

RACHEL PERRY First wife of Jimmy or Jim Jr., Thompson's son.

BEN PURCELL Army major captured in Hue. He met Thompson briefly on a jungle trail as the Viet Cong moved a dozen prisoners north in 1968.

DON RANDER An Army enlisted intelligence specialist captured in Hue during the Tet Offensive. Rander was one of only a few military POWs who had contact with Thompson during his captivity.

DAN RICKARD A colonel and senior administrator of the Infantry School, Fort Benning, Ga., site of Thompson's first training assignment after his repatriation and hospitalization.

FRANK ROSE Sergeant first class, seasoned intelligence specialist, and the only Korean War veteran on Thompson's Special Forces A-team.

LARRY RYAN Thompson's escort officer at Valley Forge Army Hospital, where he began his recuperation in March 1973.

OBE RYAN Wife of Lieutenant Colonel Larry Ryan, Thompson's escort at Valley Forge Army Hospital.

HILDA SIGDA A neighbor and close friend of Thompson's after he moved into the Fountains, a condominium complex in Alexandria, Va., in 1978.

ROBERT SIRONEN One of Thompson's closest childhood friends in Bergenfield, N.J.

ROY SIRONEN Twin brother of Robert. Both brothers were close childhood friends of Thompson's while growing up in Bergenfield.

NELSON SMITH Completed Special Forces medical training and joined Thompson's A-team in the summer of 1963.

DORIS SONGER Office secretary to Colonel Bill Guthrie and his deputy, Thompson, in the office of Army-wide training support at Fort Benning, Ga., 1974–75.

LARRY STARK A Navy employee captured in Hue during Tet. He was one of three civilian POWs to become Thompson's first cellmates after Thompson spent five years in solitary confinement.

BEAU TAYLOR An attorney on loan to the public defender's office to help defend Jim Jr. in his murder trial.

TOM THURMOND Assistant attorney general representing the state of Tennessee in Jim Jr.'s murder trial.

FRANCIS TOOMEY Thompson's roommate in Army Officer Candidate School, Fort Benning, Ga., in 1957.

EDDIE TRENT Weapons specialist on Thompson's Special Force A-team.

MARY VAIL Wife of Nathan Vail, and Alyce's friend and neighbor while the Thompson family lived on post at Fort Benning, Ga., in 1973–74.

NATHAN VAIL A retired brigadier general who, as a colonel in 1973, was director of the leadership department at the Infantry School, Fort Benning, Ga., Thompson's first training assignment after his return from Vietnam. Vail and Thompson also were on-post neighbors for a year.

ALBERT VAN DYKE Pastor of the Old North Reformed Church in Dumont, N.J., where Thompson went to Sunday school and church services as a boy. Van Dyke was pastor there throughout Thompson's nine-year captivity and emotional homecoming.

LOIS VERMILLION A friend Thompson met through a bridge group in the late 1970s in northern Virginia.

J. J. WALSH Deputy assistant commandant of the Infantry School at Fort Benning, Ga., 1973–74. Thompson had his first training assignment at the school after his return from Vietnam.

JOSEPH WEAVER One of Thompson's classmates in officer candidate school in Georgia in 1957.

STERLING WETHERELL Army chaplain at Fort Benning, Ga., 1973–75. Fort Benning was Thompson's first assignment after recovering physically from his nine-year confinement. Wetherell and his family also were neighbors of the Thompsons for the year they lived on post.

BERNIE WEISSE A neighbor and classmate of Thompson's during their childhood in Bergenfield.

RICHARD L. WHITESIDES Air Force captain and pilot of the L-19 observation plane in which Thompson was flying when shot down in March 1964. Thompson was injured in the accident and captured. Whitesides, a native of Stockton, Calif., reportedly was killed in the crash.

CHUCK WILLIS An electronics engineer with Voice of America, captured in Hue during the Tet Offensive. One of Thompson's first cellmates after five years in solitary.

DICK ZIEGLER An Army warrant officer and helicopter pilot shot down and captured near Hue in February 1968. He was one of the first American POWs to see Jim Thompson.

ILLUSTRATION CREDITS

Frontispiece: U.S. Department of Defense. Map: Designed by Chief Warrant Officer 3 Robert J. DeStatte, USA-Ret, senior analyst with the Defense Department's Office of Prisoners of War and Missing Personnel. Part Openers: Part One: U.S. Army photo; Part Two: Courtesy of Thompson family; Part Three: Courtesy of Thompson family; Part Four: Courtesy of Thompson family; Part Five: AP/Wide World Photos. Photo insert section: page 1 Courtesy of Thompson family; page 2 (top) Courtesy of Thompson family, (middle) Courtesy of Thompson family, (bottom) Courtesy of Thompson family; page 3 (top) Courtesy of Thompson family, (bottom left) Courtesy of Thompson family, (bottom right) Courtesy of Thompson family; page 4 (top) Courtesy of Thompson family, (middle) Courtesy of Thompson family, (bottom) Courtesy of Thompson family; page 5 (top) Courtesy of Thompson family, (bottom) Courtesy of Thompson family; page 6 (top) Courtesy of Nelson Smith, (bottom) Courtesy of Nelson Smith; page 7 (top) U.S. Defense Intelligence Agency, (bottom) U.S. Department of Defense; page 8 (top) U.S. Department of Defense, (bottom) U.S. Department of Defense; page 9 (top) U.S. Navy photo, R. T. Montgomery, (bottom) U.S. Department of Defense; page 10 (top) U.S. Navy photo, R. T. Montgomery, (bottom) U.S. Army; page 11 Courtesy of Thompson family; page 12 (top) U.S. Army photo, (bottom) U.S. Army photo; page 13 *The Record*; page 14 (top) *The Record*, (bottom) *The Record*; page 15 (top) U.S. Department of Defense, (bottom) U.S. Army photo, Robert Wood; page 16 (top) *Army Times*, Jeff Baum, (bottom) *Army Times*, Jeff Baum.

INDEX

ABOUT THE AUTHOR

Tom Philpott is a syndicated columnist and freelance writer. His weekly news column, "Military Update," appears in daily newspapers throughout the United States and overseas. His freelance work has appeared in numerous magazines, including *Reader's Digest*, *Washingtonian*, and *Kiplinger's*.

Before launching his syndicated column in 1994, Philpott was a senior editor and writer for Army Times Publishing Company. He has covered military affairs for more than twenty-three years, including six years (1985–1991) as senior editor of *Navy Times*.

Philpott, born in Pittsburgh in 1951, served as an information officer in the U.S. Coast Guard and is a graduate of St. Vincent College in Latrobe, Pennsylvania. He and his wife, Barbara, have two sons, Paul and Bradley.

Philpott first wrote about Jim Thompson for the *Army Times* newspaper in December 1983. Strong reader reaction encouraged him to take a closer look. He found a modern American tragedy.